ENGLISH LITERATURE,

CONSIDERED AS AN INTERPRETER

OF

ENGLISH HISTORY.

DESIGNED AS A

Manual of Instruction.

BY

HENRY COPPÉE, LL.D.,

PRESIDENT OF THE LEHIGH UNIVERSITY.

The Roman Epic abounds in moral and poetical defects; nevertheless it remains the most complete picture of the national mind at its highest elevation, the most precious document of national history, if the history of an age is revealed in its ideas, no less than in its events and incidents. — REV. C. MERIVALE.
History of the Romans under the Empire, c. xli.

SECOND EDITION.

PHILADELPHIA:
CLAXTON, REMSEN & HAFFELFINGER.
1873.

STEREOTYPED BY J. FAGAN & SON, PHILADELPHIA.

TO THE

RIGHT REVEREND WILLIAM BACON STEVENS, D.D., LL.D.,

BISHOP OF PENNSYLVANIA.

MY DEAR BISHOP:

I desire to connect your name with whatever may be useful and valuable in this work, to show my high appreciation of your fervent piety, varied learning, and elegant literary accomplishments; and, also, far more than this, to record the personal acknowledgment that no man ever had a more constant, judicious, generous and affectionate brother, than you have been to me, for forty years of intimate and unbroken association.

Most affectionately and faithfully yours,

HENRY COPPÉE.

PREFACE.

IT is not the purpose of the author to add another to the many volumes containing a chronological list of English authors, with brief comments upon each. Such a statement of works, arranged according to periods, or reigns of English monarchs, is valuable only as an abridged dictionary of names and dates. Nor is there any logical pertinence in clustering contemporary names about a principal author, however illustrious he may be. The object of this work is to present prominently the historic connections and teachings of English literature; to place great authors in immediate relations with great events in history; and thus to propose an important principle to students in all their reading. Thus it is that Literature and History are reciprocal: they combine to make eras.

Merely to establish this historic principle, it would have been sufficient to consider the greatest authors, such as Chaucer, Spenser, Shakspeare, Milton, Dryden, and Pope; but it occurred to me, while keeping this principle before me, to give also a connected view of the course of English literature, which might, in an academic curriculum, show students how and what to read for themselves. Any attempt beyond this in so condensed a work must prove a failure, and so it may well happen that some readers will fail to find a full notice, or even a mention, of some favorite author.

English literature can only be studied in the writings of the authors here only mentioned; but I hope that the work will be found to contain suggestions for making such extended reading profitable; and that teachers will find it valuable as a syllabus for fuller courses of lectures.

To those who would like to find information as to the best editions of the authors mentioned, I can only say that I at first intended and began to note editions: I soon saw that I could not do this with any degree of uniformity, and therefore determined to refer all who desire this bibliographic assistance, to *The Dictionary of Authors*, by my friend S. Austin Allibone, LL.D., in which bibliography is a strong feature. I am not called upon to eulogize that noble work, but I cannot help saying that I have found it invaluable, and that whether mentioned or not, no writer can treat of English authors without constant recurrence to its accurate columns: it is a literary marvel of our age.

It will be observed that the remoter periods of the literature are those in which the historic teachings are the most distinctly visible; we see them from a vantage ground, in their full scope, and in the interrelations of their parts. Although in the more modern periods the number of writers is greatly increased, we are too near to discern the entire period, and are in danger of becoming partisans, by reason of our limited view. Especially is this true of the age in which we live. Contemporary history is but party-chronicle: the true philosophic history can only be written when distance and elevation give due scope to our vision.

The principle I have laid down is best illustrated by the great literary masters. Those of less degree have been treated at less length, and many of them will be found in the smaller print, to save space. Those who study the book should study the small print as carefully as the other.

After a somewhat elaborate exposition of English literature, I could not induce myself to tack on an inadequate chapter on American literature; and, besides, I think that to treat the two subjects in one volume would be as incongruous as to write a joint biography of Marlborough and Washington. American literature is too great and noble, and has had too marvelous a development to be made an appendix to English literature.

If time shall serve, I hope to prepare a separate volume, exhibiting the stages of our literature in the Colonial period, the Revolutionary epoch, the time of Constitutional establishment, and the present period. It will be found to illustrate these historical divisions in a remarkable manner. H. C.

THE LEHIGH UNIVERSITY, *October*, 1872.

CONTENTS.

CHAPTER V.

THE NORMAN CONQUEST AND ITS EARLIEST LITERATURE.

CHAPTER VI.

THE MORNING TWILIGHT OF ENGLISH LITERATURE.

CHAPTER VII.

CHAUCER, AND THE EARLY REFORMATION.

CHAPTER VIII.

CHAUCER (CONTINUED). — REFORMS IN RELIGION AND SOCIETY.

CHAPTER IX.

CHAUCER (CONTINUED). — PROGRESS OF SOCIETY, AND OF LANGUAGE.

CHAPTER X.

THE BARREN PERIOD BETWEEN CHAUCER AND SPENSER.

CHAPTER XI.

SPENSER AND THE ELIZABETHAN AGE.

CHAPTER XII.

ILLUSTRATIONS OF THE HISTORY IN THE FAERIE QUEENE.

CHAPTER XIII.

THE ENGLISH DRAMA.

CHAPTER XIV.

WILLIAM SHAKSPEARE.

CHAPTER XV.

WILLIAM SHAKSPEARE (CONTINUED).

CHAPTER XVI.

BACON, AND THE RISE OF THE NEW PHILOSOPHY.

CHAPTER XVII.

THE ENGLISH BIBLE.

CHAPTER XVIII.

JOHN MILTON, AND THE ENGLISH COMMONWEALTH.

CHAPTER XIX.

THE POETRY OF MILTON.

CHAPTER XX.

COWLEY, BUTLER, AND WALTON.

CHAPTER XXI.

DRYDEN, AND THE RESTORED STUARTS.

CHAPTER XXII.

THE RELIGIOUS LITERATURE OF THE GREAT REBELLION AND OF THE RESTORATION.

CHAPTER XXIII.

THE DRAMA OF THE RESTORATION.

CHAPTER XXIV.

POPE, AND THE ARTIFICIAL SCHOOL.

CHAPTER XXV.

ADDISON, AND THE REIGN OF QUEEN ANNE.

CHAPTER XXVI.

STEELE AND SWIFT.

CHAPTER XXVII.

THE RISE AND PROGRESS OF MODERN FICTION.

CHAPTER XXVIII.

STERNE, GOLDSMITH, AND MACKENZIE.

CHAPTER XXIX.

THE HISTORICAL TRIAD IN THE SCEPTICAL AGE.

CHAPTER XXX.

SAMUEL JOHNSON AND HIS TIMES.

CHAPTER XXXI.

THE LITERARY FORGERS IN THE ANTIQUARIAN AGE.

CHAPTER XXXII.

POETRY OF THE TRANSITION SCHOOL.

CHAPTER XXXIII.

THE LATER DRAMA.

CHAPTER XXXIV.

THE NEW ROMANTIC POETRY: SCOTT.

CHAPTER XXXV.

THE NEW ROMANTIC POETRY: BYRON AND MOORE.

CHAPTER XXXVI.

THE NEW ROMANTIC POETRY (CONTINUED).

CHAPTER XXXVII.

WORDSWORTH, AND THE LAKE SCHOOL.

CHAPTER XXXVIII.

THE REACTION IN POETRY.

CHAPTER XXXIX.

THE LATER HISTORIANS.

CHAPTER XL.

THE LATER NOVELISTS AS SOCIAL REFORMERS.

CHAPTER XLI.

THE LATER WRITERS.

CHAPTER XLII.

ENGLISH JOURNALISM.

ENGLISH LITERATURE.

CHAPTER I.

THE HISTORICAL SCOPE OF THE SUBJECT.

Literature and Science. | English Literature. | General Principle. | Celts and Cymry. | Roman Conquest. | Coming of the Saxons. | Danish Invasions. | The Norman Conquest. | Changes in Language.

LITERATURE AND SCIENCE.

THERE are two words in the English language which are now used to express the two great divisions of mental production — *Science* and *Literature;* and yet, from their etymology, they have so much in common, that it has been necessary to attach to each a technical meaning, in order that we may employ them without confusion.

Science, from the participle *sciens*, of *scio*, *scire*, to know, would seem to comprise all that can be known — what the Latins called the *omne scibile*, or all-knowable.

Literature is from *litera*, a letter, and probably at one remove from *lino*, *litum*, to anoint or besmear, because in the earlier times a tablet was smeared with wax, and letters were traced upon it with a graver. Literature, in its first meaning, would, therefore, comprise all that can be conveyed by the use of letters.

But language is impatient of retaining two words which convey the same meaning; and although science had at first to do with the fact of knowing and the conditions of knowledge in the abstract, while literature meant the written record of such knowledge, a far more distinct sphere has been given to each in later times, and special functions assigned them.

In general terms, Science now means any branch of knowledge in which men search for principles reaching back to the ultimate, or for facts which establish these principles, or are classified by them in a logical order. Thus we speak of the mathematical, physical, metaphysical, and moral sciences.

Literature, which is of later development as at present used, comprises those subjects which have a relation to human life and human nature through the power of the imagination and the fancy. Technically, literature includes *history*, *poetry*, *oratory*, *the drama*, and *works of fiction*, and critical productions upon any of these as themes.

Such, at least, will be a sufficiently exact division for our purpose, although the student will find them overlapping each other's domain occasionally, interchanging functions, and reciprocally serving for each other's advantage. Thus it is no confusion of terms to speak of the poetry of science and of the science of poetry; and thus the great functions of the human mind, although scientifically distinct, co-operate in harmonious and reciprocal relations in their diverse and manifold productions.

ENGLISH LITERATURE.—English Literature may then be considered as comprising the progressive productions of the English mind in the paths of imagination and taste, and is to be studied in the works of the poets, historians, dramatists, essayists, and romancers—a long line of brilliant names from the origin of the language to the present day.

To the general reader all that is profitable in this study dates from the appearance of Chaucer, who has been justly styled the Father of English Poetry; and Chaucer even requires a glossary, as a considerable portion of his vocabulary has become obsolete and much of it has been modified; but for the student of English literature, who wishes to understand its philosophy and its historic relations, it becomes necessary to ascend to a more remote period, in order to find the origin of the language in which Chaucer wrote, and the effect produced upon him by any antecedent literary works, in the root-languages from which the English has sprung.

GENERAL PRINCIPLE. — It may be stated, as a general principle, that to understand a nation's literature, we must study the history of the people and of their language; the geography of the countries from which they came, as well as that in which they live; the concurrent historic causes which have conspired to form and influence the literature. We shall find, as we advance in this study, that the life and literature of a people are reciprocally reflective.

I. CELTS AND CYMRY. — Thus, in undertaking the study of English literature, we must begin with the history of the Celts and Cymry, the first inhabitants of the British Islands of whom we have any record, who had come from Asia in the first great wave of western migration; a rude, aboriginal people, whose languages, at the beginning of the Christian era, were included in one family, the *Celtic*, comprising the *British* or *Cambrian*, and the *Gadhelic* classes. In process of time these were subdivided thus:

The British into

Welsh, at present spoken in Wales.

Cornish, extinct only within a century.

Armorican, Bas Breton, spoken in French Brittany.

The Gadhelic into

Gaelic, still spoken in the Scottish Highlands.

Irish, or *Erse*, spoken in Ireland.

Manx, spoken in the Isle of Man.

Such are the first people and dialects to be considered as the antecedent occupants of the country in which English literature was to have its birth.

II. Roman Conquest. — But these Celtic peoples were conquered by the Romans under Cæsar and his successors, and kept in a state of servile thraldom for four hundred and fifty years. There was but little amalgamation between them and their military masters. Britain was a most valuable northern outpost of the Roman Empire, and was occupied by large garrisons, which employed the people in hard labors, and used them for Roman aggrandizement, but despised them too much to attempt to elevate their condition. Elsewhere the Romans depopulated, where they met with barbarian resistance; they made a solitude and called it peace — for which they gave a triumph and a cognomen to the conqueror; but in Britain, although harassed and endangered by the insurrections of the natives, they bore with them; they built fine cities like London and York, originally military outposts, and transformed much of the country between the Channel and the Tweed from pathless forest into a civilized residence.

III. Coming of the Saxons. — Compelled by the increasing dangers and troubles immediately around the city of Rome to abandon their distant dependencies, the Roman legions evacuated Britain, and left the people, who had become enervated, spiritless, and unaccustomed to the use of arms, a prey to their fierce neighbors, both from Scotland and from the continent.

The Saxons had already made frequent incursions into Britain, while rival Roman chieftains were contesting for preeminence, and, as early as the third century, had become so troublesome that the Roman emperors were obliged to ap-point a general to defend the eastern coast, known as *comes litoris Saxonici*, or count of the Saxon shore.[1]

These Saxons, who had already tested the goodliness of the land, came when the Romans departed, under the specious guise of protectors of the Britons against the inroads of the Picts and Scots; but in reality to possess themselves of the country. This was a true conquest of race — Teutons overrunning Celts. They came first in reconnoitring bands; then in large numbers, not simply to garrison, as the Romans had done, but to occupy permanently. From the less attractive seats of Friesland and the basin of the Weser, they came to establish themselves in a charming country, already reclaimed from barbarism, to enslave or destroy the inhabitants, and to introduce their language, religion, and social institutions. They came as a confederated people of German race — Saxons, Angles, Jutes, and Frisians;[2] but, as far as the results of their conquest are concerned, there was entire unity among them.

The Celts, for a brief period protected by them from their fierce northern neighbors, were soon enslaved and oppressed: those who resisted were driven slowly to the Welsh mountains, or into Cornwall, or across the Channel into French Brittany. Great numbers were destroyed. They left few traces of their institutions and their language. Thus the Saxon was established in its strength, and has since remained the strongest element of English ethnography.

IV. Danish Invasions. — But Saxon Britain was also to suffer from continental incursions. The Scandinavians — inhabitants of Norway, Sweden, and Denmark — impelled by the same spirit of piratical adventure which had actuated the

[1] His jurisdiction extended from Norfolk around to Sussex.

[2] This is the usually accepted division of tribes; but Dr. Latham denies that the Jutes, or inhabitants of Jutland, shared in the invasion. The difficult question does not affect the scope of our inquiry.

Saxons, began to leave their homes for foreign conquest. "Impatient of a bleak climate and narrow limits, they started from the banquet, grasped their arms, sounded their horn, ascended their ships, and explored every coast that promised either spoil or settlement."[1] To England they came as Danes; to France, as Northmen or Normans. They took advantage of the Saxon wars with the British, of Saxon national feuds, and of that enervation which luxurious living had induced in the Saxon kings of the octarchy, and succeeded in occupying a large portion of the north and east of England; and they have exerted in language, in physical type, and in manners a far greater influence than has been usually conceded. Indeed, the Danish chapter in English history has not yet been fairly written. They were men of a singularly bold and adventurous spirit, as is evinced by their voyages to Iceland, Greenland, and thence to the Atlantic coast of North America, as early as the tenth and eleventh centuries. It is more directly to our purpose to observe their character as it is displayed in their conquest of the Frankish kingdom of Neustria, in their facile reception and ready assimilation of the Roman language and arts which they found in Gaul, and in their forcible occupancy, under William the Conqueror, of Saxon England, in 1066.

V. The Norman Conquest. — The vigor of the Normans had been trained, but not weakened by their culture in Normandy. They maintained their supremacy in arms against the efforts of the kings of France. They had long cultivated intimate relations with England, and their dukes had long hankered for its possession. William, the natural son of Duke Robert — known to history and musical romance as Robert le Diable — was a man of strong mind, tenacious purpose, and powerful hand. He had obtained, by promise of Edward the Confessor, the reversion of the crown upon the

[1] Gibbon's Decline and Fall, c. lv.

death of that monarch; and when the issue came, he availed himself of that reversion and the Pope's sanction, and also of the disputed succession between Harold, the son of Godwin, and the true Saxon heir, Edgar Atheling, to make good his claim by force of arms.

Under him the Normans were united, while divisions existed in the Saxon ranks. Tostig, the brother of Harold, and Harald Hardrada, the King of Norway, combined against Harold, and, just before the landing of Duke William at Pevensey, on the coast of Sussex, Harold was obliged to march rapidly northward to Stanford bridge, to defeat Tostig and the Norwegians, and then to return with a tired army of uncertain *morale*, to encounter the invading Normans. Thus it appears that William conquered the land, which would have been invincible had the leaders and the people been united in its defence.

As the Saxons, Danes, and Normans were of the same great Teutonic family, however modified by the different circumstances of movement and residence, there was no new ethnic element introduced; and, paradoxical as it may seem, the fusion of these peoples was of great benefit, in the end, to England. Though the Saxons at first suffered from Norman oppression, the kingdom was brought into large inter-European relations, and a far better literary culture was introduced, more varied in subject, more developed in point of language, and more artistic.

Thus much, in a brief historical summary, is necessary as an introduction to our subject. From all these contests and conquests there were wrought in the language of the country important changes, which are to be studied in the standard works of its literature.

CHANGES IN LANGUAGE. — The changes and transformations of language may be thus briefly stated: — In the Celtic period, before the arrival of the Romans, the people spoke different dialects of the Celtic and Gadhelic languages, all cognate and radically similar.

These were not much affected by the occupancy of the Romans for about four hundred and fifty years, although, doubtless, Latin words, expressive of things and notions of which the British had no previous knowledge, were adopted by them, and many of the Celtic inhabitants who submitted to these conquerors learned and used the Latin language.

When the Romans departed, and the Saxons came in numbers, in the fifth and sixth centuries, the Saxon language, which is the foundation of English, became the current speech of the realm; adopting few Celtic words, but retaining a considerable number of the Celtic names of places, as it also did of Latin terminations in names.

Before the coming of the Normans, their language, called the *Langue d'oil*, or Norman French, had been very much favored by educated Englishmen; and when William conquered England, he tried to supplant the Saxon entirely. In this he was not successful; but the two languages were interfused and amalgamated, so that in the middle of the twelfth century, there had been thus created the *English language*, formed but still formative. The Anglo-Saxon was the foundation, or basis; while the Norman French is observed to be the principal modifying element.

Since the Norman conquest, numerous other elements have entered, most of them quietly, without the concomitant of political revolution or foreign invasion.

Thus the Latin, being used by the Church, and being the language of literary and scientific comity throughout the world, was constantly adding words and modes of expression to the English. The introduction of Greek into Western Europe, at the fall of Constantinople, supplied Greek words, and induced a habit of coining English words from the Greek. The establishment of the Hanoverian succession, after the fall of the Stuarts, brought in the practice and study of German, and somewhat of its phraseology; and English conquests in the East have not failed to introduce Indian words, and, what is far better, to open the way for a fuller study of comparative philology and linguistics.

In a later chapter we shall reconsider the periods referred to, in an examination of the literary works which they contain, works produced by historical causes, and illustrative of historical events.

CHAPTER II.

LITERATURE A TEACHER OF HISTORY. CELTIC REMAINS.

The Uses of Literature.
Italy, France, England.
Purpose of the Work.
Celtic Literary Remains.
Druids and Druidism.
Roman Writers.
Psalter of Cashel.
Welsh Triads and Mabinogion.
Gildas and St. Colm.

THE USES OF LITERATURE.

BEFORE examining these periods in order to find the literature produced in them, it will be well to consider briefly what are the practical uses of literature, and to set forth, as a theme, that particular utility which it is the object of these pages to inculcate and apply.

The uses of literature are manifold. Its study gives wholesome food to the mind, making it strong and systematic. It cultivates and delights the imagination and the taste of men. It refines society by elevating the thoughts and aspirations above what is sensual and sordid, and by checking the grosser passions; it makes up, in part, that "multiplication of agreeable consciousness" which Dr. Johnson calls happiness. Its adaptations in religion, in statesmanship, in legislative and judicial inquiry, are productive of noble and beneficent results. History shows us, that while it has given to the individual man, in all ages, contemplative habits, and high moral tone, it has thus also been a powerful instrument in producing the brilliant civilization of mighty empires.

A TEACHER OF HISTORY. — But apart from these its subjective benefits, it has its highest and most practical utility as a TEACHER OF HISTORY. Ballads, more powerful than laws, shouted forth from a nation's heart, have been in part the achievers, and afterward the victorious hymns, of its new-born freedom, and have been also used in after ages to reinspire the people with the spirit of their ancestors. Immortal epics not only present magnificent displays of heroism for imitation, but, like the Iliad and Odyssey, still teach the theogony, national policy, and social history of a people, after the Bema has long been silent, the temples in ruin, and the groves prostrate under the axe of repeated conquests.

Satires have at once exhibited and scourged social faults and national follies, and remained to after times as most essential materials for history.

Indeed, it was a quaint but just assertion of Hare, in his "Guesses at Truth," that in Greek history there is nothing truer than Herodotus except Homer.

Italy and France. — Passing by the classic periods, which afford abundant illustration of the position, it would be easy to exhibit the clear and direct historic teachings in purely literary works, by a reference to the literature of Italy and France. The history of the age of the Guelphs and Ghibellines is clearly revealed in the vision of Dante: the times of Louis XIV. are amply illustrated by the pulpit of Massillon, Bourdaloue, and Bridaine, and by the drama of Corneille, Racine, and Molière.

English Literature the best Illustration. — But in seeking for an illustration of the position that literature is eminently a teacher and interpreter of history, we are fortunate in finding none more striking than that presented by English literature itself. All the great events of English history find complete correspondent delineation in English literature, so that, were the purely historical record lost, we should have in the works of poetry, fiction, and the drama, correct portraitures of the character, habits, manners and customs, political sentiments, and modes and forms of religious belief among the

English people; in a word, the philosophy of English history.

In the works of Chaucer, Spenser, Shakspeare, Dryden, and Addison, are to be found the men and women, kings, nobles, and commons, descriptions of English nature, hints of the progress of science and advancement in art; the conduct of government, the force of prevailing fashions — in a word, the moving life of the time, and not its dry historic record.

"Authors," says the elder D'Israeli, "are the creators or creatures of opinion: the great form the epoch; the many reflect the age." Chameleon-like, most of them take the political, social, and religious hues of the period in which they live, while a few illustrate it perhaps quite as forcibly by violent opposition and invective.

We shall see that in Chaucer's *Canterbury Tales* and in Gower's *Vox Clamantis* are portrayed the political ferments and theological controversies of the reigns of Edward III. and Richard II. Spenser decks the history of his age in gilded mantle and flowing plumes, in his tribute to Gloriana, The Faery Queen, who is none other than Elizabeth herself. Literature partakes of the fierce polemic and religious enthusiasm which mark the troublous times of the Civil War; it becomes tawdry, tinselled, and licentious at the Restoration, and develops into numerous classes and more serious instruction, under the constitutional reigns of the house of Hanover, in which the kings were bad, but the nation prosperous because the rights of the people were guaranteed.

Many of the finest works of English literature are *purely and directly historical;* what has been said is intended to refer more particularly to those that are not — the unconscious, undesigned teachers of history, such as fiction, poetry, and the drama.

Purpose of the Work. — Such, then, is the purpose of

this volume — to indicate the teachings of history in the principal productions of English literature. Only the standard authors will be considered, and the student will not be overburdened with statistics, which it must be a part of his task to collect for himself. And now let us return to the early literature embodied in those languages which have preceded the English on British soil; or which, by their combination, have formed the English language. For, the English language may be properly compared to a stream, which, rising in a feeble source, receives in its seaward flow many tributaries, large and small, until it becomes a lordly river. The works of English literature may be considered as the ships and boats which it bears upon its bosom: near its source the craft are small and frail; as it becomes more navigable, statelier vessels are launched upon it, until, in its majestic and lakelike extensions, rich navies ride, freighted with wealth and power — the heavy ordnance of defence and attack, the products of Eastern looms, the precious metals and jewels from distant mines — the best exponents of the strength and prosperity of the nation through which flows the river of speech, bearing the treasures of mind.

Celtic Literary Remains. The Druids. — Let us take up the consideration of literature in Britain in the order of the conquests mentioned in the first chapter.

We recur to Britain while inhabited by the Celts, both before and after the Roman occupation. The extent of influence exercised by the Latin language upon the Celtic dialects cannot be determined; it seems to have been slight, and, on the other hand, it may be safely assumed that the Celtic did not contribute much to the world-absorbing Latin.

The chief feature, and a very powerful one, of the Celtic polity, was *Druidism.* At its head was a priesthood, not in the present meaning of the word, but in the more extended acceptation which it received in the middle ages, when it embraced the whole class of men of letters. Although we have very few literary remains, the system, wisdom, and works of the Druids form one of the strong foundation-stones of English literature and of English national customs, and should be studied on that account. The *Druid* proper was governor, judge, philosopher, expounder, and executioner. The *ovaidd*, or *ovates*, were the priests, chiefly concerned in the study of theology and the practice of religion. The *bards* were heroic poets of rare lyric power; they kept the national traditions in trust, and claimed the second sight and the power of prophecy. Much has been said of their human sacrifices in colossal images of wicker-work — the "*immani magnitudine simulacra*" of Cæsar — which were filled with human victims, and which crackled and disappeared in towering flame and columns of smoke, amid the loud chantings of the bards. The most that can be said in palliation of this custom is, that almost always such a scene presented the judicial execution of criminals, invested with the solemnities of religion.

In their theology, *Esus*, the God Force — the Eternal Father — has for his agents the personification of spiritual light, of immortality, of nature, and of heroism; *Camul* was the war-god; *Tarann* the thunder-god; *Heol*, the king of the sun, who inflames the soldier's heart, and gives vitality to the corn and the grape.[1]

But Druidism, which left its monuments like Stonehenge, and its strong traces in English life, now especially found in Wales and other mountainous parts of the kingdom, has not left any written record.

Roman Writers. — Of the Roman occupancy we have Roman and Greek accounts, many of them by those who took part in the doings of the time. Among the principal

[1] H. Martin, Histoire de France, i. 53.

writers are *Julius Cæsar, Tacitus, Diodorus Siculus, Strabo,* and *Suetonius.*

PSALTER OF CASHEL. — Of the later Celtic efforts, almost all are in Latin: the oldest Irish work extant is called the *Psalter of Cashel*, which is a compilation of the songs of the early bards, and of metrical legends, made in the ninth century by *Cormac Mac Culinan*, who claimed to be King of Munster and Bishop of Cashel.

THE WELSH TRIADS. — The next of the important Celtic remains is called *The Welsh Triads*, an early but progressive work of the Cymbric Celts. Some of the triads are of very early date, and others of a much later period. The work is said to have been compiled in its present form by *Caradoc of Nantgarvan* and *Jevan Brecha*, in the thirteenth century. It contains a record of "remarkable men and things which have been in the island of Britain, and of the events which befell the race of the Cymri from the age of ages," i. e. from the beginning. It has also numerous moral proverbs. It is arranged in *triads*, or sets of three.

As an example, we have one triad giving "The three of the race of the island of Britain: *Hu Gadarn*, (who first brought the race into Britain;) *Prydain*, (who first established regal government,) and *Dynwal Moelmud*, (who made a system of laws.)" Another triad presents "The three benevolent tribes of Britain: the *Cymri*, (who came with Hu Gadarn from Constantinople;) the *Lolegrwys*, (who came from the Loire,) and the *Britons*."

Then are mentioned the tribes that came with consent and under protection, viz., the *Caledonians*, the *Gwyddelian race*, and the men of *Galedin*, who came from the continent "when their country was drowned;" the last inhabited the Isle of Wight. Another mentions the three usurping tribes: the *Coranied*, the *Gwydel-Fichti*, (from Denmark,) and the *Saxons*. Although the *compilation* is so modern, most of the triads date from the sixth century.

THE MABINOGION. — Next in order of importance of the Celtic remains must be mentioned the Mabinogion, or *Tales for Youth*, a series of romantic tales, illustrative of early British life, some of which have been translated from the Celtic into English. Among these the most elaborate is the *Tale of Peredur*, a regular Romance of Arthur, entirely Welsh in costume and character.

BRITISH BARDS. — A controversy has been fiercely carried on respecting the authenticity of poems ascribed to *Aneurin*, *Taliesin*, *Llywarch Hen*, and *Merdhin*, or *Merlin*, four famous British bards of the fifth and sixth centuries, who give us the original stories respecting Arthur, representing him not as a "miraculous character," as the later histories do, but as a courageous warrior worthy of respect but not of wonder. The burden of the evidence, carefully collected and sifted by Sharon Turner,[1] seems to be in favor of the authenticity of these poems.

These works are fragmentary and legendary: they have given few elements to the English language, but they show us the condition and culture of the British mind in that period, and the nature of the people upon whom the Saxons imposed their yoke. "The general spirit [of the early British poetry] is much more Druidical than Christian,"[2] and in its mysterious and legendary nature, while it has been not without value as a historical representation of that early period, it has offered rare material for romantic poetry from that day to the present time. It is on this account especially that these works should be studied.

GILDAS. — Among the writers who must be considered as belonging to the Celtic race, although they wrote in Latin, the most prominent is *Gildas*. He was the son of Caw, (Al-

[1] Vindication of the Ancient British Poems.

[2] Craik's English Literature, i. 37.

cluyd, a British king,) who was also the father of the famous bard Aneurin. Many have supposed Gildas and Aneurin to be the same person, so vague are the accounts of both. If not, they were brothers. Gildas was a British bard, who, when converted to Christianity, became a Christian priest, and a missionary among his own people. He was born at Dumbarton in the middle of the sixth century, and was surnamed *the Wise*. His great work, the History of the Britons, is directly historical: his account extends from the first invasion of Britain down to his own time.

A true Celt, he is a violent enemy of the Roman conquerors first, and then of the Saxon invaders. He speaks of the latter as "the nefarious Saxons, of detestable name, hated alike by God and man; . . . a band of devils breaking forth from the den of the barbarian lioness."

The history of Gildas, although not of much statistical value, sounds a clear Celtic note against all invaders, and displays in many parts characteristic outlines of the British people.

ST. COLUMBANUS.—St. Colm, or Columbanus, who was born in 521, was the founder and abbot of a monastery in Iona, one of the Hebrides, which is also called Icolmkill —the Isle of Colm's Cell. The Socrates of that retreat, he found his Plato in the person of a successor, St. Adamnan, whose "Vita Sancti Columbae" is an early work of curious historical importance. St. Adamnan became abbot in 679.

A backward glance at the sparse and fragmentary annals of the Celtic people, will satisfy us that they have but slight claims to an original share in English literature. Some were in the Celtic dialects, others in Latin. They have given themes, indeed, to later scholars, but have left little trace in form and language. The common Celtic words retained in English are exceedingly few, although their number has not been decided. They form, in some sense, a portion of the foundation on which the structure of our literature has been erected, without being in any manner a part of the building itself.

CHAPTER III.

ANGLO-SAXON LITERATURE AND HISTORY.

The Lineage of the Anglo-Saxon. Earliest Saxon Poem. | Metrical Arrangement. Periphrasis and Alliteration. Beowulf. | Caedmon. Other Saxon Fragments. The Appearance of Bede.

The Lineage of the Anglo-Saxon.

THE true origin of English literature is Saxon. Anglo-Saxon is the mother tongue of the English language, or, to state its genealogy more distinctly, and to show its family relations at a glance, take the following divisions and subdivisions of the

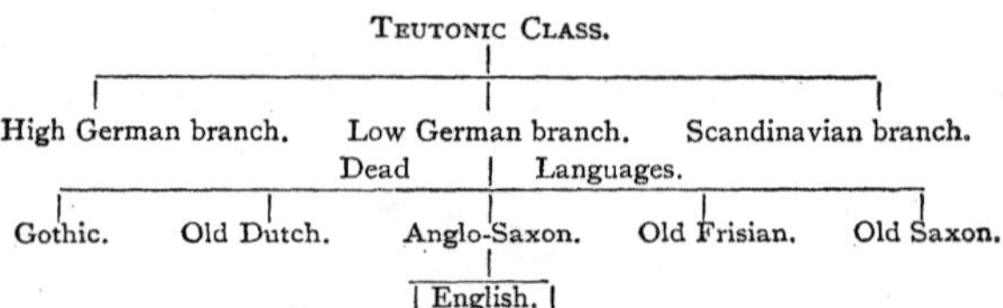

Without attempting an analysis of English to find the exact proportion of Saxon words, it must be observed that Saxon is the root-language of English; it might with propriety be called the oldest English; it has been manipulated, modified, and developed in its contact with other languages — remaining, however, *radically* the same — to become our present spoken language.

At this period of our inquiry, we have to do with the Saxon itself, premising, however, that it has many elements from the Dutch, and that its Scandinavian relations are found in many Danish words. The progress and modifications of the language in that formative process which made it the English, will be mentioned as we proceed in our inquiries.

In speaking of the Anglo-Saxon literature, we include a consideration also of those works written in Latin which are products of the times, and bear a part in the progress of the people and their literature. They are exponents of the Saxon mind, frequently of more value than the vernacular writings.

EARLIEST SAXON POEM. — The earliest literary monument in the Saxon language is the poem called Beowulf, the author and antiquity of which are alike unknown. It is at once a romantic legend and an instructive portraiture of the earliest Saxon period — "an Anglo-Saxon poetical romance," says Sharon Turner, "true in costume and manners, but with an invented story." Before proceeding to a consideration of this poem, let us look for a moment at some of the characteristics of Saxon poetry. As to its subject-matter, it is not much of a love-song, that sentiment not being one of its chief inspirations. The Saxon imagination was inflamed chiefly by the religious and the heroic in war. As to its handling, it abounded in metaphor and periphrasis, suggestive images, and parables instead of direct narrative.

METRICAL ARRANGEMENT. — As to metrical arrangement, Saxon poetry differed from our modern English as well as from the classical models, in that their poets followed no laws of metre, but arranged their vernacular verses without any distinct rules, but simply to please the ear. "To such a selection and arrangement of words as produced this effect, they added the habit of frequently omitting the usual particles, and of conveying their meaning in short and contracted phrases. The only artifices they used were those of inversion and transition."[1] It is difficult to give examples to those unacquainted

[1] Sharon Turner, History of the Anglo-Saxons, book ix., c. i.

with the language, but the following extract may serve to indicate our meaning: it is taken from Beowulf:

Crist waer a cennijd	Christ was born
Cẏninga wuldor	King of glory
On midne winter:	In mid-winter:
Mære theoden!	Illustrious King!
Ece almihtig!	Eternal, Almighty!
On thij eahteothan daeg	On the eighth day
Hael end gehaten	Saviour was called,
Heofon ricet theard.	Of Heaven's kingdom ruler.

PERIPHRASIS. — Their periphrasis, or finding figurative names for persons and things, is common to the Norse poetry. Thus Caedmon, in speaking of the ark, calls it the *sea-house, the palace of the ocean, the wooden fortress*, and by many other periphrastic names.

ALLITERATION. — The Saxons were fond of alliteration, both in prose and verse. They used it without special rules, but simply to satisfy their taste for harmony in having many words beginning with the same letter; and thus sometimes making an arbitrary connection between the sentences or clauses in a discourse, e. g.:

Firum foldan;	The ground for men
Frea almihtig;	Almighty ruler.

The nearest approach to a rule was that three words in close connection should begin with the same letter. The habit of ellipsis and transposition is illustrated by the following sentence in Alfred's prose: "So doth the moon with his pale light, that the bright stars he obscures in the heavens;" which he thus renders in poetry:

With pale light
Bright stars
Moon lesseneth.

With this brief explanation, which is only intended to be suggestive to the student, we return to Beowulf.

THE PLOT OF BEOWULF. — The poem contains six thousand lines, in which are told the wonderful adventures of the valiant viking Beowulf, who is supposed to have fallen in Jutland in the year 340. The Danish king Hrothgar, in whose great hall banquet, song, and dance are ever going on, is subjected to the stated visits of a giant, Grendel, a descendant of Cain, who destroys the Danish knights and people, and against whom no protection can be found.

Beowulf, the hero of the epic, appears. He is a great chieftain, the *heorth-geneat* (hearth-companion, or vassal) of a king named Higelac. He assembles his companions, goes over the road of the swans (the sea) to Denmark, or Norway, states his purpose to Hrothgar, and advances to meet Grendel. After an indecisive battle with the giant, and a fierce struggle with the giant's mother, who attacks him in the guise of a sea-wolf, he kills her, and then destroys Grendel. Upon the death of Hrothgar he receives his reward in being made King of the Danes.

With this occurrence the original poem ends: it is the oldest epic poem in any modern language. At a later day, new cantos were added, which, following the fortunes of the hero, record at length that he was killed by a dragon. A digest and running commentary of the poem may be found in Turner's Anglo-Saxons; and no one can read it without discerning the history shining clearly out of the mists of fable. The primitive manners, modes of life, forms of expression, are all historically delineated. In it the intimate relations between the *king* and his people are portrayed. The Saxon *cyning* is compounded of *cyn*, people, and *ing*, a son or descendant; and this etymology gives the true conditions of their rule: they were popular leaders — *elected* in the witenagemot on the death of their predecessors.[1] We observe, too, the spirit of adventure — a rude knight-errantry — which characterized these northern sea-kings

— that with such profit labor on the wide sea amid the contests of the ocean there they for riches	and for deceitful glory explore its bays in the deep waters till they sleep with their elders.

We may also notice the childish wonder of a rude, primitive, but brave people, who magnified a neighboring monarch of great skill and strength, or perhaps a malarious fen, into a giant, and who were pleased with a poem which caters to that heroic mythus which no civilization can root out of the human breast, and which gives at once charm and popularity to every epic.

CAEDMON. — Next in order, we find the paraphrase of Scripture by *Caedmon*, a monk of Whitby, who died about the year 680. The period in which he lived is especially marked by the spread of Christianity in Britain, and by a religious zeal mingled with the popular superstitions. The belief was universal that holy men had the power to work miracles. The Bible in its entire canon was known to few even among the ecclesiastics: treasure-house as it was to the more studious clerics, it was almost a sealed book to the common people. It would naturally be expected, then, that among the earliest literary efforts would be found translations and paraphrases of the most interesting portions of the Scripture narrative. It was in accordance with the spirit of the age that these productions should be attended with something of the marvellous, to give greater effect to the doctrine, and be couched in poetic language, the especial delight of people in the earlier ages of their history. Thus the writings of Caedmon are explained: he was a poor serving-brother in the

[1] Bosworth's Anglo-Saxon Dictionary.

monastery of Whitby, who was, or feigned to be, unable to improvise Scripture stories and legends of the saints as his brethren did, and had recourse to a vision before he exhibited his fluency.

In a dream, in a stall of oxen of which he was the appointed night-guard, an angelic stranger asked him to sing. "I cannot sing," said Caedmon. "Sing the creation," said the mysterious visitant. Feeling himself thus miraculously aided, Caedmon paraphrased in his dream the Bible story of the creation, and not only remembered the verses when he awoke, but found himself possessed of the gift of song for all his days.

Sharon Turner has observed that the paraphrase of Caedmon "exhibits much of a Miltonic spirit; and if it were clear that Milton had been familiar with Saxon, we should be induced to think that he owed something to Caedmon." And the elder D'Israeli has collated and compared similar passages in the two authors, in his "Amenities of Literature."

Another remarkable Anglo-Saxon fragment is called *Judith*, and gives the story of Judith and Holofernes, rendered from the Apocrypha, but with circumstances, descriptions, and speeches invented by the unknown author. It should be observed, as of historical importance, that the manners and characters of that Anglo-Saxon period are applied to the time of Judith, and so we have really an Anglo-Saxon romance, marking the progress and improvement in their poetic art.

Among the other remains of this time are the death of *Byrhtnoth*, *The Fight of Finsborough*, and the *Chronicle of King Lear and his Daughters*, the last of which is the foundation of an old play, upon which Shakspeare's tragedy of Lear is based.

It should here be noticed that Saxon literature was greatly influenced by the conversion of the realm at the close of the sixth century from the pagan religion of Woden to Christianity. It displayed no longer the fierce genius of the Scalds, inculcating revenge and promising the rewards of Walhalla; in spirit it was changed by the doctrine of love, and in form it was softened and in some degree — but only for a time — injured by the influence of the Latin, the language of the Church. At this time, also, there was a large adoption of Latin words into the Saxon, especially in theology and ecclesiastical matters.

THE ADVENT OF BEDE. — The greatest literary character of the Anglo-Saxon period, and the one who is of most value in teaching us the history of the times, both directly and indirectly, is the man who has been honored by his age as the *venerable Bede* or *Beda*. He was born at Yarrow, in the year 673, and died, after a retired but active, pious, and useful life, in 735. He wrote an Ecclesiastical history of the English, and dedicated it to the most glorious King Ceowulph of Northumberland, one of the monarchs of the Saxon Heptarchy. It is in matter and spirit a Saxon work in a Latin dress; and, although his work was written in Latin, he is placed among the Anglo-Saxon authors because it is as an Englishman that he appears to us in his subject, in the honest pride of race and country which he constantly manifests, and in the historical information which he has conveyed to us concerning the Saxons in England: of a part of the history which he relates he was an *eye-witness;* and besides, his work soon called forth several translations into Anglo-Saxon, among which that of Alfred the Great is the most noted, and would be taken for an original Saxon production.

It is worthy of remark, that after the decline of the Saxon literature, Bede remained for centuries, both in the original Latin and in the Saxon translations, a sealed and buried book; but in the later days, students of English literature and history began to look back with eager pleasure to that formative period prior to the Norman conquest, when English polity and institutions were simple and few, and when their Saxon progenitors were masters in the land.

CHAPTER IV.

THE VENERABLE BEDE AND THE SAXON CHRONICLE.

BIOGRAPHY.

BEDE was a precocious youth, whose excellent parts commended him to Bishop Benedict. He made rapid progress in Latin, Greek, and Hebrew; was a deacon at the unusual age of nineteen, and a priest at thirty. It seems probable that he always remained in his monastery, engaged in literary labor and offices of devotion until his death, which happened while he was dictating to his boy amanuensis. "Dear master," said the boy, "there is yet one sentence not written." He answered, "Write quickly." Soon after, the boy said, "The sentence is now written." He replied. "It is well; you have said the truth. Receive my head into your hands, for it is a great satisfaction to me to sit facing my holy place where I was wont to pray, that I may also sitting, call upon my Father." "And thus, on the pavement of his little cell, singing 'Glory be unto the Father, and unto the Son, and unto the Holy Ghost,' when he had named the Holy Ghost he breathed his last, and so departed to the heavenly kingdom."

HIS ECCLESIASTICAL HISTORY. — His ecclesiastical history opens with a description of Britain, including what was known of Scotland and Ireland. With a short preface concerning the Church in the earliest times, he dwells particularly upon the period, from the arrival of St. Augustine, in 597, to the year 731, a space of one hundred and thirty-four years, during nearly one-half of which the author lived. The principal written works from which he drew were the natural history of Pliny, the Hormesta of the Spanish priest *Paulus Orosius*, and the history of Gildas. His account of the coming of the Anglo-Saxons, "being the traditions of the Kentish people concerning Hengist and Horsa," has since proved to be fabulous, as the Saxons are now known to have been for a long period, during the Roman occupancy, making predatory incursions into Britain before the time of their reputed settlement.[1]

For the materials of the principal portions of his history, Bede was indebted to correspondence with those parts of England which he did not visit, and to the lives of saints and contemporary documents, which recorded the numerous miracles and wonders with which his pages are filled.

BEDE'S RECORDED MIRACLES. — The subject of these miracles has been considered at some length by Dr. Arnold,[2] in a very liberal spirit; but few readers will agree with him in concluding that with regard to some miracles, "there is no strong *a priori* improbability in their occurrence, but rather the contrary." One of the most striking of the historical lessons contained in this work, is the credulity and superstition which mark the age; and we reason justly and conclusively from the denial of the most palpable and absurd, to

[1] Kemble ("Saxon in England") suggests the resemblance between the fictitious landing of Hengist and Horsa "in three keels," and the Gothic tradition of the migration of Ostrogoths, Visigoths, and Gepidæ to the mouth of the Vistula in the same manner. Dr. Latham (English Language) fixes the Germanic immigration into Britain at the middle of the fourth, instead of the middle of the fifth century.

[2] Lectures on Modern History, lect. ii.

the repudiation of the lesser demands on our credulity. It is sufficient for us that both were eagerly believed in his day, and thus complete a picture of the age which such a view would only serve to impair, if not destroy. The theology of the age is set forth with wonderful clearness, in the numerous questions propounded by Augustine to Gregory I., the Bishop of Rome, and in the judicious answers of that prelate; in which may also be found the true relation which the Church of Rome bore to her English mission.

We have also the statement of the establishment of the archbishoprics of Canterbury and York, the bishopric of London, and others.

The last chapter but one, the twenty-third, gives an important account "of the present state of the English nation, or of all Britain;" and the twenty-fourth contains a chronological recapitulation, from the beginning of the year 731, and a list of the author's works. Bede produced, besides his history, translations of many books in the Bible, several histories of abbots and saints, books of hymns and epigrams, a treatise on orthography, and one on poetry.

To point the student to Bede's works, and to indicate their historic teachings, is all that can be here accomplished. A careful study of his Latin History, as the great literary monument of the Anglo-Saxon period, will disclose many important truths which lie beneath the surface, and thus escape the cursory reader. Wars and politics, of which the Anglo-Saxon chronicle is full, find comparatively little place in his pages. The Church was then peaceful, and not polemic; the monasteries were sanctuaries in which quiet, devotion, and order reigned. Another phase of the literature shows us how the Gentiles raged and the people were imagining a vain thing; but Bede, from his undisturbed cell, scarcely heard the howlings of the storm, as he wrote of that kingdom which promised peace and good-will.

Bede's Latin. — To the classical student, the language of

Bede offers an interesting study. The Latin had already been corrupted, and a nice discrimination will show the causes of this corruption — the effects of the other living languages, the ignorance of the clergy, and the new subjects and ideas to which it was applied.

Bede was in the main more correct than his age, and his vocabulary has few words of barbarian origin. He arose like a luminary, and when the light of his learning disappeared, but one other star appeared to irradiate the gloom which followed his setting; and that was in the person and the reign of Alfred.

OTHER WRITERS OF THIS AGE. — Among names which must pass with the mere mention, the following are, after Bede, the most illustrious in this time. *Aldhelm*, Abbot of Malmesbury, who died in the year 709, is noted for his scientific computations, and for his poetry: he is said to have translated the Psalms into Anglo-Saxon poetry.

Alcuin, the pride of two countries, England and France, was born in the year of Bede's death: renowned as an Englishman for his great learning, he was invited by Charlemagne to his court, and aided that distinguished sovereign in the scholastic and literary efforts which render his reign so illustrious. Alcuin died in 804.

The works of Alcuin are chiefly theological treatises, but he wrote a life of Charlemagne, which has unfortunately been lost, and which would have been invaluable to history in the dearth of memorials of that emperor and his age.

Alfric, surnamed Grammaticus, (died 1006,) was an Archbishop of Canterbury, in the tenth century, who wrote eighty homilies, and was, in his opposition to Romish doctrine, one of the earliest English reformers.

John Scotus Erigena, who flourished at the beginning of the ninth century, in the brightest age of Irish learning, settled in France, and is known as a subtle and learned scholastic philosopher. His principal work is a treatise "On the Division of Nature." Both names, *Scotus* and *Erigena*, indicate his Irish origin; the original *Scoti* being inhabitants of the North of Ireland.

Dunstan, (925–988,) commonly called Saint Dunstan, was a powerful and dictatorial Archbishop of Canterbury, who used the superstitions of monarch and people to enable him to exercise a marvellous supremacy in the realm. He wrote commentaries on the Benedictine rule.

These writers had but a remote and indirect bearing upon the progress of literature in England, and are mentioned rather as contemporary, than as distinct subjects of our study.

THE ANGLO-SAXON CHRONICLE. — We now reach the valuable and purely historical compilation known as the *Anglo-Saxon Chronicle*, which is a chronological arrangement of events in English history, from the birth of Christ to the year 1154, in the reign of Henry the Second. It is the most valuable epitome of English history during that long period.

It is written in Anglo-Saxon, and was begun soon after the time of Alfred, at least as a distinct work. In it we may trace the changes in the language from year to year, and from century to century, as it passed from unmixed Saxon until, as the last records are by contemporary hands, it almost melted into modern English, which would hardly trouble an Englishman of the present day to read.

The first part of the Chronicle is a table of events, many of them fabulous, which had been originally jotted down by Saxon monks, abbots, and bishops. To these partial records, King Alfred furnished additional information, as did also, in all probability, Alfric and Dunstan. These were collected into permanent form by Plegmund, Archbishop of Canterbury, who brought the annals up to the year 891; from that date they were continued in the monasteries. Of the Saxon Chronicle there are no less than seven accredited ancient copies, of which the shortest extends to the year 977, and the longest to 1154; the others extend to intermediate dates.

Its Value. — The value of the Chronicle as a statistic record of English history cannot be over-estimated; it moves before the student of English literature like a diorama, picturing the events in succession, not without glimpses of their attendant philosophy. We learn much of the nation's thoughts, troubles, mental, moral, and physical conditions, social laws, and manners. As illustrations we may refer to the romantic adventures of King Alfred; and to the conquest of Saxon England by William of Normandy — "all as God granted them," says the pious chronicler, "for the people's sins." And he afterward adds, "Bishop Odo and William the Earl built castles wide throughout the nation, and poor people distressed; and ever after it greatly grew in evil: may the end be good when God will." Although for the most part written in prose, the annals of several years are given in the alliterative Saxon verse.

A good English translation of Bede's history, and one of the Chronicle, edited by Dr. Giles, have been issued together by Bohn in one volume of his Antiquarian library. To the student of English history and of English literature, the careful perusal of both, in conjunction, is an imperative necessity.

Alfred the Great. — Among the best specimens of Saxon prose are the translations and paraphrases of King *Alfred*, justly called the Great and the Truth-teller, the noblest monarch of the Saxon period. The kingdoms of the heptarchy, or octarchy, had been united under the dominion of Egbert, the King of Wessex, in the year 827, and thus formed the kingdom of England. But this union of the kingdoms was in many respects nominal rather than really complete; as Alfred frequently subscribes himself *King of the West Saxons*. It was a confederation to gain strength against their enemies. On the one hand, the inhabitants of North, South, and West Wales were constantly rising against Wessex and Mercia; and on the other, until the accession of Alfred upon the death of his brother Ethelred, in 871, every year of the

Chronicle is marked by fierce battles with the troops and fleets of the Danes on the eastern and southern coasts.

It redounds greatly to the fame of Alfred that he could find time and inclination in his troubled and busy reign, so harassed with wars by land and sea, for the establishment of wise laws, the building or rebuilding of large cities, the pursuit of letters. and the interest of education. To give his subjects, grown-up nobles as well as children, the benefits of historical examples, he translated the work of Orosius, a compendious history of the world, a work of great repute; and to enlighten the ecclesiastics, he made versions of parts of Bede; of the Pastorale of Gregory the First; of the Soliloquies of St. Augustine, and of the work of Boethius, *De Consolatione Philosophiæ.* Beside these principal works are other minor efforts. In all his writings, he says he "sometimes interprets word for word, and sometimes meaning for meaning." With Alfred went down the last gleams of Saxon literature. Troubles were to accumulate steadily and irresistibly upon the soil of England, and the sword took the place of the pen.

THE DANES.—The Danes thronged into the realm in new incursions, until 850,000 of them were settled in the North and East of England. The Danegelt or tribute, displaying at once the power of the invaders and the cowardice and effeminacy of the Saxon monarchs, rose to a large sum, and two millions[1] of Saxons were powerless to drive the invaders away. In the year 1016, after the weak and wicked reign of the besotted *Ethelred,* justly surnamed the *Unready,* who to his cowardice in paying tribute added the cruelty of a wholesale massacre on St. Brice's Eve—since called the Danish St. Bartholomew—the heroic Edmund Ironsides could not stay the storm, but was content to divide the kingdom with *Knud* (Canute) the Great. Literary efforts were at an end. For twenty-two years the Danish kings sat upon the throne

[1] Sharon Turner.

of all England; and when the Saxon line was restored in the person of Edward the Confessor, a monarch not calculated to restore order and impart strength, in addition to the internal sources of disaster, a new element of evil had sprung up in the power and cupidity of the Normans.

Upon the death of Edward the Confessor, the claimants to the throne were *Harold*, the son of Godwin, and *William of Normandy*, both ignoring the claims of the Saxon heir apparent, Edgar Atheling. Harold, as has been already said, fell a victim to the dissensions in his own ranks, as well as to the courage and strength of William, and thus Saxon England fell under Norman rule.

THE LITERARY PHILOSOPHY. — The literary philosophy of this period does not lie far beneath the surface of the historic record. Saxon literature was expiring by limitation. During the twelfth century, the Saxon language was completely transformed into English. The intercourse of many previous years had introduced a host of Norman French words; inflections had been lost; new ideas, facts, and objects had sprung up, requiring new names. The dying Saxon literature was overshadowed by the strength and growth of the Norman, and it had no royal patron and protector since Alfred. The superior art-culture and literary attainments of the South, had long been silently making their impression in England; and it had been the custom to send many of the English youth of noble families to France to be educated.

Saxon chivalry[1] was rude and unattractive in comparison with the splendid armor, the gay tournaments, and the witching minstrelsy which signalized French chivalry; and thus the peaceful elements of conquest were as seductive as the force of arms was potent. A dynasty which had ruled for more than six hundred years was overthrown; a great chapter in English history was closed. A new order was established, and a new chapter in England's annals was begun.

[1] Turner, ch. xii.

CHAPTER V.

THE NORMAN CONQUEST AND ITS EARLIEST LITERATURE.

Norman Rule.

WITH the conquest of England, and as one of the strongest elements of its permanency, the feudal system was brought into England; the territory was surveyed and apportioned to be held by military tenure; to guard against popular insurrections, the curfew rigorously housed the Saxons at night; a new legislature, called a parliament, or talking-ground, took the place of the witenagemot, or assembly of the wise: it was a conquest not only in name but in truth; everything was changed by the conqueror's right, and the Saxons were entirely subjected.

Its Oppression. — In short, the Norman conquest, from the day of the battle of Hastings, brought the Saxon people under a galling yoke. The Norman was everywhere an oppressor. Besides his right as a conqueror, he felt a contempt for the rudeness of the Saxon. He was far more able to govern and to teach. He founded rich abbeys; schools like those of Oxford and Cambridge he expanded into universities like that of Paris. He filled all offices of profit and trust, and created many which the Saxons had not. In place of the Saxon English, which, however vigorous, was greatly wanting in what may be called the vocabulary of progress, the Norman French, drawing constantly upon the Latin, enriched by the enactments of Charlemagne and the tributes of Italy, even in its infancy a language of social comity in Western Europe, was spoken at court, introduced into the courts of law, taught in the schools, and threatened to submerge and drown out the vernacular.[1] All inducements to composition in English were wanting; delicious songs of Norman Trouvères chanted in the *Langue d'oil*, and stirring tales of Troubadours in the *Langue d'oc*, carried the taste captive away from the Saxon, as a regal banquet lures from the plain fare of the cottage board, more wholesome but less attractive.

Its Benefits. — Had this progress continued, had this grasp of power remained without hinderance or relaxation, the result would have been the destruction or amalgamation of the vigorous English, so as to form a romance language similar to the French, and only different in the amount of Northern and local words. But the Norman power, without losing its title, was to find a limit to its encroachments. This limit was fixed, *first*, by the innate hardihood and firmness of the Saxon character, which, though cast down and oppressed, retained its elasticity; which cherished its language in spite of Norman threats and sneers, and which never lost heart while waiting for better times; *secondly*, by the insular position of Great Britain, fortified by the winds and waves, which enabled her to assimilate and mould anew whatever came into her borders, to the discomfiture of further continental encroachments; constituting her, in the words of Shakspeare,

> ". . . that pale, that white-faced shore,
> Whose foot spurns back the ocean's roaring tides,
> And coops from other lands her islanders;"

and, *thirdly*, to the Crusades, which, attracting the nobles to

[1] For the discussion of the time and circumstances of the introduction of French into law processes, see Craik, i. 117.

adventures in Palestine, lifted the heel of Norman oppression off the Saxon neck, and gave that opportunity, which alone was needed, to make England in reality, if not in name — in thews, sinews, and mental strength, if not in regal state and aristocratic privilege — Saxon-England in all its future history. Other elements are still found, but the Saxon greatly predominates.

The historian of that day might well bemoan the fate of the realm, as in the Saxon Chronicle already quoted. To the philosopher of to-day, this Norman conquest and its results were of incalculable value to England, by bringing her into relations with the continent, by enduing her with a weight and influence in the affairs of Europe which she could never otherwise have attained, and by giving a new birth to a noble literature which has had no superior in any period of the world's history.

As our subject does not require, and our space will not warrant the consideration of the rise and progress of French literature, before its introduction with the Normans into England, we shall begin with the first fruits after its transplantation into British soil. But before doing so, it becomes necessary to mention certain Latin chronicles which furnished food for these Anglo-Norman poets and legendists.

WILLIAM OF MALMESBURY. — *William of Malmesbury*, the first Latin historian of distinction, who is contemporary with the Norman conquest, wrote a work called the "Heroic Deeds of the English Kings," (*Gesta Regum Anglorum*,) which extends from the arrival of the Saxons to the year 1120; another, "The New History," (*Historia Novella*,) brings the history down to 1142. Notwithstanding the credulity of the age, and his own earnest recital of numerous miracles, these works are in the main truthful, and of real value to the historical student. In the contest between Matilda and Stephen for the succession of the English crown,

William of Malmesbury is a strong partisan of the former, and his work thus stands side by side, for those who would have all the arguments, with the *Gesta Stephani*, by an unknown contemporary, which is written in the interest of Stephen.

GEOFFREY OF MONMOUTH. — More famous than the monk of Malmesbury, but by no means so truthful, stands *Geoffrey of Monmouth*, Archdeacon of Monmouth and Bishop of St. Asaph's, a writer to whom the rhyming chronicles and Anglo-Norman poets have owed so much. Walter, a Deacon of Oxford, it is said, had procured from Brittany a Welsh chronicle containing a history of the Britons from the time of one Brutus, a great-grandson of Æneas, down to the seventh century of our era. From this, partly in translation and partly in original creation, Geoffrey wrote his "History of the Britons." Catering to the popular prejudice, he revived, and in part created, the deeds of Arthur and the Knights of the Round Table — fabulous heroes who have figured in the best English poetry from that day to the present, their best presentation having been made in the Idyls of the King, (Arthur,) by Tennyson.

The popular philosophy of Geoffrey's work is found in the fact, that while in Bede and in the Saxon Chronicle the Britons had not been portrayed in such a manner as to flatter the national vanity, which seeks for remote antecedents of greatness; under the guise of the Chronicle of Brittany, Geoffrey undertook to do this. Polydore Virgil distinctly condemns him for relating "many fictitious things of King Arthur and the ancient Britons, invented by himself, and pretended to be translated by him into Latin, which he palms on the world with the sacred name of true history;" and this view is substantiated by the fact that the earlier writers speak of Arthur as a prince and a warrior, of no colossal fame — "well known, but not idolized. . . . That he was a courageous warrior is unquestionable; but that he was the miraculous Mars of the British history, from whom kings and nations shrunk in panic, is completely disproved by the temperate encomiums of his contemporary bards."[1]

It is of great historical importance to observe the firm hold taken by this fabulous character upon the English people, as evinced by the fact that he has been a popular hero of the English epic ever since. Spenser adopted him as the presiding genius of his "Fairy Queen," and Milton projected a great epic on his times, before he decided to write the Paradise Lost.

OTHER PRINCIPAL LATIN CHRONICLERS OF THE EARLY NORMAN PERIOD.

Ingulphus, Abbot of Croyland, 1075–1109: History of Croyland. Authenticity disputed.

William of Poictiers, 1070: Deeds of William the Conqueror, (Gesta Gulielmi Ducis Normannorum et Regis Anglorum.)

Ordericus Vitalis, born about 1075: general ecclesiastical history.

William of Jumièges: History of the Dukes of Normandy.

Florence of Worcester, died 1118: (Chronicon ex Chronicis,) Chronicle from the Chronicles, from the Creation to 1118, (with two valuable additions to 1141, and to 1295.)

Matthew of Westminster, end of thirteenth century (probably a fictitious name): Flowers of the Histories, (Flores Historiarum.)

Eadmer, died about 1124: history of his own time, (Historia Novorum, sive sui seculi.)

Giraldus Cambrensis, born 1146, known as Girald Barry: numerous histories, including Topographia Hiberniæ, and the Norman conquest of Ireland; also several theological works.

Henry of Huntingdon, first half of the twelfth century: History of England.

Alured of Rievaux, 1109–66: The Battle of the Standard.

Roger de Hoveden, end of twelfth century: Annales, from the end of Bede's history to 1202.

Matthew Paris, monk of St. Alban's, died 1259: Historia Major, from the Norman conquest to 1259, continued by William Rishanger to 1322.

[1] Sharon Turner's History of the Anglo-Saxons, i. 199. For an admirable summary of the bardic symbolisms and mythological types exhibited in the story of Arthur, see H. Martin, Hist. de France, liv. xx.

Ralph Higden, fourteenth century: Polychronicon, or Chronicle of Many Things; translated in the fifteenth century, by John de Trevisa; printed by Caxton in 1482, and by Wynken de Worde in 1485.

THE ANGLO-NORMAN POETS AND CHRONICLERS. — Norman literature had already made itself a name before William conquered England. Short jingling tales in verse, in ballad style, were popular under the name of *fabliaux*, and fuller epics, tender, fanciful, and spirited, called Romans, or Romaunts, were sung to the lute, in courts and camps. Of these latter, Alexander the Great, Charlemagne, and Roland were the principal heroes.

Strange as it may seem, this *langue d'oil*, in which they were composed, made more rapid progress in its poetical literature, in the period immediately after the conquest, in England than at home: it flourished by the transplantation. Its advent was with an act of heroism. Taillefer, the standard-bearer of William at Seulac, marched in advance of the army, struck the first blow, and met his death while chanting the song of Roland:

Of Charlemagne and Roland,	De Karlemaine è de Rollant,
Of Oliver and his vassals,	Et d'Olivier et des vassals,
Who died at Roncesvalles.	Ki moururent en Renchevals.

Each stanza ended with the war-shout *Aoi!* and was responded to by the cry of the Normans, *Diex aide, God to aid.* And this battle-song was the bold manifesto of Norman poetry invading England. It found an echo wherever William triumphed on English soil, and played an important part in the formation of the English language and English literature. New scenes and new victories created new inspiration in the poets; monarchs like Henry I., called from his scholarship *Beauclerc*, practised and cherished the poetic art, and thus it happened that the Norman poets in England produced works of sweeter minstrelsy and greater historical value than the *fabliaux*, *Romans*, and *Chansons de gestes* of their brethren on the continent. The conquest itself became a grand theme for their muse.

Richard Wace. — First among the Anglo-Norman poets stands Richard Wace, called Maistre Wace, reading clerk, (clerc lisant,) born in the island of Jersey, about 1112, died in 1184. His works are especially to be noted for the direct and indirect history they contain. His first work, which appeared about 1138, is entitled *Le Brut d'Angleterre* — The English Brutus — and is in part a paraphrase of the Latin history of Geoffrey of Monmouth, who had presented Brutus of Troy as the first in the line of British kings. Wace has preserved the fiction of Geoffrey, and has catered to that characteristic of the English people which, not content with homespun myths, sought for genealogies from the remote classic times. Wace's *Brut* is chiefly in octo-syllabic verse, and extends to fifteen thousand lines.

But Wace was a courtier, as well as a poet. Not content with pleasing the fancy of the English people with a fabulous royal lineage, he proceeded to gratify the pride of their Norman masters by writing, in 1171, his "Roman de Rou, et des Ducs de Normandie," an epic poem on Rollo, the first Duke of Normandy — Rollo, called the Marcher, because he was so mighty of stature that no horse could bear his weight. This Rollo compromised with Charles the Simple of France by marrying his daughter, and accepting that tract of Neustria to which he gave the name of Normandy. He was the ancestor, at six removes, of William the Conqueror, and his mighty deeds were a pleasant and popular subject for the poet of that day, when a great-grandson of William, Henry II., was upon the throne of England. The Roman de Rou contains also the history of Rollo's successors: it is in two parts; the first extending to the beginning of the reign of the third duke, Richard the Fearless, and the second, containing the story of the conquest, comes down to the time of Henry II.

himself. The second part he wrote rapidly, for fear that he would be forestalled by the king's poet *Benoit.* The first part was written in Alexandrines, but for the second he adopted the easier measure of the octo-syllabic verse, of which this part contains seventeen thousand lines. In this poem are discerned the craving of the popular mind, the power of the subject chosen, and the reflection of language and manners, which are displayed on every page.

So popular, indeed, was the subject of the Brut, indigenous as it was considered to British soil, that Wace's poem, already taken from Geoffrey of Monmouth, as Geoffrey had taken it, or pretended to take it from the older chronicle, was soon again, as we shall see, to be versionized into English.

Other Norman Writers of the Twelfth Century.

Philip de Than, about 1130, one of the Trouvères: *Li livre de crêatures* is a poetical study of chronology, and his *Bestiarie* is a sort of natural history of animals and minerals.

Benoit: Chroniques des Ducs de Normandie, 1160, written in thirty thousand octo-syllabic verses, only worthy of a passing notice, because of the appointment of the poet by the king, (Henry II.,) in order to forestall the second part of Wace's Roman de Rou.

Geoffrey, died 1146: A miracle play of St. Catherine.

Geoffrey Gaimar, about 1150: Estorie des Engles, (History of the English.)

Luc de la Barre, blinded for his bold satires by the king (Henry I.).

Mestre Thomas, latter part of twelfth century: Roman du Roi Horn. Probably the original of the "Geste of Kyng Horn."

Richard I., (Cœur de Lion,) died 1199, King of England: *Sirventes* and songs. His antiphonal song with the minstrel Blondel is said to have given information of the place of his imprisonment, and procured his release; but this is probably only a romantic fiction.

CHAPTER VI.

THE MORNING TWILIGHT OF ENGLISH LITERATURE.

Semi-Saxon Literature.
Layamon.
The Ormulum.
Robert of Gloucester.
Langland. Piers Plowman.
Piers Plowman's Creed.
Sir Jean Froissart.
Sir John Mandevil.

SEMI-SAXON LITERATURE.

MOORE, in his beautiful poem, "The Light of the Harem," speaks of that luminous pulsation which precedes the real, progressive morning:

. . . that earlier dawn
Whose glimpses are again withdrawn,
As if the morn had waked, and then
Shut close her lids of light again.

The simile is not inapt, as applied to the first efforts of the early English, or Semi-Saxon literature, during the latter part of the twelfth and the whole of the thirteenth century. That deceptive dawn, or first glimpse of the coming day, is to be found in the work of *Layamon*. The old Saxon had revived, but had been modified and altered by contact with the Latin chronicles and the Anglo-Norman poetry, so as to become a distinct language — that of the people; and in this language men of genius and poetic taste were now to speak to the English nation.

LAYAMON. — Layamon[1] was an English priest of Worcester-

[1] Craik says, (i. 198,) "Or, as he is also called, *Laweman* — for the old character represented in this instance by our modern *y*, is really only a

shire, who made a version of Wace's *Brut*, in the beginning of the thirteenth century, so peculiar, however, in its language, as to puzzle the philologist to fix its exact date with even tolerable accuracy. But, notwithstanding its resemblance, according to Mr. Ellis, to the "simple and unmixed, though very barbarous Saxon," the character of the alphabet and the nature of the rhythm place it at the close of the twelfth century, and present it as perhaps the best type of the Semi-Saxon. The poem consists partly of the Saxon alliterative lines, and partly of verses which seem to have thrown off this trammel; so that a different decision as to its date would be reached according as we consider these diverse parts of its structure. It is not improbable that, like English poets of a later time, Layamon affected a certain archaism in language, as giving greater beauty and interest to his style. The subject of the *Brut* was presented to him as already treated by three authors: first, the original Celtic poem, which has been lost; second, the Latin chronicle of Geoffrey; and, third, the French poem of Wace. Although Layamon's work is, in the main, a translation of that of Wace, he has modified it, and added much of his own. His poem contains more than thirty thousand lines.

THE ORMULUM. — Next in value to the Brut of Layamon, is the Ormulum, a series of metrical homilies, in part paraphrases of the gospels for the day, with verbal additions and annotations. This was the work of a monk named *Orm* or *Ormin*, who lived in the beginning of the thirteenth century, during the reign of King John and Henry III., and it resembles our present English much more nearly than the poem of Layamon. In his dedication of the work to his brother Walter, Orm says — and we give his words as an illustration of the language in which he wrote:

guttural, (and by no means either a *j* or a *z*,) by which it is sometimes rendered." Marsh says, "Or, perhaps, *Lagamon*, for we do not know the sound of *y* in this name."

Icc hafe don swa summ thu bad	I have done so as thou bade,
Annd forthedd te thin wille	And performed thee thine will;
Icc hafe wennd uintill Ennglissh	I have turned into English
Goddspelless hallghe lare	Gospel's holy lore,
Affterr thatt little witt tatt me	After that little wit that me
Min Drihhten hafethth lenedd	My lord hath lent.

The poem is written in Alexandrine verses, which may be divided into octo-syllabic lines, alternating with those of six syllables, as in the extract given above. He is critical with regard to his orthography, as is evinced in the following instructions which he gives to his future readers and transcriber:

And whase willen shall this booke	And whoso shall wish this book
Eft other sithe writen,	After other time to write,
Him bidde icc that he 't write right	Him bid I that he it write right,
Swa sum this booke him teacheth	So as this book him teacheth.

The critics have observed that, whereas the language of Layamon shows that it was written in the southwest of England, that of Orm manifests an eastern or northeastern origin. To the historical student, Orm discloses the religious condition and needs of the people, and the teachings of the Church. His poem is also manifestly a landmark in the history of the English language.

ROBERT OF GLOUCESTER. — Among the rhyming chroniclers of this period, Robert, a monk of Gloucester Abbey, is noted for his reproduction of the history of Geoffrey of Monmouth, already presented by Wace in French, and by Layamon in Saxon-English. But he is chiefly valuable in that he carries the chronicle forward to the end of the reign of Henry III. Written in West-country English, it not only contains a strong infusion of French, but distinctly states the prevailing influence of that language in his own day:

Vor bote a man couthe French, me tolth of him well lute
Ac lowe men holdeth to Englyss, and to her kunde speche zute.

For unless a man know French, one talketh of him little;
But *low* men hold to English, and to their natural speech yet.

The chronicle of Robert is written in Alexandrines, and, except for the French words incongruously interspersed, is almost as "barbarous" Saxon as the Brut of Layamon.

LANGLAND — PIERS PLOWMAN. — The greatest of the immediate heralds of Chaucer, whether we regard it as a work of literary art, or as an historic reflector of the age, is "The Vision of Piers Plowman," by Robert Langland, which appeared between 1360 and 1370. It stands between the Semi-Saxon and the old English, in point of language, retaining the alliterative feature of the former; and, as a teacher of history, it displays very clearly the newly awakened spirit of religious inquiry, and the desire for religious reform among the English people: it certainly was among the means which aided in establishing a freedom of religious thought in England, while as yet the continent was bound in the fetters of a rigorous and oppressive authority.

Peter, the ploughboy, intended as a representative of the common people, drops asleep on Malvern Hills, between Wales and England, and sees in his dream an array of virtues and vices pass before him — such as Mercy, Truth, Religion, Covetousness, Avarice, etc. The allegory is not unlike that of Bunyan. By using these as the personages, in the manner of the early dramas called the Moralities, he is enabled to attack and severely scourge the evil lives and practices of the clergy, and the abuses which had sprung up in the Church, and to foretell the punishment, which afterward fell upon the monasteries in the time of Henry VIII., one hundred and fifty years later:

And then shall the Abbot of Abingdon, and all his issue forever,
Have a knock of a king, and incurable the wound.

His attack is not against the Church itself, but against the clergy. It is to be remarked, in studying history through the medium of literature, that the works of a certain period, themselves the result of history, often illustrate the coming age, by being prophetic, or rather, as antecedents by suggesting consequents. Thus, this Vision of Piers Plowman indicates the existence of a popular spirit which had been slowly but steadily increasing — which sympathized with Henry II. and the priest-trammelling "Constitutions of Clarendon," even while it was ready to go on a pilgrimage to the shrine of Thomas à Becket, the illustrious victim of the quarrel between Henry and his clergy. And it points with no uncertain finger to a future of greater light and popular development, for this bold spirit of reform was strongly allied to political rights. The clergy claimed both spiritualities and temporalities from the Pope, and, being governed by ecclesiastical laws, were not like other English subjects amenable to the civil code. The king's power was thus endangered; a proud and encroaching spirit was fostered, and the clergy became dissolute in their lives. In the words of Piers Plowman:

I found these freres,
All the four orders,
Preaching the people
For profit of hem selve;
Glosed the gospel,
As hem good liked.

And again:

Ac now is Religion
A rider, a roamer about,
A leader of love days
And a lond buyer,
A pricker on a palfrey,
From manor to manor.

Piers Plowman's Creed. — The name of Piers Plowman and the conceit of his Vision became at once very popular. He stood as a representative of the peasant class rising in importance and in assertion of religious rights.

An unknown follower of Wiclif wrote a poem called "Piers Plowman's Creed," which conveys religious truth in a formula of belief. The language and the alliterative feature are similar to those of the Vision; and the invective is against the clergy, and especially against the monks and friars.

FROISSART. — Sire Jean Froissart was born about 1337. He is placed here for the observance of chronological order: he was not an English writer, but must receive special mention because his "Chronicles," although written in French, treat of the English wars in France, and present splendid pictures of English chivalry and heroism. He lived, too, for some time in England, where he figured at court as the secretary of Philippa, queen of Edward III. Although not always to be relied on as an historian, his work is unique and charming, and is very truthful in its delineation of the men and manners of that age: it was written for courtly characters, and not for the common people. The title of his work may be translated "Chronicles of France, England, Scotland, Spain, Brittany, Gascony, Flanders, and surrounding places."

SIR JOHN MANDEVIL, (1300–1371.) — We also place in this general catalogue a work which has, ever since its appearance, been considered one of the curiosities of English literature. It is a narrative of the travels of Mandevil in the East. He was born in 1300; became a doctor of medicine, and journeyed in those regions of the earth for thirty-four years. A portion of the time he was in service with a Mohammedan army; at other times he lived in Egypt, and in China, and, returning to England an old man, he brought such a budget of wonders — true and false — stories of immense birds like the roc, which figure in Arabian mythology and romance, and which could carry elephants through the air — of men with tails, which were probably orang-outangs or gorillas.

Some of his tales, which were then entirely discredited, have been ascertained by modern travellers to be true. His work was written by him first in Latin, and then in French — Latin for the savans, and French for the court — and afterward, such was the power and demand of the new English tongue, that he presented his marvels to the world in an English version. This was first printed by Wynken de Worde, in 1499.

Other Writers of the Thirteenth and Fourteenth Centuries, who preceded Chaucer.

Robert Manning, a canon of Bourne — called also Robert de Brunne: Translated a portion of Wace's *Brut*, and also a chronicle of Piers de Langtoft bringing the history down to the death of Edward I. (1307.) He is also supposed to be the author of a translation of the "Manuel des Péchés, (Handling of Sins,) the original of which is ascribed to Bishop Grostête of Lincoln.

The Ancren Riwle, or *Anchoresses' Rule*, about 1200, by an unknown writer, sets forth the duties of a monastic life for three ladies (anchoresses) and their household in Dorsetshire.

Roger Bacon, (1214–1292,) a friar of Ilchester: He extended the area of knowledge by his scientific experiments, but wrote his Opus Magus, or *greater work*, in comparison with the Opus Minus, and numerous other treatises in Latin. If he was not a writer in English, his name should be mentioned as a great genius, whose scientific knowledge was far in advance of his age, and who had prophetic glimpses of the future conquests of science.

Robert Grostête, Bishop of Lincoln, died 1253, was probably the author of the *Manuel des Pêchês*, and also wrote a treatise on the sphere.

Sir Michael Scott: He lived in the latter half of the thirteenth century; was a student of the "occult sciences," and also skilled in theology and medicine. He is referred to by Walter Scott as the "wondrous wizard, Michael Scott."

Thomas of Ercildoun — called the Rhymer — supposed by Sir Walter Scott, but erroneously, as is now believed, to be the author of "Sir Tristram."

The King of Tars is the work of an unknown author of this period.

In thus disposing of the authors before Chaucer, no attempt has been made at a nice subdivision and classification of the character of the works, or the nature of the periods, further than to trace the onward movement of the language, in its embryo state, in its birth, and in its rude but healthy infancy.

CHAPTER VII.

CHAUCER, AND THE EARLY REFORMATION.

THE BEGINNING OF A NEW ERA.

AND now it is evident, from what has been said, that we stand upon the eve of a great movement in history and literature. Up to this time everything had been more or less tentative, experimental, and disconnected, all tending indeed, but with little unity of action, toward an established order. It began to be acknowledged that though the clergy might write in Latin, and Frenchmen in French, the English should "show their fantasyes in such words as we learneden of our dame's tonge," and it was equally evident that that English must be cultivated and formed into a fitting vehicle for vigorous English thought. To do this, a master mind was required, and such a master mind appeared in the person of Chaucer. It is particularly fortunate for our historic theory that his works, constituting the origin of our homogeneous English literature, furnish forth its best and most striking demonstration.

CHAUCER'S BIRTH. — Geoffrey Chaucer was born at London about the year 1328: as to the exact date, we waive all the discussion in which his biographers have engaged, and consider this fixed as the most probable time. His parentage is unknown, although Leland, the English antiquarian, declares him to have come of a noble family, and Pitts says he was the son of a knight. He died in the year 1400, and thus was an active and observant contemporary of events in the most remarkable century which had thus far rolled over Europe — the age of Edward III. and the Black Prince, of Crecy and Poitiers, of English bills and bows, stronger than French lances; the age of Wiclif, of reformation in religion, government, language, and social order. Whatever his family antecedents, he was a courtier, and a successful one; his wife was Philippa, a sister of Lady Katherine Swinford, first the mistress and then the wife of John of Gaunt, Duke of Lancaster.

ITALIAN INFLUENCE. — From a literary point of view, the period of his birth was remarkable for the strong influence of Italian letters, which first having made its entrance into France, now, in natural course of progress, found its way into England. Dante had produced,

> . . . in the darkness prest,
> From his own soul by worldly weights, . . .

the greatest poem then known to modern Europe, and the most imaginative ever written. Thus the Italian sky was blazing with splendor, while the West was still in the morning twilight. The Divina Commedia was written half a century before the Canterbury Tales.

Boccaccio was then writing his *Filostrato*, which was to be Chaucer's model in the Troilus and Creseide, and his *Decameron*, which suggested the plan of the Canterbury Tales. His *Teseide* is also said to be the original of the Knight's Tale. Petrarch, "the worthy clerke" from whom Chaucer is said to have learned a story or two in Italy for his great work, was born in 1304, and was also a star of the first magnitude in that Italian galaxy.

Indeed, it is here worthy of a passing remark, that from that early time to a later period, many of the great products of English poetry have been watered by silver rills of imaginative genius from a remote Italian source. Chaucer's indebtedness has just been noticed. Spenser borrowed his versification and not a little of his poetic handling in the Faery Queen from Ariosto. Milton owes to Dante some of his conceptions of heaven and hell in his Paradise Lost, while his Lycidas, Arcades, Allegro and Penseroso, may be called Italian poems done into English.

In the time of Chaucer, this Italian influence marks the extended relations of English letters; and, serving to remove the trammels of the French, it gave to the now vigorous and growing English that opportunity of development for which it had so long waited. Out of the serfdom and obscurity to which it had been condemned by the Normans, it had sprung forth in reality, as in name, the English language. Books, few at the best, long used in Latin or French, were now demanded by English mind, and being produced in answer to the demand.

THE FOUNDER OF THE LITERATURE. — But there was still wanted a man who could use the elements and influences of the time — a great poet — a maker — a creator of literature. The language needed a forming, controlling, fixing hand. The English mind needed a leader and master, English imagination a guide, English literature a father.

The person who answered to this call, and who was equal to all these demands, was Chaucer. But he was something more. He claimed only to be a poet, while he was to figure in after times as historian, philosopher, and artist.

The scope of this work does not permit an examination of Chaucer's writings in detail, but the position we have taken will be best illustrated by his greatest work, the Canterbury Tales. Of the others, a few preliminary words only need be said. Like most writers in an early literary period, Chaucer began with translations, which were extended into paraphrases or versions, and thus his "'prentice hand" gained the practice and skill with which to attempt original poems.

MINOR POEMS. — His earliest attempt, doubtless, was the *Romaunt of the Rose*, an allegorical poem in French, by William de Lorris, continued, after his death in 1260, by Jean de Meun, who figured as a poet in the court of Charles le Bel, of France. This poem, esteemed by the French as the finest of their old romances, was rendered by Chaucer, with considerable alterations and improvements, into octosyllabic verse. The Romaunt portrays the trials which a lover meets and the obstacles he overcomes in pursuit of his mistress, under the allegory of a rose in an inaccessible garden. It has been variously construed — by theologians as the yearning of man for the celestial city; by chemists as the search for the philosopher's stone; by jurists as that for equity, and by medical men as the attempt to produce a panacea for all human ailments.

Next in order was his *Troilus and Creseide*, a mediæval tale, already attempted by Boccaccio in his Filostrate, but borrowed by Chaucer, according to his own account, from *Lollius*, a mysterious name without an owner. The story is similar to that dramatized by Shakspeare in his tragedy of the same title. This is in decasyllabic verse, arranged in stanzas of seven lines each.

The *House of Fame*, another of his principal poems, is a curious description — probably his first original effort — of the Temple of Fame, an immense cage, sixty miles long, and its inhabitants the great writers of classic times, and is chiefly valuable as showing the estimation in which the classic writers were held in that day. This is also in octosyllabic verses, and is further remarkable for the opulence of its imagery and its variety of description. The poet is carried in the claws of a great eagle into this house, and sees its distinguished occupants standing upon columns of different kinds of metal, according to their merits. The poem ends with the third book, very abruptly, as Chaucer awakes from his vision.

"The Legend of Good Women" is a record of the loves and misfortunes of celebrated women, and is supposed to have been written to make amends for the author's other unjust portraitures of female character.

The Canterbury Tales. — In order to give system to our historic inquiries, we shall now present an outline of the Canterbury Tales, in order that we may show—

I. The indications of a general desire in that period for a reformation in religion.

II. The social condition of the English people.

III. The important changes in government.

IV. The condition and progress of the English language.

The Canterbury Tales were begun in 1386, when Chaucer was fifty-eight years old, and in a period of comparative quiet, after the minority of Richard II. was over, and before his troubles had begun. They form a beautiful gallery of cabinet pictures of English society in all its grades, except the very highest and the lowest; and, in this respect, they supplement in exact lineaments and the freshest coloring those compendiums of English history which only present to us, on the one hand, the persons and deeds of kings and their nobles, and, on the other, the general laws which so long oppressed the lower orders of the people, and the action of which is illustrated by disorders among them. But in Chaucer we find the true philosophy of English society, the principle of the guilds, or fraternities, to which his pilgrims belong — the character and avocation of the knight, squire, yeoman, franklin, bailiff, sompnour, reeve, etc., names, many of them, now obsolete. Who can find these in our compendiums? they must be dug — and dry work it is — out of profounder histories, or found, with greater pleasure, in poems like that of Chaucer.

CHARACTERS.—Let us consider, then, a few of his principal characters which most truly represent the age and nation.

The Tabard inn at Southwark, then a suburb of "London borough without the walls," was a great rendezvous for pilgrims who were journeying to the shrine of St. Thomas à Becket, at Canterbury — that Saxon archbishop who had been murdered by the minions of Henry II. Southwark was on the high street, the old Roman highway from London to the southeast. A gathering of pilgrims here is no uncommon occurrence; and thus numbers and variety make a combination of penitence and pleasure. The host of the Tabard — doubtless a true portraiture of the landlord of that day — counts noses, that he may distribute the pewter plates. A substantial supper smokes upon the old-fashioned Saxon-English board — so substantial that the pilgrims are evidently about to lay in a good stock, in anticipation of poor fare, the fatigue of travel, and perhaps a fast or two not set down in the calendar. As soon as they attack the viands, ale and strong wines, hippocras, pigment, and claret, are served in bright pewter and wood. There were Saxon drinks for the commoner pilgrims; the claret was for the knight. Every one drinks at his will, and the miller, as we shall see, takes a little more than his head can decently carry.

First in the place of honor is the knight, accompanied by his son, the young squire, and his trusty yeoman. Then, in order of social rank, a prioress, a nun and three priests, a friar, a merchant, a poor scholar or clerk of Oxford, a sergeant of the law, a frankelein, a haberdasher, a weaver, a tapster, a dyer, a cook, a shipman, a doctor of physic, a wife of Bath, a poor parson, a ploughman, a miller, a manciple or college steward, a reeve or bailiff, a sompnour or summoner to the ecclesiastical courts, a pardoner or seller of papal indulgences (one hundred and fifty years before Luther) — an essentially English company of many social grades, bound to the most popular shrine, that of a Saxon archbishop, himself the son of a London citizen, murdered two hundred years before with the connivance of an English king. No one can read this list without thinking that if Chaucer be true and accurate in his descriptions of these persons, and make them talk as they did talk, his delineations are of inestimable value historically. He has been faithfully true. Like all great masters of the epic art, he doubtless drew them from the life; each, given in the outlines of the prologue, is a speaking portrait: even the horses they ride are as true to nature as those in the pictures of Rosa Bonheur.

And besides these historic delineations which mark the age and country, notwithstanding the loss of local and personal satire with which, to the reader of his day, the poem must have sparkled, and which time has destroyed for us, the features of our common humanity are so well portrayed, that to the latest generations will be there displayed the "forth-showing instances" of the *Idola Tribus* of Bacon, the besetting sins, frailties, and oddities of the human race.

SATIRE. — His touches of satire and irony are as light as the hits of an accomplished master of the small-sword; mere hits, but significant of deep thrusts, at the scandals, abuses, and oppressions of the age. Like Dickens, he employed his fiction in the way of reform, and helped to effect it.

Let us illustrate. While sitting at the table, Chaucer makes his sketches for the Prologue. A few of these will serve here as specimens of his powers. Take the *Doctour of Physike*, who

> Knew the cause of every maladie,
> Were it of cold or hote or wet or drie;

who also knew

> . . . the old Esculapius,
> And Dioscorides and eke Rufus,
> Old Hippocras, Rasis, and Avicen,

and many other classic authorities in medicine.

Of his diete mesurable was he,
And it was of no superfluite;

nor was it a gross slander to say of the many,

His studie was but litel on the Bible.

It was a suggestive satire which led him to hint that he was

. . . but esy of dispense;
He kepte that he wan in pestilence;
For gold in physike is a cordial;
Therefore he loved gold in special.

Chaucer deals tenderly with the lawyers; yet, granting his sergeant of the law discretion and wisdom, a knowledge of cases even "from the time of King Will," and fees and perquisites quite proportional, he adds,

Nowher so besy a man as he ther n' as,
And yet he seemed besier than he was.

His Presentations of Woman. — Woman seems to find hard judgment in this work. Madame Eglantine, the prioress, with her nasal chanting, her English-French, "of Stratford-atte-Bow," her legion of smalle houndes, and her affected manner, is not a flattering type of woman's character, and yet no doubt she is a faithful portrait of many a prioress of that day.

And the wife of Bath is still more repulsive. She tells us, in the prologue to her story, that she has buried five husbands, and, buxom still, is looking for the sixth. She is a jolly *compagnon de voyage*, had been thrice to Jerusalem, and is now seeking assoil for some little sins at Canterbury. And the host's wife, as he describes her, is not by any means a pleasant helpmeet for an honest man. The host is out of her hearing, or he would not be so ready to tell her character:

I have a wif, tho' that she poore be;
But of her tongue a blabbing shrew is she,
And yet she hath a heap of vices mo.

She is always getting into trouble with the neighbors; and when he will not fight in her quarrel, she cries,

. . . False coward, wreak thy wif;
By corpus domini, I will have thy knife,
And thou shalt have my distaff and go spin.

The best names she has for him are milksop, coward, and ape; and so we say, with him,

Come, let us pass away from this mattère.

THE PLAN PROPOSED. — With these suggestions of the nature of the company assembled "for to don their pilgrimage," we come to the framework of the story. While sitting at the table, the host proposes

That each of you, to shorten with your way,
In this viage shall tellen tales twey.

Each pilgrim should tell two stories; one on the way to Canterbury, and one returning. As, including Chaucer and the host, there are thirty-one in the company, this would make sixty-two stories. The one who told the best story should have, on the return of the company to the Tabard inn, a supper at the expense of the rest.

The host's idea was unanimously accepted; and in the morning, as they ride forth, they begin to put it into execution. Although lots are drawn for the order in which the stories shall be told, it is easily arranged by the courteous host, who recognizes the difference in station among the pilgrims, that the knight shall inaugurate the scheme, which he does by telling that beautiful story of *Palamon and Arcite*, the plot of which is taken from *Le Teseide* of Boccacio. It is received with cheers by the company, and with great delight by the host, who cries out,

> So mote I gon — this goth aright,
> Unbockled is the mail.

The next in order is called for, but the miller, who has replenished his midnight potations in the morning, and is now rolling upon his horse, swears that "he can a noble tale," and, not heeding the rebuke of the host,

> Thou art a fool, thy wit is overcome,

he shouts out a vulgar story, in all respects in direct contrast to that of the knight. As a literary device, this rude introduction of the miller breaks the stiffness and monotony of a succession in the order of rank; and, as a feature of the history, it seems to tell us something of democratic progress. The miller's story ridicules a carpenter, and the reeve, who is a carpenter, immediately repays him by telling a tale in which he puts a miller in a ludicrous position.

With such a start, the pilgrims proceed to tell their tales; but not all. There is neither record of their reaching Canterbury, nor returning. Nor is the completion of the number at all essential: for all practical purposes, we have all that can be asked; and had the work been completed, it would have added little to the historical stores which it now indirectly, and perhaps unconsciously, offers. The number of the tales (including two in prose) is twenty-four, and great additional value is given to them by the short prologue introducing each of them.

CHAPTER VIII.

CHAUCER, (CONTINUED.) — REFORMS IN RELIGION AND SOCIETY.

HISTORICAL FACTS.

LEAVING the pilgrims' cavalcade for a more philosophical consideration of the historical teachings of the subject, it may be clearly shown that the work of Chaucer informs us of a wholesome reform in religion, or, in the words of George Ellis,[1] "he was not only respected as the father of English poetry, but revered as a champion of the Reformation."

Let us recur briefly to the history. With William the Conqueror a great change had been introduced into England: under him and his immediate successors — his son William Rufus, his nephew Henry I., the usurper Stephen, and Henry II., — the efforts of the "English kings of Norman race" were directed to the establishment of their power on a strong foundation; but they began, little by little, to see that the only foundation was that of the unconquerable English people; so that popular rights soon began to be considered, and the accession of Henry II., the first of the Plantagenets, was specially grateful to the English, because he was the first since the

[1] Introduction to the Poets of Queen Elizabeth's Age.

Conquest to represent the Saxon line, being the grandson of Henry I., and son of *Matilda*, niece of Edgar Atheling. In the mean time, as has been seen, the English language had been formed, the chief element of which was Saxon. This was a strong instrument of political rights, for community of language tended to an amalgamation of the Norman and Saxon peoples. With regard to the Church in England; the insulation from Rome had impaired the influence of the Papacy. The misdeeds and arrogance of the clergy had arrayed both people and monarch against their claims, as several of the satirical poems already mentioned have shown. As a privileged class, who used their immunities to do evil and corrupt the realm, the clergy became odious to the *nobles*, whose power they shared and sometimes impaired, and to the *people*, who could now read their faults and despise their comminations, and who were unwilling to pay hard-earned wages to support them in idleness and vice. It was not the doctrine, but the practice which they condemned. With the accession of the house of Plantagenet, the people were made to feel that the Norman monarchy was a curse, without alloy. Richard I. was a knight-errant and a crusader, who cared little for the realm; John was an adulterer, traitor, and coward, who roused the people's anger by first quarrelling with the Pope, and then basely giving him the kingdom to receive it again as a papal fief. The nation, headed by the warlike barons, had forced the great charter of popular rights from John, and had caused it to be confirmed and supplemented during the long reign of his son, the weak Henry III.

Edward I. was engaged in cruel wars, both in Wales and Scotland, which wasted the people's money without any corresponding advantage.

Edward II. was deposed and murdered by his queen and her paramour Mortimer; and, however great their crime, he was certainly unworthy and unable to control a fierce and turbulent people, already clamorous for their rights. These well-known facts are here stated to show the unsettled condition of things during the period when the English were being formed into a nation, the language established, and the earliest literary efforts made. Materials for a better organization were at hand in great abundance; only proper master-builders were needed. We have seen that everything now betokened the coming of a new era, in State, Church, and literature.

The monarch who came to the throne in 1327, one year before the birth of Chaucer, was worthy to be the usher of this new era to England: a man of might, of judgment, and of forecast; the first truly *English* monarch in sympathy and purpose who had occupied the throne since the Conquest: liberal beyond all former precedent in religion, he sheltered Wiclif in his bold invectives, and paved the way for the later encroachments upon the papal supremacy. With the aid of his accomplished son, Edward the Black Prince, he rendered England illustrious by his foreign wars, and removed what remained of the animosity between Saxon and Norman.

Reform in Religion. — We are so accustomed to refer the Reformation to the time of Luther in Germany, as the grand religious turning-point in modern history, that we are apt to underrate, if not to forget, the religious movement in this most important era of English history. Chaucer and Wiclif wrote nearly half a century before John Huss was burned by Sigismond: it was a century after that that Luther burned the Pope's decretals at Wittenberg, and still later that Henry VIII. threw off the papal dominion in England. But great crises in a nation's history never arrive without premonition; — there are no moral earthquakes without premonitory throes, and sometimes these are more decisive and destructive than that which gives electric publicity. Such distinct signs appeared in the age of Chaucer, and the later history of the Church in England cannot be distinctly understood without a careful study of this period.

It is well known that Chaucer was an adherent of John of Gaunt; that he and his great protector—perhaps with no very pious intents—favored the doctrines of Wiclif; that in the politico-religious disturbances in 1382, incident to the minority of Richard II., he was obliged to flee the country. But if we wish to find the most striking religious history of the age, we must seek it in the portraitures of religious characters and events in his Canterbury Tales. In order to a proper intelligence of these, let us look for a moment at the ecclesiastical condition of England at that time. Connected with much in doctrine and ritual worthy to be retained, and, indeed, still retained in the articles and liturgy of the Anglican Church, there was much, the growth of ignorance and neglect, to be reformed. The Church of England had never had a real affinity with Rome. The gorgeous and sensual ceremonies which, in the indolent airs of the Mediterranean, were imposing and attractive, palled upon the taste of the more phlegmatic Englishmen. Institutions organized at Rome did not flourish in that higher latitude, and abuses were currently discussed even before any plan was considered for reforming them.

The Clergy.—The great monastic orders of St. Benedict, scattered throughout Europe, were, in the early and turbulent days, a most important aid and protection to Christianity. But by degrees, and as they were no longer needed, they had become corrupt, because they had become idle. The Cluniacs and Cistercians, branches of the Benedictines, are represented in Chaucer's poem by the monk and prioress, as types of bodies which needed reform.

The Grandmontines, a smaller branch, were widely known for their foppery: the young monks painted their cheeks, and washed and covered their beards at night. The cloisters became luxurious, and sheltered, and, what is worse, sanctioned lewdness and debauchery.

There was a great difference indeed between the *regular* clergy, or those belonging to orders and monasteries, and the *secular* clergy or parish priests, who were far better; and there was a jealous feud between them. There was a lamentable ignorance of the Scripture among the clergy, and gross darkness over the people. The paraphrases of Caedmon, the translations of Bede and Alfred, the rare manuscripts of the Latin Bible, were all that cast a faint ray upon this gloom. The people could not read Latin, even if they had books; and the Saxon versions were almost in a foreign language. Thus, distrusting their religious teachers, thoughtful men began to long for an English version of that Holy Book which contains all the words of eternal life. And thus, while the people were becoming more clamorous for instruction, and while Wiclif was meditating the great boon of a translated Bible, which, like a noonday sun, should irradiate the dark places and disclose the loathsome groups and filthy manifestations of cell and cloister, Chaucer was administering the wholesome medicine of satire and contempt. He displays the typical monk given up to every luxury, the costly black dress with fine fur edgings, the love-knot which fastens his hood, and his preference for pricking and hunting the hare, over poring into a stupid book in a cloister.

THE FRIAR AND THE SOMPNOUR. — His satire extends also to the friar, who has not even that semblance of virtue which is the tribute of the hypocrite to our holy faith. He is not even the demure rascal conceived by Thomson in his Castle of Indolence:

> . . . the first amid the fry,
> . . . .
> A little round, fat, oily man of God,
> Who had a roguish twinkle in his eye,
> When a tight maiden chanced to trippen by,
> . . . .
> Which when observed, he shrunk into his mew,
> And straight would recollect his piety anew.

But Chaucer's friar is a wanton and merry scoundrel, taking every license, kissing the wives and talking love-talk to the girls in his wanderings, as he begs for his Church and his order. His hood is stuffed with trinkets to give them; he is worthily known as the best beggar of his house; his eyes alight with wine, he strikes his little harp, trolls out funny songs and love-ditties. Anon, his frolic over, he preaches to the collected crowd violent denunciations of the parish priest, within the very limits of his parish. The very principles upon which these mendicant orders were established seem to be elements of evil. That they might be better than the monks, they had no cloisters and magnificent gardens, with little to do but enjoy them. Like our Lord, they were generally without a place to lay their heads; they had neither purse nor scrip. But instead of sanctifying, the itinerary was their great temptation and final ruin. Nothing can be conceived better calculated to harden the heart and to destroy the fierce sensibilities of our nature than to be a beggar and a wanderer. So that in our retrospective glance, we may pity while we condemn "the friar of orders gray." With a delicate irony in Chaucer's picture, is combined somewhat of a liking for this "worthy limitour."[1]

In the same category of contempt for the existing ecclesiastical system, Chaucer places the sompnour, or summoner to the Church courts. Of his fire-red face, scattered beard, and the bilious knobs on his cheeks, "children were sore afraid." The friar, in his tale, represents him as in league with the devil, who carries him away. He is a drinker of strong wines, a conniver at evil for bribes: for a good sum he would teach "a felon"

> . . . not to have none awe
> In swiche a case of the archdeacon's curse.

To him the Church system was nothing unless he could make profit of it.

[1] So called from his having a regular district or *limit* in which to beg.

THE PARDONERE. — Nor is his picture of the pardoner, or vender of indulgences, more flattering. He sells — to the great contempt of the poet — a piece of the Virgin's veil, a bit of the sail of St. Peter's boat, holy pigges' bones, and with these relics he made more money in each parish in one day than the parson himself in two months.

Thus taking advantage of his plot to ridicule these characters, and to make them satirize each other — as in the rival stories of the sompnour and friar — he turns with pleasure from these betrayers of religion, to show us that there was a leaven of pure piety and devotion left.

THE POOR PARSON. — With what eager interest does he portray the lovely character of the *poor parson,* the true shepherd of his little flock, in the midst of false friars and luxurious monks! — poor himself, but

> Riche was he of holy thought and work,
> . . . .
> That Cristes gospel truely wolde preche,
> His parishers devoutly wolde teche.
> . . . .
> Wide was his parish and houses fer asonder,
> But he left nought for ne rain no thonder,
> In sickness and in mischief to visite
> The ferrest in his parish, moche and lite.
> Upon his fete, and in his hand a staf,
> This noble example to his shepe he yaf,
> That first he wrought and afterward he taught.

Chaucer's description of the poor parson, which loses much by being curtailed, has proved to be a model for all poets who have drawn the likeness of an earnest pastor from that day to ours, among whom are Herbert, Cowper, Goldsmith, and Wordsworth; but no imitation has equalled this beautiful model. When urged by the host,

> Tell us a fable anon, for cocke's bones,

he quotes St. Paul to Timothy as rebuking those who tell fables; and, disclaiming all power in poetry, preaches them such a stirring discourse upon penance, contrition, confession, and the seven deadly sins, with their remedies, as must have fallen like a thunderbolt upon this careless, motly crew; and has the additional value of giving us Chaucer's epitome of sound doctrine in that bigoted and ignorant age: and, eminently sound and holy as it is, it rebukes the lewdness of the other stories, and, in point of morality, neutralizes if it does not justify the lewd teachings of the work, or in other words, the immorality of the age. This is the parson's own view: his story is the last which is told, and he tells us, in the prologue to his sermon:

> To knitte up all this feste, and make an ende;
> And Jesu for his grace wit me sende
> To showen you the way in this viage
> Of thilke parfit glorious pilgrimage,
> That hight Jerusalem celestial.

In an addendum to this discourse, which brings the Canterbury Tales to an abrupt close, and which, if genuine, as the best critics think it, was added some time after, Chaucer takes shame to himself for his lewd stories, repudiates all his "translations and enditinges of worldly vanitees," and only finds pleasure in his translations of Boethius, his homilies and legends of the saints; and, with words of penitence, he hopes that he shall be saved "atte the laste day of dome."

JOHN WICLIF.[1]—The subject of this early reformation so clearly set forth in the stories of Chaucer, cannot be fully illustrated without a special notice of Chaucer's great contemporary and co-worker, John Wiclif.

What Chaucer hints, or places in the mouths of his characters, with apparently no very serious intent, Wiclif, himself a secular priest, proclaimed boldly and as of prime import-

[1] Spelled also Wycliffe, Wicliff, and Wyklyf.

ance, first from his professor's chair at Oxford, and then from his forced retirement at Lutterworth, where he may well have been the model of Chaucer's poor parson.

Wiclif was born in 1324, four years before Chaucer. The same abuses which called forth the satires of Langland and Chaucer upon monk and friar, and which, if unchecked, promised universal corruption, aroused the martyr-zeal of Wiclif; and similar reproofs are to be found in his work entitled "Objections to Friars," and in numerous treatises from his pen against many of the doctrines and practices of the Church.

Noted for his learning and boldness, he was sent by Edward III. one of an embassy to Bruges, to negotiate with the Pope's envoys concerning benefices held in England by foreigners. There he met John of Gaunt, the Duke of Lancaster. This prince, whose immediate descendants were to play so prominent a part in later history, was the fourth son of Edward III. By the death of the Black Prince, in 1376, and of Lionel, Duke of Clarence, in 1368, he became the oldest remaining child of the king, and the father of the man who usurped the throne of England and reigned as Henry IV. The influence of Lancaster was equal to his station, and he extended his protection to Wiclif. This, combined with the support of Lord Percy, the Marshal of England, saved the reformer from the stake when he was tried before the Bishop of London on a charge of heresy, in 1377. He was again brought before a synod of the clergy at Lambeth, in 1378, but such was the favor of the populace in his behalf, and such, too, the weakness of the papal party, on account of a schism which had resulted in the election of two popes, that, although his opinions were declared heretical, he was not proceeded against.

After this, although almost sick to death, he rose from what his enemies had hoped would be his death-bed, to "again declare the evil deeds of the friars." In 1381, he lectured openly at Oxford against the doctrine of transubstantiation; and for this, after a presentment by the Church — and a partial recantation, or explaining away — even the liberal king thought proper to command that he should retire from the university. Thus, during his latter years, he lived in retirement at his little parish of Lutterworth, escaping the dangers of the troublous time, and dying — struck with paralysis at his chancel — in 1384, sixteen years before Chaucer.

TRANSLATION OF THE BIBLE. — The labors of Wiclif which produced the most important results, were not his violent lectures as a reformer, but the translation of the Bible into English, the very language of the common people, greatly to the wrath of the hierarchy and its political upholders. This, too, is his chief glory: as a reformer he went too fast and too far; he struck fiercely at the root of authority, imperilling what was good, in his attack upon what was evil. In pulling up the tares he endangered the wheat, and from him, as a progenitor, came the Lollards, a fanatical, violent, and revolutionary sect.

But his English Bible, the parent of the later versions, cannot be too highly valued. For the first time, English readers could search the whole Scriptures, and judge for themselves of doctrine and authority: there they could learn how far the traditions and commandments of men had encrusted and corrupted the pure word of truth. Thus the greatest impulsion was given to a reformation in doctrine; and thus, too, the exclusiveness and arrogance of the clergy received the first of many sledge-hammer blows which were to result in their confusion and discomfiture.

"If," says Froude,[1] "the Black Prince had lived, or if Richard II. had inherited the temper of the Plantagenets, the ecclesiastical system would have been spared the misfortune of a longer reprieve."

THE ASHES OF WICLIF. — The vengeance which Wiclif es-

[1] Am. ed., i. 94.

caped during his life was wreaked upon his bones. In 1428, the Council of Constance ordered that if his bones could be distinguished from those of other, faithful people, they should "be taken out of the ground and thrown far off from Christian burial." On this errand the Bishop of Lincoln came with his officials to Lutterworth, and, finding them, burned them, and threw the ashes into the little stream called the Swift. Fuller, in his Church History, adds: "Thus this brook has conveyed his ashes into Avon, Avon into Severn, Severn into the narrow seas, they into the main ocean; and thus the ashes of Wiclif are the emblem of his doctrine, which now is dispersed all the world over;" or, in the more carefully selected words of an English laureate of modern days,[1]

> . . . this deed accurst,
> An emblem yields to friends and enemies,
> How the bold teacher's doctrine, *sanctified*
> *By truth*, shall spread, throughout the world dispersed.

[1] Wordsworth, Ecc. Son., xvii.

CHAPTER IX.

CHAUCER, (CONTINUED.) — PROGRESS OF SOCIETY, AND OF LANGUAGE.

Social Life.

A FEW words must suffice to suggest to the student what may be learned, as to the condition of society in England, from the Canterbury Tales.

All the portraits are representatives of classes. But an inquiry into the social life of the period will be more systematic, if we look first at the nature and condition of chivalry, as it still existed, although on the eve of departure, in England. This is found in the portraits of certain of Chaucer's pilgrims — the knight, the squire, and the yeoman; and in the special prologues to the various tales. The *knight*, as the representative of European chivalry, comes to us in name at least from the German forests with the irrepressible Teutons. *Chivalry* in its rude form, however, was destined to pass through a refining and modifying process, and to obtain its name in France. Its Norman characteristic is found in the young *ecuyer* or squire, of Chaucer, who aspires to equal his father in station and renown; while the English type of the man-at-arms (*l'homme d'armes*) is found in their attendant yeoman, the *tiers état* of English chivalry, whose bills and bows served Edward III. at Cressy and Poictiers, and, a little later, made Henry V. of England king of France in prospect, at Agincourt. Chivalry, in its palmy days, was an institution of great merit and power; but its humanizing purpose now accomplished, it was beginning to decline.

What a speaking picture has Chaucer drawn of the knight, brave as a lion, prudent in counsel, but gentle as a woman. His deeds of valor had been achieved, not at Cressy and Calais, but — what both chieftain and poet esteemed far nobler warfare — in battle with the infidel, at Algeçiras, in Poland, in Prussia, and Russia. Thrice had he fought with sharp lances in the lists, and thrice had he slain his foe; yet he was

> Of his port as meke as is a mayde;
> He never yet no vilainie ne sayde
> In all his life unto ne manere wight,
> He was a very parfit gentil knight.

The entire paradox of chivalry is here presented by the poet. For, though Chaucer's knight, just returned from the wars, is going to show his devotion to God and the saints by his pilgrimage to the hallowed shrine at Canterbury, when he is called upon for his story, his fancy flies to the old romantic mythology. Mars is his god of war, and Venus his mother of loves, and, by an anachronism quite common in that day, Palamon and Arcite are mediæval knights trained in the school of chivalry, and aflame, in knightly style, with the light of love and ladies' eyes. These incongruities marked the age.

Such was the flickering brightness of chivalry in Chaucer's time, even then growing dimmer and more fitful, and soon to "pale its ineffectual fire" in the light of a growing civilization. Its better principles, which were those of truth, virtue, and holiness, were to remain; but its forms, ceremonies, and magnificence were to disappear.

It is significant of social progress, and of the levelling influence of Christianity, that common people should do their pilgrimage with community of interest as well as danger, and in easy, tale-telling conference with those of higher station. The franklin, with white beard and red face, has been lord of the sessions and knight of the shire. The merchant, with forked beard and Flaundrish beaver hat, discourses learnedly of taxes and ship-money, and was doubtless drawn from an existing original, the type of a class. Several of the personages belong to the guilds which were so famous in London, and

> Were alle yclothed in o livere
> Of a solempne and grete fraternite.

GOVERNMENT. — Closely connected with this social progress, was the progress in constitutional government, the fruit of the charters of John and Henry III. After the assassination of Edward II. by his queen and her paramour, there opened upon England a new historic era, when the bold and energetic Edward III. ascended the throne — an era reflected in the poem of Chaucer. The king, with Wiclif's aid, checked the encroachments of the Church. He increased the representation of the people in parliament, and — perhaps the greatest reform of all — he divided that body into two houses, the peers and the commons, giving great consequence to the latter in the conduct of the government, and introducing that striking feature of English legislation, that no ministry can withstand an opposition majority in the lower house; and another quite as important, that no tax should be imposed without its consent. The philosophy of these great facts is to be found in the democratic spirit so manifest among the pilgrims; a spirit tempered with loyalty, but ready, where their liberties were encroached upon, to act with legislative vigor, as well as individual boldness.

Not so directly, but still forcibly, does Chaucer present the results of Edward's wars in France, in the status of the knight, squire, and yeoman, and of the English sailor, and in the changes introduced into the language and customs of the English thereby.

CHAUCER'S ENGLISH. — But we are to observe, finally, that Chaucer is the type of progress in the language, giving it himself the momentum which carried it forward with only technical modifications to the days of Spenser and the Virgin Queen. The *House of Fame* and other minor poems are written in the octosyllabic verse of the Trouvères, but the *Canterbury Tales* give us the first vigorous English handling of the decasyllabic couplet, or iambic pentameter, which was to become so polished an instrument afterward in the hands of Dryden and Pope. The English of all the poems is simple and vernacular.

It is known that Dante had at first intended to compose the Divina Commedia in Latin. "But when," he said to the sympathizing Frate Ilario, "I recalled the condition of the present age, and knew that those generous men for whom, in better days, these things were written, had abandoned (*ahi dolore*) the liberal arts into vulgar hands, I threw aside the delicate lyre which armed my flank, and attuned another more befitting the ears of moderns." It seems strange that he should have thus regretted what to us seems a noble and original opportunity of double creation — poem and language. What Dante thus bewailed was his real warrant for immortality. Had he written his great work in Latin, it would have been consigned, with the Italian latinity of the middle ages, to oblivion; while his Tuscan still delights the ear of princes and lazzaroni. Professorships of the Divina Commedia are instituted in Italian universities, and men are considered accomplished when they know it by heart.

What Dante had done, not without murmuring, Chaucer did more cheerfully in England. Claimed by both universities as a collegian, perhaps without truth, he certainly was an educated man, and must have been sorely tempted by Latin hexameters; but he knew his mission, and felt his power. With a master hand he moulded the language. He is reproached for having introduced "a wagon-load of foreign words," i. e. Norman words, which, although frowned upon by some critics, were greatly needed, were eagerly adopted, and constituted him the "well of English undefiled," as he was called by Spenser. It is no part of our plan to consider Chaucer's language or diction, a special study which the reader can pursue for himself. Occleve, in his work "*De Regimine Principium*," calls him "the honour of English tonge," "floure of eloquence," and "universal fadir in science," and, above all, "the firste findere of our faire language." To Lydgate he was the "Floure of Poetes throughout all Bretaine." Measured by our standard, he is not always musical, "and," in the language of Dryden, "many of his verses are lame for want of half a foot, and sometimes a whole one;" but he must be measured by the standards of his age, by the judgment of his contemporaries, and by a thorough intelligence of the language as he found it and as he left it. Edward III., a practical reformer in many things, gave additional importance to English, by restoring it in the courts of law, and administering justice to the people in their own tongue. When we read of the *English* kings of this early period, it is curious to reflect that these monarchs, up to the time of Edward I., spoke French as their vernacular tongue, while English had only been the mixed, corrupted language of the lower classes, which was now brought thus by king and poet into honorable consideration.

HIS DEATH.—Chaucer died on the 25th of October, 1400, in his little tenement in the garden of St. Mary's Chapel, Westminster, and left his works and his fame to an evil and unappreciative age. His monument was not erected until one hundred and fifty-six years afterward, by Nicholas Brigham. It stands in the "poets' corner" of Westminster Abbey, and has been the nucleus of that gathering-place of the sacred dust which once enclosed the great minds of England. The inscription, which justly styles him "Anglorum vates ter maximus," is not to be entirely depended upon as to the "annus Domini," or "tempora vitae," because of the turbulent and destructive reigns that had intervened — evil times for literary effort, and yet making material for literature and history, and producing that wonderful magician, the printing-press, and paper, by means of which the former things might be disseminated, and Chaucer brought nearer to us than to them.

HISTORICAL FACTS. — The year before Chaucer died, Richard II. was starved in his dungeon. Henry, the son of John of Gaunt, represented the usurpation of Lancaster, and the realm was convulsed with the revolts of rival aristocracy; and, although Prince Hal, or Henry V., warred with entire success in France, and got the throne of that kingdom away from Charles VI., (the Insane,) he died leaving to his infant son, Henry VI., an inheritance which could not be secured. The rival claimant of York, Edward IV., had a strong party in the kingdom: then came the wars of the Roses; the murders and treason of Richard III.; the sordid valor of Henry VII.; the conjugal affection of Henry VIII.; the great religious earthquake all over Europe, known as the Reformation; constituting all together an epoch too stirring and unsettled to permit literature to flourish; an epoch which gave birth to no great poet or mighty master, but which contained only the seeds of things which were to germinate and flourish in a kindlier age.

In closing this notice of Chaucer, it should be remarked that no English poet has been more successful in the varied delineation of character, or in fresh and charming pictures of Nature. Witty and humorous, sententious and didactic, solemn and pathetic, he not only pleases the fancy, but touches the heart.

JOHN GOWER. — Before entering upon the barren period from Chaucer to Spenser, however, there is one contemporary of Chaucer whom we must not omit to mention; for his works, although of little literary value, are historical signs of the times: this is *John Gower*, styled variously Sir John and Judge Gower, as he was very probably both a knight and a justice. He seems to owe most of his celebrity to his connection, however slight, with Chaucer; although there is no doubt of his having been held in good repute by the literary patrons and critics of his own age. His fame rests upon three works, or rather three parts of one scheme — *Speculum Meditantis*, *Vox Clamantis*, and *Confessio Amantis*. The first of these, *the mirror of one who meditates*, was in French verse, and was, in the main, a treatise upon virtue and repentance, with inculcations to conjugal fidelity much disregarded at that time. This work has been lost. The *Vox Clamantis*, or *voice of one crying in the wilderness*, is directly historical, being a chronicle, in Latin elegiacs, of the popular revolts of Wat Tyler in the time of Richard II., and a sermon on fatalism, which, while it calls for a reformation in the clergy, takes ground against Wiclif, his doctrines, and adherents. In the later books he discusses the military and the lawyers; and thus he is the voice of one crying, like the Baptist in the wilderness, against existing abuses and for the advent of a better order. The *Confessio Amantis*, now principally known because it contains a eulogium of Chaucer, which in his later editions he left out, is in English verse, and was composed at the instance of Richard II. The general argument of this Lover's Confession is a dialogue between the lover and a priest of Venus, who, in the guise of a confessor, applies the breviary of the Church to the confessions of love.[1] The poem is interspersed with introductory or recapitulatory Latin verses.

CHAUCER AND GOWER. — That there was for a time a

[1] "The Joyous Science, as the profession of minstrelsy was termed, had its various ranks, like the degrees in the Church and in chivalry." — *Sir Walter Scott*, (*The Betrothed.*)

mutual admiration between Chaucer and Gower, is shown by their allusion to each other. In the penultimate stanza of the Troilus and Creseide, Chaucer calls him "O Morall Gower," an epithet repeated by Dunbar, Hawes, and other writers; while in the *Confessio Amantis*, Gower speaks of Chaucer as his disciple and poet, and alludes to his poems with great praise. That they were at any time alienated from each other has been asserted, but the best commentators agree in thinking without sufficient grounds.

The historical teachings of Gower are easy to find. He states truths without parable. His moral satires are aimed at the Church corruptions of the day, and yet are conservative; and are taken, says Berthelet, in his dedication of the Confessio to Henry VIII., not only out of "poets, orators, historic writers, and philosophers, but out of the Holy Scripture"—the same Scripture so eloquently expounded by Chaucer, and translated by Wiclif. Again, Gower, with an eye to the present rather than to future fame, wrote in three languages—a tribute to the Church in his Latin, to the court in his French, and to the progressive spirit of the age in his English. The latter alone is now read, and is the basis of his fame. Besides three poems, he left, among his manuscripts, fifty French sonnets, (cinquantes balades,) which were afterward printed by his descendant, Lord Gower, Duke of Sutherland.

GOWER'S LANGUAGE.—Like Chaucer, Gower was a reformer in language, and was accused by the "severer etymologists of having corrupted the purity of the English by affecting to introduce so many foreign words and phrases;" but he has the tribute of Sir Philip Sidney (no mean praise) that Chaucer and himself were the leaders of a movement, which others have followed, "to beautifie our mother tongue," and thus the *Confessio Amantis* ranks as one of the formers of our language, in a day when it required much moral courage to break away from the trammels of Latin and French, and at the same time to compel them to surrender their choicest treasures to the English.

Gower was born in 1325 or 1326, and outlived Chaucer. It has been generally believed that Chaucer was his poetical pupil. The only evidence is found in the following vague expression of Gower in the Confessio Amantis:

> And greet well Chaucer when ye meet
> As *my disciple* and my poete.
> For in the flower of his youth,
> In sondry wise as he well couth,
> Of ditties and of songes glade
> The which he for my sake made.

It may have been but a patronizing phrase, warranted by Gower's superior rank and station; for to the modern critic the one is the uprising sun, and the other the pale star scarcely discerned in the sky. Gower died in 1408, eight years after his more illustrious colleague.

Other Writers of the Period of Chaucer.

John Barbour, Archdeacon of Aberdeen, a Scottish poet, born about 1320: wrote a poem concerning the deeds of King Robert I. in achieving the independence of Scotland. It is called *Broite* or *Brute*, and in it, in imitation of the English, he traces the Scottish royal lineage to Brutus. Although by no means equal to Chaucer, he is far superior to any other English poet of the time, and his language is more intelligible at the present day than that of Chaucer or Gower. Sir Walter Scott has borrowed from Barbour's poem in his "Lord of the Isles."

Blind Harry — name unknown: wrote the adventures of Sir William Wallace, about 1460.

James I. of Scotland, assassinated at Perth, in 1437. He wrote "The Kings Quhair," (Quire or Book,) describing the progress of his attachment to the daughter of the Earl of Somerset, while a prisoner in England, during the reign of Henry IV.

Thomas Occleve, flourished about 1420. His principal work is in Latin; De Regimine Principum, (concerning the government of princes.)

John Lydgate, flourished about 1430: wrote *Masks* and *Mummeries*, and nine books of tragedies translated from Boccaccio.

Robert Henryson, flourished about 1430: Robin and Makyne, a pastoral; and a continuation of Chaucer's Troilus and Creseide, entitled "The Testament of Fair Creseide."

William Dunbar, died about 1520: the greatest of Scottish poets, called "The Chaucer of Scotland." He wrote "The Thistle and the Rose," "The Dance," and "The Golden Targe."

CHAPTER X.

THE BARREN PERIOD BETWEEN CHAUCER AND SPENSER.

Greek Literature. Invention of Printing. Caxton. Contemporary History. | Skelton. Wyatt. Surrey. | Sir Thomas More. Utopia, and other Works. Other Writers.

THE STUDY OF GREEK LITERATURE.

HAVING thus mentioned the writers whom we regard as belonging to the period of Chaucer, although some of them, like Henryson and Dunbar, flourished at the close of the fifteenth century, we reach those of that literary epoch which may be regarded as the transition state between Chaucer and the age of Elizabeth: an epoch which, while it produced no great literary work, and is irradiated by no great name, was, however, a time of preparation for the splendid advent of Spenser and Shakspeare.

Incident to the dangers which had so long beset the Eastern or Byzantine Empire, which culminated in the fall of Constantinople — and to the gradual but steady progress of Western Europe in arts and letters, which made it a welcome refuge for the imperilled learning of the East — Greek letters came like a fertilizing flood across the Continent into England. The philosophy of Plato, the power of the Athenian drama, and the learning of the Stagyrite, were a new impulse to literature. Before the close of the fifteenth century, Greek was taught at Oxford, and men marvelled as they read that "musical and prolific language, that gives a soul to the objects of sense, and a body to the abstractions of philosophy," a knowledge of which had been before entirely lost in the

West. Thus was perfected what is known as the revival of letters, when classical learning came to enrich and modify the national literatures, if it did temporarily retard the vernacular progress. The Humanists carried the day against the Obscurantists; and, as scholarship had before consisted in a thorough knowledge of Latin, it now also included a knowledge of Greek, which presented noble works of poetry, eloquence, and philosophy, and gave us a new idiom for the terminologies of science.

INVENTION OF PRINTING. — Nor was this all. This great wealth of learning would have still remained a dead letter to the multitude, and, in the main, a useless treasure even to scholars, had it not been for a simple yet marvellous invention of the same period. In Germany, some obscure mechanics, at Harlem, at Mayence, and at Strasbourg, were at work upon a machine which, if perfected, should at once extend letters a hundred-fold, and by that process revolutionize literature. The writers before, few as they were, had been almost as numerous as the readers; hereafter the readers were to increase in a geometrical proportion, and each great writer should address millions. Movable types, first of wood and then of metal, were made, the latter as early as 1441. Schœffer, Guttenberg, and Faust brought them to such perfection that books were soon printed and issued in large numbers. But so slowly did the art travel, partly on account of want of communication, and partly because it was believed to partake of necromancy, and partly, too, from the phlegmatic character of the English people, that thirty years elapsed before it was brought into England. The art of printing came in response to the demand of an age of progress: it was needed before; it was called for by the increasing number of readers, and when it came it multiplied that number largely.

WILLIAM CAXTON.—That it did at last come to England was

due to William Caxton, a native of Kent, and by vocation a mercer, who imported costly continental fabrics into England, and with them some of the new books now being printed in Holland. That he was a man of some eminence is shown by his having been engaged by Edward IV. on a mission to the Duke of Burgundy, with power to negotiate a treaty of commerce; that he was a person of skill and courtesy is evinced by his being retained in the service of Margaret, Duchess of York, when she married Charles, Duke of Burgundy. While in her train, he studied printing on the Continent, and is said to have printed some books there. At length, when he was more than sixty years old, he returned to England; and, in 1474, he printed what is supposed to be the first book printed in England, "The Game and Playe of the Chesse." Thus it was a century after Chaucer wrote the Canterbury Tales that printing was introduced into England. Caxton died in 1491, but his workmen continued to print, and among them Wynken de Worde stands conspicuous. Among the earlier works printed by Caxton were the Canterbury Tales, the Book of Fame, and the Troilus and Creseide of Chaucer.

Contemporary History. — It will be remembered that this was the stormy period of the Wars of the Roses. The long and troubled reign of Henry VI. closed in sorrow in 1471. The titular crown of France had been easily taken from him by Charles VII. and Joan of Arc; and although Richard of York, the great-grandson of Edward III., had failed in his attempts upon the English throne, yet *his* son Edward, afterward the Fourth, was successful. Then came the patricide of Clarence, the accession and cruelties of Richard III., the battle of Bosworth, and, at length, the union of the two houses in the persons of Henry VII. (Henry Tudor of Lancaster) and Elizabeth of York. Thus the strife of the succession was settled, and the realm had rest to reorganize and start anew in its historic career.

The weakening of the aristocracy by war and by execution gave to the crown a power before unknown, and made it a fearful coigne of vantage for Henry VIII., whose accession was in 1509. People and parliament were alike subservient, and gave their consent to the unjust edicts and arbitrary cruelties of this terrible tyrant.

In his reign the old English quarrel between Church and State — which during the civil war had lain dormant — again rose, and was brought to a final issue. It is not unusual to hear that the English Reformation grew out of the ambition of a libidinous monarch. This is a coincidence rather than a cause. His lust and his marriages would have occurred had there been no question of Pope or Church; conversely, had there been a continent king upon the throne, the great political and religious events would have happened in almost the same order and manner. That "knock of a king" and "incurable wound" prophesied by Piers Plowman were to come. Henry only seized the opportunity afforded by his ungodly passions as the best pretext, where there were many, for setting the Pope at defiance; and the spirit of reformation so early displayed, and awhile dormant from circumstances, and now strengthened by the voice of Luther, burst forth in England. There was little demur to the suppression of the monasteries; the tomb of St. Thomas à Becket was desecrated amidst the insulting mummeries of the multitude; and if Henry still burned Lutherans — because he could not forget that he had in earlier days denounced Luther — if he still maintained the six bloody articles[1] — his reforming spirit is shown in the execution of Fisher and More, by the anathema which he drew upon himself from the Pope, and by Henry's retaliation upon the friends and kinsmen of Cardinal Pole, the papal legate.

[1] 1st, the real presence; 2d, celibacy; 3d, monastic vows; 4th, low mass; 5th, auricular confession; 6th, withholding the cup from the laity.

Having thus briefly glanced at the history, we return to the literary products, all of which reflect more or less of the historic age, and by their paucity and poverty indicate the existence of the causes so unfavorable to literary effort. This statement will be partially understood when we mention, as the principal names of this period, Skelton, Wyatt, Surrey, and Sir Thomas More, men whose works are scarcely known to the ordinary reader, and which are yet the best of the time.

SKELTON.—John Skelton, poet, priest, and buffoon, was born about the year 1460, and educated at what he calls "Alma parens, O Cantabrigensis." Tutor to Prince Henry, afterward Henry VIII., he could boast, "The honour of England I lernyd to spelle." That he was highly esteemed in his day we gather from the eulogium of Erasmus, then for a short time professor of Greek at Oxford: "Unum Brittanicarum literarum lumen et decus." By another contemporary he is called the "inventive Skelton." As a priest he was not very holy; for, in a day when the marriage of the clergy was worse than their incontinence, he contracted a secret marriage. He enjoyed for a time the patronage of Wolsey, but afterward joined his enemies and attacked him violently. He was *laureated:* this does not mean, as at present, that he was poet laureate of England, but that he received a degree of which that was the title.

His works are direct delineations of the age. Among these are "monodies" upon *Kynge Edwarde the forthe*, and the *Earle of Northumberlande*. He corrects for Caxton "The boke of the Eneydos composed by Vyrgyle." He enters heartily into numerous literary quarrels; is a reformer to the extent of exposing ecclesiastical abuses in his *Colin Clout;* and scourges the friars and bishops alike; and in this work, and his "Why come ye not to Courte?" he makes a special target of Wolsey, and the pomp and luxury of his household.

He calls him "Mad Amelek, like to Mamelek" (Mameluke), and speaks

> Of his wretched original
> And his greasy genealogy.
> He came from the sank (blood) royal
> That was cast out of a butcher's stall.

This was the sorest point upon which he could touch the great cardinal and prime minister of Henry VIII.

Historically considered, one work of Skelton is especially valuable, for it places him among the first of English dramatists. The first effort of the modern drama was the *miracle play;* then came the *morality;* after that the *interlude,* which was soon merged into regular tragedy and comedy. Skelton's "Magnyfycence," which he calls "a goodly interlude and a merie," is, in reality, a morality play as well as an interlude, and marks the opening of the modern drama in England.

The peculiar verse of Skelton, styled *skeltonical,* is a sort of English anacreontic. One example has been given; take, as another, the following lampoon of Philip of Spain and the armada:

> A skeltonicall salutation
> Or condigne gratulation
> And just vexation
> Of the Spanish nation,
> That in bravado
> Spent many a crusado
> In setting forth an armado
> England to invado.
>
> Who but Philippus,
> That seeketh to nip us,
> To rob us and strip us,
> And then for to whip us,
> Would ever have meant
> Or had intent
> Or hither sent
> Such strips of charge, etc., etc.

It varies from five to six syllables, with several consecutive rhymes.

His "Merie Tales" are a series of short and generally broad stories, suited to the vulgar taste: no one can read them without being struck with the truly historic character of the subjects and the handling, and without moralizing upon the age which they describe. Skelton, a contemporary of the

French Rabelais, seems to us a weak English portrait of that great author; like him a priest, a buffoon, a satirist, and a lampooner, but unlike him in that he has given us no English *Gargantua* and *Pantagruel* to illustrate his age.

WYATT.—The next writer who claims our attention is Sir Thomas Wyatt, the son of Sir Henry Wyatt. He was born in 1503, and educated at Cambridge. Early a courtier, he was imperilled by his attachment to Anne Boleyn, conceded, if not quite Platonic, yet to have never led him to criminality. Several of his poems were inspired by her charms. The one best known begins—

What word is that that changeth not,
Though it be turned and made in twain?
It is mine ANNA, God it wot, etc.

That unfortunate queen—to possess whose charms Henry VIII. had repudiated Catherine of Arragon, and who was soon to be brought to the block after trial on the gravest charges—which we do not think substantiated—was, however, frivolous and imprudent, and liked such impassioned attentions—indeed, may be said to have suffered for them.

Wyatt was styled by Camden "splendide doctus," but his learning, however honorable to him, was not of much benefit to the world; for his works are few, and most of them amatory—"songs and sonnets"—full of love and lovers: as a makeweight, in *foro conscientiæ*, he paraphrased the penitential Psalms. An excellent comment this on the age of Henry VIII., when the monarch possessed with lust attempted the reformation of the Church. That Wyatt looked with favor upon the Reformation is indicated by one of his remarks to the king: "Heavens! that a man cannot repent him of his sins without the Pope's leave!" Imprisoned several times during the reign of Henry, after that monarch's death he favored the accession of Lady Jane Grey, and, with other of her adherents, was executed for high treason on the 11th of April, 1554. We have spoken of the spirit of the age. Its criticism was no better than its literature; for Wyatt, whom few read but the literary historian, was then considered

> A hand that taught what might be said in rhyme,
> That reft Chaucer the glory of his wit."

The glory of Chaucer's wit remains, while Wyatt is chiefly known because he was executed.

SURREY.—A twin star, but with a brighter lustre, was Henry Howard, Earl of Surrey, a writer whose works are remarkable for purity of thought and refinement of language. Surrey was a gay and wild young fellow—distinguished in the tournament which celebrated Henry's marriage with Anne of Cleves; now in prison for eating meat in Lent, and breaking windows at night; again we find him the English marshal when Henry invaded France in 1544. He led a restless life, was imperious and hot-tempered to the king, and at length quartered the king's arms with his own, thus assuming royal rights and imperilling the king's dignity. On this charge, which was, however, only a pretext, he was arrested and executed for high treason in 1547, before he was thirty years old.

Surrey is the greatest poetical name of Henry the Eighth's reign, not so much for the substance of his poems as for their peculiar handling. He is claimed as the introducer of blank verse—the iambic pentameter without rhyme, occasionally broken for musical effect by a change in the place of the cæsural pause. His translation of the Fourth Book of the Æneid, imitated perhaps from the Italian version of the Cardinal de Medici, is said to be the first specimen of blank verse in English. How slow its progress was is proved by Johnson's remarks upon the versification of Milton.[1] Thus in his blank

[1] "The Earl of Surrey is said to have translated one of Virgil's books

verse Surrey was the forerunner of Milton, and in his rhymed pentameter couplet one of the heralds of Dryden and Pope.

Sir Thomas More. — In a bird's-eye view of literature, the division into poetry and prose is really a distinction without a difference. They are the same body in different clothing, at labor and at festivity — in the working suit and in the court costume. With this remark we usher upon the literary scene Thomas More, in many respects one of the most remarkable men of his age — scholar, jurist, statesman, gentleman, and Christian; and, withal, a martyr to his principles of justice and faith. In a better age, he would have retained the highest honors: it is not to his discredit that in that reign he was brought to the block.

He was born in 1480. A very precocious youth, a distinguished career was predicted for him. He was greatly favored by Henry VIII., who constantly visited him at Chelsea, hanging upon his neck, and professing an intensity of friendship which, it is said, More always distrusted. He was the friend and companion of Erasmus during the residence of that distinguished man in England. More was gifted as an orator, and rose to the distinction of speaker of the House of Commons; was presented with the great seal upon the dismissal of Wolsey, and by his learning, his affability, and his kindness, became the most popular, as he seemed to be the most prosperous man in England. But, the test of Henry's friendship and of More's principles came when the king desired his concurrence in the divorce of Catherine of Arragon. He resigned the great seal rather than sign the marriage articles of

without rhyme, and, besides our tragedies, a few short poems had appeared in blank verse. . . . These petty performances cannot be supposed to have much influenced Milton; . . . finding blank verse easier than rhyme, he was desirous of persuading himself that it is better.' — *Lives of the Poets — Milton.*

Anne Boleyn, and would not take the oath as to the lawfulness of that marriage. Henry's kindness turned to fury, and More was a doomed man. A devout Romanist, he would not violate his conscience by submitting to the act of supremacy which made Henry the head of the Church, and so he was tried for high treason, and executed on the 6th of July, 1535. There are few scenes more pathetic than his last interview with his daughter Margaret, in the Tower, and no death more calmly and beautifully grand than his. He kissed the executioner and forgave him. "Thou art," said he, "to do me the greatest benefit that I can receive: pluck up thy spirit man, and be not afraid to do thine office."

UTOPIA. — His great work, and that which best illustrates the history of the age, is his Utopia, (ου τοπος, not a place.) Upon an island discovered by a companion of Vespuccius, he established an imaginary commonwealth, in which everybody was good and everybody happy. Purely fanciful as is his Utopia, and impossible of realization as he knew it to be while men are what they are, and not what they ought to be, it is manifestly a satire on that age, for his republic shunned English errors, and practised social virtues which were not the rule in England.

Although More wrote against Luther, and opposed Henry's Church innovations, we are struck with his Utopian claim for great freedom of inquiry on all subjects, even religion; and the bold assertion that no man should be punished for his religion, because "a man cannot make himself believe anything he pleases," as Henry's six bloody articles so fearfully asserted he must. The Utopia was written in Latin, but soon translated into English. We use the adjective *utopian* as meaning wildly fanciful and impossible: its true meaning is of high excellence, to be striven for — in a word, human perfection.

OTHER WORKS. — More also wrote, in most excellent English prose, a history of the princes, Edward V. and his brother Richard of York, who were murdered in the Tower; and a history of their murderer and uncle, Richard III. This Richard — and we need not doubt his accuracy of statement, for he was born five years before Richard fell at Bosworth — is the short, deformed youth, with his left shoulder higher than the right; crafty, stony-hearted, and cruel, so strikingly presented by Shakspeare, who takes More as his authority. "Not letting (sparing) to kiss whom he thought to kill . . . friend and foe was indifferent where his advantage grew; he spared no man's death whose life withstood his purpose. He slew, with his own hands, King Henry VI., being a prisoner in the Tower."

With the honorable name of More we leave this unproductive period, in which there was no great growth of any kind, but which was the planting-time, when seeds were sown that were soon to germinate and bloom and astonish the world. The times remind us of the dark saying in the Bible, "Out of the eater came forth meat; out of the strong came sweetness."

The art of printing had so increased the number of books, that public libraries began to be collected, and, what is better, to be used. The universities enlarged their borders, new colleges were added to Cambridge and Oxford; new foundations laid. The note of preparation betokened a great advent; the scene was fully prepared, and the actors would not be wanting.

Upon the death of Henry VIII., in 1547, Edward VI., his son by Jane Seymour, ascended the throne, and during his minority a protector was appointed in the person of his mother's brother, the Earl of Hertford, afterward Duke of Somerset. Edward was a sickly youth of ten years old, but his reign is noted for the progress of reform in the Church, and especially for the issue of the *Book of Common Prayer*, which must be considered of literary importance, as, although with decided modifications, and an interruption in its use during the brief reign of Mary, it has been the ritual of worship in the Anglican Church ever since. It superseded the Latin services — of which it was mainly a translation rearranged and modified — finally and completely, and containing, as it does, the whole body of doctrine, it was the first clear manifesto of the creeds and usages of that Church, and a strong bond of union among its members.

Other Writers of the Period.

Thomas Tusser, 1527–1580: published, in 1557, "A Hundreth Good Points of Husbandrie," afterward enlarged and called, "Five Hundred Points of Good Husbandrie, united to as many of Good Huswiferie;" especially valuable as a picture of rural life and labor in that age.

Alexander Barklay, died 1552: translated into English poetry the *Ship of Fools*, by Sebastian Brandt, of Basle.

Reginald Pecock, Bishop of St. Asaph and of Chichester: published, in 1449, "The Repressor of Overmuch Blaming of the Clergy." He attacked the Lollards, but was suspected of heresy himself, and deprived of his bishopric.

John Fisher, 1459–1535: was made Bishop of Rochester in 1504; opposed the Reformation, and refused to approve of Henry's divorce from Catherine of Arragon; was executed by the king. The Pope sent him a cardinal's hat while he was lying under sentence. Henry said he would not leave him a head to put it on. Wrote principally sermons and theological treatises.

Hugh Latimer, 1472–1555: was made Bishop of Worcester in 1535. An ardent supporter of the Reformation, who, by a rude, homely eloquence, influenced many people. He was burned at the stake at the age of eighty-three, in company with Ridley, Bishop of London, by Queen Mary. His memorable words to his fellow-martyr are: "We shall this day light a candle in England which, I trust, shall never be put out."

John Leland, or Laylonde, died 1552: an eminent antiquary, who, by order of Henry VIII., examined, *con amore*, the records of libraries, cathedrals, priories, abbeys, colleges, etc., and has left a vast amount of curious antiquarian learning behind him. He became insane by reason of the pressure of his labors.

George Cavendish, died 1557: wrote "The Negotiations of Woolsey, the Great Cardinal of England," etc., which was republished as the "Life and Death of Thomas Woolsey." From this, it is said, Shakspeare drew in writing his "Henry VIII."

Roger Ascham, 1515–1568: specially famous as the successful instructor of Elizabeth and Lady Jane Grey, whom he was able to imbue with a taste for classical learning. He wrote a treatise on the use of the bow, called *Toxophilus*, and *The Schoolmaster*, which contains many excellent and judicious suggestions, worthy to be carried out in modern education. It was highly praised by Dr. Johnson. It was written for the use of the children of Sackville, Lord Buckhurst.

CHAPTER XI.

SPENSER AND THE ELIZABETHAN AGE.

The Great Change.

WITH what joy does the traveller in the desert, after a day of scorching glow and a night of breathless heat, descry the distant trees which mark the longed-for well-spring in the emerald oasis, which seems to beckon with its branching palms to the converging caravans, to come and slake their fever-thirst, and escape from the threatening sirocco !

The pilgrim arrives at the caravansery : not the long, low stone house, unfurnished and bare, which former experience had led him to expect; but a splendid palace. He dismounts ; maidens purer and more beautiful than fabled houris, accompanied by slaves bearing rare dishes and goblets of crusted gold, offer him refreshments : perfumed baths, couches of down, soft and soothing music are about him in delicious combination. Surely he is dreaming ; or if this be real, were not the burning sun and the sand of the desert, the panting camel and the dying horse of an hour ago but a dream ?

Such is not an overwrought illustration of English literature in the long, barren reach from Chaucer to Spenser, as compared with the freshness, beauty, and grandeur of the geniuses which adorned Elizabeth's court, and tended to make her reign as illustrious in history as the age of Pericles, of Augustus, or of Louis XIV. Chief among these were Spenser and Shakspeare. As the latter has been truly characterized as not for an age, but for all time, the former may be more justly considered as the highest exponent and representative of that period. The Faerie Queene, considered only as a grand heroic poem, is unrivalled in its pictures of beautiful women, brave men, daring deeds, and Oriental splendor; but in its allegorical character, it is far more instructive, since it enumerates and illustrates the cardinal virtues which should make up the moral character of a gentleman: add to this, that it is teeming with history, and in its manifold completeness we have, if not an oasis in the desert, more truly the rich verge of the fertile country which bounds that desert, and which opens a more beautiful road to the literary traveller as he comes down the great highway: wearied and worn with the factions and barrenness of the fifteenth century, he fairly revels with delight in the fertility and variety of the Elizabethan age.

EDWARD AND MARY. — In pursuance of our plan, a few preliminary words will present the historic features of that age. In the year 1547, Henry VIII., the royal Bluebeard, sank, full of crimes and beset with deathbed horrors, into a dishonorable grave.[1] A poor, weak youth, his son, Edward VI., seemed sent by special providence on a short mission of six years, to foster the reformed faith, and to give the land a brief rest after the disorders and crimes of his father's reign.

After Edward came Queen Mary, in 1553 — the bloody Mary, who violently overturned the Protestant system, and avenged her mother against her father by restoring the Papal

[1] From this dishonor Mr. Froude's researches among the statute books have not been able to lift him, for he gives system to horrors which were before believed to be eccentric; and, while he fails to justify the monarch, implicates a trembling parliament and a servile ministry, as if their sharing the crime made it less odious.

sway and making heresy the unpardonable sin. It may seem strange, in one breath to denounce Henry and to defend his daughter Mary; but severe justice, untempered with sympathy, has been meted out to her. We acknowledge all her recorded actions, but let it be remembered that she was the child of a basely repudiated mother, Catherine of Arragon, who, as the daughter of Ferdinand and Isabella of Spain, was a Catholic of the Catholics. Mary had been declared illegitimate; she was laboring under an incurable disease, affecting her mind as well as her body; she was the wife of Philip II. of Spain, a monster of iniquity, whose sole virtue — if we may so speak — was his devotion to his Church. She inherited her bigotry from her mother, and strengthened it by her marriage; and she thought that in persecuting heretics she was doing God service, which would only be a perfect service when she should have burned out the bay-tree growth of heresy and restored the ancient faith.

Such were her character and condition as displayed to the English world; but we know, in addition, that she bore her sufferings with great fortitude; that, an unloved wife, she was a pattern of conjugal affection and fidelity; that she was a dupe in the hands of designing men and a fierce propaganda; and we may infer that, under different circumstances and with better guidance, the real elements of her character would have made her a good monarch and presented a far more pleasing historical portrait.

Justice demands that we should say thus much, for even with these qualifications, the picture of her reign is very dark and painful. After a sad and bloody rule of five years — a reign of worse than Roman proscription, or later French terrors — she died without leaving a child. There was but one voice as to her successor. Delirious shouts of joy were heard throughout the land: "God save Queen Elizabeth!" "No more burnings at Smithfield, nor beheadings on Tower green! No more of Spanish Philip and his pernicious bigots! Toleration, freedom, light!" The people of England were ready for a golden age, and the golden age had come.

ELIZABETH. — And who was Elizabeth? The daughter of the dishonored Anne Boleyn, who had been declared illegitimate, and set out of the succession; who had been kept in ward; often and long in peril of her life; destined, in all human foresight, to a life of sorrow, humiliation, and obscurity; her head had been long lying "'twixt axe and crown," with more probability of the former than the latter.

Wonderful was the change. With her began a reign the like of which the world had never seen; a great and brilliant crisis in English history, in which the old order passed away and the new was inaugurated. It was like a new historic fulfilment of the prophecy of Virgil:

> Magnus . . . sæclorum nascitur ordo;
> Jam redit et *Virgo*, redeunt Saturnia regna.

Her accession and its consequences were like the scenes in some fairy tale. She was indeed a Faerie Queene, as she was designated in Spenser's magnificent allegory. Around her clustered a new chivalry, whose gentle deeds were wrought not only with the sword, but with the pen. Stout heart, stalwart arm, and soaring imagination, all wore her colors and were amply rewarded by her smiles; and whatever her personal faults — and they were many — as a monarch, she was not unworthy of their allegiance.

SIDNEY. — Before proceeding to a consideration of Spenser's great poem, it is necessary to mention two names intimately associated with him and with his fame, and of special interest in the literary catalogue of Queen Elizabeth's court, brilliant and numerous as that catalogue was.

Among the most striking characters of this period was Sir Philip Sidney, whose brief history is full of romance and attraction; not so much for what he did as for what he personally was, and gave promise of being. Whenever we seek for an historical illustration of the *gentleman*, the figure of Sidney rises in company with that of Bayard, and claims distinction. He was born at Pennshurst in Kent, on the 29th of November, 1554. He was the nephew of Robert Dudley, Earl of Leicester, the chief favorite of the queen. Precocious in grace, dignity, and learning, Sidney was educated both at Oxford and Cambridge, and in his earliest manhood he was a *prud'homme*, handsome, elegant, learned, and chivalrous; a statesman, a diplomatist, a soldier, and a poet; "not only of excellent wit, but extremely beautiful of face. Delicately chiselled Anglo-Norman features, smooth, fair cheek, a faint moustache, blue eyes, and a mass of amber-colored hair," distinguished him among the handsome men of a court where handsome men were in great request.

He spent some time at the court of Charles IX. of France — which, however, he left suddenly, shocked and disgusted by the massacre of St. Bartholomew's Eve — and extended his travels into Germany. The queen held him in the highest esteem — although he was disliked by the Cecils, the constant rivals of the Dudleys; and when he was elected to the crown of Poland, the queen refused him permission to accept, because she would not lose "the brightest jewel of her crown — her Philip," as she called him to distinguish him from her sister Mary's Philip, Philip II. of Spain. A few words will finish his personal story. He went, by the queen's permission, with his uncle Leicester to the Low Countries, then struggling, with Elizabeth's assistance, against Philip of Spain. There he was made governor of Flushing — the key to the navigation of the North Seas — with the rank of general of horse. In a skirmish near Zutphen (South Fen) he served as a volunteer; and, as he was going into action fully armed, seeing his old friend Sir William Pelham without cuishes upon his thighs, prompted by mistaken but chivalrous generosity, he took off his own, and had his thigh broken by a musket-ball. This was on the 2d of October, 1586, N. S. He lingered for twenty days, and then died at Arnheim, mourned by all. The story of his passing the untasted water to the wounded soldier, will never become trite: "This man's necessity is greater than mine," was an immortal speech which men like to quote.[1]

SIDNEY'S WORKS. — But it is as a literary character that we must consider Sidney; and it is worthy of special notice that his works could not have been produced in any other age. The principal one is the *Arcadia*. The name, which was adopted from Sannazzaro, would indicate a pastoral — and this was eminently the age of English pastoral — but it is in reality not such. It presents indeed sylvan scenes, but they are in the life of a knight. It is written in prose, interspersed with short poems, and was inspired by and dedicated to his literary sister Mary, the Countess of Pembroke. It was called indeed the *Countess of Pembroke's Arcadia*. There are many scenes of great beauty and vigor; there is much which represents the manners of the age, but few persons can now peruse it with pleasure, because of the peculiar affectations of style, and its overload of ornament. There grew naturally in the atmosphere of the court of a regnant queen, an affected, flattering, and inflated language, known to us as *Euphuism*. Of this John Lilly has been called the father, but we really only owe to him the name, which is taken from his two works, *Euphues*, *Anatomy of Wit*, and *Euphues and his England*. The speech of the Euphuist is hardly caricatured in Sir Walter Scott's delineation of Sir Piercie Shafton in "The Monastery." The gallant men of that day affected this form of address to fair ladies, and fair ladies liked to be greeted in

[1] The reader's attention is called — or recalled — to the masterly etching of Sir Philip Sidney, in Motley's History of the United Netherlands. The low chant of the *cuisse rompue* is especially pathetic.

such language. Sidney's works have a relish of this diction, and are imbued with the spirit which produced it.

Defence of Poesie. — The second work to be mentioned is his "Defence of Poesie." Amid the gayety and splendor of that reign, there was a sombre element. The Puritans took gloomy views of life: they accounted amusements, dress, and splendor as things of the world; and would even sweep away poetry as idle, and even wicked. Sir Philip came to its defence with the spirit of a courtier and a poet, and the work in which he upholds it is his best, far better in style and sense than his Arcadia. It is one of the curiosities of literature, in itself, and in its representation of such a social condition as could require a defence of poetry. His *Astrophel and Stella* is a collection of amatory poems, disclosing his passion for Lady Rich, the sister of the Earl of Essex. Although something must be allowed to the license of the age, in language at least, yet still the *Astrophel and Stella* cannot be commended for its morality. The sentiments are far from Platonic, and have been severely censured by the best critics. Among the young gallants of Euphuistic habitudes, Sidney was known as *Astrophel;* and Spenser wrote a poem mourning the death of Astrophel: *Stella,* of course, was the star of his worship.

Gabriel Harvey. — Among the friends of both Sidney and Spenser, was one who had the pleasure of making them acquainted — Gabriel Harvey. He was born, it is believed, in 1545, and lived until 1630. Much may be gathered of the literary character and tendencies of the age by a perusal of the "three proper and wittie familiar letters" which passed between Spenser and himself, and the "four letters and certain sonnets," containing valuable notices of contemporary poets. He also prefixed a poem entitled *Hobbinol,* to the Faery Queene. But Harvey most deserves our notice because he was the champion of the hexameter verse in English, and imbued even Spenser with an enthusiasm for it.

Each language has its own poetic and rhythmic capacities. Actual experiment and public taste have declared their verdict against hexameter verse in English. The genius of the Northern languages refuses this old heroic measure, which the Latins borrowed from the Greeks, and all the scholarship and finish of Longfellow has not been able to establish it in English. Harvey was a pedant so thoroughly tinctured with classical learning, that he would trammel his own language by ancient rules, instead of letting it grow into the assertion of its own rules.

EDMUND SPENSER — THE SHEPHERD'S CALENDAR. — Having noticed these lesser lights of the age of Spenser, we return to a brief consideration of that poet, who, of all others, is the highest exponent and representative of literature in the age of Queen Elizabeth, and whose works are full of contemporary history.

Spenser was born in the year of the accession of Queen Mary, 1553, at London, and of what he calls "a house of ancient fame." He was educated at Cambridge, where he early displayed poetic taste and power, and he went, after leaving college, to reside as a tutor in the North of England. A love affair with "a skittish female," who jilted him, was the cause of his writing the *Shepherd's Calendar*, which he soon after took with him in manuscript to London, as the first fruits of a genius that promised far nobler things.

Harvey introduced him to Sidney, and a tender friendship sprang up between them: he spent much of his time with Sidney at Pennshurst, and dedicated to him the *Shepherd's Calendar*. He calls it "an olde name for a newe worke." The plan of it is as follows: There are twelve parts, corresponding to twelve months: these he calls *aeglogues*, or goatherde's songs, (not *eclogues* or εκλογαι — well-chosen words.)

It is a rambling work in varied melody, interspersed and relieved by songs and lays.

HIS ARCHAISMS.—In view of its historical character, there are several points to be observed. It is of philological importance to notice that in the preliminary epistle, he explains and defends his use of archaisms—for the language of none of his poems is the current English of the day, but always that of a former period—saying that he uses old English words "restored as to their rightful heritage;" and it is also evident that he makes new ones, in accordance with just principles of philology. This fact is pointed out, lest the cursory reader should look for the current English of the age of Elizabeth in Spenser's poems.

How much, or rather how little he thought of the poets of the day, may be gathered from his saying that he "scorns and spews the rakebelly rout of ragged rymers." It further displays the boldness of his English, that he is obliged to add "a Glosse or Scholion," for the use of the reader.

Another historical point worthy of observation is his early adulation of Elizabeth, evincing at once his own courtiership and her popularity. In "February" (Story of the Oak and Briar) he speaks of "colours meete to clothe a mayden queene." The whole of "April" is in her honor:

> Of fair Eliza be your silver song,
> That blessed wight,
> The floure of virgins, may she flourish long,
> In princely plight.

In "September" "he discourseth at large upon the loose living of Popish prelates," an historical trait of the new but cautious reformation of the Marian Church, under Elizabeth. Whether a courtier like Spenser could expect the world to believe in the motto with which he concludes the epilogue, "Merce non mercede," is doubtful, but the words are significant; and it is not to his discredit that he strove for both.

HIS GREATEST WORK. — We now approach *The Faerie Queene,* the greatest of Spenser's works, the most remarkable poem of that age, and one of the greatest landmarks in English literature and English history. It was not published in full until nearly all the great events of Elizabeth's reign had transpired, and it is replete with the history of nearly half a century in the most wonderful period of English history. To courtly readers of that day the history was only pleasantly illustrative — to the present age it is invaluable for itself: the poem illustrates the history.

He received, through the friendship of Sidney, the patronage of his uncle, Robert Dudley, Earl of Leicester — a powerful nobleman, because, besides his family name, and the removal of the late attainder, which had been in itself a distinction, he was known to be the lover of the queen: for whatever may be thought of her conduct, we know that in recommending him as a husband to the widowed Queen of Scots, she said she would have married him herself had she designed to marry at all; or, it may be said, she would have married him had she dared, for that act would have ruined her.

Spenser was a loyal and enthusiastic subject, a poet, and a scholar. From these characteristics sprang the Faerie Queene. After submitting the first book to the criticism of his friend and his patron, he dedicated the work to "The most high, mighty, and magnificent empress, renowned for piety, virtue, and all gracious government, Elizabeth, by the grace of God Queen of England, France, and Ireland, and of Virginia." [1]

[1] This last claim of title was based upon the voyages of the Cabots, and the unsuccessful colonial efforts of Raleigh and Gilber .

CHAPTER XII.

ILLUSTRATIONS OF THE HISTORY IN THE FAERIE QUEENE.

THE FAERIE QUEENE.

THE Faerie Queene is an allegory, in many parts capable of more than one interpretation. Some of the characters stand for two, and several of them even for three distinct historical personages.

The general plan and scope of the poem may be found in the poet's letter to his friend, Sir Walter Raleigh. It is designed to enumerate and illustrate the moral virtues which should characterize a noble or gentle person — to present "the image of a brave knight perfected in the twelve private morall vertues, as Aristotle hath devised." It appears that the author designed twelve books, but he did not accomplish his purpose. The poem, which he left unfinished, contains but six books or legends, each of which relates the adventures of a knight who is the patron and representative of a special virtue.

Book I. gives the adventures of St. George, the Red-Cross Knight, by whom is intended the virtue of Holiness.

Book II., those of Sir Guyon, or Temperance.

Book III., Britomartis, a lady-knight, or Chastity.

Book IV., Cambel and Triamond, or Friendship.

Book V., Sir Artegal, or Justice.

Book VI., Sir Calydore, or Courtesy.

The perfect hero of the entire poem is King Arthur, chosen "as most fitte, for the excellency of his person, being made famous by many men's former workes, and also furthest from the daunger of envy and suspition of present time."

It was manifestly thus, too, that the poet solved a difficult and delicate problem: he pleased the queen by adopting this mythic hero, for who else was worthy of her august hand?

And in the person of the faerie queene herself Spenser informs us: "I mean *glory* in my general intention, but in my particular, I conceive the most excellent and glorious person of our sovereign, the *Queene*."

Did we depend upon the poem for an explanation of Spenser's design, we should be left in the dark, for he intended to leave the origin and connection of the adventures for the twelfth book, which was never written; but he has given us his plan in the same preliminary letter to Raleigh.

The Plan Proposed. — "The beginning of my history," he says, "should be in the twelfth booke, which is the last; where I devise that the Faerie Queene kept her Annual Feaste XII days; uppon which XII severall days the occasions of the XII severall adventures hapned, which being undertaken by XII severall knights, are in these XII books handled and discoursed."

First, a tall, clownish youth falls before the queen and desires a boon, which she might not refuse, viz. the achievement of any adventure which might present itself. Then appears a fair lady, habited in mourning, and riding on an ass, while behind her comes a dwarf, leading a caparisoned war-horse, upon which was the complete armor of a knight. The lady falls before the queen and complains that her father and mother, an ancient king and queen, had, for many years, been shut up by a dragon in a brazen castle, and begs that one of the knights may be allowed to deliver them.

The young clown entreats that he may take this adventure, and notwithstanding the wonder and misgiving of all, the armor is found to fit him well, and when he had put it on, "he seemed the goodliest man in all the company, and was well liked by the lady, and eftsoones taking on him knighthood, and mounting on that strounge courser, he went forth with her on that adventure; where beginneth the First Booke."

In a similar manner, other petitions are urged, and other adventures undertaken.

ILLUSTRATIONS OF THE HISTORY. — The history in this poem lies directly upon the surface. Elizabeth was the Faery Queen herself—faery in her real person, springing Cinderella-like from durance and danger to the most powerful throne in Europe. Hers was a reign of faery character, popular and august at home, after centuries of misrule and civil war; abroad English influence and power were exerted in a magical manner. It is she who holds a court such as no Englishman had ever seen; who had the power to transform common men into valiant warriors, elegant courtiers, and great statesmen; to send forth her knights upon glorious adventures — Sidney to die at Zutphen, Raleigh to North and South America, Frobisher — with a wave of her hand as he passes down the Thames — to try the northwest passage to India; Effingham, Drake, and Hawkins to drive off to the tender mercy of northern storms the Invincible Armada, and then to point out to the coming generations the distant fields of English enterprise.

"Chivalry was dying; the abbey and the castle were soon together to crumble into ruins; and all the forms, desires, beliefs, convictions of the old world were passing away, never to return;"[1] but this virgin queen was the founder of a new

[1] Froude, i. 65.

chivalry, whose deeds were not less valiant, and far more useful to civilization.

It is not our purpose, for it would be impossible, to interpret all the history contained in this wonderful poem: a few of the more striking presentations will be indicated, and thus suggest to the student how he may continue the investigation for himself.

THE KNIGHT AND THE LADY. — In the First Book we are at once struck with the fine portraiture of the Red Crosse Knight, the Patron of Holinesse, which we find in the opening lines:

> A gentle knight was pricking on the plain,
> Ycladd in mighty arms and silver shield.

As we read we discover, without effort, that he is the St. George of England, or the impersonation of England herself, whose red-cross banner distinguishes her among the nations of the earth. It is a description of Christian England with which the poet thus opens his work:

> And on his brest a bloodie cross he bore,
>   The dear remembrance of his dying Lord,
> For whose sweet sake that glorious badge he wore,
>   And dead, as living ever, Him adored.
> Upon his shield the like was also scored,
> For sovereign hope which in his help he had.

Then follows his adventure — that of St. George and the Dragon. By slaying this monster, he will give comfort and aid to a peerless lady, the daughter of a glorious king; this fair lady, *Una*, who has come a long distance, and to whom, as a champion, the Faery Queene has presented the red-cross knight. Thus is presented the historic truth that the reformed and suffering Church looked to Queen Elizabeth for succor and support, for the Lady Una is one of several portraitures of the Church in this poem.

As we proceed in the poem, the history becomes more apparent. The Lady Una, riding upon a lowly ass, shrouded by a veil, covered with a black stole, "as one that inly mourned," and leading "a milk-white lamb," is the Church. The ass is the symbol of her Master's lowliness, who made even his triumphant entry into Jerusalem upon "a colt the foal of an ass;" the lamb, the emblem of the innocence and of the helplessness of the "little flock;" the black stole is meant to represent the Church's trials and sorrows in her former history as well as in that naughty age. The dragon is the old serpent, her constant and bitter foe, who, often discomfited, returns again and again to the attack in hope of her overthrow.

THE WOOD OF ERROR. — The adventures of the knight and the lady take them first into the Wood of Error, a noble and alluring grove, within which, however, lurks a loathsome serpent. The knight rushes upon this female monster with great boldness, but

. . . Wrapping up her wreathed body round,
She leaped upon his shield and her huge train
All suddenly about his body wound,
That hand and foot he strove to stir in vain.
God help the man so wrapt in Error's endless chain.

The Lady Una cries out:

. . . Now, now, sir knight, shew what ye bee,
Add faith unto thy force, and be not faint.
Strangle her, else she sure will strangle thee.

He follows her advice, makes one desperate effort, Error is slain, and the pilgrimage resumed.

Thus it is taught that the Church has waged successful battle with Error in all its forms — paganism, Arianism, Socinianism, infidelity; and in all ages of her history, whether crouching in the lofty groves of the Druids, or in the more insidious forms of later Christian heresy.

THE HERMITAGE. — On leaving the Wood of Error, the knight and Lady Una encounter a venerable hermit, and are led into his hermitage. This is *Archimago*, a vile magician thus disguised, and in his retreat foul spirits personate both knight and lady, and present these false doubles to each. Each sees what seems to be the other's fall from virtue, and, horrified by the sight, the real persons leave the hermitage by separate ways, and wander, in inextricable mazes lost, until fortune and faery bring them together again and disclose the truth.

Here Spenser, who was a zealous Protestant, designs to present the monastic system, the disfavor into which the monasteries had fallen, and the black arts secretly studied among better arts in the cloisters, especially in the period just succeeding the Norman conquest.

THE CRUSADES. — As another specimen of the historic interpretation, we may trace the adventures of England in the Crusades, as presented in the encounter of St. George with *Sansfoy*, (without faith,) or the Infidel.

From the hermitage of Archimago,

> The true St. George had wandered far away,
> Still flying from his thoughts and jealous fear,
> Will was his guide, and grief led him astray;
> At last him chanced to meet upon the way
> A faithless Saracen all armed to point,
> In whose great shield was writ with letters gay
> SANSFOY: full large of limb, and every joint
> He was, and carèd not for God or man a point.

Well might the poet speak of Mohammedanism as large of limb, for it had stretched itself like a Colossus to India, and through Northern Africa into Spain, where it threatened Christendom, beyond the Pyrenees. It was then that the unity of the Church, the concurrence of Europe in one form of Christianity, made available the enthusiasm which succeeded in stemming the torrent of Islam, and setting bounds to its conquests.

It is not our purpose to pursue the adventures of the Church, but to indicate the meaning of the allegory and the general interpretation; it will give greater zest to the student to make the investigation for himself, with the all-sufficient aids of modern criticism.

Assailed in turn by error in doctrine, superstition, hypocrisy, enchantments, lawlessness, pride, and despair, the red-cross knight overcomes them all, and is led at last by the Lady Una into the House of Holiness, a happy and glorious house. There, anew equipped with the shield of Faith, the helmet of Salvation, and the sword of the Spirit, he goes forth to greater conquests; the dragon is slain, the Lady Una triumphant, the Church delivered, and Holiness to the Lord established as the law of his all-subduing kingdom on earth.

BRITOMARTIS. — In the third book the further adventures of the red-cross knight are related, but a heroine divides our attention with him. *Britomartis*, or Chastity, finds him attacked by six lawless knights, who try to compel him to give up his lady and serve another. Here Britomartis represents Elizabeth, and the historic fact is the conflict of English Protestantism carried on upon land and sea, in the Netherlands, in France, and against the Invincible Armada of Philip. The new mistress offered him in the place of Una is the Papal Church, and the six knights are the nations fighting for the claims of Rome.

The valiant deeds of Britomartis represent also the power of chastity, to which Scott alludes when he says,

> She charmed at once and tamed the heart,
> Incomparable Britomarte.[1]

And here the poet pays his most acceptable tribute to the Virgin Queen. She is in love with Sir Artegal — abstract justice. She has encountered him in fierce battle, and he has conquered her. It was the fond boast of Elizabeth that

[1] Introduction to fifth canto of Marmion.

she lived for her people, and for their sake refused to marry. The following portraiture will be at once recognized :

> And round about her face her yellow hair
>   Having, thro' stirring, loosed its wonted band,
> Like to a golden border did appear,
>   Framèd in goldsmith's forge with cunning hand;
>   Yet goldsmith's cunning could not understand
> To frame such subtle wire, so shiny clear,
>   For it did glisten like the glowing sand,
> The which Pactòlus with his waters sheer,
> Throws forth upon the rivage, round about him near.

This encomium upon Elizabeth's hair recalls the description of another courtier, that it was like the last rays of the declining sun. Ill-natured persons called it red.

SIR ARTEGAL, OR JUSTICE. — As has been already said, Artegal, or Justice, makes conquest of Britomartis or Elizabeth. It is no earthly love that follows, but the declaration of the queen that in her continued maidenhood justice to her people shall be her only spouse. Such, whatever the honest historian may think, was the poet's conceit of what would best please his royal mistress.

It has been already stated that by Gloriana, the Faerie Queene, the poet intended the person of Elizabeth in her regnant grandeur: Britomartis represents her chastity. Not content with these impersonations, Spenser introduces a third: it is Belphœbe, the abstraction of virginity; a character for which, however, he designs a dual interpretation. Belphœbe is also another representation of the Church; in describing her he rises to great splendor of language :

> . . . her birth was of the morning dew,
> And her conception of the glorious prime.

We recur, as we read, to the grandeur of the Psalmist's words, as he speaks of the coming of her Lord : "In the day of thy power shall the people offer thee free-will offerings with a holy worship; the dew of thy birth is of the womb of the morning.''

ELIZABETH. — In the fifth book a great number of the statistics of contemporary history are found. A cruel sultan, urged on by an abandoned sultana, is Philip with the Spanish Church. Mercilla, a queen pursued by the sultan and his wife, is another name for Elizabeth, for he tells us she was

> . . . a maiden queen of high renown;
> For her great bounty knowen over all.

Artegal, assuming the armor of a pagan knight, represents justice in the person of Solyman the Magnificent, making war against Philip of Spain. In the ninth canto of the sixth book, the court of Elizabeth is portrayed; in the tenth and eleventh, the war in Flanders — so brilliantly described in Mr. Motley's history. The Lady Belge is the United Netherlands; Gerioneo, the oppressor, is the Duke of Alva; the Inquisition appears as a horrid but nameless monster, and minor personages occur to complete the historic pictures.

The adventure of Sir Artegal in succor of the Lady Irena, (Erin,) represents the proceedings of Elizabeth in Ireland, in enforcing the Reformation, abrogating the establishments of her sister Mary, and thus inducing Tyrone's rebellion, with the consequent humiliation of Essex.

MARY QUEEN OF SCOTS. — With one more interpretation we close. In the fifth book, Spenser is the apologist of Elizabeth for her conduct to her cousin, Mary Queen of Scots, and he has been very delicate in his distinctions. It is not her high abstraction of justice, Sir Artegal, who does the murderous deed, but his man *Talus*, retributive justice, who, like a limehound, finds her hidden under a heap of gold, and drags her forth by her fair locks, in such rueful plight that even Artegal pities her:

Yet for no pity would he change the course
  Of justice which in Talus hand did lie,
Who rudely haled her forth without remorse,
  Still holding up her suppliant hands on high,
  And kneeling at his feet submissively;
But he her suppliant hands, those *hands of gold*,
  And eke her feet, those feet of *silver try*,
Which sought unrighteousness and justice sold,
Chopped off and nailed on high that all might them behold.

She was a royal lady, a regnant queen: her hands held a golden sceptre, and her feet pressed a silver footstool. She was thrown down the castle wall, and drowned "in the dirty mud."

"But the stream washed away her guilty blood." Did it wash away Elizabeth's bloody guilt? No. For this act she stands in history like Lady Macbeth, ever rubbing her hands, but "the damned spot" will not out at her bidding. Granted all that is charged against Mary, never was woman so meanly, basely, cruelly treated as she.

What has been said is only in partial illustration of the plan and manner of Spenser's great poem: the student is invited and encouraged to make an analysis of the other portions himself. To the careless reader the poem is harmonious, the pictures beautiful, and the imagery gorgeous; to the careful student it is equally charming, and also discloses historic pictures of great value.

It is so attractive that the critic lingers unconsciously upon it. Spenser's tributes to the character of woman are original, beautiful, and just, and the fame of his great work, originally popular and designed for a contemporary purpose only, has steadily increased. Next to Milton, he is the most learned of the British poets. Warton calls him the *serious Spenser*. Thomson says he formed himself upon Spenser. He took the ottava rima, or eight-lined stanza of the Italian poets, and by adding an Alexandrine line, formed it into what has since been called the Spenserian stanza, which has been imitated by many great poets since, and by Byron, the greatest of them, in his Childe Harold. Of his language it has already been said that he designedly uses the archaic, or that of Chaucer; or, as Pope has said,

Spenser himself affects the obsolete.

The plan of the poem, neglecting the unities of an epic, is like that of a general history, rambling and desultory, or like the transformations of a fairy tale, as it is: his descriptions are gorgeous, his verse exceedingly melodious, and his management of it very graceful. The Gerusalemme Liberata of Tasso appeared while he was writing the Faery Queene, and he imitated portions of that great epic in his own, but his imitations are finer than the original.

HIS OTHER WORKS. — His other works need not detain us: Hymns in honor of Love and Beauty, Prothalamion, and Epithalamion, Mother Hubbard's Tale, Amoretti or Sonnets, The Tears of the Muses or Brittain's Ida, are little read at the present day. His Astrophel is a tender "pastoral elegie" upon the death of the most noble and valorous knight, Sir Philip Sidney; and is better known for its subject than for itself. This was a favorite theme of the friendly and sensitive poet; he has also written several elegies and æglogues in honor of Sidney.

SPENSER'S FATE. — The fate of Spenser is a commentary upon courtiership, even in the reign of Elizabeth, the Faery Queene. Her requital of his adoration was an annual pension of fifty pounds, and the ruined castle and unprofitable estate of Kilcolman in Ireland, among a half-savage population, in a period of insurrections and massacres, with the requirement that he should reside upon his grant. An occasional visit from Raleigh, then a captain in the army, a rambler along the banks of the picturesque Mulla, and the composition and arrangement of the great poem with the suggestions of his friend, were at once his labors and his only recreations. He sighed after the court, and considered himself as hardly used by the queen.

At length an insurrection broke out, and his home was set on fire: he fled from his flaming castle, and in the confusion his infant child was left behind and burned to death. A few months after, he died in London, on January 16, 1598–9, broken-hearted and poor, at an humble tavern in King Street. Buried at the expense of the Earl of Essex, Ann Countess of Dorset bore the expense of his monument in Westminster Abbey, in gratitude for his noble championship of woman. Upon that are inscribed these words: *Anglorum poetarum nostri seculi facile princeps* — truer words, great as is the praise, than are usually found in monumental inscriptions.

Whatever our estimate of Spenser, he must be regarded as the truest literary exponent and representative of the age of Elizabeth, almost as much her biographer as Miss Strickland, and her historian as Hume: indeed, neither biographer nor historian could venture to draw the lineaments of her character without having recourse to Spenser and his literary contemporaries.

Other Writers of the Age of Spenser.

Richard Hooker, 1553–1598: educated at Oxford, he became Master of the Temple in London, a post which he left with pleasure to take a country parish. He wrote a famous work, entitled "A Treatise on the Laws of Ecclesiastical Polity," which is remarkable for its profound learning, powerful logic, and eloquence of style. In it he defends the position of the Church of England, against Popery on the one hand and Calvinism on the other.

Robert Burton, 1576–1639: author of "The Anatomy of Melancholie," an amusing and instructive medley of quotations and classical anecdotes, showing a profound erudition. In this all the causes and effects of melancholy are set forth with varied illustrations. His *nom de plume* was Democritus, Jr., and he is an advocate of the laughing philosophy.

Thomas Hobbes, 1588–1679: tutor to Charles II., when Prince of Wales, and author of the *Leviathan.* This is a philosophical treatise, in which he advocates monarchical government, as based upon the fact that all men are selfish, and that human nature, being essentially corrupt, requires an iron control: he also wrote upon *Liberty and Necessity*, and on *Human Nature.*

John Stow, 1525–1605: tailor and antiquary. Principally valuable for his "Annales," "Summary of English Chronicles," and "A Survey of London." The latter is the foundation of later topographical descriptions of the English metropolis.

Raphael Hollinshed, or Holinshed, died about 1580: his *Chronicles of Englande, Scotlande, and Irelande,* were a treasure-house to Shakspeare, from which he drew materials for King Lear, Cymbeline, Macbeth, and other plays.

Richard Hakluyt, died 1616: being greatly interested in voyages and travels, he wrote works upon the adventures of others. Among these are, "Divers Voyages Touching the Discoverie of America," and "Four Voyages unto Florida," which have been very useful in the compilation of early American history.

Samuel Purchas, 1577–1628: like Hakluyt, he was exceedingly industrious in collecting material, and wrote "Hakluyt's Posthumus, or Purchas, his Pilgrimes," a history of the world "in Sea Voyages and Land Travels."

Sir Walter Raleigh, 1552–1618: a man famous for his personal strength and comeliness, vigor of mind, valor, adventures, and sufferings. A prominent actor in the stirring scenes of Elizabeth's reign, he was high in the favor of the queen. Accused of high treason on the accession of James I., and imprisoned under sentence of death, an unsuccessful expedition to South America in search of El Dorado, which caused complaints from the Spanish king, led to his execution under the pending sentence. He wrote, chiefly in prison, a History of the World, in which he was aided by his literary friends, and which is highly commended. It extends to the end of the second Macedonian war. Raleigh was also a poet, and wrote several special treatises.

William Camden, 1551–1623: author of Britannia, or a chorographic description of the most flourishing kingdoms of England, Scotland, Ireland, and the adjacent islands, from the earliest antiquity. This work, written in Latin, has been translated into English. He also wrote a sketch of the reign of Elizabeth.

George Buchanan, 1506–1581: celebrated as a Latin writer, an historian, a poet, and an ecclesiastical polemic. He wrote a *History of Scotland,* a Latin version of the Psalms, and a satire called *Chamæleon.* He was a man of profound learning and indomitable courage; and when told, just before his death, that the king was incensed at his treatise *De Jure Regni*, he answered that he was not concerned at that, for he was "going to a place where there were few kings."

Thomas Sackville, Earl Dorset, Lord Buckhurst, 1536–1608: author, or rather originator of "The Mirror for Magistrates," showing by illustrious, unfortunate examples, the vanity and transitory character of human success. Of Sackville and his portion of the Mirror for Magistrates, Craik says they "must be considered as forming the connecting link between the Canterbury Tales and the Fairy Queen."

Samuel Daniel, 1562–1619: an historian and a poet. His chief work is "The Historie of the Civile Warres between the Houses of York and Lancaster," "a production," says Drake, "which reflects great credit on the age in which it was written." This work is in poetical form; and, besides it, he wrote many poems and plays, and numerous sonnets.

Michael Drayton, 1563–1631: a versatile writer, most favorably known through his *Polyolbion*, a poem in thirty books, containing a detailed description of the topography of England, in Alexandrine verses. His *Barons' Wars* describe the civil commotions during the reign of Edward II.

Sir John Davies, 1570–1626: author of *Nosce Teipsum* and *The Orchestra*. The former is commended by Hallam; and another critic calls it "the best poem, except Spenser's Faery Queen, in Queen Elizabeth's, or even in James VI.'s time."

John Donne, 1573–1631: a famous preacher, Dean of St. Paul's: considered at the head of the metaphysical school of poets: author of *Pseudo-Martyr*, *Polydoron*, and numerous sermons. He wrote seven *satires*, which are valuable, but his style is harsh, and his ideas far-fetched.

Joseph Hall, 1574–1656: an eminent divine, author of six books of *satires*, of which he called the first three *toothless*, and the others *biting* satires. These are valuable as presenting truthful pictures of the manners and morals of the age and of the defects in contemporary literature.

Sir Fulke Greville, Lord Brooke, 1554–1628: he wrote the Life of Sidney, and requested to have placed upon his tomb, "The friend of Sir Philip Sidney." He was also the author of numerous treatises: "Monarchy," "Humane Learning," "Wars," etc., and of two tragedies.

George Chapman, 1557–1634: author of a translation of Homer, in verses of fourteen syllables. It retains much of the spirit of the original, and is still considered one of the best among the numerous versions of the ancient poet. He also wrote *Cæsar and Pompey*; *Byron's Tragedy*, and other plays.

CHAPTER XIII.

THE ENGLISH DRAMA.

Origin of the Drama.	First Comedy.	Christopher Marlowe.
Miracle Plays.	Early Tragedies.	Other Dramatists.
Moralities.		Playwrights and Morals.

ORIGIN OF THE ENGLISH DRAMA.

TO the Elizabethan period also belongs the glory of having produced and fostered the English drama, itself so marked a teacher of history, not only in plays professedly historical, but also in the delineations of national character, the indications of national taste, and the satirical scourgings of the follies of the day. A few observations are necessary as to its feeble beginnings. The old Greek drama indeed existed as a model, especially in the tragedies of Euripides and the comedies of Aristophanes; but until the fall of Constantinople, these were a dead letter to Western Europe, and when the study of Greek was begun in England, they were only open to men of the highest education and culture; whereas the drama designed for the people was to cater in its earlier forms to the rude tastes and love of the marvellous which are characteristic of an unlettered people. And, besides, the Roman drama of Plautus and of Terence was not suited to the comprehension of the multitude, in its form and its preservation of the unities. To gratify the taste for shows and excitement, the people already had the high ritual of the Church, but they demanded something more: the Church itself acceded to this demand, and dramatized Scripture at once for their amusement and instruction. Thus the *mys-*

teria or *miracle play* originated, and served a double purpose.

"As in ancient Greece, generations before the rise of the great dramas of Athens, itinerant companies wandered from village to village, carrying their stage furniture in their little carts, and acted in their booths and tents the grand stories of the mythology — so in England the mystery players haunted the wakes and fairs, and in barns or taverns, taprooms, or in the farm-house kitchen, played at saints and angels, and transacted on their petty stage the drama of the Christian faith." [1]

THE MYSTERY, OR MIRACLE PLAY. — The subjects of these dramas were taken from such Old Testament narratives as the creation, the lives of the patriarchs, the deluge; or from the crucifixion, and from legends of the saints: the plays were long, sometimes occupying portions of several days consecutively, during seasons of religious festival. They were enacted in monasteries, cathedrals, churches, and church-yards. The *mise en scène* was on two stages or platforms, on the upper of which were represented the Persons of the Trinity, and on the lower the personages of earth; while a yawning cellar, with smoke arising from an unseen fire, represented the infernal regions. This device is similar in character to the plan of Dante's poem — Hell, Purgatory, and Paradise.

The earliest of these mysteries was performed somewhere about the year 1300, and they held sway until 1600, being, however, slowly supplanted by the *moralities*, which we shall presently consider. Many of these *mysteries* still remain in English, and notices of them may be found in *Collier's History of Dramatic Poetry*.

A miracle play was performed to celebrate the birth of Philip II. of Spain. They are still performed in Andalusia, and one written within a few years for such representation, was enacted at Seville, with great pomp of scenic effect,

[1] Froude, i. 73.

in the Holy Week of 1870. Similar scenes are also witnessed by curious foreigners at the present day in the Ober-Ammergau of Bavaria. These enable the traveller of to-day to realize the former history.

To introduce a comic element, the devil was made to appear with horns, hoof, and tail, to figure with grotesque malignity throughout the play, and to be reconsigned at the close to his dark abode by the divine power.

Moralities. — As the people became enlightened, and especially as religious knowledge made progress, such childish shows were no longer able to satisfy them. The drama undertook a higher task of instruction in the form of what was called a *morality*, or *moral play*. Instead of old stories reproduced to please the childish fancy of the ignorant, genius invented scenes and incidents taken indeed from common life, but the characters were impersonal; they were the ideal virtues, *morality*, *hope*, *mercy*, *frugality*, and their correlative vices. The *mystery* had endeavored to present similitudes; the *moralities* were of the nature of allegory, and evinced a decided progress in popular intelligence.

These for a time divided the interest with the mysteries, but eventually superseded them. The impersonality of the characters enabled the author to make hits at political circumstances and existent follies with impunity, as the multitude received advice and reproof addressed to them abstractly, without feeling a personal sting, and the government would not condescend to notice such abstractions. The moralities were enacted in court-yards or palaces, the characters generally being personated by students, or merchants from the guilds. A great improvement was also made in the length of the play, which was usually only an hour in performance. The public taste was so wedded to the devil of the mysteries, that he could not be given up in the moral plays: he kept his place; but a rival buffoon appeared in the person of *the vice,* who tried conclusions with the archfiend in serio-comic style until the close of the performance, when Satan always carried the vice away in triumph, as he should do.

The moralities retained their place as legitimate drama throughout the sixteenth century, and indeed after the modern drama appeared. It is recorded that Queen Elizabeth, in 1601, then an old woman, witnessed one of these plays, entitled "The Contention between Liberality and Prodigality." This was written by Lodge and Greene, two of the regular dramatists, after Ben Jonson had written "Every Man in his Humour," and while Shakspeare was writing Hamlet. Thus the various progressive forms of the drama overlapped each other, the older retaining its place until the younger gained strength to assert its rights and supersede its rival.

THE INTERLUDE. — While the moralities were slowly dying out, another form of the drama had appeared as a connecting link between them and the legitimate drama of Shakspeare. This was the *interlude,* a short play, in which the *dramatis personæ* were no longer allegorical characters, but persons in real life, usually, however, not all bearing names even assumed, but presented as a friar, a curate, a tapster, etc. The chief characteristic of the interlude was, however, its satire; it was a more outspoken reformer than the morality, scourged the evils of the age with greater boldness, and plunged into religious controversy with the zeal of opposing ecclesiastics. The first and principal writer of these interludes was John Heywood, a Roman Catholic, who wrote during the reign of Henry VIII., and, while a professed jester, was a great champion of his Church.

As in all cases of progress, literary and scientific, the lines of demarcation cannot be very distinctly drawn, but as the morality had superseded the mystery, and the interlude the morality, so now they were all to give way before the regular drama. The people were becoming more educated; the greater spread of classical knowledge had caused the dramatists to study and assimilate the excellences of Latin and Greek models; the power of the drama to instruct and refine, as well as to amuse, was acknowledged, and thus its capability of improvement became manifest. The forms it then assumed were more permanent, and indeed have remained almost unchanged down to our own day.

What is called the *first* comedy in the language cannot be expected to show a very decided improvement over the last interludes or moralities, but it bears those distinctive marks which establish its right to the title.

THE FIRST COMEDY. — This was *Ralph Roister Doister*, which appeared in the middle of the sixteenth century: (a printed copy of 1551 was discovered in 1818.) Its author was Nicholas Udall, the master of Eton, a clergyman, but very severe as a pedagogue; an ultra Protestant, who is also accused of having stolen church plate, which may perhaps mean that he took away from the altar what he regarded as popish vessels and ornaments. He calls the play "a comedy and interlude," but claims that it is imitated from the Roman drama. It is regularly divided into acts and scenes, in the form of our modern plays. The plot is simple: Ralph, a gay Lothario, courts as gay a widow, and the by-play includes a designing servant and an intriguing lady's-maid: these are the stock elements of a hundred comedies since.

Contemporary with this was *Gammer Gurton's Needle*, supposed to be written, but not conclusively, by John Still, Bishop of Bath and Wells, about 1560. The story turns upon the loss of a steel needle — a rare instrument in that day, as it was only introduced into England from Spain during the age of Elizabeth. This play is a coarser piece than Ralph Roister Doister; the buffoon raises the devil to aid him in finding the lost needle, which is at length found, by very palpable proof, to be sticking in the seat of Goodman Hodge's breeches.

THE FIRST TRAGEDY. — Hand in hand with these first comedies came the earliest tragedy, *Gorboduc*, by Sackville and Norton, known under another name as *Ferrex and Porrex;* and it is curious to observe that this came in while the moralities still occupied the stage, and before the interludes had disappeared, as it was played before the queen at White Hall, in 1562. It is also to be noted that it introduced a chorus like that of the old Greek drama. Ferrex and Porrex are the sons of King Gorboduc: the former is killed by the latter, who in turn is slain by his own mother. Of Gorboduc, Lamb says, "The style of this old play is stiff and cumbersome, like the dresses of the times. There may be flesh and blood underneath, but we cannot get at it."

With the awakened interest of the people, the drama now made steady progress. In 1568 the tragedy of *Tancred and Gismunda*, based upon one of the stories of Boccaccio, was enacted before Elizabeth.

A license for establishing a regular theatre was got out by Burbage in 1574. Peele and Greene wrote plays in the new manner: Marlowe, the greatest name in the English drama, except those of Shakspeare and Ben Jonson, gave to the world his *Tragical History of the Life and Death of Doctor Faustus*, which many do not hesitate to compare favorably with Goethe's great drama, and his *Rich Jew of Malta*, which contains the portraiture of Barabas, second only to the Shylock of Shakspeare. Of Marlowe a more special mention will be made.

PLAYWRIGHTS AND MORALS. — It was to the great advantage of the English regular drama, that the men who wrote were almost in every case highly educated in the classics, and thus able to avail themselves of the best models. It is equally true that, owing to the religious condition of the times, when Puritanism launched forth its diatribes against all amusements, they were men in the opposition, and in most cases of irregular lives. Men of the world, they took their characters from among the persons with whom they associated; and so we find in their plays traces of the history of the age, in the appropriation of classical forms, in the references to religious and political parties, and in their delineation of the morals, manners, and follies of the period: if the drama of the present day owes to them its origin and nurture, it also retains as an inheritance many of the faults and deformities from which in a more refined period it is seeking to purge itself. It is worthy of notice, that as the drama owes everything to popular patronage, its moral tone reflects of necessity the moral character of the people who frequent it, and of the age which sustains it.

CHRISTOPHER MARLOWE.—Among those who may be regarded as the immediate forerunners and ushers of Shakspeare, and who, although they prepared the way for his advent, have been obscured by his greater brilliance, the one most deserving of special mention is Marlowe.

Christopher Marlowe was born at Canterbury, about the year 1564. He was a wild, irregular genius, of bad morals and loose life, but of fine imagination and excellent powers of expression. He wrote only tragedies.

His *Tamburlaine the Great* is based upon the history of that *Timour Leuk*, or *Timour the Lame*, the great Oriental conqueror of the fourteenth century:

> So large of limb, his joints so strongly knit,
> Such breadth of shoulders as might mainly bear
> Old Atlas' burthen.

The descriptions are overdrawn, and the style inflated, but the subject partakes of the heroic, and was popular still, though nearly two centuries had passed since the exploits of the historic hero.

The Rich Jew of Malta is of value, as presenting to us Barabas the Jew as he appeared to Christian suspicion and hatred in the fifteenth century. As he sits in his country-house with heaps of gold before him, and receives the visits of merchants who inform him of the safe arrival of his ships, it is manifest that he gave Shakspeare the first ideal of his Shylock, upon which the greater dramatist greatly improved.

The Tragicall Life and Death of Doctor John Faustus certainly helped Goethe in the conception and preparation of his modern drama, and contains many passages of rare power. Charles Lamb says: "The growing horrors of Faustus are awfully marked by the hours and half-hours which expire and bring him nearer and nearer to the enactment of his dire compact. It is indeed an agony and bloody sweat."

Edward II. presents in the assassination scene wonderful power and pathos, and is regarded by Hazlitt as his best play.

Marlowe is the author of the pleasant madrigal, called by Izaak Walton "that smooth song":

> Come live with me and be my love.

The playwright, who had led a wild life, came to his end in a tavern brawl: he had endeavored to use his dagger upon one of the waiters, who turned it upon him, and gave him a wound in the head of which he died, in 1593.

His talents were of a higher order than those of his contemporaries; he was next to Shakspeare in power, and was called by Phillips "a second Shakspeare."

Other Dramatic Writers before Shakspeare.

Thomas Lodge, 1556–1625: educated at Oxford. Wrote *The Wounds of Civil War*, and other tragedies. Rosalynd, a novel, from which Shakspeare drew in his *As You Like It.* He translated *Josephus* and *Seneca.*

Thomas Kyd, died about 1600: *The Spanish Tragedy, or, Hieronymo is Mad Again.* This contains a few highly wrought scenes, which have been variously attributed to Ben Jonson and to Webster.

Robert Tailor: wrote *The Hog hath Lost his Pearl*, a comedy, published in 1614. This partakes of the character of the *morality.*

John Marston: wrote *Antonio and Mellida*, 1602; *Antonio's Revenge*, 1602; *Sophonisba, a Wonder of Women*, 1606; *The Insatiate Countess*, 1603, and many other plays. Marston ranks high among the immediate predecessors of Shakspeare, for the number, variety, and vigorous handling of his plays.

George Peele, born about 1553: educated at Oxford. Many of his pieces are broadly comic. The principal plays are: *The Arraignment of Paris, Edward I.*, and *David and Bethsabe.* The latter is overwrought and full of sickish sentiment.

Thomas Nash, 1558–1601: a satirist and polemic, who is best known for his controversy with Gabriel Harvey. Most of his plays were written in conjunction with others. He was imprisoned for writing *The Isle of Dogs*, which was played, but not published. He is very licentious in his language.

John Lyly, born about 1553: wrote numerous smaller plays, but is chiefly known as the author of *Euphues, Anatomy of Wit*, and *Euphues and his England.*

Robert Greene, died 1592: educated at Cambridge. Wrote *Alphonsus, King of Arragon, James IV., George-a-Greene, Friar Bacon and Friar Bungay*, and other plays. After leading a profligate life, he left behind him a pamphlet entitled, "A Groat's-worth of Wit, bought with a Million of Repentance:" this is full of contrition, and of advice to his fellow-actors and fellow-sinners. It is mainly remarkable for its abuse of Shakspeare, "an upstart crow, beautified with our feathers;" "Tygre's heart wrapt in a player's hide;" "an absolute Johannes factotum, in his own conceyt the onely *shakescene* in the country."

Most of these dramatists wrote in copartnership with others, and many of the plays which bear their names singly, have parts composed by colleagues. Such was the custom of the age, and it is now very difficult to declare the distinct authorship of many of the plays.

CHAPTER XIV.

WILLIAM SHAKSPEARE.

The Power of Shakspeare.	What is known.	Literary Habitudes.
Meagre Early History.	Marries, and goes to London.	Variety of the Plays.
Doubts of his Identity.	"Venus" and "Lucrece."	Table of Dates and Sources.
	Retirement and Death.	

THE POWER OF SHAKSPEARE.

WE have now reached, in our search for the historic teachings in English literature, and in our consideration of the English drama, the greatest name of all, the writer whose works illustrate our position most strongly, and yet who, eminent type as he is of British culture in the age of Elizabeth, was truly and pithily declared by his friend and contemporary, Ben Jonson, to be "not for an age, but for all time." It is also singularly true that, even in such a work as this, Shakspeare really requires only brief notice at our hands, because he is so universally known and read: his characters are among our familiar acquaintance; his simple but thoughtful words are incorporated in our common conversation; he is our every-day companion. To eulogize him to the reading public is

> To gild refined gold, to paint the lily,
> To lend a perfume to the violet . . .

The Bible and Shakspeare have been long conjoined as the two most necessary books in a family library; and Mrs. Cowden Clarke, the author of the Concordance to Shakspeare, has pointedly and truthfully said: "A poor lad, possessing no other book, might on this single one make himself a gentleman and a scholar: a poor girl, studying no other volume, might become a lady in heart and soul."

Meagre Early History. — It is passing strange, considering the great value of his writings, and his present fame, that of his personal history so little is known. In the words of Steevens, one of his most successful commentators: "All that is known, with any degree of certainty, concerning Shakspeare, is — that he was born at Stratford upon Avon — married and had children there — went to London, where he commenced actor, and wrote poems and plays — returned to Stratford, made his will, died, and was buried."

This want of knowledge is in part due to his obscure youth, during which no one could predict what he would afterward achieve, and therefore no one took notes of his life: to his own apparent ignorance and carelessness of his own merits, and to the low repute in which plays, and especially playwrights, were then held; although they were in reality making their age illustrious in history. The pilgrim to Stratford sees the little low house in which he is said to have been born, purchased by the nation, and now restored into a smart cottage: within are a few meagre relics of the poet's time; not far distant is the foundation — recently uncovered — of his more ambitious residence in New Place, and a mulberry-tree, which probably grew from a slip of that which he had planted with his own hand. Opposite is the old Falcon Inn, where he made his daily potations. Very near rises, above elms and lime-trees, the spire of the beautiful church on the bank of the Avon, beneath the chancel of which his remains repose, with those of his wife and daughter, overlooked by his bust, of which no one knows the maker or the history, except that it dates from his own time. His bust is of life-size, and was originally painted to imitate nature — eyes of hazel, hair and beard auburn, doublet scarlet, and sleeveless gown of black. Covered by a false taste with white paint to imitate marble, while it destroyed identity and age: it has since been recolored from traditional knowledge, but it is too rude to give us the expression of his face.

The only other probable likeness is that from an old picture, an engraving of which, by Droeshout, is found in the first folio edition of his plays, published in 1623, seven years after his death: it was said by Ben Jonson to be a good likeness. We are very fortunate in having these, unsatisfactory as they are, for it is simple truth that beyond these places and things, there is little, if anything, to illustrate the personal history of Shakspeare. All that we can know of the man is found in his works.

DOUBTS OF HIS IDENTITY. — This ignorance concerning him has given rise to numerous doubts as to his literary identity, and many efforts have been made to find other authors for his dramas. Among the most industrious in this deposing scheme, have been Miss Delia Bacon and Mr. Nathaniel Holmes, who concur in attributing his best plays to Francis Bacon. That Bacon did not acknowledge his own work, they say, is because he rated the dramatic art too far beneath his dignity to confess any complicity with it. In short, he and other great men of that day wrote immortal works which they were ashamed of, and were willing to father upon the common actor and stage-manager, one William Shakspeare!

While it is not within the scope of this volume to enter into the controversy, it is a duty to state its existence, and to express the judgment that these efforts have been entirely unsuccessful, but have not been without value in that they have added a little to the meagre history by their researches, and have established the claims of Shakspeare on a firmer foundation than before.

WHAT IS KNOWN. — William Shakspeare (spelt *Shackspeare* in the body of his will, but signed *Shakspeare*) was the third of eight children, and the eldest son of John Shakspeare and Mary Arden: he was born at the beautiful rural town of Stratford, on the little river Avon, on the 23d of April, 1564. His father, who was of yeoman rank, was probably a dealer in wool and leather. Aubrey, a gossiping chronicler of the next generation, says he was a butcher, and some biographers assert that he was a glover. He may have exercised all these crafts together, but it is more to our purpose to know that in his best estate he was a property holder and chief burgess of the town. Shakspeare's mother seems to have been of an older family. Neither of them could write. Shakspeare received his education at the free grammar-school, still a well-endowed institution in the town, where he learned the "small Latin and less Greek" accorded to him by Ben Jonson at a later day.

There are guesses, rather than traditions, that he was, after the age of fifteen, a student in a law-office, that he was for a time at one of the universities, and also that he was a teacher in the grammar-school. These are weak inventions to account for the varied learning displayed in his dramas. His love of Nature and his power to delineate her charms were certainly fostered by the beautiful rural surroundings of Stratford; beyond this it is idle to seek to penetrate the obscure processes of his youth.

MARRIES, AND GOES TO LONDON. — Finding himself one of a numerous and poor family, to the support of which his father's business was inadequate, he determined to shift for himself, and to push his fortunes in the best way he could.

Whether he regarded matrimony as one element of success we do not know, but the preliminary bond of marriage between himself and Anne Hathaway, was signed on the 28th of November, 1582, when he was eighteen years old. The woman was seven years older than himself; and it is a sad commentary on the morality of both, that his first child, Susanna, was baptized on the 25th of May, 1583.

Strolling bands of players, in passing through England, were in the habit of stopping at Stratford, and setting upon wheels their rude stage with weather-stained curtains; and these, it should be observed, were the best dramatic companies of the time, such as the queen's company, and those in the service of noblemen like Leicester, Warwick, and others. If he did not see he must have heard of the great pageant in 1575, when Leicester entertained Queen Elizabeth at Kenilworth, which is so charmingly described by Sir Walter Scott. Young Shakspeare became stage-struck, and probably joined one of these companies, with other idle young men of the neighborhood.

Various legends, without sufficient foundation of truth, are related of him at this time, which indicate that he was of a frolicsome and mischievous turn: among these is a statement that he was arraigned for deer-poaching in the park of Sir Thomas Lucy, of Charlecote. A satirical reference to Sir Thomas in one of his plays,* leads us to think that there is some truth in the story, although certain of his biographers have denied it.

In February, 1584–5, he became the father of twins, Hamnet and Judith, and in 1586, leaving his wife and children at Stratford, he went up with a theatrical company to London, where for three years he led a hard and obscure life. He was at first a menial at the theatre; some say he held gentlemen's horses at the door, others that he was call-boy, prompter, scene-shifter, minor actor. At length he began to find his true vocation in altering and adapting plays for the stage. This earlier practice, in every capacity, was of great value to him when he began to write plays of his own. As an actor he never rose above mediocrity. It is said that he played such parts as the Ghost in Hamlet, and Adam in As You Like It; but off the stage he became known for a ready wit and convivial humor.

His ready hand for any work caused him to prosper steadily,

* Opening scene of The Merry Wives of Windsor.

and so in 1589 we find his name the twelfth on the list of sixteen shareholders in the Blackfriars Theatre, one of the first play-houses built in London. That he was steadily growing in public favor, as well as in private fortune, might be inferred from Spenser's mention of him in the "Tears of the Muses," published in 1591, if we were sure he was the person referred to. If he was, this is the first great commendation he had received:

The man whom nature's self had made,
  To mock herself and truth to imitate,
With kindly counter under mimic shade,
  Our pleasant Willie.

There is, however, a doubt whether the reference is to him, as he had written very little as early as 1591.

VENUS AND ADONIS. — In 1593 appeared his *Venus and Adonis*, which he now had the social position and interest to dedicate to the Earl of Southampton. It is a harmonious and beautiful poem, but the display of libidinous passion in the goddess, however in keeping with her character and with the broad taste of the age, is disgusting to the refined reader, even while he acknowledges the great power of the poet. In the same year was built the Globe Theatre, a hexagonal wooden structure, unroofed over the pit, but thatched over the stage and the galleries. In this, too, Shakspeare was a shareholder.

THE RAPE OF LUCRECE. — The *Rape of Lucrece* was published in 1594, and was dedicated to the same nobleman, who, after the custom of the period, became Shakspeare's patron, and showed the value of his patronage by the gift to the poet of a thousand pounds.

Thus in making poetical versions of classical stories, which formed the imaginative pabulum of the age, and in readapting older plays, the poet was gaining that skill and power which were to produce his later immortal dramas.

These, as we shall see, he began to write as early as 1589, and continued to produce until 1612.

Retirement and Death. — A few words will complete his personal history: His fortune steadily increased; in 1602 he was the principal owner of the Globe; then, actuated by his home feeling, which had been kept alive by annual visits to Stratford, he determined, as soon as he could, to give up the stage, and to take up his residence there. He had purchased, in 1597, the New Place at Stratford, but he did not fully carry out his plan until 1612, when he finally retired with ample means and in the enjoyment of an honorable reputation. There he exercised a generous hospitality, and led a quiet rural life. He planted a mulberry-tree, which became a pilgrim's shrine to numerous travellers; but a ruthless successor in the ownership of New Place, the Reverend Francis Gastrell, annoyed by the concourse of visitors, was Vandal enough to cut it down. Such was the anger of the people that he was obliged to leave the place, which he did after razing the mansion to the ground. His name is held in great detestation at Stratford now, as every traveller is told his story.

Shakspeare's death occurred on his fifty-second birthday, April 23d, 1616. He had been ill of a fever, from which he was slowly recovering, and his end is said to have been the result of an over-conviviality in entertaining Drayton and Ben Jonson, who had paid him a visit at Stratford.

His son Hamnet had died in 1596, at the age of twelve. In 1607, his daughter Susannah had married Dr. Hall; and in 1614 died Judith, who had married Thomas Quiney. Shakspeare's wife survived him, and died in 1623.

Literary Habitudes. — Such, in brief, is the personal

history of Shakspeare: of his literary habitudes we know nothing. The exact dates of the appearance of his plays are, in most cases, doubtful. Many of these had been printed singly during his life, but the first complete edition was published in folio, in 1623. It contains *thirty-six* plays, and is the basis of the later editions, which contain thirty-*seven*. Many questions arise which cannot be fully answered: Did he write all the plays contained in the volume? Are the First Part of Henry VI., Titus Andronicus,[1] and Pericles his work? Did he not write others not found among these? Had he, as was not uncommon then and later, collaboration in those which bear his name? Was he a Beaumont to some Fletcher, or a Sackville to some Norton? Upon these questions generations of Shakspearean scholars have expended a great amount of learned inquiry ever since his day, and not without results: it is known that many of his dramas are founded upon old plays, as to plots; and that he availed himself of the labor of others in casting his plays.

But the real value of his plays, the insight into human nature, the profound philosophy, "the myriad-soul" which they display, are Shakspeare's only. By applying just rules of evidence, we conclude that he did write thirty-five of the plays attributed to him, and that he did not write, or was not the chief writer of others. It is certainly very strong testimony on these points, that seven years after his death, and *three years before that of Bacon*, a large folio should have been published by his professional friends Heminge and Condell, prefaced with ardent eulogies, claiming thirty-six plays as his, and that it did not meet with the instant and indignant cry that his claims were false. The players of that day were an envious and carping set, and the controversy would have been fierce from the very first, had there been just grounds for it.

VARIETY OF PLAYS. — No attempt will be made to analyze

[1] Rev. A. Dyce attributes this play to Marlowe or Kyd.

any of the plays of Shakspeare: that is left for the private study and enjoyment of the student, by the use of the very numerous aids furnished by commentators and critics. It will be found often that in their great ardor, the dramatist has been treated like the Grecian poet:

> [Shakspeare's] critics bring to view
> Things which [Shakspeare] never knew.

Many of the plays are based upon well-known legends and fictional tales, some of them already adopted in old plays: thus the story of King Lear and his daughters is found in Holinshed's Chronicle, and had been for years represented; from this Shakspeare has borrowed the story, but has used only a single passage. The play is intended to represent the ancient Celtic times in Britain, eight hundred years before Christ; and such is its power and pathos, that we care little for its glaring anachronisms and curious errors. In Holinshed are also found the stories of Cymbeline and Macbeth, the former supposed to have occurred during the Roman occupancy of Britain, and the latter during the Saxon period.

With these before us, let us observe that names, chronology, geography, costumes, and customs are as nothing in his eyes. His aim is human philosophy: he places his living creations before us, dressing them, as it were, in any garments most conveniently at hand. These lose their grotesqueness as his characters speak and act. Paternal love and weakness, met by filial ingratitude; these are the lessons and the fearful pictures of Lear: sad as they are, the world needed them, and they have saved many a later Lear from expulsion and storm and death, and shamed many a Goneril and Regan, while they have strengthened the hearts of many a Cordelia since. Chastity and constancy shine like twin stars from the forest of Cymbeline. And what have we in Macbeth? Mad ambition parleying with the devil, in the guise of a woman lost to all virtue save a desire to aggrandize her husband and herself. These have a pretence of history; but Hamlet, with hardly that pretence, stands alone supreme in varied excellence. Ambition, murder, resistless fate, filial love, the love of woman, revenge, the power of conscience, paternal solicitude, infinite jest: what a volume is this!

TABLE OF DATES AND SOURCES. — The following table, which presents the plays in chronological order,[1] the times when they were written, as nearly as can be known, and the sources whence they were derived, will be of more service to the student than any discursive remarks upon the several plays.

	Plays.	Dates.	Sources.
1.	Henry VI., first part . . .	1589	Denied to Shakspeare; attributed to Marlowe or Kyd.
2.	Pericles	1590	From the "Gesta Romanorum."
3.	Henry VI., second part .	1591	" an older play.
4.	Henry VI., third part . .	1591	" " " "
5.	Two Gentlemen of Verona	1591	" an old tale.
6.	Comedy of Errors . . .	1592	" a comedy of Plautus.
7.	Love's Labor Lost . . .	1592	" an Italian play.
8.	Richard II.	1593	" Holinshed and other chronicles.
9.	Richard III.	1593	From an old play and Sir Thomas More's History.
10.	Midsummer Night's Dream	1594	Suggested by Palamon and Arcite, The Knight's Tale, of Chaucer.
11.	Taming of the Shrew . .	1596	From an older play.
12.	Romeo and Juliet	1596	" " old tale. Boccaccio.
13.	Merchant of Venice . . .	1597	" Gesta Romanorum, with suggestions from Marlowe's Jew of Malta.
14.	Henry IV., part 1 . . .	1597	From an old play.
15.	Henry IV., part 2 . . .	1598	" " "
16.	King John	1598	" " "
17.	All 's Well that Ends Well .	1598	" Boccaccio.

[1] The dates as determined by Malone are given: many of them differ from those of Drake and Chalmers.

	Plays.	Dates.	Sources.
18.	Henry V.	1599	From an older play.
19.	As You Like It	1600	Suggested in part by Lodge's novel, Rosalynd.
20.	Much Ado About Nothing	1600	Source unknown.
21.	Hamlet	1601	From the Latin History of Scandinavia, by Saxo, called Grammaticus.
22.	Merry Wives of Windsor .	1601	Said to have been suggested by Elizabeth.
23.	Twelfth Night	1601	From an old tale.
24.	Troilus and Cressida . .	1602	Of classical origin, through Chaucer.
25.	Henry VIII.	1603	From the chronicles of the day.
26.	Measure for Measure . .	1603	" an old tale.
27.	Othello	1604	" " " "
28.	King Lear	1605	" Holinshed.
29.	Macbeth	1606	" "
30.	Julius Cæsar	1607	" Plutarch's Parallel Lives.
31.	Antony and Cleopatra . .	1608	" " " "
32.	Cymbeline	1609	" Holinshed.
33.	Coriolanus	1610	" Plutarch.
34.	Timon of Athens	1610	" " and other sources.
35.	Winter's Tale	1611	" a novel by Greene.
36.	Tempest	1612	" Italian Tale.
37.	Titus Andronicus	1593	Denied to Shakspeare; probably by Marlowe or Kyd.

CHAPTER XV.

WILLIAM SHAKSPEARE, (CONTINUED.)

THE GROUNDS OF HIS FAME.

FROM what has been said, it is manifest that as to his plots and historical reproductions, Shakspeare has little merit but taste in selection; and indeed in most cases, had he invented the stories, his merit would not have been great: what then is the true secret of his power and of his fame? This question is not difficult to answer.

First, these are due to his wonderful insight into human nature, and the philosophy of human life: he dissects the human mind in all its conditions, and by this vivisection he displays its workings as it lives and throbs; he divines the secret impulses of all ages and characters — childhood, boyhood, manhood, girlhood, and womanhood; men of peace, and men of war; clowns, nobles, and kings. His large heart was sympathetic with all, and even most so with the lowly and suffering; he shows us to ourselves, and enables us to use that knowledge for our profit. All the virtues are held up to our imitation and praise, and all the vices are scourged and rendered odious in our sight. To read Shakspeare aright is of the nature of honest self-examination, that most difficult and most necessary of duties.

CREATION OF CHARACTER. — Second: He stands supreme

in the creation of character, which may be considered the distinguishing mark of the highest literary genius. The men and women whom he has made are not stage-puppets moved by hidden strings; they are real. We know them as intimately as the friends and acquaintances who visit us, or the people whom we accost in our daily walks.

And again, in this varied delineation of character, Shakspeare less than any other author either obtrudes or repeats himself. Unlike Byron, he is nowhere his own hero: unlike most modern novelists, he fashions men who, while they have the generic human resemblance, differ from each other like those of flesh and blood around us: he has presented a hundred phases of love, passion, ambition, jealousy, revenge, treachery, and cruelty, and each distinct from the others of its kind; but lest any character should degenerate into an allegorical representation of a single virtue or vice, he has provided it with the other lineaments necessary to produce in it a rare human identity.

The stock company of most writers is limited, and does arduous duty in each new play or romance; so that we detect in the comic actor, who is now convulsing the pit with laughter, the same person who a little while ago died heroically to slow music in the tragedy. Each character in Shakspeare plays but one part, and plays it skilfully and well. And who has portrayed the character of woman like Shakspeare? — the grand sorrow of the repudiated Catharine, the incorruptible chastity of Isabella, the cleverness of Portia, the loves of Jessica and of Juliet, the innocent curiosity of Miranda, the broken heart and crazed brain of the fair Ophelia.

In this connection also should be noticed his powers of grouping and composition; which, in the words of one of his biographers, "present to us pictures from the realms of spirits and from fairyland, which in deep reflection and in useful maxims, yield nothing to the pages of the philosophers, and which glow with all the poetic beauty that an exhaustless fancy could shower upon them."

IMAGINATION AND FANCY. — And this brings us to notice, in the third place, his rare gifts of imagination and of fancy; those instruments of the representative faculty by which objects of sense and of mind are held up to view in new, varied, and vivid lights. Many of his tragedies abound in imaginative pictures, while there are not in the realm of Fancy's fairy frostwork more exquisite representations than those found in the *Tempest* and the *Midsummer Night's Dream.*

POWER OF EXPRESSION. — Fourth, Shakspeare is remarkable for the power and felicity of his expression. He adapts his language to the persons who use it, and thus we pass from the pompous grandiloquence of king and herald to the common English and coarse conceits of clown and nurse and grave-digger; from the bombastic speech of Glendower and the rhapsodies of Hotspur to the slang and jests of Falstaff.

But something more is meant by felicity of expression than this. It applies to the apt words which present pithy bits of household philosophy, and to the beautiful words which convey the higher sentiments and flights of fancy; to the simple words couching grand thoughts with such exquisite aptness that they seem made for each other, so that no other words would do as well, and to the dainty songs, like those of birds, which fill his forests and gardens with melody. Thus it is that orators and essayists give dignity and point to their own periods by quoting Shakspeare.

Such are a few of Shakspeare's high merits, which constitute him the greatest poet who has ever used the English tongue — poet, moralist, and philosopher in one.

HIS FAULTS. — If it be necessary to point out his faults, it should be observed that most of them are those of the age and of his profession. To both may be charged the vulgarity and lewdness of some of his representations; which, however, err in this respect far less than the writings of his contemporaries.

Again: in the short time allowed for the presentation of a play, before a restless audience, as soon as the plot was fairly shadowed, the hearers were anxious for the *dénouement*. And so Shakspeare, careless of future fame, frequently displays a singular disparity between the parts. He has so much of detail in the first two acts, that in order to preserve the symmetry, five or six more would be necessary. Thus conclusions are hurried, when, as works of art, they should be the most elaborated.

He has sometimes been accused of obscurity in expression, which renders some of his passages difficult to be understood by commentators; but this, in most cases, is the fault of his editors. The cases are exceptional and unimportant. His anachronisms and historical inaccuracies have already been referred to. His greatest admirers will allow that his wit and humor are very often forced and frequently out of place; but here, too, he should be leniently judged. These sallies of wit were meant rather to "tickle the ears of the groundlings" than as just subjects for criticism by later scholars. We know that old jokes, bad puns, and innuendoes are needed on the stage at the present day. Shakspeare used them for the same ephemeral purpose then; and had he sent down corrected versions to posterity, they would have been purged of these.

INFLUENCE OF ELIZABETH. — Enough has been said to show in what manner Shakspeare represents his age, and indeed many former periods of English history. There are numerous passages which display the influence of Elizabeth. It was at her request that he wrote the *Merry Wives of Windsor*, in which Falstaff is depicted as a lover: the play of Henry VIII., criticizing the queen's father, was not produced until after her death. His pure women, like those of Spenser, are drawn after a queenly model. It is known that

Elizabeth was very susceptible to admiration, but did not wish to be considered so; and Shakspeare paid the most delicate and courtly tribute to her vanity, in those exquisite lines from the *Midsummer Night's Dream*, showing how powerless Cupid was to touch her heart:

A certain aim he took
At a fair vestal, throned by the west;
And loos'd his love-shaft smartly from his bow,
As it should pierce a hundred thousand hearts:
But I might see young Cupid's fiery shaft
Quench'd in the chaste beams of the wat'ry moon;
And *the imperial votaress passed on*,
In maiden meditation, fancy free.

SHAKSPEARE'S SONNETS. — Before his time, the sonnet had been but little used in England, the principal writers being Surrey, Sir Walter Raleigh, Sidney, Daniel, and Drayton. Shakspeare left one hundred and fifty-four, which exhibit rare poetical power, and which are most of them addressed to a person unknown, perhaps an ideal personage, whose initials are W. H. Although chiefly addressed to a man, they are of an amatory nature, and dwell strongly upon human frailty, infidelity, and treachery, from which he seems to have suffered: the mystery of these poems has never been penetrated. They were printed in 1609. "Our language," says one of his editors, "can boast no sonnets altogether worthy of being placed by the side of Shakspeare's, except the few which Milton poured forth — so severe and so majestic."

It need hardly be said that Shakspeare has been translated into all modern languages, in whole or in part. In French, by Victor Hugo and Guizot, Leon de Wailly and Alfred de Vigny; in German, by Wieland, A. W. Schlegel, and Bürger; in Italian, by Leoni and Carcano, and in Portuguese by La Silva. Goethe's Apprenticeship of Wilhelm Meister is a long and profound critique of Hamlet; and to the Germans he is quite as familiar and intelligible as to the English.

IRELAND: COLLIER. — The most celebrated forgery of Shakspeare was that by Samuel Ireland, the son of a Shakspearean scholar, who was an engraver and dealer in curiosities. He wrote two plays, called *Vortigern* and *Henry the Second*, which he said he had discovered; and he forged a deed with Shakspeare's autograph. By these he imposed upon his father and many others, but eventually confessed the forgery.

One word should be said concerning the Collier controversy. John Payne Collier was a lawyer, born in 1789, and is known as the author of an excellent history of *English Dramatic Poetry to the Time of Shakspeare*, and *Annals of the Stage to the Restoration*. In the year 1849, he came into possession of a copy of the folio edition of Shakspeare, published in 1632, *full of emendations*, by an early owner of the volume. In 1852 he published these, and at once great enthusiasm was excited, for and against the emendations: many thought them of great value, while others even went so far as to accuse Mr. Collier of having made some of them himself. The chief value of the work was that it led to new investigations, and has thus thrown additional light upon the works of Shakspeare.

CONCORDANCE. — The student is referred to a very complete concordance of Shakspeare, by Mrs. Mary Cowden Clarke, the labor of many years, by which every line of Shakspeare may be found, and which is thus of incalculable utility to the Shakspearean scholar.

OTHER DRAMATIC WRITERS OF THE AGE OF SHAKSPEARE.

Ben Jonson, 1573–1637: this great dramatist, who deserves a larger space, was born in London; his father became a Puritan preacher, but after his death, his mother's second husband put the boy at brick-making. His spirit revolted at this, and he ran away, and served as a soldier in the Low Countries. On his return he killed Gabriel Spencer, a fellow-actor, in a duel, and was for some time imprisoned. His first play was a comedy entitled *Every Man in his Humour*, acted in 1598. This was succeeded, the next year, by *Every Man out of his Humour.* He wrote a great number of both tragedies and comedies, among which the principal are *Cynthia's Revels*, *Sejanus*, *Volpone*, *Catiline's Conspiracy*, and *The Alchemist.* In 1616, he received a pension from the crown of one hundred marks, which was increased by Charles I., in 1630, to one hundred pounds. He was the friend of Shakspeare, and had many wit-encounters with him. In these, Fuller compares Jonson to a great Spanish galleon, "built far higher in learning, solid and slow in performance," and Shakspeare to an "English man-of-war, lesser in bulk, but lighter in sailing, could turn with all tides, tack about and take advantage of all winds, by the quickness of his wit and invention."

Massinger, 1548–1640: born at Salisbury. Is said to have written thirty-eight plays, of which only eighteen remain. The chief of these is the *Virgin Martyr*, in which he was assisted by Dekker. The best of the others are *The City Madam* and *A New Way to Pay Old Debts*, *The Fatal Dowry*, *The Unnatural Combat*, and *The Duke of Milan.* *A New Way to Pay Old Debts* keeps its place upon the modern stage.

John Ford, born 1586: author of *The Lover's Melancholy*, *Love's Sacrifice*, *Perkin Warbeck*, and *The Broken Heart.* He was a pathetic delineator of love, especially of unhappy love. Some of his plots are unnatural, and abhorrent to a refined taste.

Webster (dates unknown): this author is remarkable for his handling of gloomy and terrible subjects. His best plays are *The Devil's Law Case*, *Appius and Virginia*, *The Duchess of Malfy*, and *The White Devil.* Hazlitt says "his *White Devil* and *Duchess of Malfy* come the nearest to Shakspeare of anything we have upon record."

Francis Beaumont, 1586–1615, and John Fletcher, 1576–1625: joint authors of plays, numbering fifty-two. A prolific union, in which it is difficult to determine the exact authorship of each. Among the best plays are *The Maid's Tragedy*, *Philaster*, and *Cupid's Revenge.* Many of the plots are licentious, but in monologues they frequently rise to eloquence, and in descriptions are picturesque and graphic.

Shirley, 1594–1666: delineates fashionable life with success. His best plays are *The Maid's Revenge*, *The Politician*, and *The Lady of Pleasure.* The last suggested to Van Brugh his character of Lady Townly, in *The Provoked Husband.* Lamb says Shirley "was the last of a great race, all of whom spoke the same language, and had a set of moral feelings and notions in common. A new language and quite a new turn of tragic and comic interest came in at the Restoration."

Thomas Dekker, died about 1638: wrote, besides numerous tracts, twenty-eight plays. The principal are *Old Fortunatus*, *The Honest Whore*, and *Satiro-Mastix*, *or*, *The Humorous Poet Untrussed.* In the last, he satirized Ben Jonson, with whom he had quarrelled, and who had ridiculed him in *The Poetaster.* In the Honest Whore are found those beautiful lines so often quoted:

> . . . the best of men
> That e'er wore earth about him was a sufferer;
> A soft, meek, patient, humble, tranquil spirit;
> The first true gentleman that ever breathed.

Extracts from the plays mentioned may be found in Charles Lamb's "Specimens of English Dramatic Poets who lived about the time of Shakspeare."

CHAPTER XVI.

BACON, AND THE RISE OF THE NEW PHILOSOPHY.

BIRTH AND EARLY LIFE OF BACON.

CONTEMPORARY with Shakspeare, and almost equal to him in English fame at least, is Francis Bacon, the founder of the system of experimental philosophy in the Elizabethan age. The investigations of the one in the philosophy of human life, were emulated by those of the other in the realm of general nature, in order to find laws to govern further progress, and to evolve order and harmony out of chaos.

Bacon was born in London, on the 22d of January, 1560–61, to an enviable social lot. His father, Sir Nicholas Bacon, was for twenty years lord keeper of the great seal, and was eulogized by George Buchanan as "Diu Britannici regni secundum columen." His mother was Anne Cook, a person of remarkable acquirements in language and theology. Francis Bacon was a delicate, attractive, and precocious child, noticed by the great, and kindly called by the queen "her little lord keeper." Ben Jonson refers to this when he writes, at a later day:

> England's high chancellor, the destined heir
> In his soft cradle to his father's chair.

Thus, in his early childhood, he became accustomed to the

forms and grandeur of political power, and the modes by which it was to be striven for.

In his thirteenth year he was entered at Trinity College, Cambridge, then, as now, the more mathematical and scientific of the two universities. But, like Gibbon at Oxford, he thought little of his alma mater, under whose care he remained only three years. It is said that at an early age he disliked the Logic of Aristotle, and began to excogitate his system of Induction: not content with the formal recorded knowledge, he viewed the universe as a great storehouse of facts to be educed, investigated, and philosophically classified.

After leaving the university, he went in the suite of Sir Amyas Paulet, the English ambassador, to France; and recorded the observations made during his travels in a treatise *On the State of Europe*, which is thoughtful beyond his years. The sudden death of his father, in February, 1579–80, recalled him to England, and his desire to study led him to apply to the government for a sinecure, which would permit him to do so without concern as to his support. It is not strange — considering his youth and the entire ignorance of the government as to his abilities — that this was refused. He then applied himself to the study of the law; and whatever his real ability, the jealousy of the Cecils no doubt prompted the opinion of the queen, that he was not very profound in the branch he had chosen, an opinion which was fully shared by the blunt and outspoken Lord Coke, who was his rival in love, law, and preferment. Prompted no doubt by the coldness of Burleigh, he joined the opposition headed by the Earl of Essex, and he found in that nobleman a powerful friend and generous patron, who used his utmost endeavors to have Bacon appointed attorney-general, but without success. To compensate Bacon for his failure, Essex presented him with a beautiful villa at Twickenham on the Thames, which was worth £2,000.

TREATMENT OF ESSEX. — Essex was of a bold, eccentric, and violent temper. It is not to the credit of Bacon that when Essex, through his rashness and eccentricities, found himself arraigned for treason, Bacon deserted him, and did not simply stand aloof, but was the chief agent in his prosecution. Nor is this all: after making a vehement and effective speech against him, as counsel for the prosecution — a speech which led to his conviction and execution — Bacon wrote an uncalled-for and malignant paper, entitled "A Declaration of the Treasons of Robert, Earl of Essex."

A high-minded man would have aided his friend; a cautious man would have remained neutral; but Bacon was extravagant, fond of show, eager for money, and in debt: he sought only to push his own fortunes, without regard to justice or gratitude, and he saw that he had everything to gain from his servility to the queen, and nothing from standing by his friend. Even those who thought Essex justly punished, regarded Bacon with aversion and contempt, and impartial history has not reversed their opinion.

HIS APPOINTMENTS. — He strove for place, and he obtained it. In 1590 he was appointed counsel extraordinary to the queen: such was his first reward for this conduct, and such his first lesson in the school where thrift followed fawning. In 1593 he was brought into parliament for Middlesex, and there he charmed all hearers by his eloquence, which has received the special eulogy of Ben Jonson. In his parliamentary career is found a second instance of his truckling to power: in a speech touching the rights of the crown, he offended the queen and her ministers; and as soon as he found they resented it, he made a servile and unqualified apology.

At this time he began to write his *Essays*, which will be referred to hereafter, and published two treatises, one on *The Common Law*, and one on *The Alienation Office*.

In 1603 he was, by his own seeking, among the crowd of gentlemen knighted by James I. on his accession; and in 1604 he added fortune to his new dignity by marrying Alice Barnham, "a handsome maiden," the daughter of a London alderman. He had before addressed the dowager Lady Hatton, who had refused him and bestowed her hand upon his rival, Coke.

In 1613 he attained to the long-desired dignity of attorney-general, a post which he filled with power and energy, but which he disgraced by the torture of Peacham, an old clergyman, who was charged with having written treason in a sermon which he never preached nor published. As nothing could be extorted from him by the rack, Bacon informed the king that Peacham "had a dumb devil." It should be some palliation of this deed, however, that the government was quick and sharp in ferretting out treason, and that torture was still authorized.

In 1616 he was sworn of the privy council, and in the next year inherited his father's honors, being made lord keeper of the seal, principally through the favor of the favorite Buckingham. His course was still upward: in 1618 he was made lord high chancellor, and Baron Verulam, and the next year he was created Viscount St. Albans. Such rapid and high promotion marked his great powers, but it belonged to the period of despotism. James had been ruling without a parliament. At length the necessities of the government caused the king to summon a parliament, and the struggle began which was to have a fatal issue twenty-five years later. Parliament met, began to assert popular rights, and to examine into the conduct of ministers and high officials; and among those who could ill bear such scrutiny, Bacon was prominent.

His Fall. — The charges against him were varied and numerous, and easy of proof. He had received bribes; he had given false judgments for money; he had perverted justice to secure the smiles of Buckingham, the favorite; and when a commission was appointed to examine these charges he was convicted. With abject humility, he acknowledged his guilt, and implored the pity of his judges. The annals of biography present no sorrier picture than this. "Upon advised consideration of the charges," he wrote, "descending into my own conscience, and calling my memory to account so far as I am able, I do plainly and ingenuously confess that I am guilty of corruption, and do renounce all defence. O my lords, spare a broken reed!"

It is useless for his defenders, among whom the chief are Mr. Basil Montagu and Mr. Hepworth Dixon, to inform us that judges in that day were ill paid, and that it was the custom to receive gifts. If Bacon had a defence to make and did not make it, he was a coward or a sycophant: if what he said is true, he was a dishonest man, an unjust judge. He was sentenced to pay a fine of £40,000, and to be imprisoned in the Tower at the king's pleasure: the fine was remitted, and the imprisonment lasted but two days, a result, no doubt foreseen, of his wretched confession. This was the end of his public career. In retirement, with a pension of £1,200, making, with his other means, an annual income of £2,500, this "meanest of mankind" set himself busily to work to prove to the world that he could also be the "wisest and brightest;"[1] a duality of fame approached by others, but never equalled. He was, in fact, two men in one: a dishonest, truckling politician, and a large-minded and truth-seeking philosopher.

Begins his Philosophy. — Retired in disgrace from his places at court, the rest of his life was spent in developing

[1] If parts allure thee, think how Bacon shined
The wisest, brightest, meanest of mankind.
Pope, Essay on Man.

his *Instauratio Magna*, that revolution in the very principles and institutes of science—that philosophy which, in the words of Macaulay, "began in observations, and ended in arts." A few words will suffice to close his personal history. While riding in his coach, he was struck with the idea that snow would arrest animal putrefaction. He alighted, bought a fowl, and stuffed it with snow, with his own hands. He caught cold, stopped at the Earl of Arundel's mansion, and slept in damp sheets; fever intervened, and on Easter Day, 1626, he died, leaving his great work unfinished, but in such condition that the plan has been sketched for the use of the philosophers who came after him.

He is said to have made the first sketch of the *Instauratio* when he was twenty-six years old, but it was much modified in later years. He fondly called it also *Temporis Partus Maximus*, the greatest birth of Time. After that he wrote his *Advancement of Learning in* 1605, which was to appear in his developed scheme, under the title *De Augmentis Scientiarum*, written in 1623. His work advanced with and was modified by his investigations.

In 1620 he wrote the *Novum Organum*, which, when it first appeared, called forth from James I. the profane *bon mot* that it was like the peace of God, "because it passeth all understanding." Thus he was preparing the component parts, and fitting them into his system, which has at length become quite intelligible. A clear notion of what he proposed to himself and what he accomplished, may be found in the subjoined meagre sketch, only designed to indicate the outline of that system, which it will require long and patient study to master thoroughly.

THE GREAT RESTORATION, (MAGNA INSTAURATIO.)—He divided it into six parts, bearing a logical relation to each other, and arranged in the proper order of study.

I. Survey and extension of the sciences, (*De Augmentis*

Scientiarum.) "Gives the substance or general description of the knowledge which mankind *at present possesses.*" That is, let it be observed, not according to the received system and divisions, but according to his own. It is a new presentation of the existent state of knowledge, comprehending "not only the things already invented and known, but also those omitted and wanted," for he says the intellectual globe, as well as the terrestrial, has its broils and deceits.

In the branch "*De Partitione Scientiarum,*" he divides all human learning into *History,* which uses the memory; *Poetry,* which employs the imagination; and *Philosophy,* which requires the reason: divisions too vague and too few, and so overlapping each other as to be of little present use. Later classifications into numerous divisions have been necessary to the progress of scientific research.

II. Precepts for the interpretation of nature, (*Novum Organum.*) This sets forth "the doctrine of a more perfect use of the reason, and the true helps of the intellectual faculties, so as to raise and enlarge the powers of the mind." "A kind of logic, by us called," he says, "the art of interpreting nature: differing from the common logic . . . in three things, the end, the order of demonstrating, and the grounds of inquiry."

Here he discusses induction; opposes the syllogism; shows the value and the faults of the senses — as they fail us, or deceive us — and presents in his *idola* the various modes and forms of deception. These *idola,* which he calls the deepest fallacies of the human mind, are divided into four classes: Idola Tribus, Idola Specus, Idola Fori, Idola Theatri. The first are the errors belonging to the whole human race, or *tribe;* the second — *of the den* — are the peculiarities of individuals; the third — *of the market-place* — are social and conventional errors; and the fourth — *those of the theatre* — include Partisanship, Fashion, and Authority.

III. Phenomena of the Universe, or Natural and Experimental History, on which to found Philosophy, (*Sylva Sylva-*

rum.) "Our natural history is not designed," he says, "so much to please by vanity, or benefit by gainful experiments, as to afford light to the discovery of causes, and hold out the breasts of philosophy." This includes his patient search for facts — nature *free*, as in the history of plants, minerals, animals, etc. — nature *put to the torture*, as in the productions of art and human industry.

IV. Ladder of the Understanding, (*Scala Intellectûs.*) "Not illustrations of rules and precepts, but perfect models, which will exemplify the second part of this work, and represent to the eye the whole progress of the mind, and the continued structure and order of invention, in the most chosen subjects, after the same manner as globes and machines facilitate the more abstruse and subtle demonstrations in mathematics."

V. Precursors or anticipations of the second philosophy, (*Prodromi sive anticipationes philosophiæ secundæ.*) "These will consist of such things as we have invented, experienced, or added by the same common use of the understanding that others employ"— a sort of scaffolding, only of use till the rest are finished — a set of suggestive helps to the attainment of this second philosophy, which is the goal and completion of his system.

VI. Second Philosophy, or Active Science, (*Philosophia Secunda.*) "To this all the rest are subservient — *to lay down that philosophy* which shall flow from the just, pure, and strict inquiry hitherto proposed." "To perfect this is beyond both our abilities and our hopes; yet we shall lay the foundations of it, and recommend the superstructure to posterity."

An examination of this scheme will show a logical procession from the existing knowledge, and from existing defects, by right rules of reason, and the avoidance of deceptions, with a just scale of perfected models, to the *second philosophy*, or science in useful practical action, diffusing light and comfort throughout the world.

In a philosophic instead of a literary work, these heads would require great expansion in order adequately to illustrate the scheme in its six parts. This, however, would be entirely out of our province, which is to present a brief outline of the works of a man who occupies a prominent place in the intellectual realm of England, as a profound philosopher, and as a writer of English prose; only as one might introduce a great man in a crowd: those who wish to know the extent and character of his greatness must study his works.

They were most of them written in Latin, but they have been ably translated and annotated, and are within the ready reach and comprehension of students. The best edition in English, is that by Spedding, Ellis, and Heath, which has been republished in America.

Bacon's Defects. — Further than this tabular outline, neither our space nor the scope of our work will warrant us in going; but it is important to consider briefly the elements of Bacon's remarkable fame. His system and his knowledge are superseded entirely. Those who have studied physics and chemistry at the present day, know a thousand-fold more than Bacon could; for such knowledge did not exist in his day. But he was one of those — and the chief one — who, in that age of what is called the childhood of experimental philosophy, helped to clear away the mists of error, and prepare for the present sunshine of truth. "I have been laboring," says some writer, (quoted by Bishop Whately, Pref. to Essay XIV.,) "to render myself useless." Such was Bacon's task, and such the task of the greatest inventors, discoverers, and benefactors of the human race.

Nor did Bacon rank high even as a natural philosopher or physicist in his own age: he seems to have refused credence to the discoveries of Copernicus and Galileo, which had stirred the scientific world into great activity before his day; and his investigations in botany and vegetable physiology are crude and full of errors.

His mind, eminently philosophic, searched for facts only to establish principles and discover laws; and he was often impatient or obstinate in this search, feeling that it trammelled him in his haste to reach conclusions.

In the consideration of the reason, he unduly despised the *Organon* of Aristotle, which, after much indignity and misapprehension, still remains to elucidate the universal principle of reasoning, and published his new organon — *Novum Organum* — as a sort of substitute for it: Induction unjustly opposed to the Syllogism. In what, then, consists that wonderful excellence, that master-power which has made his name illustrious?

HIS FAME. — I. He labored earnestly to introduce, in the place of fanciful and conjectural systems — careful, patient investigation: the principle of the procurement of well-known facts, in order that, by severe induction, philosophy might attain to general laws, and to a classification of the sciences. The fault of the ages before him had been hasty, careless, often neglected observation, inaccurate analysis, the want of patient successive experiment. His great motto was experiment, and again and again experiment; and the excellent maxims which he laid down for the proper conduct of experimental philosophy have outlived his own facts and system and peculiar beliefs. Thus he has fitly been compared to Moses. He led men, marshalled in strong array, to the vantage ground from which he showed them the land of promise, and the way to enter it; while he himself, after all his labors, was not permitted to enjoy it. Such men deserve the highest fame; and thus the most practical philosophers of to-day revere the memory of him who showed them from the mountain-top, albeit in dim vision, the land which they now occupy.

II. Again, Bacon is the most notable example among natural philosophers of a man who worked for science and truth alone, with a singleness of purpose and entire unconcern as to immediate and selfish rewards. Bacon the philosopher was in the strongest contrast to Bacon the politician. He left, he said, his labors to posterity ; his name and memory to foreign nations, and "to (his) own country, after some time is past over." His own time could neither appreciate nor reward them. Here is an element of greatness worthy of all imitation: he who works for popular applause, may have his reward, but it is fleeting and unsatisfying; he who works for truth alone, has a grand inner consequence while he works, and his name will be honored, if for nothing else, for this loyalty to truth. After what has been said of his servility and dishonesty, it is pleasing to contemplate this unsullied side of his escutcheon, and to give a better significance to the motto on his monument — *Sic sedebat.*

HIS ESSAYS. — Bacon's *Essays*, or *Counsels Civil and Moral*, are as intelligible to the common mind as his philosophy is dry and difficult. They are short, pithy, sententious, telling us plain truths in simple language: he had been writing them through several years. He dedicated them, under the title of *Essays*, to Henry, Prince of Wales, the eldest son of King James I., a prince of rare gifts, and worthy such a dedication, who unfortunately died in 1612. They show him to be the greatest master of English prose in his day, and to have had a deep insight into human nature.

Bacon is said to have been the first person who applied the word *essay* in English to such writings: it meant, as the French word shows, a little trial-sketch, a suggestion, a few loose thoughts — a brief of something to be filled in by the reader. Now it means something far more — a long composition, dissertation, disquisition. The subjects of the essays, which number sixty-eight, are such as are of universal interest — fame, studies, atheism, beauty, ambition, death, empire, sedition, honor, adversity, and suchlike.

The Essays have been ably edited and annotated by Archbishop Whately, and his work has been republished in America.

CHAPTER XVII.

THE ENGLISH BIBLE.

Early Versions.	Wiclif; Tyndale.	King James's Bible.
The Septuagint.	Coverdale; Cranmer.	Language of the Bible.
The Vulgate.	Geneva; Bishop's Bible.	Revision.

Early Versions of the Scriptures.

WHEN we consider the very extended circulation of the English Bible in the version made by direction of James I., we are warranted in saying that no work in the language, viewed simply as a literary production, has had a more powerful historic influence over the world of English-speaking people.

Properly to understand its value as a version of the inspired writings, it is necessary to go back to the original history, and discover through what precedent forms they have come into English.

All the canonical books of the Old Testament were written in Hebrew. The apocryphal books were produced either in a corrupted dialect, or in Greek.

The Septuagint.—Limiting our inquiry to the canonical books, and rejecting all fanciful traditions, it is known that about 286 or 285 B. C., Ptolemy Philadelphus, King of Egypt, probably at the instance of his librarian, Demetrius Phalereus, caused seventy-two Jews, equally learned in Hebrew and in Greek, to be brought to Alexandria, to prepare a Greek version of the Hebrew Scriptures. This was for the use of the Alexandrian Jews. The version was called the Septuagint, or translation of the seventy. The various portions of the translation are of unequal merit, the rendering of the Pentateuch being the best; but the completed work was of great value, not only to the Jews dispersed in the countries where Greek had been adopted as the national language, but it opened the way for the coming of Christianity: the study of its prophecies prepared the minds of men for the great Advent, and the version was used by the earlier Christians as the historic ground of their faith.

The books of the New Testament were written in Greek, with the probable exception of St. Matthew's Gospel, which, if written in Hebrew, or Aramæan, was immediately translated into Greek.

Contemporary with the origin of Christianity, and the vast extension of the Roman Empire, the Latin had become the all-absorbing tongue; and, as might be expected, numerous versions of the whole and of parts of the Scriptures were made in that language, and one of these complete versions, which grew in favor, almost superseding all others, was called the *Vetus Itala*.

THE VULGATE. — St. Jerome, a doctor of the Latin Church in the latter part of the fourth century, undertook, with the sanction of Damasus, the Bishop of Rome, a new Latin version upon the basis of the *Vetus Itala*, bringing it nearer to the Septuagint in the Old Testament, and to the original Greek of the New.

This version of Jerome, corrected from time to time, was approved by Gregory I., (the Great,) and, since the seventh century, has been used by the Western Church, under the name of the *Vulgate*, (from *vulgatus* — for general or common use.) The Council of Trent, in the sixteenth century, declared it alone to be authentic.

Throughout Western Europe this was used, and made the basis of further translations into the national languages. It was from the Vulgate that Aldhelm made his Anglo-Saxon version of the Psalter in 706; Bede, his entire Saxon Bible in the same period; Alfred, his portion of the Psalms; and other writers, fragmentary translations.

As soon as the newly formed English language was strong enough, partial versions were attempted in it: one by an unknown hand, as early as 1290; and one by John de Trevisa, about one hundred years later.

WICLIF: TYNDALE. — Wiclif's Bible was translated from the Latin Vulgate, and issued about 1378. If it be asked why he did not go to the original sources, and thus avoid the errors of successive renderings, the answer is plain: he was not sufficiently acquainted with Hebrew and Greek to translate from them. Wiclif's translation was eagerly sought, and was multiplied by the hands of skilful scribes. Its popularity was very great, as is attested by the fact that when, in the House of Lords, in the year 1390, a bill was offered to suppress it, the measure signally failed. The first copy of Wiclif's Bible was not printed until the year 1731.

About a century after Wiclif, the Greek language and the study of Greek literature came into England, and were of great effect in making the forthcoming translations more accurate.

First among these new translators was William Tyndale, who was born about the year 1477. He was educated at Oxford and Cambridge, and left England for fear of persecution. He translated the Scriptures from the Greek, and printed the volume at Antwerp — the first printed translation of the Scriptures in English — in the year 1526. This work was largely circulated in England. It was very good for a first translation, and the language is very nearly that of King James's Bible. It met the fury of the Church, all the copies which could be found being burned by Tonstall, Bishop of London, at St. Paul's Cross. When Sir Thomas More asked how Tyndale subsisted abroad, he was pithily answered that Tyndale was supported by the Bishop of London, who sent over money to buy up his books. To the fame of being a translator of the Scriptures, Tyndale adds that of martyrdom. He was seized, at the instance of Henry VIII., in Antwerp, and condemned to death by the Emperor of Germany. He was strangled in the year 1536, at Villefort, near Brussels, praying, just before his death, that the Lord would open the King of England's eyes.

The Old Testament portion of Tyndale's Bible is principally from the Septuagint, and has many corruptions and errors, which have been corrected by more modern translators.

MILES COVERDALE: CRANMER'S BIBLE. — In 1535, Miles Coverdale, a co-laborer of Tyndale, published "Biblia; The Bible, that is, the Holy Scriptures of the Olde and New Testament, faithfully and truly translated out of the Douche and Latyn into Englishe: Zurich." In the next year, 1536, Coverdale issued another edition, which was dedicated to Henry VIII., who ordered a copy to be placed in every parish church in England. This translation is in part that of Tyndale, and is based upon it. Another edition of this appeared in 1537, and was called Matthew's Bible, probably a pseudonym of Coverdale. Of this, from the beginning to the end of Chronicles is Tyndale's version. The rest of the Old Testament is Coverdale's translation. The entire New Testament is Tyndale's. This was published by royal license. Strange mutation! The same king who had caused Tyndale to be strangled for publishing the English Scriptures at Antwerp, was now spreading Tyndale's work throughout the parishes of England. Coverdale published many editions, among which the most noted was Cranmer's Bible, issued in 1539, so called because Cranmer wrote a preface to it. Coverdale led an eventful life, being sometimes in exile and prisoner, and at others in high favor. He was Bishop of Exeter, from which see he was ejected by Mary, in 1553. He died in 1568, at the age of eighty-one.

THE GENEVAN: BISHOPS' BIBLE. — In the year 1557 he had aided those who were driven away by Mary, in publishing a version of the Bible at Geneva. It was much read in England, and is known as the Genevan Bible. The Great Bible was an edition of Coverdale issued in 1562. The Bishops' Bible was so called because, at the instance of Archbishop Parker, it was translated by a royal commission, of whom eight were bishops. And in 1571, a canon was passed at Canterbury, requiring a large copy of this work to be in every parish church, and in the possession of every bishop and dignitary among the clergy. Thus far every new edition and issue had been an improvement on what had gone before, and all tended to the production of a still more perfect and permanent translation. It should be mentioned that Luther, in Germany, after ten years of labor, from 1522 to 1532, had produced, unaided, his wonderful German version. This had helped the cause of translations everywhere.

KING JAMES'S BIBLE. — At length, in 1603, just after the accession of James I., a conference was held at Hampton Court, which, among other tasks, undertook to consider what objections could be made to the Bishops' Bible. The result was that the king ordered a new version which should supersede all others. The number of eminent and learned divines appointed to make the translation was fifty-four; seven of these were prevented by disability of one kind or another. The remaining forty-seven were divided into six classes, and the labor was thus apportioned: ten, who sat at Westminster, translated from Genesis through Kings; eight, at Cambridge, undertook the other historical books and the Hagiographa, including the Psalms, Proverbs, Job, Daniel, Ezra, Nehemiah, Ruth, Esther, and a few other books; seven at Oxford, the four greater Prophets, the Lamentations of Jeremiah, and the twelve minor Prophets; eight, also at Oxford, the four Gospels, the Acts of the Apostles, and the Revelation of St. John;

seven more at Westminster, the Epistles of St. Paul, and the remaining canonical books; and five more at Cambridge, the Apocryphal books. The following was the mode of translation: Each individual in one of the classes translated himself every book confided to that class; each class then met and compared these translations, and thus completed their task. The work thus done was sent by each class to all the other classes; after this, all the classes met together, and while one read the others criticized. The translation was commenced in the year 1607, and was finished in three years. The first public issue was in 1611, when the book was dedicated to King James, and has since been known as King James's Bible. It was adopted not only in the English Church, but by all the English people, so that the other versions have fallen into entire disuse, with the exception of the Psalms, which, according to the translation of Cranmer's Bible, were placed in the Book of Common Prayer, where they have since remained, constituting the Psalter. It should be observed that the Psalter, which is taken principally from the Vulgate, is not so near the original as the Psalms in King James's version: the language is, however, more musical and better suited to chanting in the church service.

The Language of the Bible. — There have been numerous criticisms, favorable and adverse, to the language of King James's Bible. It is said to have been written in older English than that of its day, and Selden remarks that "it is rather translated into English words than into English phrase." The Hebraisms are kept, and the phraseology of that language is retained. This leads to the opinion of Bishop Horsley, that the adherence to the Hebrew idiom is supposed to have at once enriched and adorned our language. Bishop Middleton says "the style is simple, it is harmonious, it is energetic, and, which is of no small importance, use has made it familiar, and time has rendered it sacred." That it has lasted two hundred and fifty years without a rival, is the strongest testimony in favor of its accuracy and the beauty of its diction. Philologically considered, it has been of inestimable value as a strong rallying-point for the language, keeping it from wild progress in any and every direction. Many of our best words, which would otherwise have been lost, have been kept in current use because they are in the Bible. The peculiar language of the Bible expresses our most serious sentiments and our deepest emotions. It is associated with our holiest thoughts, and gives phraseology to our prayers. It is the language of heavenly things, but not only so: it is interwreathed in our daily discourse, kept fresh by our constant Christian services, and thus we are bound by ties of the same speech to the devout men of King James's day.

REVISION. — There are some inaccuracies and flaws in the translation which have been discerned by the superior excellence of modern learning. In the question now mooted of a revision of the English Bible, the correction of these should be the chief object. A version in the language of the present day, in the course of time would be as archaic as the existing version is now; and the private attempts which have been made, have shown us the great danger of conflicting sectarian views.

In any event, it is to be hoped that those who authorize a new translation will emulate the good sense and judgment of King James, by placing it in the hands of the highest learning, most liberal scholarship, and most devoted piety.

CHAPTER XVIII.

JOHN MILTON, AND THE ENGLISH COMMONWEALTH.

Historical Facts. | Cromwell. | Other Prose Works.
Charles I. | Birth and Early Works. | Effects of the Restoration.
Religious Extremes. | Views of Marriage. | Estimate of his Prose.

Historical Facts.

IT is Charles Lamb who says "Milton almost requires a solemn service to be played before you enter upon him." Of Milton, the poet of *Paradise Lost*, this is true; but for Milton the statesman, the politician, and polemic, this is neither necessary nor appropriate. John Milton and the Commonwealth! Until the present age, Milton has been regarded almost solely as a poet, and as the greatest imaginative poet England has produced; but the translation and publication of his prose works have identified him with the political history of England, and the discovery in 1823, of his *Treatise on Christian Doctrine*, has established him as one of the greatest religious polemics in an age when every theological sect was closely allied to a political party, and thus rendered the strife of contending factions more bitter and relentless. Thus it is that the name of John Milton, as an author, is fitly coupled with the commonwealth, as a political condition.

It remains for us to show that in all his works he was the strongest literary type of history in the age in which he lived. Great as he would have been in any age, his greatness is mainly English and historical. In his literary works may be traced every cardinal event in the history of that period: he aided in the establishment of the Commonwealth, and of that Commonwealth he was one of the principal characters. His pen was as sharp and effective as the sabres of Cromwell's Ironsides.

A few words of preliminary history must introduce him to our reader. Upon the death of Queen Elizabeth, in 1603, James I. ascended the throne with the highest notions of kingly prerogative and of a church establishment; but the progress of the English people in education and intelligence, the advance in arts and letters which had been made, were vastly injurious to the autocratic and aristocratic system which James had received from his predecessor. His foolish arrogance and contempt for popular rights incensed the people thus enlightened as to their own position and importance. They soon began to feel that he was not only unjust, but ungrateful: he had come from a rustic throne in Scotland, where he had received £5,000 per annum, with occasional presents of fruits, grain, and poultry, to the greatest throne in Europe; and, besides, the Stuart family, according to Thackeray, "as regards mere lineage, were no better than a dozen English and Scottish houses that could be named."

They resisted his illegal taxes and forced loans; they clamored against the unconstitutional Court of High Commission; they despised his arrogant favorites; and what they might have patiently borne from a gallant, energetic, and handsome monarch, they found it hard to bear from a pedantic, timid, uncouth, and rickety man, who gave them neither glory nor comfort. His eldest son, Prince Henry, the universal favorite of the nation, had died in 1612, before he was eighteen.

Charles I. — When, after a series of struggles with the parliament, which he had reluctantly convened, James died in 1625, Charles I. came to an inheritance of error and misfortune. Imbued with the principles of his father, he, too, insisted upon "governing the people of England in the seventeenth century as they had been governed in the sixteenth," while in reality they had made a century of progress. The cloud increased in blackness and portent; he dissolved the parliament, and ruled without one; he imposed and collected illegal and doubtful taxes; he made forced loans, as his father had done; he was artful, capricious, winding and doubling in his policy; he made promises without intending to perform them; and found himself, finally, at direct issue with his parliament and his people. First at war with the political principles of the court, the nation soon found itself in antagonism with the religion and morals of the court. Before the final rupture, the two parties were well defined, as Cavaliers and Roundheads: each party went to extremes, through the spite and fury of mutual opposition. The Cavaliers affected a recklessness and dissoluteness greater than they really felt to be right, in order to differ most widely from those purists who, urged by analogous motives, decried all amusements as evil. Each party repelled the other to the extreme of opposition.

Religious Extremes. — Loyalty was opposed by radicalism, and the invectives of both were bitter in the extreme. The system and ceremonial of a gorgeous worship restored by Laud, and accused by its opposers of formalism and idolatry, were attacked by a spirit of excess, which, to religionize daily life, took the words of Scripture, and especially those of the Old Testament, as the language of common intercourse, which issued them from a gloomy countenance, with a nasal twang, and often with a false interpretation.

As opposed to the genuflections of Laud and the pomp of his ritual, the land swarmed with unauthorized preachers; then came out from among the Presbyterians the Independents; the fifth-monarchy men, shouting for King Jesus; the Seekers, the Antinomians, who, like Trusty Tomkins, were elect by the fore-knowledge of God, who were not under the law but under grace, and who might therefore gratify every lust, and give the rein to every passion, because they were sealed to a certain salvation. Even in the army sprang up the Levellers, who wished to abolish monarchy and aristocracy, and to level all ranks to one. To each religious party, there was a political character, ranging from High Church and the divine right of kings, to absolute levellers in Church and State. This disintegrating process threatened not only civil war, with well-defined parties, but entire anarchy in the realm of England. It was long resisted by the conservative men of all opinions. At length the issue came: the king was a prisoner, without a shadow of power.

The parliament was still firm, and would have treated with the king by a considerable majority; but Colonel Pride surrounded it with two regiments, excluded more than two hundred of the Presbyterians and moderate men; and the parliament, thus *purged*, appointed the High Court of Justice to try the king for treason.

Charles I. fell before the storm. His was a losing cause from the day he erected his standard at Nottingham, in 1642, to that on which, after his noble bearing on the scaffold, the masked executioner held up his head and cried out, "This is the head of a traitor."

With a fearful consistency the Commons voted soon after to abolish monarchy and the upper house, and on their new seal inscribed, "On the first year of freedom by God's blessing restored, 1648." The dispassionate historian of the present day must condemn both parties; and yet, out of this fierce travail of the nation, English constitutional liberty was born.

Cromwell. — The power which the parliament, under the dictation of the army, had so furiously wielded, passed into the hands of Cromwell, a mighty man, warrior, statesman, and fanatic, who mastered the crew, seized the helm, and guided the ship of State as she drove furiously before the wind. He became lord protector, a king in everything but the name. We need not enter into an analysis of these parties: the history is better known than any other part of the English annals, and almost every reader becomes a partisan. Cromwell, the greatest man of his age, was still a creature of the age, and was led by the violence of circumstances to do many things questionable and even wicked, but with little premeditation: like Rienzi and Napoleon, his sudden elevation fostered an ambition which robbed him of the stern purpose and pure motives of his earlier career.

The establishment of the commonwealth seemed at first to assure the people's liberty; but it was only in seeming, and as the sequel shows, they liked the rule of the lord protector less than that of the unfortunate king; for, ten years after the beheading of Charles I., they restored the monarchy in the person of his son, Charles.

Such, very briefly and in mere outline, was the political situation. And now to return to Milton: It is claimed that of all the elements of these troublous times, he was the literary type, and this may be demonstrated —

I. By observing his personal characteristics and political appointments.

II. By the study of his prose works; and

III. By analyzing his poems.

Birth and Early Works. — John Milton was born on the 9th of December, 1608, in London. His grandfather, John Mylton, was a Papist, who disinherited his son, the poet's father, for becoming a Church-of-England man. His mother was a gentlewoman. Milton was born just in time to grow up with the civil troubles. When the outburst came in 1642, he was thirty-four years old, a solemn, cold, studious, thoughtful, and dogmatic Puritan. In 1624 he entered Christ College, Cambridge, where, from his delicate and beautiful face and shy airs, he was called the "Lady of the College." It is said that he left the university on account of peculiar views in theology and politics; but eight years after, in 1632, he took his degree as master of arts. Meanwhile, in December, 1629, he had celebrated his twenty-first birthday, when the Star of Bethlehem was coming into the ascendant, with that pealing, organ-like hymn, "On the Eve of Christ's Nativity"—the worthiest poetic tribute ever laid by man, along with the gold, frankincense, and myrrh of the Eastern sages, at the feet of the Infant God:

> See how from far upon the Eastern road,
>   The star-led wizards haste with odours sweet;
> O run, prevent them with thy humble ode,
>   And lay it lowly at his blessed feet;
>   Have thou the honour first thy Lord to greet,
> And join thy voice unto the angel choir,
> From out his secret altar touched with hallowed fire.

Some years of travel on the Continent matured his mind, and gave full scope to his poetic genius. At Paris he became acquainted with Grotius, the illustrious writer upon public law; and in Rome, Genoa, Florence, and other Italian cities, he became intimate with the leading minds of the age. He returned to England on account of the political troubles.

MILTON'S VIEWS OF MARRIAGE.—In the consideration of Milton's personality, we do not find in him much to arouse our heart-sympathy. His opinions concerning marriage and divorce, as set forth in several of his prose writings, would, if generally adopted, destroy the sacred character of divinely appointed wedlock. His views may be found in his essay on *The Doctrine and Discipline of Divorce;* in his *Tetrachordon, or the four chief places in Scripture, which treat of Marriage, or Nullities in Marriage;* in his *Colasterion*, and in his translation of Martin Bucer's *Judgment Concerning Divorce*, addressed to the Parliament of England. Where women were concerned he was a hard man and a stern master.

In 1643 he married Mary Powell, the daughter of a Cavalier; and, taking her from the gay life of her father's house, he brought her into a gloom and seclusion almost insupportable. He loved his books better than he did his wife. He fed and sheltered her, indeed, but he gave her no tender sympathy. Then was enacted in his household the drama of the rebellion in miniature; and no doubt his domestic troubles had led to his extended discussion of the question of divorce. He speaks, too, almost entirely in the interest of husbands. With him woman is not complementary to man, but his inferior, to be cherished if obedient, to minister to her husband's welfare, but to have her resolute spirit broken after the manner of Petruchio, the shrew-tamer. In all this, however, Milton was eminently a type of the times. It was the canon law of the established Church of England at which he aimed, and he endeavored to lead the parliament to legislation upon the most sacred ties and relations of human life. Happily, English morals were too strong, even in that turbulent period, to yield to this unholy attempt. It was a day when authority was questioned, a day for "extending the area of freedom," but he went too far even for emancipated England; and the mysterious power of the marriage tie has always been reverenced as one of the main bulwarks of that righteousness which exalteth a nation.

His apology for Smectymnuus is one of his pamphlets against Episcopacy, and receives its title from the initial letters of the names of five Puritan ministers, who also engaged in controversy: they were Stephen Marshall, Edward Calamy, Thomas Young, Matthew Newcome, William Spenston. The Church of England never had a more intelligent and relentless enemy than John Milton.

Other Prose Works. — Milton's prose works are almost all of them of an historical character. Appointed Latin Secretary to the Council, he wrote foreign dispatches and treatises upon the persons and events of the day. In 1644 he published his *Areopagitica*, a noble paper in favor of *Unlicensed Printing*, and boldly directed against the Presbyterian party, then in power, which had continued and even increased the restraints upon the press. No stouter appeal for the freedom of the press was ever heard, even in America. But in the main, his prose pen was employed against the crown and the Church, while they still existed; against the king's memory, after the unfortunate monarch had fallen, and in favor of the parliament and all its acts. Milton was no trimmer; he gave forth no uncertain sound; he was partisan to the extreme, and left himself no loop-hole of retreat in the change that was to come.

A famous book appeared in 1649, not long after Charles's execution, proclaimed to have been written by King Charles while in prison, and entitled *Eikon Basilike*, or *The Kingly Image*, being the portraiture of his majesty in his solitude and suffering. It was supposed that it might influence the people in favor of royalty, and so Milton was employed to answer it in a bitter invective, an unnecessary and heartless attack upon the dead king, entitled *Eikonoklastes*, or *The Image-breaker*. The Eikon was probably in part written by the king, and in part by Bishop Gauden, who indeed claimed its authorship after the Restoration.

Salmasius having defended Charles in a work of dignified and moderate tone, Milton answered in his first *Defensio pro Populo Anglicano;* in which he traverses the whole ground of popular rights and kingly prerogative, in a masterly and eloquent manner. This was followed by a second *Defensio*. For the two he received £1,000, and by his own account accelerated the disease of the eyes which ended in complete blindness.

No pen in England worked more powerfully than his in behalf of the parliament and the protectorate, or to stay the flood tide of loyalty, which bore upon its sweeping heart the restoration of the second Charles. He wrote the last foreign despatches of Richard Cromwell, the weak successor of the powerful Oliver; but nothing could now avail to check the return of monarchy. The people were tired of turmoil and sick of blood; they wanted rest, at any cost. The powerful hand of Cromwell was removed, and astute Monk used his army to secure his reward. The army, concurring with the popular sentiment, restored the Stuarts. The conduct of the English people in bringing Charles back stamped Cromwell as a usurper, and they have steadily ignored in their list of governors—called monarchs—the man through whose efforts much of their liberty had been achieved; but history asserts itself, and the benefits of the "Great Rebellion" are gratefully acknowledged by the people, whether the protectorate appears in the court list or not.

The Effect of the Restoration. — Charles II. came back to such an overwhelming reception, that he said, in his witty way, it must have been his own fault to stay away so long from a people who were so glad to see him when he did come. This restoration forced Milton into concealment: his public day was over, and yet his remaining history is particularly interesting. Inheriting weak eyes from his mother, he had overtasked their powers, especially in writing the *Defensiones*, and had become entirely blind. Although his person was included in the general amnesty, his polemical works were burned by the hangman; and the pen that had so powerfully battled for a party, now returned to the service of its first love, poetry. His loss of power and place was the world's gain. In his forced seclusion, he produced the greatest of English poems — religious, romantic, and heroic.

Estimate of his Prose. — Before considering his poems, we may briefly state some estimate of his prose works. They comprise much that is excellent, are full of learning, and contain passages of rarest rhetoric. He said himself, that in prose he had only "the use of his left hand;" but it was the left hand of a Milton. To the English scholar they are chiefly of historical value: many of them are written in Latin, and lose much of their terseness in a translation which retains classical peculiarities of form and phrase.

His *History of England from the Earliest Times* is not profound, nor philosophical; he followed standard chronicle authorities, but made few, if any, original investigations, and gives us little philosophy. His tractate on *Education* contains peculiar views of a curriculum of study, but is charmingly written. He also wrote a treatise on *Logic.* Little known to the great world outside of his poems, there is one prose work, discovered only in 1823, which has been less read, but which contains the articles of his Christian belief. It is a tractate on Christian doctrine: no one now doubts its genuineness; and it proves him to have been a Unitarian, or High Arian, by his own confession. This was somewhat startling to the great orthodox world, who had taken many of their conceptions of supernatural things from Milton's *Paradise Lost;* and yet a careful study of that poem will disclose similar tendencies in the poet's mind. He was a Puritan whose theology was progressive until it issued in complete isolation: he left the Presbyterian ranks for the Independents, and then, startled by the rise and number of sects, he retired within himself and stood almost alone, too proud to be instructed, and dissatisfied with the doctrines and excesses of his earlier colleagues.

In 1653 he lost his wife, Mary Powell, who left him three daughters. He supplied her place in 1656, by marrying Catherine Woodstock, to whom he was greatly attached, and who also died fifteen months after. Eight years afterward he married his third wife, Elizabeth Minshull, who survived him.

CHAPTER XIX.

THE POETRY OF MILTON.

THE BLIND POET.

MILTON'S blindness, his loneliness, and his loss of power, threw him upon himself. His imagination, concentrated by these disasters and troubles, was to see higher things in a clear, celestial light: there was nothing to distract his attention, and he began that achievement which he had long before contemplated—a great religious epic, in which the heroes should be celestial beings and our sinless first parents, and the scenes Heaven, Hell, and the Paradise of a yet untainted Earth. His first idea was to write an epic on King Arthur and his knights: it is well for the world that he changed his intention, and took as a grander subject the loss of Paradise, full as it is of individual interest to mankind.

In a consideration of his poetry, we must now first recur to those pieces which he had written at an earlier day. Before settling in London, he had, as we have seen, travelled fifteen months on the Continent, and had been particularly interested by his residence in Italy, where he visited the blind Galileo. The poems which most clearly show the still powerful influence of Italy in all European literature, and upon him especially, are the *Arcades*, *Comus*, *L'Allegro*, *Il Penseroso*, and *Lycidas*, each beautiful and finished, and although Italian in their taste, yet full of true philosophy couched in charming verse.

The *Arcades,* (Arcadians,) composed in 1684, is a pastoral masque, enacted before the Countess Dowager of Derby at Harefield, by some noble persons of her family. The *Allegro* is the song of Mirth, the nymph who brings with her

> Jest and youthful jollity,
> Quips and cranks, and wanton wiles,
> Nods and becks and wreathèd smiles,
> . . . .
> Sport that wrinkled Care derides,
> And Laughter holding both his sides.

The poem is like the nymph whom he addresses,

> Buxom, blithe, and debonaire.

The *Penseroso* is a tribute to tender melancholy, and is designed as a pendant to the *Allegro:*

> Pensive nun devout and pure,
> Sober, steadfast, and demure,
> All in a robe of darkest grain,
> Flowing with majestic train.

We fall in love with each goddess in turn, and find comfort for our varying moods from "grave to gay."

Burke said he was certain Milton composed the *Penseroso* in the aisle of a cloister, or in an ivy-grown abbey.

Comus is a noble poem, philosophic and tender, but neither pastoral nor dramatic, except in form; it presents the power of chastity in disarming *Circe, Comus,* and all the libidinous sirens. *L'Allegro* and *Il Penseroso* were written at Horton, about 1633.

Lycidas, written in 1637, is a tender monody on the loss of a friend named King, in the Irish Channel, in that year, and is a classical pastoral, tricked off in Italian garb. What it loses in adherence to classic models and Italian taste, is more than made up by exquisite lines and felicitous phrases. In it he calls fame "that last infirmity of noble mind." Perhaps he has nowhere written finer lines than these:

> So sinks the day-star in the ocean bed,
> And yet anon repairs his drooping head,
> And tricks his beams, and with new-spangled ore
> *Flames in the forehead of the morning sky.*

Besides these, Milton wrote Latin poems with great vigor, if not with remarkable grace; and several Italian sonnets and poems, which have been much admired even by Italian critics. The sonnet, if not of Italian origin, had been naturalized there when its birth was forgotten; and this practice in the Italian gave him that power to produce them in English which he afterward used with such effect.

PARADISE LOST. — Having thus summarily disposed of his minor poems, each of which would have immortalized any other man, we come to that upon which his highest fame rests; which is familiarly known by men who have never read the others, and who are ignorant of his prose works; which is used as a parsing exercise in many schools, and which, as we have before hinted, has furnished Protestant pulpits with pictorial theology from that day to this. It occupied him several years in the composition; from 1658, when Cromwell died, through the years of retirement and obscurity until 1667. It came forth in an evil day, for the merry monarch was on the throne, and an irreligious court gave tone to public opinion.

The hardiest critic must approach the *Paradise Lost* with wonder and reverence. What an imagination, and what a compass of imagination! Now with the lost peers in Hell, his glowing fancy projects an empire almost as grand and glorious as that of God himself. Now with undazzled, presumptuous gaze he stands face to face with the Almighty, and records the words falling from His lips; words which he has dared to place in the mouth of the Most High — words at the utterance of which

> . . . ambrosial fragrance filled
> All heaven, and in the blessed spirits elect
> Sense of new joy ineffable diffused.

Little wonder that in his further flight he does not shrink from colloquy with the Eternal Son — in his theology not the equal of His Father — or that he does not fear to describe the fearful battle between Christ with his angelic hosts against the kingdom of darkness:

> . . . At his right hand victory
> Sat eagle-winged: beside him hung his bow
> And quiver with three-bolted thunder stored.
> . . . .
> . . . Them unexpected joy surprised,
> When the great ensign of Messiah blazed,
> Aloft by angels borne his sign in heaven.

How heart-rending his story of the fall, and of the bitter sorrow of our first parents, whose fatal act

> Brought death into the world and all our woe,
> With loss of Eden, till one greater Man
> Restore us, and regain the blissful seat.

How marvellous is the combat at Hell-gate, between Satan and Death; how terrible the power at which "Hell itself grew darker"! How we strive to shade our mind's eye as we enter again with him into the courts of Heaven. How refreshingly beautiful the perennial bloom of Eden:

> Picta velut primo Vere coruscat humus.

What a wonderful story of the teeming creation related to our first parents by the lips of Raphael:

When from the Earth appeared
The tawny lion, pawing to get free
His hinder parts, then springs as broke from bonds,
And rampant shakes his brinded mane.

And withal, how compact the poem, how perfect the drama. It is Paradise, perfect in beauty and holiness; attacked with devilish art; in danger; betrayed; lost!

Forth reaching to the fruit, she plucked and ate;
Earth felt the wound, and Nature from her seat,
Sighing through all her works gave signs of woe
That all was lost!

Unit-like, complete, brilliant, sublime, awful, the poem dazzles criticism, and belittles the critic. It is the grandest poem ever written. It almost sets up a competition with Scripture. Milton's Adam and Eve walk before us instead of the Adam and Eve of Genesis. Milton's Satan usurps the place of that grotesque, malignant spirit of the Bible, which, instead of claiming our admiration, excites only our horror, as he goes about like a roaring lion seeking whom he may devour. He it is who can declare

The mind is its own place, and in itself
Can make a Heaven of Hell, a Hell of Heaven.
What matter where, if I be still the same,
And what I should be?

MILTON AND DANTE. — It has been usual for the literary critic to compare Milton and Dante; and it is certain that in the conception, at least, of his great themes, Milton took Dante for his guide. Without an odious comparison, and conceding the great value, principally historical, of the *Divina Commedia*, it must be said that the palm remains with the English poet. Take, for a single illustration, the fall of the arch-fiend. Dante's Lucifer falls with such force that he makes a conical hole in the earth to its centre, and forces out a hill on the other side — a physical prediction, as the antipodes had not yet been established. The cavity is the seat of Hell; and the mountain, that of Purgatory. So mathematical is his fancy, that in vignette illustrations we have right-lined drawings of these surfaces and their different circles. Science had indeed progressed in Milton's time, but his imagination scorns its aid; everything is with him grandly ideal, as well as rhetorically harmonious:

> . . . Him the Almighty power,
> Hurled headlong flaming from th' ethereal sky,
> With hideous ruin and combustion down
> To bottomless perdition, there to dwell
> In adamantine chains and penal power,
> Who durst defy th' Omnipotent in arms.

And when a lesser spirit falls, what a sad Æolian melody describes the downward flight:

> . . . How he fell
> From Heaven they fabled thrown by angry Jove,
> Sheer o'er the crystal battlements: from morn
> To noon he fell, from noon to dewy eve
> A summer's day; and with the setting sun,
> Dropt from the zenith like a falling star.

The heavenly colloquies to which we have alluded between the Father and the Son, involve questions of theology, and present peculiar views — such as the subordination of the Son, and the relative unimportance of the third Person of the Blessed Trinity. They establish Milton's Arianism almost as completely as his Treatise on Christian Doctrine.

His Faults. — Grand, far above all human efforts, his poems fail in these representations. God is a spirit; he is here presented as a body, and that by an uninspired pen. The poet has not been able to carry us up to those infinite heights, and so his attempt only ends in a humanitarian philosophy: he has been obliged to lower the whole heavenly hierarchy to bring it within the scope of our objective comprehension. He blinds our poor eyes by the dazzling effulgence of that light which is

> . . . of the Eternal co-eternal beam.

And it must be asserted that in this attempt Milton has done injury to the cause of religion, however much he has vindicated the power of the human intellect and the compass of the human imagination. He has made sensuous that which was entirely spiritual, and has attempted with finite powers to realize the Infinite.

The fault is not so great when he delineates created intelligences, ranging from the highest seraph to him who was only "less than archangel ruined." We gaze, unreproved by conscience, at the rapid rise of Pandemonium; we watch with eager interest the hellish crew as they "open into the hill a spacious wound, and dig out ribs of gold." We admire the fabric which springs

> . . . like an exhalation, with the sound
> Of dulcet symphonies and voices sweet.

Nothing can be grander or more articulately realized than that arched roof, from which,

> Pendent by subtle magic, many a row
> Of starry lamps and blazing cressets, fed
> With naphtha and asphaltus, yields the light
> As from a sky.

It is an illustrative criticism that while the painter's art has seized these scenes, not one has dared to attempt his heavenly descriptions with the pencil. Art is less bold or more reverent than poetry, and rebukes the poet.

Characteristics of the Age. — And here it is particularly to our purpose to observe, that in this very boldness of entrance into the holy of holies — in this attempted grasp with finite hands of infinite things, Milton was but a sublimated type of his age, and of the Commonwealth, when man, struggling for political freedom, went, as in the later age of the French Illuminati, too far in the regions of spirit and of faith. As Dante, with a powerful satire, filled his poem with the personages of the day, assigning his enemies to the *girone* of the Inferno, so Milton vents his gentler spleen by placing cowls and hood and habits in the limbo of vanity and paradise of fools:

> . . . all these upwhirled aloft
> Fly o'er the backside of the world far off,
> Into a limbo large and broad, since called
> The paradise of fools.

It was a setting forth of that spirit which, when the Cavaliers were many of them formalists, and the Puritans many of them fanatics, led to the rise of many sects, and caused rude soldiers to bellow their own riotous fancies from the pulpit. In the suddenness of change, when the earthly throne had been destroyed, men misconceived what was due to the heavenly; the fancy which had been before curbed by an awe for authority, and was too ignorant to move without it, now revelled unrebuked among the mysteries which are not revealed to angelic vision, and thus "fools rushed in where angels fear to tread."

The book could not fail to bring him immense fame, but personally he received very little for it in money — less than £20.

PARADISE REGAINED. — It was Thomas Ellwood, Milton's Quaker friend, who, after reading the *Paradise Lost*, suggested the *Paradise Regained.* This poem will bear no comparison with its great companion. It may, without irreverence, be called "The gospel according to John Milton." Beauties it does contain; but the very foundation of it is false. Milton makes man regain Paradise by the success of Christ in withstanding the Devil's temptations in the wilderness; a new presentation of his Arian theology, which is quite transcendental; whereas, in our opinion, the gate of Paradise was opened only "by His precious death and burial; His glorious resurrection and ascension; and by the coming of the Holy Ghost." But if it is immeasurably inferior in its conception and treatment, it is quite equal to the *Paradise Lost* in its execution.

A few words as to Milton's vocabulary and style must close our notice of this greatest of English poets. With regard to the first, the Latin element, which is so manifest in his prose works, largely predominates in his poems, but accords better with the poetic license. In a list of authors which Mr. Marsh has prepared, down to Milton's time, which includes an analysis of the sixth book of the *Paradise Lost,* he is found to employ only eighty per cent. of Anglo-Saxon words—less than any up to that day. But his words are chosen with a delicacy of taste and ear which astonishes and delights; his works are full of an adaptive harmony, the suiting of sound to sense. His rhythm is perfect. We have not space for extended illustrations, but the reader will notice this in the lady's song in Comus—the address to

> Sweet Echo, sweeter nymph that liv'st unseen
> Within thy airy shell,
> By slow Meander's margent green!
> . . . .
> Sweet queen of parley, daughter of the sphere,
> So may'st thou be translated to the skies,
> And give resounding grace to all heaven's harmonies.

And again, the description of Chastity, in the same poem, is inimitable in the language:

> So dear to Heaven is saintly Chastity,
> That when a soul is found sincerely so,
> A thousand liveried angels lackey her.

HIS SCHOLARSHIP.—It is unnecessary to state the well-known fact, attested by all his works, of his elegant and versatile scholarship. He was the most learned man in England in his day. If, like J. C. Scaliger, he did not commit Homer to memory in twenty-one days, and the whole of the Greek poets in three months, he had all classical learning literally at his fingers' ends, and his works are absolutely glistening with drops which show that every one has been dipped in that Castalian fountain which, it was fabled, changed the earthly flowers of the mind into immortal jewels.

Nor need we refer to what every one concedes, that a vein of pure but austere morals runs through all his works; but Puritan as he was, his myriad fancy led him into places which Puritanism abjured: the cloisters, with their dim religious light, in *Il Penseroso* — and anon with mirth he cries:

> Come and trip it as you go,
> On the light fantastic toe.

SONNETS. — His sonnets have been variously estimated: they are not as polished as his other poems, but are crystal-like and sententious, abrupt bursts of opinion and feeling in fourteen lines. Their masculine power it was which caused Wordsworth, himself a prince of sonneteers, to say:

> In his hand,
> The thing became a trumpet, whence he blew
> Soul-animating strains . . .

That to his dead wife, whom he saw in a vision; that to Cyriac Skinner on his blindness, and that to the persecuted Waldenses, are the most known and appreciated. That to Skinner is a noble assertion of heart and hope:

> Cyriac, this three-years-day these eyes, though clear
> To outward view, of blemish and of spot,
> Bereft of light, their seeing have forgot:
> Nor to their idle orbs doth sight appear
> Of sun, or moon, or star, throughout the year,
> Or man, or woman. Yet I argue not
> Against Heaven's hand or will, nor bate a jot
> Of heart or hope; but still bear up and steer

Right onward. What supports me, dost thou ask?
The conscience friend to have lost them over-plied
In liberty's defence, my noble task,
Of which all Europe talks from side to side,
This thought might lead me through the world's vain mask
Content, though blind, had I no better guide.

Milton died in 1674, of gout, which had long afflicted him; and he left his name and works to posterity. Posterity has done large but mistaken justice to his fame. Men have not discriminated between his real merits and his faults: all parties have conceded the former, and conspired to conceal the latter. A just statement of both will still establish his great fame on the immutable foundations of truth — a fame, the honest pursuit of which caused him, throughout his long life,

To scorn delights, and live laborious days.

No writer has ever been the subject of more uncritical, ignorant, and senseless panegyric: like Bacon, he is lauded by men who never read his works, and are entirely ignorant of the true foundation of his fame. Nay, more; partisanship becomes very warlike, and we are reminded in this controversy of the Italian gentleman, who fought three duels in maintaining that Ariosto was a better poet than Tasso: in the third he was mortally wounded, and he confessed before dying that he had never read a line of either. A similar logomachy has marked the course of Milton's champions; words like sharp swords have been wielded by ignorance, and have injured the poet's true fame.

He now stands before the world, not only as the greatest English poet, except Shakspeare, but also as the most remarkable example and illustration of the theory we have adopted, that literature is a very vivid and permanent interpreter of contemporary history. To those who ask for a philosophic summary of the age of Charles I. and Cromwell, the answer may be justly given: "Study the works of John Milton, and you will find it."

CHAPTER XX.

COWLEY, BUTLER, AND WALTON.

COWLEY AND MILTON.

IN contrast with Milton, in his own age, both in political tenets and in the character of his poetry, stood Cowley, the poetical champion of the party of king and cavaliers during the civil war. Historically he belongs to two periods — antecedent and consequent — that of the rebellion itself, and that of the Restoration: the latter was a reaction from the former, in which the masses changed their opinions, in which the Puritan leaders were silenced, and in which the constant and consistent Cavaliers had their day of triumph. Both parties, however, modified their views somewhat after the whirlwind of excitement had swept by, and both deprecated the extreme violence of their former actions. This is cleverly set forth in a charming paper of Lord Macaulay, entitled *Cowley and Milton.* It purports to be the report of a pleasant colloquy between the two in the spring of 1665, "set down by a gentleman of the Middle Temple." Their principles are courteously expressed, in a retrospective view of the great rebellion.

COWLEY'S LIFE AND WORKS. — Abraham Cowley, the posthumous son of a grocer, was born in London, in the year 1618. He is said to have been so precocious that he read

Spenser with pleasure when he was twelve years old; and he published a volume of poems, entitled "Poetical Blossoms," before he was fifteen. After a preliminary education at Westminster school, he was entered at Trinity College, Cambridge, in 1636, and while there he published, in 1638, two comedies, one in English, entitled *Love's Riddle,* and one in Latin, *Naufragium Joculare, or, The Merry Shipwreck.*

When the troubles which culminated in the civil war began to convulse England, Cowley, who was a strong adherent of the king, was compelled to leave Cambridge; and we find him, when the war had fairly opened, at Oxford, where he was well received by the Royal party, in 1643. He vindicated the justice of this reception by publishing in that year a satire called *Puritan and Papist.* Upon the retirement of the queen to Paris, he was one of her suite, and as secretary to Viscount St. Albans he conducted the correspondence in cipher between the queen and her unfortunate husband.

He remained abroad during the civil war and the protectorate, returning with Charles II. in 1660. "The Blessed Restoration" he celebrated in an ode with that title, and would seem to have thus established a claim to the king's gratitude and bounty. But he was mistaken. Perhaps this led him to write a comedy, entitled *The Cutter of Coleman Street,* in which he severely censured the license and debaucheries of the court: this made the arch-debauchee, the king himself, cold toward the poet, who at once issued *A Complaint;* but neither satire nor complaint helped him to the desired preferment. He quitted London a disappointed man, and retired to the country, where he died on the 28th of July, 1667.

His poems bear the impress of the age in a remarkable degree. His *Mistress, or, Love Verses,* and his other Anacreontics or paraphrases of Anacreon's odes, were eminently to the taste of the luxurious and immoral court of Charles II. His *Davideis* is an heroic poem on the troubles of King David.

His *Poem on the Late Civil War*, which was not published until 1679, twelve years after his death, is written in the interests of the monarchy.

His varied learning gave a wide range to his pen. In 1661 appeared his *Proposition for the Advancement of Experimental Philosophy*, which was followed in the next year by *Two Books of Plants*, which he increased to six books afterward — devoting two to herbs, two to flowers, and two to trees. If he does not appear in them to be profound in botanical researches, it was justly said by Dr. Johnson that in his mind "botany turned into poetry."

His prose pen was as ready, versatile, and charming as his poetic pencil. He produced discourses or essays on commonplace topics of general interest, such as *myself; the shortness of life; the uncertainty of riches; the danger of procrastination*, etc. These are well written, in easy-flowing language, evincing his poetic nature, and many of them are more truly poetic than his metrical pieces.

HIS FAME. — Cowley had all his good things in his lifetime; he was the most popular poet in England, and is the best illustration of the literary taste of his age. His poetry is like water rippling in the sunlight, brilliant but dazzling and painful: it bewilders with far-fetched and witty conceits: varied but full of art, there is little of nature or real passion to be found even in his amatory verses. He suited the taste of a court which preferred an epigram to a proverb, and a repartee to an apothegm; and, as a consequence, with the growth of a better culture and a better taste, he has steadily declined in favor, so that at the present day he is scarcely read at all. Two authoritative opinions mark the history of this decline: Milton, in his own day, placed him with Spenser and Shakspeare as one of the three greatest English poets; while Pope, not much more than half a century later, asks:

> Who now reads Cowley? If he pleases yet,
> His moral pleases, not his pointed wit.

Still later, Dr. Johnson gives him the credit of having been the first to master the Pindaric ode in English; while Cowper expresses, in his Task, regret that his "splendid wit" should have been

> Entangled in the cobwebs of the schools.

But if he is neglected in the present day as a household poet, he stands prominently forth to the literary student as an historic personage of no mean rank, a type and representative of his age, country, and social conditions.

Samuel Butler.

Butler's Career. — The author of Hudibras, a satirical poem which may as justly be called a comic history of England as any of those written in prose in more modern times, was born in Worcestershire, on the 8th of February, 1612. The son of poor parents, he received his education at a grammar school. Some, who have desired to magnify his learning, have said that he was for a time a student at Cambridge; but the chronicler Aubrey, who knew him well, denies this. He was learned, but this was due to the ardor with which he pursued his studies, when he was clerk to Mr. Jeffreys, an eminent justice of the peace, and as an inmate of the mansion of the Countess of Kent, in whose fine library he was associated with the accomplished Selden.

We next find him domiciled with Sir Samuel Luke, a Presbyterian and a parliamentary soldier, in whose household he saw and noted those characteristics of the Puritans which he afterward ridiculed so severely in his great poem, a poem which he was quietly engaged in writing during the protectorate of Cromwell, in hope of the coming of a day when it could be issued to the world.

This hope was fulfilled by the Restoration. In the new

order he was appointed secretary to the Earl of Carbery, and steward of Ludlow Castle; and he also increased his frugal fortunes by marrying a widow, Mrs. Herbert, whose means, however, were soon lost by bad investments.

HUDIBRAS. — The only work of merit which Butler produced was *Hudibras*. This was published in three parts: the first appeared in 1663, the second in 1664, and the third not until 1678. Even then it was left unfinished; but as the interest in the third part seems to flag, it is probable that the author did not intend to complete it. His death, two years later, however, settled the question.

The general idea of the poem is taken from Don Quixote. As in that immortal work, there are two heroes. Sir Hudibras, corresponding to the Don, is a Presbyterian justice of the peace, whose features are said to have been copied from those of the poet's former employer, Sir Samuel Luke. For this, Butler has been accused of ingratitude, but the nature of their connection does not seem to have been such as to warrant the charge. Ralph the squire, the humble Sancho of the poem, is a cross-grained dogmatic Independent.

These two the poet sends forth, as a knight-errant with a squire, to correct existing abuses of all kinds — political, religious, and scientific. The plot is rambling and disconnected, but the author contrives to go over the whole ground of English history in his inimitable burlesque. Unlike Cervantes, who makes his reader always sympathize with his foolish heroes, Butler brings his knight and squire into supreme contempt; he lashes the two hundred religious sects of the day, and attacks with matchless ridicule all the Puritan positions. The poem is directly historical in its statement of events, tenets, and factions, and in its protracted religious discussions: it is indirectly historical in that it shows how this ridicule of the Puritans, only four years after the death of Cromwell, delighted the merry monarch and his vicious court, and was greatly acceptable to the large majority of the English people. This fact marks the suddenness of the historic change from the influence of Puritanism to that of the restored Stuarts.

Hudibras is written in octosyllabic verse, frequently not rising above doggerel: it is full of verbal "quips and cranks and wanton wiles:" in parts it is eminently epigrammatic, and many of its happiest couplets seem to have been dashed off without effort. Walpole calls Butler "the Hogarth of poetry;" and we know that Hogarth illustrated Hudibras. The comparison is not inapt, but the pictorial element in Hudibras is not its best claim to our praise. This is found in its string of proverbs and maxims elucidating human nature, and set forth in such terse language that we are inclined to use them thus in preference to any other form of expression.

Hudibras is the very prince of *burlesques;* it stands alone of its kind, and still retains its popularity. Although there is much that belongs to the age, and much that is of only local interest, it is still read to find apt quotations, of which not a few have become hackneyed by constant use. With these, pages might be filled; all readers will recognize the following:

He speaks of the knight thus:

On either side he would dispute,
Confute, change hands, and still confute:
. . . .
For rhetoric, he could not ope
His mouth but out there flew a trope.

Again: he refers, in speaking of religious characters, to

Such as do build their faith upon
The holy text of pike and gun,
And prove their doctrine orthodox,
By apostolic blows and knocks;
Compound for sins they are inclined to
By damning those they have no mind to.

Few persons of the present generation have patience to read Hudibras through. Allibone says "it is a work to be studied once and gleaned occasionally." Most are content to glean frequently, and not to study at all.

His Poverty and Death. — Butler lived in great poverty, being neglected by a monarch and a court for whose amusement he had done so much. They laughed at the jester, and let him starve. Indeed, he seems to have had few friends; and this is accounted for quaintly by Aubrey, who says: "Satirical wits disoblige whom they converse with, and consequently make to themselves many enemies, and few friends; and this was his manner and case."

The best known of his works, after Hudibras, is the *Elephant in the Moon*, a satire on the Royal Society.

It is significant of the popularity of Hudibras, that numerous imitations of it have been written from his day to ours.

Butler died on the 25th of September, 1680. Sixty years after, the hand of private friendship erected a monument to him in Westminster Abbey. The friend was John Barber, Lord Mayor of London, whose object is thus stated: "That he who was destitute of all things when alive, might not want a monument when he was dead." Upon the occasion of erecting this, Samuel Wesley wrote:

While Butler, needy wretch, was yet alive,
No generous patron would a dinner give;
See him, when starved to death and turned to dust,
Presented with a monumental bust.
The poet's fate is here in emblem shown,
He asked for bread, and he received a stone.

To his own age he was the prince of jesters; to English literature he has given its best illustration of the burlesque in rhetoric. To the reader of the present day he presents rare historical pictures of his day, of far greater value than his wit or his burlesque.

Izaak Walton.

If men are to be measured by their permanent popularity, Walton deserves an enthusiastic mention in literary annals, not for the greatness of his achievements, but for his having touched a chord in the human heart which still vibrates without hint of cessation wherever English is spoken.

Izaak Walton was born at Stafford, on the 9th of August, 1593. In his earlier life he was a linen-draper, but he had made enough for his frugal wants by his shop to enable him to retire from business in 1643, and then he quietly assumed a position as *pontifex piscatorum.* His fishing-rod was a sceptre which he swayed unrivalled for forty years. He gathered about him in his house and on the borders of fishing streams an admiring and congenial circle, principally of the clergy, who felt it a privilege to honor the retired linen-draper. There must have been a peculiar charm, a personal magnetism about him, which has also imbued his works. His first wife was Rachel Floud, a descendant of the ill-fated Cranmer; and his second was Anne Ken, the half-sister of the saintly Bishop Ken. Whatever may have been his deficiencies of early education, he was so constant and varied a reader that he made amends for these.

The Complete Angler. — His first and most popular work was *The Complete Angler, or, The Contemplative Man's Recreation.* It has been the delight of all sorts of people since, and has gone through more than forty respectable editions in England, besides many in America. Many of these editions are splendidly illustrated and sumptuous. The dialogues are pleasant and natural, and his enthusiasm for the art of angling is quite contagious.

His Lives. — Nor is Walton less esteemed by a smaller but more appreciative circle for his beautiful and finished biographies or *Lives* of Dr. Donne, Wotton, Richard Hooker, George Herbert, and Bishop Robert Sanderson.

Here Walton has bestowed and received fame: the simple but exquisite portraitures of these holy and worthy men have made them familiar to posterity; and they, in turn, by the virtues which Walton's pen has made manifest, have given distinction to the hand which portrayed them. Walton's good life was lengthened out to fourscore and ten. He died at the residence of his son-in-law, the Reverend William Hawkins, prebendary of Winchester Cathedral, in 1683. Bishop Jebb has judiciously said of his *Lives:* "They not only do ample justice to individual piety and learning, but throw a mild and cheerful light upon the manners of an interesting age, as well as upon the venerable features of our mother Church." Less, however, than any of his contemporaries can Walton be appreciated by a sketch of the man: his works must be read, and their spirit imbibed, in order to know his worth.

Other Writers of the Age.

George Wither, born in Hampshire, June 11, 1588, died May 2, 1667: he was a voluminous and versatile writer. His chief work is *The Shepherd's Hunting*, which, with beautiful descriptions of rural life, abounds in those strained efforts at wit and curious conceits, which were acceptable to the age, but which have lost their charm in a more sensible and philosophic age. Wither was a Parliament man, and was imprisoned and ill-treated after the Restoration. He, and most of those who follow, were classed by Dr. Johnson as *metaphysical poets.*

Francis Quarles, 1592–1644: he was a Royalist, but belongs to the literary school of Withers. He is best known by his collection of moral and religious poems, called *Divine Emblems,* which were accompanied with quaint engraved illustrations. These allegories are full of unnatural conceits, and are many of them borrowed from an older source. He was immensely popular as a poet in his own day, and there was truth in the statement of Horace Walpole, that "Milton was forced to wait till the world had done admiring Quarles."

George Herbert, 1593–1632: a man of birth and station, Herbert entered the Church, and as the incumbent of the living at Bemerton, he illustrated in his own piety and devotion "the beauty of holiness." Conscientious and self-denying in his parish work, he found time to give forth those devout breathings which in harmony of expression, fervor of piety, and simplicity of thought, have been a goodly heritage to the Church ever since, while they still retain some of those "poetical surprises" which mark the literary taste of the age. His principal work is *The Temple, or, Sacred Poems and Private Ejaculations.* The short lyrics which form the stones of this temple are upon the rites and ceremonies of the Church and other sacred subjects: many of them are still in great favor, and will always be. In his portraiture of the *Good Parson,* he paints himself. He magnifies the office, and he fulfilled all the requirements he has laid down.

Robert Herrick, 1591–1674: like Herbert, Herrick was a clergyman, but, unlike Herbert, he was not a holy man. He wrote Anacreontic poems, full of wine and love, and appears to us like a reveller masking in a surplice. Being a cavalier in sentiment, he was ejected from his vicarage in 1648, and went to London, where he assumed the lay habit. In 1647 he published *Hesperides,* a collection of small poems of great lyric beauty, Anacreontic, pastoral, and amatory, but containing much that is coarse and indelicate. In 1648 he in part atoned for these by publishing his *Noble Numbers,* a collection of pious pieces, in the beginning of which he asks God's forgiveness for his "unbaptized rhymes," "writ in my wild, unhallowed times." The best comment upon his works may be found in the words of a reviewer: "Herrick trifled in this way solely in compliment to the age; whenever he wrote to please himself, he wrote from the heart to the heart." His *Litanie* is a noble and beautiful penitential petition.

Sir John Suckling, 1609–1641: a writer of love songs. That by which he is most favorably known is his exquisite *Ballad upon a Wedding.* He was a man of versatile talents; an officer in the army of Gustavus Adolphus, and a captain of horse in the army of Charles I. He wrote several plays, of which the best are *Aglaura* and *The Discontented Colonel.* While evidently tinctured by the spirit of the age, he exceeded his contemporaries in the purity of his style and manliness of his expression. His wit is not so forced as theirs.

Edmund Waller, 1605–1687: he was a cousin of John Hampden. By great care and adroitness he seems to have trimmed between the two parties in the civil war, but was suspected by both. His poetry was like himself, artificial and designed to please, but has little depth of sentiment. Like other poets, he praised Cromwell in 1654 in *A Pan-*

egyric, and welcomed Charles II. in 1660, upon *His Majesty's Happy Return*. His greatest benefaction to English poetry was in refining its language and harmonizing its versification. He has all the conceits and strained wit of the metaphysical school.

Sir William Davenant, 1605–1668: he was the son of a vintner, but sometimes claimed to be the natural son of Shakspeare, who was intimate with his father and mother. An ardent Loyalist, he was imprisoned at the beginning of the civil war, but escaped to France. He is best known by his heroic poem *Gondibert*, founded upon the reign of King Aribert of Lombardy, in the seventh century. The French taste which he brought back from his exile, is shown in his own dramas, and in his efforts to restore the theatre at the Restoration. His best plays are the *Cruel Brother* and *The Law against Lovers*. He was knighted by Charles I., and succeeded Ben Jonson as poet laureate. On his monument in Westminster Abbey are these words: "O rare Sir William Davenant."

Charles Cotton, 1630–1687: he was a wit and a poet, and is best known as the friend of Izaak Walton. He made an addition to *Walton's Complete Angler*, which is found in all the later editions. The companion of Walton in his fishing excursions on the river Dove, Cotton addressed many of his poems to his "Adopted Father." He made travesties upon Virgil and Lucian, which are characterized by great licentiousness; and wrote a gossiping and humorous *Voyage to Ireland*.

Henry Vaughan, 1614–1695: he was called the *Silurist*, from his residence in Wales, the country of the Silures. He is favorably known by the *Silex Scintillans, or, Sacred Poems and Private Ejaculations*. With a rigid religious tone, he has all the attempt at rhetorical effect which mark the metaphysical school, but his language is harsher and more rugged. He has more heart than most of his colleagues, and extracts of great terseness and beauty are still made from his poems. He reproves the corruptions of the age, and while acknowledging an indebtedness, he gives us a clue to his inspiration: "The first, that with any effectual success attempted a diversion of this foul and overflowing stream, was that blessed man, Mr. George Herbert, whose holy life and verse gained many pious converts, of whom I am the least."

The Earl of Clarendon, 1608–1674: Edward Hyde, afterward the Earl of Clarendon, played a conspicuous part in the history of England during his life, and also wrote a history of that period, which, although in the interests of the king's party, is an invaluable key to a knowledge of English life during the rebellion and just after the Restoration. A member of parliament in 1640, he rose rapidly in favor with the king, and was knighted in 1643. He left England in charge of the Prince of Wales in 1646, and at once began his History of the Great Rebellion, which was to occupy him for many years before its completion. After the death of Charles I., he was the companion of his son's exile, and often without means for himself and his royal master, he was chancellor of the exchequer. At the Restoration in 1660, Sir Edward Hyde was created Earl of Clarendon, and entered upon the real duties of his office. He retained his place for seven years, but became disagreeable to Charles as a troublesome monitor, and at the same time incurred the hatred of the people. In 1667 he was accused of high treason, and made his escape to France. Neglected by his master, ignored by the French monarch, he wandered about in France, from time to time petitioning his king to permit him to return and die in England, but without success. Seven years of exile, which he reminded the king "was a time prescribed and limited by God himself for the expiation of some of his greatest judgments," passed by, and the ex-chancellor died at Rouen. He had begun his history in exile as the faithful servant of a dethroned prince; he ended it in exile, as the cast-off servant of an ungrateful monarch. As a writer of contemporary history, Clarendon has given us the form and color of the time. The book is in title and handling a Royalist history. Its faults are manifest: first those of partisanship; and secondly, those which spring from his absence, so that much of the work was written without an observant knowledge. His delineation of character is wonderful: the men of the times are more pictorially displayed than in the portraits of Van Dyk. The style is somewhat too pompous, being more that of the orator than of the historian, and containing long and parenthetic periods. Sir Walter Scott says: "His characters may match those of the ancient historians, and one thinks he would know the very men if he were to meet them in society." Macaulay concedes to him a strong sense of moral and religious obligation, a sincere reverence for the laws of his country, and a conscientious regard for the honor and interests of the crown; but adds that "his temper was sour, arrogant, and impatient of opposition." No one can rightly understand the great rebellion without reading Clarendon's history of it.

CHAPTER XXI.

DRYDEN, AND THE RESTORED STUARTS.

THE COURT OF CHARLES II.

THE antithetic literature which takes its coloring from the great rebellion, was now to give place to new forms not immediately connected with it, but incident to the Restoration. Puritanism was now to be oppressed, and the country was to be governed, under a show of constitutional right, more arbitrarily than ever before. The moral rebound, too, was tremendous; the debaucheries of the cavaliers of Charles I. were as nothing in comparison with the lewdness and filth of the court of Charles II. To say that he brought in French fashions and customs, is to do injustice to the French: there never was a viler court in Europe than his own. It is but in accordance with our historical theory that the literature should partake of and represent the new condition of things; and the most remarkable illustrations of this are to be found in the works of Dryden.

It may indeed with truth be said that we have now reached the most absolute of the literary types of English history. There was no great event, political or social, which is not mirrored in his poems; no sentiment or caprice of the age which does not there find expression; no kingly whim which he did not prostitute his great powers to gratify; no change of creed, political or religious, of which he was not the recorder — few indeed, where royal favor was concerned, to which he was not the convert. To review the life of Dryden himself, is therefore to enter into the chronicle and philosophy of the times in which he lived. With this view, we shall dwell at some length upon his character and works.

EARLY LIFE.—Dryden was born on the 10th of August, 1631, and died on the 1st of May, 1700. He lived, therefore, during the reign of Charles I., the interregnum of Parliament, the protectorate of Cromwell, the restoration and reign of Charles II., and the reign of James II.; he saw and suffered from the accession of William and Mary — a wonderful and varied volume in English history. And of all these Dryden was, more than any other man, the literary type. He was of a good family, and was educated at Westminster and Cambridge, where he gave early proofs of his literary talents.

His father, a zealous Presbyterian, had reared his children in his own tenets; we are not therefore astonished to find that his earliest poetical efforts are in accordance with the political conditions of the day. He settled in London, under the protection of his kinsman, Sir Gilbert Pickering, who was afterward one of the king's judges in 1649, and one of the council of eight who controlled the kingdom after Charles lost his head. As secretary to Sir Gilbert, young Dryden learned to scan the political horizon, and to aspire to preferment.

CROMWELL'S DEATH, AND DRYDEN'S MONODY.—But those who had depended upon Cromwell, forgot that he was not England, and that his breath was in his nostrils. The time of his departure was at hand. He had been offered the crown (April 9, 1656,) by a subservient parliament, and wanted it; but his friends and family opposed his taking it;

and the officers of the army, influenced by Pride, sent such a petition against it, that he felt obliged to refuse it. After months of mental anxiety and nervous torture — fearing assassination, keeping arms under his pillow, never sleeping above three nights together in the same chamber, disappointed that even after all his achievements, and with all his cunning efforts, he had been unable to put on the crown, and to be numbered among the English sovereigns — Cromwell died in 1658, leaving his title as Lord Protector to his son Richard, a weak and indolent man, who, after seven months' rule, fled the kingdom at the Restoration, to return after a generation had passed away, a very old man, to die in his native land. The people of Hertfordshire knew Richard Cromwell as the excellent and benevolent Mr. Clarke.

Very soon after the death of Oliver Cromwell, Dryden, not yet foreseeing the Restoration, presented his tribute to the Commonwealth, in the shape of "Heroic Stanzas on the Death of Oliver Cromwell; written after his funeral." A few stanzas will show his political principles, and are in strange contrast with what was soon to follow:

How shall I then begin, or where conclude,
  To draw a fame so truly circular?
For, in a round, what order can be showed,
  Where all the parts so equal perfect are?

He made us freemen of the continent,
  Whom nature did like captives treat before;
To nobler preys the English lion sent,
  And taught him first in Belgian walks to roar.

His ashes in a peaceful urn shall rest;
  His name a great example stands, to show
How strangely high endeavors may be blest,
  Where piety and valor jointly go.

THE RESTORATION. — Cromwell died in September: early in the next year these stanzas were written. One year later was the witness of a great event, which stirred England to its very depths, because it gave vent to sentiments for some time past cherished but concealed. The Long Parliament was dissolved on the 10th of March, 1660. The new parliament meets April 25th; it is almost entirely of Royalist opinions; it receives Sir John Granville, the king's messenger, with loud acclamations; the old lords come forth once more in velvet, ermine, and lawn. It is proclaimed that General Monk, the representative of the army, soon to be Duke of Albemarle, has gone from St. Albans to Dover,

> To welcome home again discarded faith.

The strong are as tow, and the maker as a spark. From the house of every citizen, lately vocal with the praises of the Protector, issues a subject ready to welcome his king with the most enthusiastic loyalty.

Royal proclamations follow each other in rapid succession: at length the eventful day has come — the 29th of May, 1660. All the bells of London are ringing their merriest chimes; the streets are thronged with citizens in holiday attire; the guilds of work and trade are out in their uniforms; the army, late the organ of Cromwell, is drawn up on Black Heath, and is cracking its myriad throat with cheers. In the words of Master Roger Wildrake, "There were bonfires flaming, music playing, rumps roasting, healths drinking; London in a blaze of light from the Strand to Rotherhithe." At length the sound of herald trumpets is heard; the king is coming; a cry bursts forth which the London echoes have almost forgotten: "God save the king! The king enjoys his own again!"

It seems to the dispassionate reader almost incredible that the English people, who shed his father's blood, who rallied round the Parliament, and were fulsome in their praises of the Protector, should thus suddenly change; but, allowing for "the madness of the people," we look for strength and consistency to the men of learning and letters. We feel sure that he who sang his eulogy of Cromwell dead, can have now no lyric burst for the returning Stuart. We are disappointed.

DRYDEN'S TRIBUTE.—The first poetic garland thrown at the feet of the restored king was Dryden's *Astræa Redux*, a poem on *The happy restoration of his sacred majesty Charles II.* To give it classic force, he quotes from the Pollio as a text,

> Jam redit et virgo, redeunt saturnia regna;

thus hailing the saturnian times of James I. and Charles I. A few lines of the poem complete the curious contrast:

> While our cross stars deny us Charles his bed,
> Whom our first flames and virgin love did wed,
> For his long absence church and state did groan;
> Madness the pulpit, faction seized the throne.
> . . . .
> How great were then our Charles his woes, who thus
> Was forced to suffer for himself and us.
> . . . .
> Oh happy prince whom Heaven hath taught the way,
> By paying vows to have more vows to pay:
> Oh happy age! oh, times like those alone
> By Fate reserved for great Augustus' throne,
> When the joint growth of arts and arms foreshow
> The world a monarch, and that monarch you!

The contrast assumes a clearer significance, if we remember that the real time which elapsed between the publications of these two poems was less than two years.

This is greatly to Dryden's shame, as it is to Waller's, who did the same thing; but it must be clearly pointed out that in this the poets were really a type of all England, for whose suffrages they wrote thus. From this time the career of Dryden was intimately associated with that of the restored king. He wrote an ode for the coronation in 1661, and a poetical tribute to Clarendon, the Lord High Chancellor, the king's better self.

To Dryden, as a writer of plays, we shall recur in a later chapter, when the other dramatists of the age will be considered.

A concurrence of unusual events in 1665, brought forth the next year the "Annus Mirabilis," or *Wonderful Year*, in which these events are recorded with the minuteness of a chronicle. This is indeed its chief value; for, praised as it was at the time, it does not so well bear the analysis of modern criticism.

ANNUS MIRABILIS.—It describes the great naval battle with the Dutch; the fire of London; and the ravages of the plague. The detail with which these are described, and the frequent felicity of expression, are the chief charm of the poem. In the refreshingly simple diary of Pepy's, we find this jotting under date of 3d February, 1666–7: "*Annus Mirabilis.* I am very well pleased this night with reading a poem I brought home with me last night from Westminster Hall, of Dryden's, upon the present war: a very good poem."

Dryden's subserviency, aided by the power of his pen, gained its reward. In 1668, on the death of Sir William Davenant, he was appointed Laureate, and historiographer to the king, with an annual salary of £200. He soon became the most famous literary man in England. Milton, the Puritan, was producing his wonderful visions in darkened retirement, while at court, or in the seat of honor on the stage, or in his sacred chair at Will's Coffee-house in Covent Garden (near the fire-place in winter, and carried into the balcony in summer), "Glorious John" was the observed of all observers. Of Will's Coffee-house, Congreve says, in *Love for Love*, "Oh, confound that Will's Coffee-house; it has ruined more young men than the Royal Oak Lottery:" this speaks at once of the fashion and social license of the time.

Charles II. was happy to have so fluent a pen, to lampoon

or satirize his enemies, or to make indecent comedies for his amusement; while Dryden's aim seems to have been scarcely higher than preferment at court and honored contemporary notoriety for his genius. But if the great majority lauded and flattered him, he was not without his share in those quarrels of authors, which were carried on at that day not only with goose-quills, but with swords and bludgeons. It is recorded that he was once waylaid by the hired ruffians of the Earl of Rochester, and beaten almost to death: these broils generally had a political as well as a social significance. In his quarrels with the literary men, he used the shafts of satire. His contest with Thomas Shadwell has been preserved in his satire called McFlecknoe. Flecknoe was an Irish priest who wrote dull plays; and in this poem Dryden proposes Shadwell as his successor on the throne of dulness. It was the model or suggester of Pope's *Dunciad;* but the model is by no means equal to the copy.

Absalom and Achitophel. — Nothing which he had yet written is so true an index to the political history as his "Absalom and Achitophel," which he published in 1681. The history may be given in few words. Charles II. had a natural son by an obscure woman named Lucy Walters. This boy had been created Duke of Monmouth. He was put forward by the designing Earl of Shaftesbury as the head of a faction, and as a rival to the Duke of York. To ruin the Duke was their first object; and this they attempted by inflaming the people against his religion, which was Roman Catholic. If they could thus have him and his heirs put out of the succession to the throne, Monmouth might be named heir apparent; and Shaftesbury hoped to be the power behind the throne.

Monmouth was weak, handsome, and vain, and was in truth a puppet in wicked hands; he was engaged in the Rye-house plot, and schemed not only against his uncle, but against the person of his father himself. To satirize and expose these plots and plotters, Dryden (at the instance of the king, it is said,) wrote *Absalom and Achitophel,* in which are introduced, under Scripture names, many of the principal political characters of the day, from the king down to Titus Oates. The number of the names is 61. Charles is, of course, David, and Monmouth, the wayward son, is Absalom. Shaftesbury is Achitophel, and Dr. Oates figures as Corah. The Ethnic plot is the popish plot, and Gath is that land of exile where Charles so long resided. Strong in his praise of David, the poet is discreet and delicate in his handling of Absalom; his instinct is as acute as that of Falstaff: "Beware! instinct, the lion will not touch a true prince," or touch him so gently that the lion at least will not suffer. Thus, Monmouth is represented as

> Half loath, and half consenting to the ill,
> For royal blood within him struggled still;
> He thus replied: "And what pretence have I
> To take up arms for public liberty?
> My father governs with unquestioned right,
> The faith's defender and mankind's delight;
> Good, gracious, just, observant of the laws,
> And heaven by wonders has espoused his cause."

But he may, and does, roundly rate Achitophel, who tempts with satanic seductions, and proves to the youth, from the Bible, his right to the succession, peaceably or forcibly obtained. Among those who conspired with Monmouth were honest hearts seeking for the welfare of the realm. Chief of these were Lord Russel and Sidney, of whom the latter was in favor of a commonwealth; and the former, only sought the exclusion of the Roman Catholic Duke of York, and the redress of grievances, but not the assassination or deposition of the king. Both fell on the scaffold; but they have both been considered martyrs in the cause of civil liberty.

And here we must pause to say that in the literary structure, language, and rhythm of the poem, Dryden had made a great step toward that mastery of the rhymed pentameter couplet, which is one of his greatest claims to distinction.

Death of Charles.—At length, in 1685, Charles II., after a sudden and short illness, was gathered to his fathers. His life had been such that England could not mourn: he had prostituted female honor, and almost destroyed political virtue; sold English territory and influence to France for beautiful strumpets; and at the last had been received, on his death-bed, into the Roman Catholic Church, while nominally the supreme head of the Anglican communion. England cannot mourn, but Dryden tortures language into crocodile tears in his *Threnodia Augustalis, sacred to the happy memory of King Charles II.* A few lines will exhibit at once the false statements and the absolute want of a spark of sorrow—dead, inanimate words, words, words!

> Thus long my grief has kept me drunk:
> Sure there 's a lethargy in mighty woe;
> Tears stand congealed, and cannot flow.
> . . . .
> Tears for a stroke foreseen, afford relief;
> But unprovided for a sudden blow,
> Like Niobe, we marble grow,
> And petrify with grief!

Dryden's Conversion.—The Duke of York succeeded as James II.: he was an open and bigoted Roman Catholic, who at once blazoned forth the death-bed conversion of his brother; and who from the first only limited his hopes to the complete restoration of the realm to popery. Dryden's course was at once taken; but his instinct was at fault, as but three short years were to show. He gave in his adhesion to the new king's creed; he who had been Puritan with the commonwealth, and churchman with the Restoration, became Roman Catholic with the accession of a popish king. He had written the *Religio Laici* to defend the tenets of the Church of England against the attacks of papists and dissenters; and he now, to leave the world in no doubt as to his reasons and his honesty, published a poem entitled the *Hind and Panther*, which might in his earlier phraseology have been justly styled "The Christian experience of pious John Dryden." It seems a shameless act, but it is one exponent of the loyalty of that day. There are some critics who believe him to have been sincere, and who insist that such a man "is not to be sullied by suspicion that rests on what after all might prove a fortuitous coincidence." But such frequent changes with the government — with a reward for each change — tax too far even that charity which "thinketh no evil." Dryden's pen was eagerly welcomed by the Roman Catholics. He began to write at once in their interest, and thus to further his own. Dr. Johnson says: "That conversion will always be suspected which apparently concerns with interest. He that never finds his error till it hinders his progress toward wealth or honor, will not be thought to love truth only for herself."

In this long poem of 2,000 lines, we have the arguments which conducted the poet to this change. The different beasts represent the different churches and sects. The Church of Rome is thus represented:

> A milk-white hind, immortal and unchanged,
> Fed on the lawns, and in the forest ranged;
> Without unspotted, innocent within,
> She feared no danger, for she knew no sin.

The other beasts were united to destroy her; but she could "venture to drink with them at the common watering-place under the protection of her friend the kingly lion."

The Panther is the Church of England:

> The Panther, sure the noblest, next the hind,
> And fairest creature of the spotted kind;

Oh, could her inborn stains be washed away,
She were too good to be a beast of prey!

Then he introduces —

The *Bloody Bear*, an *Independent* beast; the *Quaking Hare*, for the *Quakers;* the *Bristled Baptist Boar.*

In this fable, quite in the style of Æsop, we find the Dame, *i.e.*, the Hind, entering into the subtle points of theology, and trying to prove her position. The poem, as might be supposed, was well received, and perhaps converted a few to the monarch's faith; for who were able yet to foresee that the monarch would so abuse his power, as to be driven away from his throne amid the execrations of his subjects.

The harmony of Dryden and the power of James could control progressive England no longer. Like one man, the nation rose and uttered a mighty cry to William of Orange. James, trembling, flies hither and thither, and at length, fearing the fate of his father, he deserts his throne; the commons call this desertion abdication, and they give the throne to his nephew William and his daughter Mary. Such was the end of the restored Stuarts; and we can have no regret that it is: whatever sympathy we may have had with the sufferings of Charles I., —and the English nation shared it, as is proved by the restoration of his son, — we can have none with his successors: they threw away their chances; they dissipated the most enthusiastic loyalty; they squandered opportunities; and had no enemies, even the bitterest, who were more fatal than themselves. And now it was manifest that Dryden's day was over. Nor does he shrink from his fate. He neither sings a Godspeeding ode to the runaway king, nor a salutatory to the new comers.

Dryden's Fall. — Stripped of his laureate-wreath and all his emoluments, he does not sit down to fold his hands and repine. Sixty years of age, he girds up his loins to work manfully for his living. He translates from the classics; he renders Chaucer into modern English: in 1690 he produced a play entitled Don Sebastian, which has been considered his dramatic master-piece, and, as if to inform the world that age had not dimmed the fire of his genius, he takes as his caption,—

> . . . . nec tarda senectus
> Debilitat vires animi, mutat que vigorem.

This latter part of his life claims a true sympathy, because he is every inch a man.

It must not be forgotten that Dryden presented Chaucer to England anew, after centuries of neglect, almost oblivion; for which the world owes him a debt of gratitude. This he did by modernizing several of the Canterbury Tales, and thus leading English scholars to seek the beauties and instructions of the original. The versions themselves are by no means well executed, it must be said. He has lost the musical words and fresh diction of the original, as a single comparison between the two will clearly show. Perhaps there is no finer description of morning than is contained in these lines of Chaucer:

> The besy lark, the messager of day,
> Saleweth in hir song the morwe gray;
> And firy Phebus riseth up so bright
> That all the orient laugheth of the sight.

How expressive the words: the *busy* lark; the sun rising like a strong man; *all the orient* laughing. The following version by Dryden, loses at once the freshness of idea and the felicity of phrase:

> The morning lark, the messenger of day,
> Saluted in her song the morning gray;
> And soon the sun arose with beams so bright
> That all the horizon laughed to see the joyous sight.

The student will find this only one of many illustrations of the manner in which Dryden has belittled Chaucer in his versions.

ODES. — Dryden has been regarded as the first who used the heroic couplet with entire mastery. In his hands it is bold and sometimes rugged, but always powerful and handled with great ease: he fashioned it for Pope to polish. Of this, his larger poems are full of proof. But there is another verse, of irregular rhythm, in which he was even more successful, — lyric poetry as found in the irregular ode, varying from the short line to the "Alexandrine dragging its slow length along;" the staccato of a harp ending in a lengthened flow of melody.

> Thus long ago,
> Ere heaving billows learned to blow,
> While organs yet were mute;
> Timotheus to his breathing flute
> And sounding lyre
> Could swell the soul to rage, or kindle soft desire.

When he became a Roman Catholic, St. Cecilia, "inventress of the vocal frame," became his chief devotion; and the *Song on St. Cecilia's Day* and *An Ode to St. Cecilia*, are the principal illustrations of this new power.

Gray, who was remarkable for his own lyric power, told Dr. Beattie that if there were any excellence in his own numbers, he had learned it wholly from Dryden.

The *Ode on St. Cecilia's Day*, also entitled "*Alexander's Feast*," in which he portrays the power of music in inspiring that famous monarch to love, pity, and war, has to the scholar the perfect excellence of the best Greek lyric. It ends with a tribute to St. Cecilia.

> At last divine Cecilia came,
> Inventress of the vocal frame:
> Now let Timotheus yield the prize,
> Or both divide the crown.

He raised a mortal to the skies;
She drew an angel down.

Dryden's prose, principally in the form of prefaces and dedications, has been admired by all critics; and one of the greatest has said, that if he had turned his attention entirely in that direction, he would have been *facile princeps* among the prose writers of his day. He has, in general terms, the merit of being the greatest refiner of the English language, and of having given system and strength to English poetry above any writer up to his day; but more than all, his works are a transcript of English history — political, religious, and social — as valuable as those of any professed historian. Dryden married Lady Elizabeth Howard, the daughter of an earl, who, it is said, was not a congenial companion, and who afterwards became insane. He died from a gangrene in the foot. He declared that he died in the profession of the Roman Catholic faith; which raises a new doubt as to his sincerity in the change. Near the monument of old father Chaucer, in Westminster, is one erected, by the Duke of Buckingham, to Dryden. It merely bears name and date, as his life and works were supposed to need no eulogy.

CHAPTER XXII.

THE RELIGIOUS LITERATURE OF THE GREAT REBELLION AND OF THE RESTORATION.

The English Divines.
Hall.
Chillingworth.
Taylor.
Fuller.
Sir T. Browne.
Baxter.
Fox.
Bunyan.
South.
Other Writers.

THE ENGLISH DIVINES.

HAVING come down, in the course of English Literature, to the reign of William and Mary, we must look back for a brief space to consider the religious polemics which grew out of the national troubles and vicissitudes. We shall endeavor to classify the principal authors under this head from the days of Milton to the time when the Protestant succession was established on the English throne.

The Established Church had its learned doctors before the civil war, many of whom contributed to the literature; but when the contest between king and parliament became imminent, and during the progress of the quarrel, these became controversialists,—most of them on the side of the unfortunate but misguided monarch,—and suffered with his declining fortunes.

To go over the whole range of theological literature in this extended period, would be to study the history of the times from a theological point of view. Our space will only permit a brief notice of the principal writers.

HALL.—First among these was Joseph Hall, who was born in 1574. He was educated at Cambridge, and was appointed to the See of Exeter in 1624, and transferred to that of Norwich in 1641, the year before Charles I. ascended the throne. The scope of his writings was quite extensive. As a theological writer, he is known by his numerous sermons, his *Episcopacy by Divine Right Asserted,* his *Christian Meditations,* and various commentaries and *Contemplations* upon the Scriptures. He was also a poet and a satirist, and excelled in this field. His *Satires — Virgidemiarium* — were published at the early age of twenty-three; but they are highly praised by the critics, who rank him also, for eloquence and learning, with Jeremy Taylor. He suffered for his attachment to the king's cause, was driven from his see, and spent the last portion of his life in retirement and poverty. He died in 1656.

CHILLINGWORTH. — The next in chronological order is William Chillingworth, who was born in 1602, and is principally known as the champion of Protestantism against Rome and Roman innovations. While a student at Oxford, he had been won over to the Roman Catholic Church by John Perse, a famous Jesuit; and he went at once to pursue his studies in the Jesuit college at Douay. He was so notable for his acuteness and industry, that every effort was made to bring him back. Archbishop Laud, his god-father, was able to convince him of his errors, and in two months he returned to England. A short time after this he left the Roman Catholics, and became tenfold more a Protestant than before. He entered into controversies with his former friends the Jesuits, and in answer to one of their treatises entitled, *Mercy and Truth, or Charity maintained by the Roman Catholics,* he wrote his most famous work, *The Religion of Protestants a Safe Way to Salvation.* Chillingworth was a warm adherent of Charles I.; and was captured by the parliamentary forces in 1643. He died the next year. His double change of faith gave him the full range of the controversial field; and, in addition to this knowledge, the clearness of his language and the perspicuity of his logic gave great effect to his writings. Tillotson calls him "the glory of this age and nation."

TAYLOR. — One of the greatest names in the annals of the English Church and of English literature is that of Jeremy Taylor. He was the son of a barber, and was born at Cambridge in 1613. A remarkably clever youth, he was educated at Cambridge, and soon owed his preferment to his talents, eloquence, and learning. An adherent of the king, he was appointed chaplain in the royal army, and was several times imprisoned. When the king's cause went down, and during the protectorate of Cromwell, he retired to Wales, where he kept a school, and was also chaplain to the Earl of Carberry. The vicissitudes of fortune compelled him to leave for a while this retreat, and he became a teacher in Ireland. The restoration of Charles II. gave him rest and preferment: he was made Bishop of Down and Connor. Taylor is now principally known for his learned, quaint, and eloquent discourses, which are still read. A man of liberal feelings and opinions, he wrote on "The liberty of prophesying, showing the unreasonableness of prescribing to other men's faith, and the iniquity of persecuting different opinions:" the title itself being a very liberal discourse. He upholds the Ritual in *An Apology for fixed and set Forms of Worship.* In this he considers the divine precepts to be contained within narrow limits, and that beyond this everything is a matter of dispute, so that we cannot unconditionally condemn the opinions of others.

His *Great Exemplar of Sanctity and Holy Life,* his *Rule and Exercises of Holy Living and of Holy Dying,* and his *Golden Grove,* are devotional works, well known to modern Christians of all denominations. He has been praised alike by Roman Catholic divines and many Protestant Christians not of the Anglican Church. There is in all his writings a splendor of imagery, combined with harmony of style, and wonderful variety, readiness, and accuracy of scholarship. His quotations from the whole range of classic authors would furnish the Greek and Latin armory of any modern writer. What Shakspeare is in the Drama, Spenser in the Allegory, and Milton in the religious Epic, Taylor may claim to be in the field of purely religious literature. He died at Lisburn, in 1667.

FULLER. — More quaint and eccentric than the writers just mentioned, but a rare representative of his age, stands Thomas Fuller. He was born in 1608; at the early age of twelve, he entered Cambridge, and, after completing his education, took orders. In 1631, he was appointed prebendary of Salisbury. Thence he removed to London in 1641, when the civil war was about to open. When the king left London, in 1642, Fuller preached a sermon in his favor, to the great indignation of the opposite party. Soon after, he was appointed to a chaplaincy in the royal army, and not only preached to the soldiers, but urged them forward in battle. In 1646 he returned to London, where he was permitted to preach, under *surveillance*, however. He seems to have succeeded in keeping out of trouble until the Restoration, when he was restored to his prebend. He did not enjoy it long, as he died in the next year, 1661. His writings are very numerous, and some of them are still read. Among these are *Good Thoughts in Bad Times, Good Thoughts in Worse Times,* and *Mixt Contemplations in Better Times.* The *bad* and *worse* times mark the progress of the civil war: the *better* times he finds in the Restoration.

One of his most valuable works is *The Church History of Britain, from the birth of Christ to* 1648, in 11 books. Criticized as it has been for its puns and quibbles and its occasional caricatures, it contains rare descriptions and very vivid stories of the important ecclesiastical eras in England.

Another book containing important information is his

History of the Worthies of England, a posthumous work, published by his son the year after his death. It contains accounts of eminent Englishmen in different countries; and while there are many errors which he would perhaps have corrected, it is full of odd and interesting information not to be found collated in any other book.

Representing and chronicling the age as he does, he has perhaps more individuality than any writer of his time, and this gives a special interest to his works.

SIR THOMAS BROWNE. — Classed among theological writers, but not a clergyman, Sir Thomas Browne is noted for the peculiarity of his subjects, and his diction. He was born in 1605, and was educated at Oxford. He studied medicine, and became a practising physician. He travelled on the continent, and returning to England in 1633, he began to write his most important work, *Religio Medici*, at once a transcript of his own life and a manifesto of what the religion of a physician should be. It was kept in manuscript for some time, but was published without his knowledge in 1642. He then revised the work, and published several editions himself. No description of the treatise can give the reader a just idea of it; it requires perusal. The criticism of Dr. Johnson is terse and just: it is remarkable, he says, for "the novelty of paradoxes, the dignity of sentiment, the quick succession of images, the multitude of abstruse allusions, the subtilty of disquisition, and the strength of language." As the portraiture of an inner life, it is admirable; and the accusation of heterodoxy brought against him on account of a few careless passages is unjust.

Among his other works are *Essays on Vulgar Errors* (*Pseudoxia Epidemica*), and *Hydriotaphica* or *Urne burial;* the latter suggested by the exhumation of some sepulchral remains in Norfolk, which led him to treat with great learning of the funeral rites of all nations. To this he afterwards added *The*

Garden of Cyrus, or The Quincunxial Lozenge, in which, in the language of Coleridge, he finds quincunxes "in heaven above, in the earth below, in the mind of man, in tones, optic nerves, in the roots of trees, in leaves, in everything." He died in 1682.

Numerous sects, all finding doctrine and forms in the Bible, were the issue of the religious and political controversies of the day. Without entering into a consideration or even an enumeration of these, we now mention a few of the principal names among them.

RICHARD BAXTER.—Among the most devout, independent, and popular of the religious writers of the day, Richard Baxter occupies a high rank. He was born in 1615, and was ordained a clergyman in 1638. In the civil troubles he desired to remain neutral, and he opposed Cromwell when he was made Protector. In 1662 he left the Church, and was soon the subject of persecution: he was always the champion of toleration. In prison, poor, hunted about from place to place, he was a martyr in spirit. During his great earthly troubles he was solaced by a vision, which he embodied in his popular work, *The Saints' Everlasting Rest;* and he wrote with great fervor *A Call to the Unconverted.* He was a very voluminous writer; the brutal Judge Jeffries, before whom he appeared for trial, called him "an old knave, who had written books enough to load a cart." He wrote a paraphrase of the New Testament, and numerous discourses. Dr. Johnson advised Boswell, when speaking of Baxter's works: "Read any of them; they are all good." He continued preaching until the close of his life, and died peacefully in 1691.

GEORGE FOX.—The founder of the Society of Friends was born in 1624, in an humble condition of life, and at an early age was apprenticed to a shoemaker and grazier. Uneducated and unknown, he considered himself as the subject of special religious providence, and at length as supernaturally called of God. Suddenly abandoning his servile occupation, he came out in 1647, at the age of twenty-three, as the founder of a new sect; an itinerant preacher, he rebuked the multitudes which he assembled by his fervent words. Much of his success was due to his earnestness and self-abnegation. He preached in all parts of England, and visited the American colonies. The name Quaker is said to have been applied to this sect in 1650, when Fox, arraigned before Judge Bennet, told him to "tremble at the word of the Lord." The establishment of this sect by such a man is one of the strongest illustrations of the eager religious inquiry of the age.

The works of Fox are a very valuable *Journal of his Life and Travels; Letters and Testimonies; Gospel Truth Demonstrated*,—all of which form the best statement of the origin and tenets of his sect. Fox was a solemn, reverent, absorbed man; a great reader and fluent expounder of the Scriptures, but fanatical and superstitious; a believer in witchcraft, and in his power to detect witches. The sect which he founded, and which has played so respectable a part in later history, is far more important than the founder himself. He died in London in 1690.

William Penn.—The fame of Fox in America has been eclipsed by that of his chief convert William Penn. In an historical or biographical work, the life of Penn would demand extended mention; but his name is introduced here only as one of the theological writers of the day. He was born in 1644, and while a student at Oxford was converted to the Friends' doctrine by the preaching of Thomas Loe, a colleague of George Fox. The son of Admiral Sir William Penn, he was the ward of James II., and afterwards Lord Proprietary and founder of Pennsylvania. Persecuted for his tenets, he was frequently imprisoned for his preaching and writings. In 1668 he wrote *Truth Exalted* and *The Sandy*

Foundation, and when imprisoned for these, he wrote in jail his most famous work, *No Cross, no Crown.*

After the expulsion of James II., Penn was repeatedly tried and acquitted for alleged attempts to aid the king in recovering his throne. The malignity of Lord Macaulay has reproduced the charges, but reversed, most unjustly, the acquittals. His record occupies a large space in American history, and he is reverenced for having established a great colony on the basis of brotherly love. Poor and infirm, he died in 1718.

ROBERT BARCLAY, who was born in 1648, is only mentioned in this connection on account of his Latin apology for the Quakers, written in 1676, and translated since into English.

JOHN BUNYAN.—Among the curious religious outcroppings of the civil war, none is more striking and singular than John Bunyan. He produced a work of a decidedly polemical character, setting forth his peculiar doctrines, and—a remarkable feature in the course of English literature—a story so interesting and vivid that it has met with universal perusal and admiration. It is at the same time an allegory which has not its equal in the language. Rhetoricians must always mention the Pilgrim's Progress as the most splendid example of the allegory.

Bunyan was born in Elston, Bedfordshire, in 1628. The son of a tinker, his childhood and early manhood were idle and vicious. A sudden and sharp rebuke from a woman not much better than himself, for his blasphemy, set him to thinking, and he soon became a changed man. In 1653 he joined the Baptists, and soon, without preparation, began to preach. For this he was thrown into jail, where he remained for more than twelve years. It was during this period that, with no other books than the Bible and Fox's Book of Martyrs, he excogitated his allegory. In 1672 he was released through the influence of Barlow, Bishop of Lincoln. He immediately began to preach, and continued to do so until 1688, when he died from a fever brought on by exposure.

In his first work, *Grace Abounding to the Chief of Sinners*, he gives us his own experience,—fearful dreams of early childhood, his sins and warnings in the parliamentary army, with divers temptations, falls, and struggles.

Of his great work, *The Pilgrim's Progress*, it is hardly necessary to speak at length. The story of the Pilgrim, Christian, is known to all English readers, large and little; how he left the City of Destruction, and journeyed towards the Celestial City; of his thrilling adventures; of the men and things that retarded his progress, and of those who helped him forward. No one has ever discoursed with such vivid description and touching pathos of the Land of Beulah, the Delectable Mountains, the Christian's inward rapture at the glimpse of the Celestial City, and his faith-sustaining descent into the Valley of the Shadow of Death! As a work of art, it is inimitable; as a book of religious instruction, it is more to be admired for sentiment than for logic; its influence upon children is rather that of a high-wrought romance than of godly precept. It is a curious reproduction, with a slight difference in cast, of the morality play of an earlier time. Mercy, Piety, Christian, Hopeful, Greatheart, Faithful, are representatives of Christian graces; and, as in the morality, the Prince of Darkness figures as Apollyon.

Bunyan also wrote *The Holy War*, an allegory, which describes the contest between Immanuel and Diabolus for the conquest of the city of Mansoul. This does not by any means share the popularity of *The Pilgrim's Progress*. The language of all his works is common and idiomatic, but precise and strong: it is the vigorous English of an unpretending man, without the graces of the schools, but expressing his meaning with remarkable clearness. Like Milton's Paradise Lost, Bunyan's allegory has been improperly placed by many persons on a par with the Bible as a body of Christian doctrine, and for instruction in righteousness.

ROBERT SOUTH.— This eccentric clergyman was born in 1633. While king's scholar at Dr. Busby's school in London, he led the devotions on the day of King Charles' execution, and prayed for his majesty by name. At first a Puritan, he became a churchman, and took orders. He was learned and eloquent; but his sermons, which were greatly admired at the time, contain many oddities, forced conceits, and singular anti-climaxes, which gained for him the appellation of the witty churchman.

He is accused of having been too subservient to Charles II.; and he also is considered as displaying not a little vindictiveness in his attacks on his former colleagues the Puritans. He is only known to this age by his sermons, which are still published and read.

OTHER THEOLOGICAL WRITERS.

Isaac Barrow, 1630–1677: a man of varied learning, a traveller in the East, and an oriental scholar. He was appointed Professor of Greek at Cambridge, and also lectured on Mathematics. He was a profound thinker and a weighty writer, principally known by his courses of sermons on the Decalogue, the Creed, and the Sacraments.

Edward Stillingfleet, 1635–1699: a clergyman of the Church of England, he was appointed Bishop of Worcester. Many of his sermons have been published. Among his treatises is one entitled, *Irenicum, a Weapon-Salve for the Church's Wounds, or the Divine Right of Particular Forms of Church Government Discussed and Examined.* "The argument," says Bishop Burnet, "was managed with so much learning and skill that none of either side ever undertook to answer it." He also wrote *Origines Sacræ, or a Rational Account of the Christian Faith*, and various treatises in favor of Protestantism and against the Church of Rome.

William Sherlock, 1678–1761: he was Dean of St. Paul's, and a writer of numerous doctrinal discourses, among which are those on *The Trinity*, and on *Death and the Future Judgment.* His son, Thomas

Sherlock, D.D., born 1678, was also a distinguished theological writer.

Gilbert Burnet, 1643–1715: he was very much of a politician, and played a prominent part in the Revolution. He was made Bishop of Salisbury in 1689. He is principally known by his *History of the Reformation*, written in the Protestant interest, and by his greater work, the *History of my Own Times*. Not without a decided bias, this latter work is specially valuable as the narration of an eye-witness. The history has been variously criticized for prejudice and inaccuracy; but it fills what would otherwise have been a great vacuum in English historical literature.

John Locke, 1632–1704. In a history of philosophy, the name of this distinguished philosopher would occupy a prominent place, and his works would require extended notice. But it is not amiss to introduce him briefly in this connection, because his works all have an ethical significance. He was educated as a physician, and occupied several official positions, in which he suffered from the vicissitudes of political fortune, being once obliged to retreat from persecution to Holland. His *Letters on Toleration* is a noble effort to secure the freedom of conscience: his *Treatises on Civil Government* were specially designed to refute Sir John Filmer's *Patriarcha*, and to overthrow the principle of the *Jus Divinum*. His greatest work is an *Essay on the Human Understanding*. This marks an era in English thought, and has done much to invite attention to the subject of intellectual philosophy. He derives our ideas from the two sources, *sensation* and *reflection;* and although many of his views have been superseded by the investigations of later philosophers, it is due to him in some degree that their inquiries have been possible.

Diarists and Antiquarians.

John Evelyn, 1620–1705. Among the unintentional historians of England, none are of more value than those who have left detailed and gossiping diaries of the times in which they lived: among these Evelyn occupies a prominent place. He was a gentleman of education and position, who, after the study of law, travelled extensively, and resided several years in France. He had varied accomplishments. His *Sylva* is a discourse on forest trees and on the propagation of timber in his majesty's dominions. To this he afterwards added *Pomona*, or a treatise on fruit trees. He was also the author of an essay on *A Parallel of the Ancient Architecture with the Modern*. But the work by which he is now best known is his *Diary* from 1641 to 1705; it is a necessary companion to the study of the history of that period; and has been largely consulted by modern writers in making up the historic record of the time.

Samuel Pepys, 1637–1703. This famous diarist was the son of a London tailor. He received a collegiate education, and became a connoisseur in literature and art. Of a prying disposition, he saw all that he could of the varied political, literary, and social life of England; and has recorded what he saw in a diary so quaint, simple, and amusing, that it has retained its popularity to the present day, and has greatly aided the historian both in facts and philosophy. He held an official position as secretary in the admiralty, the duties of which he discharged with great system and skill. In addition to this *Diary*, we have also his *Correspondence*, published after his death, which is historically of great importance. In both diary and correspondence he has the charm of great *naïveté*,—as of a curious and gossiping observer, who never dreamed that his writings would be made public. Men and women of social station are painted in pre-Raphaelite style, and figure before us with great truth and vividness.

Elias Ashmole, 1617–1693. This antiquarian and virtuoso is principally known as the founder of the Ashmolean Museum at Oxford. He studied law, chemistry, and natural philosophy. Besides an edition of the manuscript works of certain English chemists, he wrote *Bennevennu*,—the description of a Roman road mentioned in the Itinerary of Antoninus,—and a *History of the Order of the Garter*. His *Diary* was published nearly a century after his death, but is by no means equal in value to those of Evelyn and Pepys.

John Aubrey, 1627–1697: a man of curious mind, Aubrey investigated the supernatural topics of the day, and presented them to the world in his *Miscellanies*. Among these subjects it is interesting to notice "blows invisible," and "knockings," which have been resuscitated in the present day. He was a "perambulator," and, in the words of one of his critics, "picked up information on the highway, and scattered it everywhere as authentic." His most valuable contribution to history is found in his *Letters Written by Eminent Persons in the 17th and 18th Centuries, with Lives of Eminent Men*. The searcher for authentic material must carefully scrutinize Aubrey's *facts*; but, with much that is doubtful, valuable information may be obtained from his pages.

CHAPTER XXIII.

THE DRAMA OF THE RESTORATION.

The License of the Age.	Vanbrugh.	Otway.
Dryden.	Farquhar.	Rowe.
Wycherley.	Etherege.	Lee.
Congreve.	Tragedy.	Southern.

THE LICENSE OF THE AGE.

THERE is no portion of the literature of this period which so fully represents and explains the social history of the age as the drama. With the restoration of Charles it returned to England, after a time in which the chief faults had been too great rigor in morals. The theatres had been closed, all amusements checked, and even poetry and the fine arts placed under a ban. In the reign of Charles I., Prynne had written his *Histrio Mastix*, or Scourge of the Stage, in which he not only denounced all stage plays, but music and dancing; and also declaimed against hunting, festival days, the celebration of Christmas, and Maypoles. For this he was indicted in the Star Chamber for libel, and was sentenced to stand in the pillory, to lose his ears, to pay the king a fine of £5000, and to be imprisoned for life. For his attack there was much excuse in the license of the former period; but when puritanism, in its turn, was brought under the three spears, the drama was to come back tenfold more injurious and more immoral than before.

From the stern and gloomy morals of the Commonwealth we now turn to the debaucheries of the court,—from cropped heads and dark cloaks to plumes and velvet, gold lace and embroidery,—to the varied fashions of every kind for which Paris has always been renowned, and which Charles brought back with him from his exile;—from prudish morals to indiscriminate debauchery; from the exercisings of brewers' clerks, the expounding of tailors, the catechizing of watermen, to the stage, which was now loudly petitioned to supply amusement and novelty. Macaulay justly says: "The restraints of that gloomy time were such as would have been impatiently borne, if imposed by men who were universally believed to be saints; these restraints became altogether insupportable when they were known to be kept up for the profit of hypocrites! It is quite certain that if the royal family had never returned, there would have been a great relaxation of manners." It is equally certain, let us add, that morals would not have been correspondingly relaxed. The revulsion was terrible. In no period of English history was society ever so grossly immoral; and the drama, which we now come to consider, displays this immorality and license with a perfect delineation.

The English people had always been fond of the drama in all its forms, and were ready to receive it even contaminated as it was by the licentious spirit of the time. An illiterate and ignorant people cannot think for themselves; they act upon the precepts and example of those above them in knowledge and social station: thus it is that a dissolute monarch and a subservient aristocracy corrupt the masses.

DRYDEN'S PLAYS.—Although Dryden's reputation is based on his other poems, and although his dramas have conduced scarcely at all to his fame, he did play a principal part in this department of literary work. Dryden made haste to answer the call, and his venal muse wrote to please the town. The names of many of his plays and personages are foreign; but their vitality is purely English. Of his first play, *The Duke of Guise*, which was unsuccessful, he tells us: "I undertook this as the fairest way which the Act of Indemnity had left us, as setting forth the rise of the great rebellion, and of exposing the villanies of it upon the stage, to precaution posterity against the like errors;"—a rebellion the master-spirit of which he had eulogized upon his bier!

His second play, *The Wild Gallant*, may be judged by the fact that it won for him the favor of Charles II. and of his mistress, the Duchess of Cleveland. Pepys saw it "well acted;" but says, "It hath little good in it." It is not our purpose to give a list of Dryden's plays; besides their occasional lewdness, they are very far inferior to his poems, and are now rarely read except by the historical student. They paid him in ready money, and he cannot ask payment from posterity in fame.

On the 13th of January, 1667–8, (we are told by Pepys,) the ladies and the Duke of Monmouth acted *The Indian Emperour* at court.

The same chronicler says: *The Maiden Queene* was "mightily commended for the regularity of it, and the strain and wit;" but of the *Ladys à la Mode* he says it was "so mean a thing" that, when it was announced for the next night, the pit "fell a laughing, because the house was not a quarter full."

But Dryden, as a playwright, does not enjoy the infamous honor of a high rank among his fellow-dramatists. The proper representations of the drama in that age were, in Comedy, Wycherley, Congreve, Vanbrugh, and Farquhar; and, in Tragedy, Otway, Rowe, and Lee.

WYCHERLEY.—Of the comedists of this period, where all were evil, William Wycherley was the worst. In his four plays, *Love in a Wood*, *The Gentleman Dancing-Master*, *The Country Wife*, and *The Plain Dealer*, he outrages all decency, ridicules honesty and virtue, and makes vice always triumphant. As a young man, profligate with pen and in his life, he was a wicked old man; for, when sixty-four years of age, he published a miscellany of verses of which Macaulay says: "The style and versification are beneath criticism: the morals are those of Rochester." And yet it is sad to be obliged to say that his characters pleased the age, because such men and women really lived then, and acted just as he describes them. He depicted vice to applaud and not to punish it. Wycherley was born in 1640, and died in 1715.

CONGREVE. — William Congreve, who is of the same school of morals, is far superior as a writer; indeed, were one name to be selected in illustration of our subject, it would be his. He was born in 1666, and, after being educated at Trinity College, Dublin, was a student at the Middle Temple. His first play, *The Old Bachelor*, produced in his twenty-first year, was a great success, and won for him the patronage of Lord Halifax. His next, *The Double Dealer*, caused Dryden to proclaim him the equal of Shakspeare! Perhaps his most famous comedy is *Love for Love*, which is besides an excellent index to the morality of the age. The author was quoted and caressed; Pope dedicated to him his Translation of the Iliad; and Voltaire considered him the most successful English writer of comedy. His merit consists in some degree of originality, and in the liveliness of his colloquies. His wit is brilliant and flashing, but, in the words of Thackeray, the world to him "seems to have had no moral at all."

How much he owed to the French school, and especially to Molière, may be judged from the fact that a whole scene in *Love for Love* is borrowed from the *Don Juan* of Molière. It is that in which Trapland comes to collect his debt from Valentine Legend. Readers of Molière will recall the scene between Don Juan, Sganarelle and M. Dimanche, which is here, with change of names, taken almost word for word. His men are gallants neither from love or passion, but from the custom of the age, of which it is said, "it would break

Mr. Tattle's heart to think anybody else should be beforehand with him;" and Mr. Tattle was the type of a thousand fine gentlemen in the best English society of that day.

His only tragedy, *The Mourning Bride,* although far below those of Shakspeare, is the best of that age; and Dr. Johnson says he would go to it to find the most poetical paragraph in the range of English poetry. Congreve died in 1729, leaving his gains to the Duchess of Marlborough, who cherished his memory in a very original fashion. She had a statue of him in ivory, which went by clockwork, and was daily seated at her table; and another wax-doll imitation, whose feet she caused to be blistered and anointed by physicians, as the poet's gouty extremities had been.

Congreve was not ashamed to vindicate the drama, licentious as it was. In the year 1698, Jeremy Collier, a distinguished nonjuring clergyman, published *A Short View of the Immorality and Profaneness of the English Stage;* a very vigorous and severe criticism, containing a great deal of wholesome but bitter truth. Congreve came to the defence of the stage, and his example was followed by his brother dramatists. But Collier was too strong for his enemies, and the defences were very weak. There yet existed in England that leaven of purity which has steadily since been making its influence felt.

VANBRUGH. — Sir John Vanbrugh (born in 1666, died in 1726) was an architect as well as a dramatist, but not great in either rôle. His principal dramas are *The Provoked Wife, The City Wives' Confederacy,* and *The Journey to London* (finished by Colley Cibber). His personages are vicious and lewd, but quite real; and his wit is constant and flowing. *The Provoked Wife* is so licentious a play that it is supposed Vanbrugh afterwards conceived and began his *Provoked Husband* to make some amends for it. This latter play, however, he did not complete: it was finished after his death by Cibber, who says in the Prologue:

> This play took birth from principles of truth,
> To make amends for errors past of youth.
> . . . .
> Though vice is natural, 't was never meant
> The stage should show it but for punishment.
> Warm with such thoughts, his muse once more took flame,
> Resolved to bring licentious life to shame.

If Vanbrugh was not born in France, it is certain that he spent many years there, and there acquired the taste and handling of the comic drama, which then had its halcyon days under Molière. His dialogue is very spirited, and his humor is greater than that of Congreve, who, however, excelled him in wit.

The principal architectural efforts of Vanbrugh were the design for Castle Howard, and the palace of Blenheim, built for Marlborough by the English nation, both of which are greater titles to enduring reputation than any of his plays.

FARQUHAR. — George Farquhar was born in Londonderry, in 1678, and began his studies at Trinity College, Dublin, but was soon stage-struck, and became an actor. Not long after, he was commissioned in the army, and began to write plays in the style and moral tone of the age. Among his nine comedies, those which present that tone best are his *Love in a Bottle*, *The Constant Couple*, *The Recruiting Officer*, and *The Beaux' Stratagem*. All his productions were hastily written, but met with great success from their gayety and clever plots, especially the last two mentioned, which are not, besides, so immoral as the others, and which are yet acted upon the British stage.

ETHEREGE. — Sir George Etherege, a coxcomb and a diplomatist, was born in 1636, and died in 1694. His plays are, equally with the others mentioned, marked by the licentiousness of the age, which is rendered more insidious by their elegance. Among them are *The Comical Revenge, or Love in a Tub*, and *The Man of Mode, or Sir Fopling Flutter.*

Tragedy.

The domain of tragedy, although perhaps not so attractive to the English people as comedy, was still sufficiently so to invite the attention of the literati. The excitement which is produced by exaggerated scenes of distress and death has always had a charm for the multitude; and although the principal tragedies of this period are based upon heroic stories, many of them of classic origin, the genius of the writer displayed itself in applying these to his own times, and in introducing that "touch of nature" which "makes the whole world kin." Human sympathy is based upon a community of suffering, and the sorrows of one age are similar to those of another. Besides, tragedy served, in the period of which we are speaking, to give variety and contrast to what would otherwise have been the gay monotony of the comic muse.

Otway.—The first writer to be mentioned in this field is Thomas Otway (born in 1651, died in 1685). He led an irregular and wretched life, and died, it is said, from being choked by a roll of bread which, after great want, he was eating too ravenously.

His style is extravagant, his pathos too exacting, and his delineation of the passions sensational and overwrought. He produced in his earlier career *Alcibiades* and *Don Carlos*, and, later, *The Orphan*, and *The Soldier's Fortune*. But the piece by which his fame was secured is *Venice Preserved*, which, based upon history, is fictional in its details. The original story is found in the Abbé de St. Real's *Histoire de la Conjuration du Marquis de Bedamar*, or the account of a Spanish conspiracy in which the marquis, who was ambassador, took part. It is still put upon the stage, with the omission, however, of the licentious comic portions found in the original play.

NICHOLAS ROWE, who was born in 1673, a man of fortune and a government official, produced seven tragedies, of which *The Fair Penitent, Lady Jane Grey,* and *Jane Shore* are the best. His description of the lover, in the first, has become a current phrase: "That haughty, gallant, gay Lothario,"—the prototype of false lovers since. The plots are too broad, but the moral of these tragedies is in most cases good.

In *Jane Shore*, he has followed the history of the royal mistress, and has given a moral lesson of great efficacy.

NATHANIEL LEE, 1657–1692: was a man of dissolute life, for some time insane, and met his death in a drunken brawl. Of his ten tragedies, the best are *The Rival Queens*, and *Theodosius, or The Force of Love.* The rival queens of Alexander the Great—Roxana and Statira—figure in the first, which is still presented upon the stage. It has been called, with just critical point, "A great and glorious flight of a bold but frenzied imagination, having as much absurdity as sublimity, and as much extravagance as passion; the poet, the genius, the scholar are everywhere visible."

THOMAS SOUTHERN, 1659–1746: wrote *Isabella, or The Fatal Marriage*, and *Oronooko.* In the latter, although yielding to the corrupt taste of the time in his comic parts, he causes his captive Indian prince to teach that period a lesson by his pure and noble love for Imoinda. Oronooko is a prince taken by the English at Surinam and carried captive to England.

These writers are the best representatives of those who in tragedy and comedy form the staple of that age. Their models were copied in succeeding years; but, with the expulsion of the Stuarts, morals were somewhat mended; and while light, gay, and witty productions for the stage were still in demand, the extreme licentiousness was repudiated by the public; and the plays of Cibber, Cumberland, Colman, and Sheridan, reflecting these better tastes, are free from much of the pollution to which we have referred.

CHAPTER XXIV.

POPE, AND THE ARTIFICIAL SCHOOL.

Contemporary History. | The Messiah. | Essay on Man.
Birth and Early Life. | The Iliad. | The Artificial School.
Essay on Criticism. | Value of the Translation. | Estimate of Pope.
Rape of the Lock. | The Odyssey. | Other Writers.

ALEXANDER POPE is at once one of the greatest names in English literature and one of the most remarkable illustrations of the fact that the literature is the interpreter of English history. He was also a man of singular individuality, and may, in some respects, be considered a *lusus naturæ* among the literary men of his day.

CONTEMPORARY HISTORY. — He was born in London on the 21st of May, 1688, the year which witnessed the second and final expulsion of the Stuarts, in direct line, and the accession of a younger branch in the persons of Mary and her husband, William of Orange. Pope comes upon the literary scene with the new order of political affairs. A dynasty had been overthrown, and the power of the parliament had been established; new charters of right had secured the people from kingly oppression; but there was still a strong element of opposition and sedition in the Jacobite party, which had by no means abandoned the hope of restoring the former rule. They were kept in check, indeed, during the reign of William and Mary, but they became bolder upon the accession of Queen Anne. They hoped to find their efforts facilitated by the fact that she was childless; and they even asserted that upon her death-bed she had favored the succession of the pretender, whom they called James III.

In 1715, the year after the accession of George I., the electoral prince of Hanover,—whose grandmother was the daughter of James I., — they broke out into open rebellion. The pretender landed in Scotland, and made an abortive attempt to recover the throne. The nation was kept in a state of excitement and turmoil until the disaster of Culloden, and the final defeat of Charles Edward, the young pretender, in 1745, one year after the death of Pope.

These historical facts had a direct influence upon English society: the country was divided into factions; and political conflicts sharpened the wits and gave vigor to the conduct of men in all ranks. Pope was an interpreter of his age, in politics, in general culture, and in social manners and morals. Thus he was a politician among the statesmen Bolingbroke, Buckingham, Oxford, Sunderland, Halifax, Harley, and Marlborough. His *Essay on Criticism* presents to us the artificial taste and technical rules which were established as a standard in literature. His *Essay on Man*, his *Moral Epistles*, and his *Universal Prayer* are an index to the semi-Christian, semi-Grecian ethics of an age too selfish to be orthodox, and too progressive to be intolerant. His *Rape of the Lock* is a striking picture of social life, sketched by the hand of a gentle satire. His translations of Homer, and their great success, are significant of a more extended taste for scholarship; not attended, however, with many incentives to originality of production. The nobles were still the patrons of literature, and they fancied old things which were grand, in new and gaudy English dresses. The age was also marked by rapid and uniform progress in the English language. The sonorous, but cumbrous English of Milton had been greatly improved by Dryden; and we have seen, also, that the terse and somewhat crude diction of Dryden's earlier works had been polished and rendered more harmonious in his later poems.

This harmony of language seemed to Pope and to his

patrons the chief aim of the poet, and to make it still more tuneful and melodious was the purpose of his life.

Birth and Early Life. — Pope was the son of a respectable linen-draper, who had achieved a competency and retired to enjoy it. The mother of the poet must have been a good one, to have retained the ardent and eulogistic affection of her son to the close of her life, as she did. This attachment is a marked feature in his biography, and at last finds vent in her epitaph, in which he calls her "*mater optima, mulierum amantissima.*"

Pope was a sickly, dwarfed, precocious child. His early studies in Latin and Greek were conducted by priests of the Roman Catholic Church, to which his parents belonged; but he soon took his education into his own hands. Alone and unaided he pursued his classical studies, and made good progress in French and German.

Of his early rhyming powers he says:

"I lisped in numbers, for the numbers came."

At the age of twelve, he was taken to Will's Coffee-house, to see the great Dryden, upon whom, as a model, he had already determined to fashion himself.

His first efforts were translations. He made English versions of the first book of the *Thebais* of Statius; several of the stories of Chaucer, and one of Ovid's Epistles, all of which were produced before he was fifteen.

Essay on Criticism.—He was not quite twenty-one when he wrote his *Essay on Criticism*, in which he lays down the canons of just criticism, and the causes which prevent it. In illustration, he attacks the multitude of critics of that day, and is particularly harsh in his handling of a few among them. He gained a name by this excellent poem, but he made many enemies, and among them one John Dennis, whom he had satirized under the name of Appius. Dennis was his life-long foe.

Perhaps there is no better proof of the lasting and deserved popularity of this Essay, than the numerous quotations from it, not only in works on rhetoric and literary criticism, but in our ordinary intercourse with men. Couplets and lines have become household words wherever the English language is spoken. How often do we hear the sciolist condemned in these words:

> A little learning is a dangerous thing;
> Drink deep, or touch not the Pierian spring?

Irreverence and rash speculation are satirized thus:

> Nay, fly to altars; there they 'll talk you dead,
> For fools rush in where angels fear to tread.

We may waive a special notice of his *Pastorals*, which, like those of Dryden, are but clever imitations of Theocritus and anachronisms of the Alexandrian period. Of their merits, we may judge from his own words. "If they have any merit, it is to be attributed to some good old authors, whose works as I had leisure to study, so I hope I have not wanted care to imitate."

Rape of the Lock. — The poem which displays most originality of invention is the *Rape of the Lock*. It is, perhaps, the best and most charming specimen of the mock-heroic to be found in English; and it is specially deserving of attention, because it depicts the social life of the period in one of its principal phases. Miss Arabella Fermor, one of the reigning beauties of London society, while on a pleasure party on the Thames, had a lock of her hair surreptitiously cut off by Lord Petre. Although it was designed as a joke, the belle was very angry; and Pope, who was a friend of both persons, wrote this poem to assuage her wrath and to reconcile them. It has all the system and construction of an epic.

The poet describes, with becoming delicacy, the toilet of the lady, at which she is attended by obsequious sylphs.

The party embark upon the river, and the fair lady is described in the splendor of her charms:

This nymph, to the destruction of mankind,
Nourished two locks, which graceful hung behind
In equal curls, and well conspired to deck,
With shining ringlets, the smooth, ivory neck.
. . . .
Fair tresses man's imperial race ensnare,
And beauty draws us by a single hair.

Surrounding sylphs protect the beauty; and one to whom the lock has been given in charge, flutters unfortunately too near, and is clipped in two by the scissors that cut the lock. It is a rather extravagant conclusion, even in a mock-heroic poem, that when the strife was greatest to restore the lock, it flew upward:

A sudden star, it shot through liquid air,
And drew behind a radiant trail of hair,

and thus, and always, it

Adds new glory to the shining sphere.

With these simple and meagre materials, Pope has constructed an harmonious poem in which the sylphs, gnomes, and other sprites of the Rosicrucian philosophy find appropriate place and service. It failed in its principal purpose of reconciliation, but it has given us the best mock-heroic poem in the language. As might have been expected, it called forth bitter criticisms from Dennis; and there were not wanting those who saw in it a political significance. Pope's pleasantry was aroused at this, and he published *A Key to the Lock*, in which he further mystifies these sage readers: Belinda becomes Great Britain; the Baron is the Earl of Oxford; and Thalestris is the Duchess of Marlborough.

THE MESSIAH.—In 1712 there appeared in one of the numbers of *The Spectator*, his *Messiah, a Sacred Eclogue*, written with the purpose of harmonizing the prophecy of Isaiah and the singular oracles of the Pollio, or Fourth Eclogue of Virgil. Elevated in thought and grand in diction, the Messiah has kept its hold upon public favor ever since, and portions of it are used as hymns in general worship. Among these will be recognized that of which the opening lines are:

> Rise, crowned with light, imperial Salem, rise;
> Exalt thy towering head and lift thine eyes.

In 1713 he published a poem on *Windsor Forest*, and an *Ode on St. Cecilia's Day*, in imitation of Dryden. He also furnished the beautiful prologue to Addison's Cato.

TRANSLATION OF THE ILIAD. — He now proposed to himself a task which was to give him more reputation and far greater emolument than anything he had yet accomplished — a translation of the Iliad of Homer. This was a great desideratum, and men of all parties conspired to encourage and reward him. Chapman's Homer, excellent as it was, was not in a popular measure, and was known only to scholars.

In the execution of this project, Pope labored for six years — writing by day and dreaming of his work at night; translating thirty or forty lines before rising in the morning, and jotting down portions even while on a journey. Pope's polished pentameters, when read, are very unlike the full-voiced hexameters of Homer; but the errors in the translation are comparatively few and unimportant, and his own poetry is in his best vein. The poem was published by subscription, and was a great pecuniary success. This was in part due to the blunt importunity of Dean Swift, who said: "The author shall not begin to print until I have a thousand guineas for him." Parnell, one of the most accomplished Greek scholars of the day, wrote a life of Homer, to be prefixed to the work; and many of the critical notes were written by Broome, who had translated the Iliad into English prose. Pope was not without poetical rivals. Tickell produced a translation of the first book of the Iliad, which was certainly revised, and many thought partly written, by Addison. A coolness already existing between Pope and Addison was increased by this circumstance, which soon led to an open rupture between them. The public, however, favored Pope's version, while a few of the *dilettanti* joined Addison in preferring Tickell's.

The pecuniary results of Pope's labors were particularly gratifying. The work was published in six quarto volumes, and had more than six hundred subscribers, at six guineas a copy: the amount realized by Pope on the first and subsequent issues was upwards of five thousand pounds — an unprecedented payment of bookseller to author in that day.

VALUE OF THE TRANSLATION. — This work, in spite of the criticism of exact scholars, has retained its popularity to the present time. Chapman's Homer has been already referred to. Since the days of Pope numerous authors have tried their hands upon Homer, translating the whole or a part. Among these is a very fine poem by Cowper, in blank verse, which is praised by the critics, but little read. Lord Derby's translation is distinguished for its prosaic accuracy. The recent version of our venerable poet, Wm. C. Bryant, is acknowledged to be at once scholarly, accurate, and harmonious, and will be of permanent value and reputation. But the exquisite tinkling of Pope's lines, the pleasant refrain they leave in the memory, like the chiming of silver bells, will cause them to last, with undiminished favor, unaffected by more correct rivals, as long as the language itself. "A very pretty poem, Mr. Pope," said the great Bentley; "but pray do not call it Homer." Despite this criticism of the Greek scholar, the world has taken it for Homer, and knows Homer almost solely through this charming medium.

The Iliad was issued in successive years, the last two volumes appearing in 1720. Of course it was savagely attacked by Dennis; but Pope had won more than he had hoped for, and might laugh at his enemies.

With the means he had inherited, increased by the sale of his poem, Pope leased a villa on the Thames, at Twickenham, which he fitted up as a residence for life. He laid out the grounds, built a grotto, and made his villa a famous spot.

Here he was smitten by the masculine charms of the gifted Lady Mary Wortley Montagu, who figures in many of his verses, and particularly in the closing lines of the *Epistle of Eloisa to Abelard.* It was a singular alliance, destined to a speedy rupture. On her return from Turkey, in 1718, where her husband had been the English ambassador, she took a home near Pope's villa, and, at his request, sat for her portrait. When, later, they became estranged, she laughed at the poet, and his coldness turned into hatred.

THE ODYSSEY. — The success of his version of the Iliad led to his translation of the Odyssey; but this he did with the collaboration of Fenton and Broome, the former writing four and the latter six books. The volumes appeared successively in 1725–6, and there was an appendix containing the *Batrachomiomachia,* or Battle of the Frogs and Mice, translated by Parnell. For this work Pope received the lion's share of profits, his co-laborers being paid only £800.

Among his miscellaneous works must be mentioned portions of *Martinus Scriblerus.* One of these, *Peri Bathous,* or *Art of Sinking in Poetry,* was the germ of The Dunciad.

Like Dryden, he was attacked by the *soi-disant* poets of the day, and retorted in similar style and taste. In imitation of Dryden's *MacFlecknoe,* he wrote *The Dunciad,* or epic of the Dunces, in the first edition of which Theobald was promoted to the vacant throne. It roused a great storm. Authors besieged the publisher to hinder him from publishing it, while booksellers and agents were doing all in their power to procure it. In a later edition a new book was added, deposing Theobald and elevating Colley Cibber to the throne of Dulness. This was ill-advised, as the ridicule, which was justly applied to Theobald, is not applicable to Cibber.

ESSAY ON MAN. — The intercourse of the poet with the gifted but sceptical Lord Bolingbroke is apparent in his *Essay on Man*, in which, with much that is orthodox and excellent, the principles and influence of his lordship are readily discerned. The first part appeared in 1732, and the second some years later. The opinion is no longer held that Bolingbroke wrote any part of the poem; he has only infected it. It is one of Pope's best poems in versification and diction, and abounds with pithy proverbial sayings, which the English world has been using ever since as current money in conversational barter. Among many that might be selected, the following are well known:

All are but parts of one stupendous whole
Whose body nature is, and God the soul.

Know thou thyself, presume not God to scan;
The proper study of mankind is man.

A wit's a feather, and a chief's a rod;
An honest man 's the noblest work of God.

Among the historical teachings of Pope's works and career, and also among the curiosities of literature, must be noticed the publication of Pope's letters, by Curll the bookseller, without the poet's permission. They were principally letters to Henry Cromwell, Wycherley, Congreve, Steele, Addison, and Swift. There were not wanting those who believed that it was a trick of the poet himself to increase his notoriety;

but such an opinion is hardly warranted. These letters form a valuable chapter in the social and literary history of the period.

Pope's Death and Character. — On the 30th of May, 1744, Pope passed away, after a long illness, during which he said he was "dying of a hundred good symptoms." Indeed, so frail and weak had he always been, that it was a wonder he lived so long. His weakness of body seems to have acted upon his strong mind, which must account for much that is satirical and splenetic in his writings. Very short, thin, and ill-shaped, his person wanted the compactness necessary to stand alone, until it was encased in stays. He needed a high chair at table, such as children use; but he was an epicure, and a fastidious one; and despite his infirmities, his bright, intellectual eye and his courtly manners caused him to be noted quite as much as his defects.

The Artificial School. — Pope has been set forth as the head of the *Artificial School.* This is, perhaps, rather a convenient than an exact designation. He had little of original genius, but was an apt imitator and reproducer — what in painting would be an excellent copyist. His greatest praise, however, is that he reduced to system what had gone before him; his poems present in themselves an art of poetry, with technical canons and illustrations, which were long after servilely obeyed, and the influence of which is still felt to-day.

And this artificial school was in the main due to the artificial character of the age. Nature seemed to have lost her charms; pastorals were little more than private theatricals, enacted with straw hats and shepherd's crook in drawing-rooms or on close-clipped lawns. Culture was confined to court and town, and poets found little inducement to consult the heart or to woo nature, but wrote what would please the town or court. This taste gave character to the technical standards, to which Pope, more than any other writer, gave system and coherence. Most of the literati were men of the town; many were fine gentlemen with a political bias; and thus it is that the school of poets of which Pope is the unchallenged head, has been known as the Artificial School.

In the passage of time, and with the increase of literature, the real merits of Pope were for some time neglected, or misrepresented. The world is beginning to discern and recognize these again. Learned, industrious, self-reliant, controversial, and, above all, harmonious, instead of giving vent to the highest fancies in simple language, he has treated the common-place — that which is of universal interest — in melodious and splendid diction. But, above all, he stands as the representative of his age: a wit among the comic dramatists who were going out and the essayists who were coming in; a man of the world with Lady Mary and the gay parties on the Thames; a polemic, who dealt keen thrusts and who liked to see them rankle, and who yet writhed in agony when the *riposte* came; a Roman Catholic in faith and a latitudinarian in speech; — such was Pope as a type of that world in which he lived.

A poet of the first rank he was not; he invented nothing; but he established the canons of poetry, attuned to exquisite harmony the rhymed couplet which Dryden had made so powerful an instrument, improved the language, discerned and reconnected the discordant parts of literature; and thus it is that he towers above all the poets of his age, and has sent his influence through those that followed, even to the present day.

Other Writers of the Period.

Matthew Prior, 1664–1721: in his early youth he was a waiter in his uncle's tap-room, but, surmounting all difficulties, he rose to be a distinguished poet and diplomatist. He was an envoy to France, where he was noted for his wit and ready repartee. His love songs are somewhat immoral, but exquisitely melodious. His chief poems are: *Alma*, a philosophic piece in the vein of Hudibras; *Solomon*, a Scripture poem; and, the best of all, *The City and Country Mouse*, a parody on Dryden's *Hind and Panther*, which he wrote in conjunction with Mr. Montague. He was imprisoned by the Whigs in 1715, and lost all his fortune. He was distinguished by having Dr. Johnson as his biographer, in the *Lives of the Poets*.

John Arbuthnot, 1667–1735: born in Scotland. He was learned, witty, and amiable. Eminent in medicine, he was physician to the court of Queen Anne. He is chiefly known in literature as the companion of Pope and Swift, and as the writer with them of papers in the Martinus Scriblerus Club, which was founded in 1714, and of which Pope, Gay, Swift, Arbuthnot, Harvey, Atterbury, and others, were the principal members. Arbuthnot wrote a *History of John Bull*, which was designed to render the war then carried on by Marlborough unpopular, and certainly conduced to that end.

John Gay, 1688–1732: he was of humble origin, but rose by his talents, and figured at court. He wrote several dramas in a mock-tragic vein. Among these are *What D'ye Call It?* and *Three Hours after Marriage;* but that which gave him permanent reputation is his *Beggar's Opera*, of which the hero is a highwayman, and the characters are prostitutes and Newgate gentry. It is interspersed with gay and lyrical songs, and was rendered particularly effective by the fine acting of Miss Elizabeth Fenton, in the part of *Polly*. The *Shepherd's Week*, a pastoral, contains more real delineations of rural life than any other poem of the period. Another curious piece is entitled, *Trivia, or the Art of Walking the Streets of London.*

Thomas Parnell, 1679–1718: he was the author of numerous poems, among which the only one which has retained popular favor is *The Hermit*, a touching poem founded upon an older story. He wrote the life of Homer prefixed to Pope's translation; but it was very much altered by Pope.

Thomas Tickell, 1686–1740: particularly known as the friend of Addison. He wrote a translation of the First Book of Homer's Iliad, which was corrected by Addison, and contributed several papers to *The Spectator*. But he is best known by his *Elegy* upon Addison, which Dr. Johnson calls a very "elegant funeral poem."

Isaac Watts, 1674–1765: this great writer of hymns was born at Southampton, and became one of the most eminent of the dissenting ministers of England. He is principally known by his metrical versions of the Psalms, and by a great number of original hymns, which have been generally used by all denominations of Christians since. He also produced many hymns for children, which have become familiar as household words. He had a lyrical ear, and an easy, flowing diction, but is sometimes careless in his versification and incorrect in his theology. During the greater part of his life the honored guest of Sir Thomas Abney, he devoted himself to literature. Besides many sermons, he produced a treatise on *The First Principles of Geology and Astronomy;* a work on *Logic, or the Right Use of the Reason in the Inquiry after Truth;* and *A Supplement on the Improvement of the Mind.* These latter have been superseded as text-books by later and more correct inquiry.

Edward Young, 1681–1765: in his younger days he sought preferment at court, but being disappointed in his aspirations, he took orders in the Church, and led a retired life. He published a satire entitled, *The Love of Fame, the Universal Passion,* which was quite successful. But his chief work, which for a long time was classed with the highest poetic efforts, is the *Night Thoughts*, a series of meditations, during nine nights, on Life, Death, and Immortality. The style is somewhat pompous, the imagery striking, but frequently unnatural; the occasional descriptions majestic and vivid; and the effect of the whole is grand, gloomy, and peculiar. It is full of apothegms, which have been much quoted; and some of his lines and phrases are very familiar to all.

He wrote papers on many topics, and among his tragedies the best known is that entitled *The Revenge.* Very popular in his own day, Young has been steadily declining in public favor, partly on account of the superior claims of modern writers, and partly because of the morbid and gloomy views he has taken of human nature. His solemn admonitions throng upon the reader like phantoms, and cause him to desire more cheerful company. A sketch of the life of Young may be found in Dr. Johnson's *Lives of the Poets.*

CHAPTER XXV.

ADDISON, AND THE REIGN OF QUEEN ANNE.

The Character of the Age.

TO cater further to the Artificial Age, the literary cravings of which far exceeded those of any former period, there sprang up a school of Essayists, most of whom were also poets, dramatists, and politicians. Among these Addison, Steele, and Swift stand pre-eminent. Each of them was a man of distinct and interesting personality. Two of them — Addison and Swift — presented such a remarkable contrast, that it has been usual for writers on this period of English Literature to bring them together as foils to each other. This has led to injustice towards Swift; they should be placed in juxtaposition because they are of the same period, and because of their joint efforts in the literary development of the age. The period is distinctly marked. We speak as currently of the wits and the essayists of Queen Anne's reign as we do of the authors of the Elizabethan age.

A glance at contemporary history will give us an intelligent clue to our literary inquiries, and cause us to observe the historical character of the literature.

To a casual observer, the reign of Queen Anne seems particularly untroubled and prosperous. English history calls it the time of "Good Queen Anne;" and it is referred to with great unction by the *laudator temporis acti*, in unjust comparison with the period which has since intervened, as well as with that which preceded it.

QUEEN ANNE. — The queen was a Protestant, as opposed to the Romanists and Jacobites; a faithful wife, and a tender mother in her memory of several children who died young. She was merciful, pure, and gracious to her subjects. Her reign was tolerant. There was plenty at home; rebellion and civil war were at least latent. Abroad, England was greatly distinguished by the victories of Marlborough and Eugene. But to one who looks through this veil of prosperity, a curious history is unfolded. The fires of faction were scarcely smouldering. It was the transition period between the expiring dynasty of the direct line of Stuarts and the coming of the Hanoverian house. Women took part in politics; sermons like that of Sacheverell against the dissenters and the government were thundered from the pulpit. Volcanic fires were at work; the low rumblings of an earthquake were heard from time to time, and gave constant cause of concern to the queen and her statesmen. Men of rank conspired against each other; the moral license of former reigns seems to have been forgotten in political intrigue. When James II. had been driven out in 1688, the English conscience compromised on the score of the divine right of kings, by taking his daughter Mary and her husband as joint monarchs. To do this, they affected to call the king's son by his second wife, born in that year, a pretender. It was said that he was the child of another woman, and had been brought to the queen's bedside in a warming-pan, that James might be able to present, thus fraudulently, a Roman Catholic heir to the throne. In this they did the king injustice, and greater injustice to the queen, Maria de Modena, a pleasing and innocent woman, who had, by her virtues and personal popularity alone, kept the king on his throne, in spite of his pernicious measures.

When the dynasty was overthrown, the parliament had presented to William and Mary *A Bill of Rights*, in which the people's grievances were set forth, and their rights enumerated and insisted upon; and this was accepted by the monarchs as a condition of their tenure.

Mary died in 1695, and when William followed her, in 1702, Anne, the second daughter of James, ascended the throne. Had she refused the succession, there would have been a furious war between the Jacobites and the Hanoverians. In 1714, Anne died childless, but her reign had bridged the chasm between the experiment of William and Mary and the house of Hanover. In default of direct heirs to Queen Anne, the succession was in this Hanoverian house; represented in the person of the Electress Sophia, the granddaughter of James I., through his daughter, Elizabeth of Bohemia. But this lineage of blood had lost all English affinities and sympathies.

Meanwhile, the child born to James II., in 1688, had grown to be a man, and stood ready, on the death of Queen Anne, to re-affirm his claim to the throne. It was said that, although, on account of the plottings of the Jacobites, a price had been put upon his head, the queen herself wished him to succeed, and had expressed scruples about her own right to reign. She greatly disliked the family of Hanover, and while she was on her death-bed, the pretender had been brought to England, in the hope that she would declare him her successor. The elements of discord asserted themselves still more strongly. Whigs and Tories in politics, Romanists and Protestants in creed, Jacobite and Hanoverian in loyalty, opposed each other, harassing the feeble queen, and keeping the realm in continual ferment.

WHIGS AND TORIES.—The Whigs were those who declared that kingly power was solely for the good of the subject; that the reformed creed was the religion of the realm; that James had forfeited the throne, and that his son was a pretender; and that the power justly passed to the house of Hanover. The Tories asserted that monarchs ruled by *divine right* only; and that if, when religion was at stake, the king might be deposed, this could not affect the succession.

Anne escaped her troubles by dying, in 1714. Sophia, the Electress of Hanover, who had only wished to live, she said, long enough to have engraved upon her tombstone: "Here lies Sophia, Queen of England," died, in spite of this desire, only a few weeks before the queen; and the new heir to the throne was her son, George Louis of Brunswick-Luneburg, electoral prince of Hanover.

He came cautiously and selfishly to the throne of England; he felt his way, and left a line of retreat open; he brought not a spice of honest English sentiment, but he introduced the filth of the electoral court. As gross in his conduct as Charles II., he had indeed a prosperous reign, because it was based upon a just and tolerant Constitution; because the English were in reality not governed by a king, but by well-enacted laws.

The effect of all this political turmoil upon the leading men in England had been manifest; both parties had been expectant, and many of the statesmen had been upon the fence, ready to get down on one side or the other, according to circumstances. Marlborough left the Tories and joined the Whigs; Swift, who had been a Whig, joined the Tories. The queen's first ministry had consisted of Whigs and the more moderate Tories; but as she fell away from the Marlboroughs, she threw herself into the hands of the Tories, who had determined, and now achieved, the downfall of Marlborough.

Such was the reign of good Queen Anne. With this brief sketch as a preliminary, we return to the literature, which, like her coin, bore her image and carried it into succeeding reigns. In literature, the age of Queen Anne extends far beyond her lifetime.

ADDISON.—The principal name of this period is that of Joseph Addison. He was the son of the rector of Milston, in Wiltshire, and was born in 1672. Old enough in 1688 to appreciate the revolution, as early as he could wield his pen, he used it in the cause of the new monarchs. At the age of fifteen he was sent from the Charter-House to Oxford; and there he wrote some Latin verses, for which he was rewarded by a university scholarship. After pursuing his studies at Oxford, he began his literary career. In his twenty-second year he wrote a poetical address to Dryden; but he chiefly sought preferment through political poetry. In 1695 he wrote a poem to the king, which was well received; and in 1699 he received a pension of £300. In 1701 he went upon the Continent, and travelled principally in France and Italy. On his return, he published his travels, and a *Poetical Epistle from Italy*, which are interesting as delineating continental scenes and manners in that day. Of the travels, Dr. Johnson said, "they might have been written at home;" but he praised the poetical epistle as the finest of Addison's poetical works.

Upon the accession of Queen Anne, he continued to pay his court in verse. When the great battle of Blenheim was fought, in 1704, he at once published an artificial poem called *The Campaign*, which has received the fitting name of the *Rhymed Despatch*. Eulogistic of Marlborough and descriptive of his army manœuvres, its chief value is to be found in its historical character, and not in any poetic merit. It was a political paper, and he was rewarded for it by the appointment of Commissioner of Appeals, in which post he succeeded the philosopher Locke.

The spirit of this poem is found in the following lines:

Fiction may deck the truth with spurious rays,
And round the hero cast a borrowed blaze;
Marlboro's exploits appear divinely bright,
And proudly shine in their own native light.

If we look for a contrast to this poem, indicating with it the two political sides of the question, it may be found in Swift's tract on *The Conduct of the Allies*, which asserts that the war had been maintained to gratify the ambition and greed of Marlborough, and also for the benefit of the Allies. Addison was appointed, as a reward for his poem, Under-Secretary of State.

To this extent Addison was the historian by purpose. A moderate partisan, he eulogized King William, Marlborough, Lord Somers, Lord Halifax, and others, and thus commended himself to the crown; and in several elegant articles in *The Spectator*, he sought to mitigate the fierce party spirit of the time.

Sir Roger de Coverley. — But it is the unconscious historian with whom we are most charmed, and by whom we are best instructed. It is in this character that Addison presents himself in his numerous contributions to *The Spectator*, *The Tatler*, and *The Guardian*. Amid much that is now considered pedantic and artificial, and which, in those faults, marks the age, are to be found as striking and truthful delineations of English life and society in that day as Chaucer has given us of an earlier period.

Those who no longer read *The Spectator* as a model of style and learning, must continue to prize it for these rare historic teachings. The men and women walk before us as in some antique representation in a social festival, when grandmothers' brocades are taken out, when curious fashions are displayed, when Honoria and Flavia, Fidelia and Gloriana dress and speak and ogle and flirt just as Addison saw and photographed them. We have their subjects of interest, their forms of gossip, the existing abuses of the day, their taste in letters, their opinions upon the works of literature, in all their freshness.

The fullest and most systematic of these social delineations is found in the sketch of *The Club* and *Sir Roger de Coverley.* The creation of character is excellent. Each member, individual and distinct, is also the type of a class.

THE CLUB. — There is Will Honeycomb, the old beau, "a gentleman who, according to his years, should be in the decline of his life, but having ever been careful of his person, and always had an easy fortune, time has made but very little impression, either by wrinkles on his forehead or traces on his brain." He knew from what French woman this manner of curling the hair came, who invented hoops, and whose vanity to show her foot brought in short dresses. He is a woman-killer, sceptical about marriage ; and at length he gives the fair sex ample satisfaction for his cruelty and egotism by marrying, unknown to his friends, a farmer's daughter, whose face and virtues are her only fortune.

Captain Sentry, the nephew of Sir Roger, is, it may be supposed, the essayist's ideal of what an English officer should be — a courageous soldier and a modest gentleman.

Sir Andrew Freeport is the retired merchant, drawn to the life. He is moderate in politics, as expediency in that age would suggest. Thoroughly satisfied of the naval supremacy of England, he calls the sea, "the British Common." He is the founder of his own fortune, and is satisfied to transmit to posterity an unsullied name, a goodly store of wealth, and the title he has so honorably won.

In *The Templar,* we have a satire upon a certain class of lawyers. It is indicative of that classical age, that he understands Aristotle and Longinus better than Littleton and Coke, and is happy in anything but law — a briefless barrister, but a gentleman of consideration.

But the most charming, the most living portrait is that of Sir Roger de Coverley, an English country gentleman, as he ought to be, and as not a few really were. What a generous humanity for all wells forth from his simple and loving heart!

He has such a mirthful cast in his behavior that he is rather loved than esteemed. Repulsed by a fair widow, several years before, he keeps his sentiment alive by wearing a coat and doublet of the same cut that was in fashion at the time, which, he tells us, has been out and in twelve times since he first wore it. All the young women profess to love him, and all the young men are glad of his company.

Last of all is the clergyman, whose piety is all reverence, and who talks and acts "as one who is hastening to the object of all his wishes, and conceives hope from his decays and infirmities."

It is said that Addison, warned by the fate of Cervantes, — whose noble hero, Don Quixote, was killed by another pen, — determined to conduct Sir Roger to the tomb himself; and the knight makes a fitting end. He congratulates his nephew, Captain Sentry, upon his succession to the inheritance; he is thoughtful of old friends and old servants. In a word, so excellent was his life, and so touching the story of his death, that we feel like mourners at a real grave. Indeed he did live, and still lives, — one type of the English country gentleman one hundred and fifty years ago. Other types there were, not so pleasant to contemplate; but Addison's Sir Roger de Coverley and Fielding's Squire Allworthy vindicate their class in that age.

Addison's Hymns. — Addison appears to us also as the writer of beautiful hymns, and has paraphrased some of the Psalms. In this, like Watts, he catered to a decided religious craving of that day. In a Protestant realm, and by reason of religious controversy, the fine old hymns of the Latin church, which are now renewing their youth in an English dress, had fallen into disrepute: hymnody had, to some extent, superseded the plain chant. Hymns were in demand. Poets like Addison and Watts provided for this new want; and from the beauty of his few contributions, our great regret is that Addison wrote so few. Every one he did write is a gem in many collections. Among them we have that admirable paraphrase of the *Twenty-third Psalm:*

> The Lord my pasture shall prepare,
> And feed me with a shepherd's care;

and the hymn

> When all Thy mercies, O my God,
> My rising soul surveys.

None, however, is so beautiful, stately, and polished as the Divine Ode, so pleasant to all people, little and large,—

> The spacious firmament on high.

His Person and Character.—In closing this brief sketch of Addison, a few words are necessary as to his personality, and an estimate of his powers. In 1716 he married the Countess-Dowager of Warwick, and parted with independence to live with a coronet. His married life was not happy. The lady was cold and exacting; and, it must be confessed, the poet loved a bottle at the club-room or tavern better than the luxuries of Holland House; and not infrequently this conviviality led him to excess. He died in 1719, in his forty-eighth year, and made a truly pious end. He wished, he said, to atone for any injuries he had done to others, and sent for his sceptical and dissolute step-son, Lord Warwick, to show him how a Christian could die. A monument has been erected to his memory in the Poets' Corner of Westminster Abbey, and the closing words of the inscription upon it calls him "the honor and delight of the English nation."

As a man, he was grave and retiring: he had a high opinion of his own powers; in company he was extremely diffident; in the main, he was moral, just, and consistent. His intemperance was in part the custom of the age and in part a physical failing, and it must have been excessive to be distinguished in that age. In the Latin-English of Dr. Johnson, "It is not unlikely that Addison was first seduced to excess by the manumission which he obtained from the servile timidity of his sober hours." This failing must be regarded as a blot on his fame.

He was the most accomplished writer of his own age, and in elegance of style superior to all who had gone before him.

In the words of his epitaph, his prose papers "encouraged the good and reformed the improvident, tamed the wicked, and in some degree made them in love with virtue." His poetry is chiefly of historical value, in that it represents so distinctly the Artificial School; but it is now very little read. His drama entitled *Cato* was modelled upon the French drama of the classical school, with its singular preservation of the unities. But his contributions to *The Spectator* and other periodicals are historically of great value. Here he abandons the artificial school; nothing in his delineations of character is simply statuesque or pictorial. He has done for us what the historians have left undone. They present processions of automata moving to the sound of trumpet and drum, ushered by Black Rod or Garter King-at-arms; but in Addison we find that Promethean heat which relumes their life; the galvanic motion becomes a living stride; the puppet eyes emit fire; the automata are men. Thus it is, that, although *The Spectator*, once read as a model of taste and style, has become antiquated and has been superseded, it must still be resorted to for its life-like portraiture of men and women, manners and customs, and will be found truer and more valuable for these than history itself.

CHAPTER XXVI.

STEELE AND SWIFT.

Sir Richard Steele.	Jonathan Swift — Poems.	M. B. Drapier.
Periodicals.	The Tale of a Tub.	Gulliver's Travels.
The Crisis.	Battle of the Books.	Stella and Vanessa.
His Last Days.	Pamphlets.	His Character and Death.

CONTEMPORARY with Addison, and forming with him a literary fraternity, Steele and Swift were besides men of distinct prominence, and clearly represent the age in which they lived.

SIR RICHARD STEELE. — If Addison were chosen as the principal literary figure of the period, a sketch of his life would be incomplete without a large mention of his lifelong friend and collaborator, Steele. If to Bacon belongs the honor of being the first writer and the namer of the English *essay*, Steele may claim that of being the first periodical essayist.

He was born in Dublin, in 1671, of English parents; his father being at the time secretary to the Lord Lieutenant of Ireland. He received his early education at the Charter-House school, in London, an institution which has numbered among its pupils many who have gained distinguished names in literature. Here he met and formed a permanent friendship with Addison. He was afterwards entered as a student at Merton College, Oxford; but he led there a wild and reckless life, and leaving without a degree, he enlisted as a private in the Horse Guards. Through the influence of his friends, he was made a cornet, and afterwards a captain, in the Fusileers; but this only gave him opportunity for continued dissipation. His principles were better than his conduct; and, haunted by conscience, he made an effort to reform himself by writing a devotional work called *The Christian Hero;* but there was such a contrast between his precepts and his life, that he was laughed at by the town. Between 1701 and 1704 he produced his three comedies, *The Funeral, or Grief à la Mode; The Tender Husband*, and *The Lying Lover*. The first two were successful upon the stage, but the last was a complete failure. Disgusted for the time with the drama, he was led to find his true place as the writer of those light, brilliant, periodical essays which form a prominent literary feature of the reign of Queen Anne. These *Essays* were comments, suggestions, strictures, and satires upon the age. They were of immediate and local interest then, and have now a value which the writers did not foresee: they are unconscious history.

PERIODICALS.—The first of these periodicals was *The Tatler*, a penny sheet, issued tri-weekly, on post-days. The first number appeared on the 12th of April, 1709, and asserted the very laudable purpose "to expose the deceits, sins, and vanities of the former age, and to make virtue, simplicity, and plain-dealing the law of social life." "For this purpose," in the words of Dr. Johnson,* "nothing is so proper as the frequent publication of short papers, which we read not as study, but amusement. If the subject be slight, the treatise is short. The busy may find time, and the idle may find patience." One *nom de plume* of Steele was *Isaac Bickerstaff*, which he borrowed from Swift, who had issued party pamphlets under that name.

The Tatler was a success. The fluent pen of Addison gave it valuable assistance; and in January, 1711, it was merged

* Life of Addison.

into, rather than superseded by, *The Spectator*, which was issued six days in the week.

In this new periodical, Steele wrote the paper containing the original sketch of Sir Roger de Coverley and The Club; but, as has been already said, Addison adopted, elaborated, and finished this in several later papers. Steele had been by far the larger contributor to *The Tatler*. Of all the articles in *The Spectator*, Steele wrote two hundred and forty, and Addison two hundred and seventy-four; the rest were by various hands. In March, 1713, when *The Spectator* was commencing its seventh volume, *The Guardian* made its appearance. For the first volume of *The Guardian*, Addison wrote but one paper; but for the second he wrote more than Steele. Of the one hundred and seventy-six numbers of that periodical, eighty-two of the papers were by Steele and fifty-three by Addison. If the writings of Addison were more scholarly and elegant, those of Steele were more vivacious and brilliant; and together they have produced a series of essays which have not been surpassed in later times, and which are vividly delineative of their own.

THE CRISIS. — The career of Steele was varied and erratic. He held several public offices, was a justice of the peace, and a member of parliament. He wrote numerous political tracts, which are not without historical value. For one pamphlet of a political character, entitled *The Crisis*, he was expelled from parliament for libel; but upon the death of Queen Anne, he again found himself in favor. He was knighted in 1715, and received several lucrative appointments.

He was an eloquent orator, and as a writer rapid and brilliant, but not profound. Even thus, however, he catered to an age at once artificial and superficial. Very observant of what he saw, he rushed to his closet and jotted down his views in electrical words, which made themselves immediately and distinctly felt.

HIS LAST DAYS. — Near the close of his life he produced a very successful comedy, entitled *The Conscious Lover*, which would have been of pecuniary value to him, were it not that he was already overwhelmed with debt. His end was a sad one; but he reaped what his extravagance and recklessness had sown. Shattered in health and ruined in fortune, he retreated from the great world into homely retirement in Wales, where he lived, poor and hidden, in a humble cottage at Llangunnor. His end was heralded by an attack of paralysis, and he died in 1729.

After his death, his letters were published; and in the private history which they unfold, he appears, notwithstanding all his follies, in the light of a tender husband and of an amiable and unselfish man. He had principle, but he lacked resolution; and the wild, vacillating character of his life is mirrored in his writings, where *The Christian Hero* stands in singular contrast to the comic personages of his dramas. He was a genial critic. His exuberant wit and humor reproved without wounding; he was not severe enough to be a public censor, nor pedantic enough to be the pedagogue of an age which often needed the lash rather than the gentle reproof, and upon which a merciful clemency lost its end if not its praises. He deserves credit for an attempt, however feeble, to reward virtue upon the stage, after the wholesale rewards which vice had reaped in the age of Charles II.

Steele has been overshadowed, in his connection with Addison, by the more dignified and consistent career, the greater social respectability, and the more elegant and scholarly style of his friend; and yet in much that they jointly accomplished, the merit of Steele is really as great, and conduces much to the reputation of Addison. The one husbanded and cherished his fame; the other flung it away or lavished it upon his colleagues. As contributors to history, they claim an equal share of our gratitude and praise.

Jonathan Swift. — The grandfather of Swift was vicar of Goodrich, in Herefordshire. His father and mother were both English, but he was born in Dublin, in the year 1667. A posthumous child, he came into the world seven months after his father's death. From his earliest youth, he deplored the circumstances among which his lot had been cast. He was dependent upon his uncle, Godwin Swift, himself a poor man; but was not grateful for his assistance, always saying that his uncle had given him the education of a dog. At the University of Dublin, where he was entered, he did not bear a good character: he was frequently absent from his duties and negligent of his studies; and although he read history and poetry, he was considered stupid as well as idle. He was more than once admonished and suspended, but at length received his degree, *Speciali gratia;* which special act of grace implied that he had not fairly earned it. Piqued by this, he set to work in real earnest, and is said to have studied eight hours a day for eight years. Thus, from an idle and unsuccessful collegian, he became a man of considerable learning and a powerful writer.

He was a distant connection of Sir William Temple, through Lady Temple; and he went, by his mother's advice, to live with that distinguished man at his seat, Shene, in Moor Park, as private secretary.

In this position Swift seems to have led an uncomfortable life, ranking somewhere between the family and the upper servants. Sir William Temple was disposed to be kind, but found it difficult to converse with him on account of his moroseness and other peculiarities. At Shene he met King William III., who talked with him, and offered him a captaincy in the army. This Swift declined, knowing his unfitness for the post, and doubtless feeling the promptings of a higher ambition. It was also at Shene that he met a young girl, whose history was thenceforth to be mingled with his in sadness and sorrow, during their lives. This was Esther Johnson, the daughter of Temple's housekeeper, and surmised, at a later day, to be the natural daughter of Temple himself. When the young secretary first met her, she was fourteen years of age, very clever and beautiful; and they fell in love with each other.

We cannot dwell at length upon the events of his life. His versatile pen was prolific of poetry, sentimental and satirical; of political allegories of great potency, of fiction erected of impossible materials, and yet so creating and peopling a world of fancy as to illude the reader into temporary belief in its truth.

POEMS. — His poems are rather sententious than harmonious. His power, however, was great; he managed verse as an engine, and had an entire mastery over rhyme, which masters so many would-be poets. His *Odes* are classically constructed, but massive and cumbrous. His satirical poems are eminently historical, ranging over and attacking almost every topic, political, religious, and social. Among the most characteristic of his miscellaneous verses are *Epigrams and Epistles*, *Clever Tom Pinch Going to be Hanged*, *Advice to Grub Street Writers*, *Helter-Skelter*, *The Puppet Show*, and similar odd pieces, frequently scurrilous, bitter, and lewd in expression. The writer of English history consults these as he does the penny ballads, lampoons, and caricatures of the day, — to discern the *animus* of parties and the methods of hostile factions.

But it is in his inimitable prose writings that Swift is of most value to the historical student. Against all comers he stood the Goliath of pamphleteers in the reign of Queen Anne, and there arose no David who could slay him.

THE TALE OF A TUB. — While an unappreciated student at the university, he had sketched a satirical piece, which he finished and published in 1704, under the title of *The Tale of a Tub.* As a tub is thrown overboard at sea to divert a whale, so this is supposed to be a sop cast out to the *Leviathan* of Hobbes, to prevent it from injuring the vessel of state. The story is a satire aimed against the Roman Catholics on the one hand, and the Presbyterians on the other, in order that he may exalt the Church of England as, in his judgment, free from the errors of both, and a just and happy medium between the two extremes. His own opinion of its merits is well known: in one of his later years, when his hand had lost its cunning, he is said to have exclaimed, as he picked it up, "What a genius I had when I wrote that book!" The characters of the story are *Peter* (representing St. Peter, or the Roman Catholic Church), *Martin* (Luther, or the Church of England), and *Jack* (John Calvin, or the Presbyterians). By their father's will each had been left a suit of clothes, made in the fashion of his day. To this Peter added laces and fringes; Martin took off some of the ornaments of doubtful taste; but Jack ripped and tore off the trimmings of his dress to such an extent that he was in danger of exposing his nakedness. It is said that the invective was so strong and the satire so bitter, that they presented a bar to that preferment which Swift might otherwise have obtained.

He appears at this time to have cared little for public opinion, except that it should fear his trenchant wit and do homage to his genius.

THE BATTLE OF THE BOOKS. — In the same year, 1704, he also published *The Battle of the Books*, the idea of which was taken from a French work of Courtraye, entitled "*Histoire de la guerre nouvellement déclarée entre les Anciens et les Modernes.*" Swift's work was written in furtherance of the views of his patron, Temple, who had some time before engaged in the controversy as to the relative merits of ancient and modern learning, and who, in the words of Macaulay, "was so absurd as to set up his own authority against that of Bentley on questions of Greek history and philology."

The Battle of the Books is of present value, as it affords information upon the opinions then held on a question which, in various forms, has been agitating the literary world ever since. In it Swift compares Dryden, Wotten, and Bentley with the old authors in St. James's Library, where the battle of the books is said to have taken place.

Upon the death of Sir William Temple, in 1699, Swift had gone to London. He was ambitious of power and money, and when he found little chance of preferment among the Whigs, he became a Tory. It must be said, in explanation of this change, that, although he had called himself a Whig, he had disliked many of their opinions, and had never heartily espoused their cause. Like others already referred to, he watched the political horizon, and was ready for a change when circumstances should warrant it. This change and its causes are set forth in his *Bickerstaff's Ridicule of Astrology* and *Sacramental Test.*

The Whigs tried hard to retain him; the Tories were rejoiced to receive him, and modes of preferment for him were openly canvassed. One of these was to make him Bishop of Virginia, with metropolitan powers in America; but it failed. He was also recommended for the See of Hereford; but persons near the queen advised her "to be sure that the man she was going to make a bishop was a Christian." Thus far he had only been made rector of Agher and vicar of Laracor and Rathbeggin.

VARIOUS PAMPHLETS. — His *Argument Against the Abolition of Christianity,* Dr. Johnson calls "a very happy and judicious irony." In 1710 he wrote a paper, at the request of the Irish primate, petitioning the queen to remit the first-fruits and twentieth parts to the Irish clergy. In 1712, ten days before the meeting of parliament, he published his *Con-*

duct of the Allies, which, exposing the greed of Marlborough, persuaded the nation to make peace. A supplement to this is found in *Reflections on the Barrier Treaty*, in which he shows how little English interests had been consulted in that negotiation.

His pamphlet on *The Public Spirit of the Whigs*, in answer to Steele's *Crisis*, was so terrible a bomb-shell thrown into the camp of his former friends, and so insulting to the Scotch, that £300 were offered by the queen, at the instance of the Scotch lords, for the discovery of the author; but without success.

At last his versatile and powerful pen obtained some measure of reward: in 1713 he was made Dean of St. Patrick's, in Dublin, with a stipend of £700 per annum. This was his greatest and last preferment.

On the accession of George I., in the following year, he paid his court, but was received with something more than coldness. He withdrew to his deanery in Dublin, and, in the words of Johnson, "commenced Irishman for life, and was to contrive how he might be best accommodated in a country where he considered himself as in a state of exile." After some misunderstanding between himself and his Irish fellow-citizens, he espoused their cause so warmly that he became the most popular man in Ireland. In 1721 he could write to Pope, "I neither know the names nor the number of the family which now reigneth, further than the prayer-book informeth me." His letters, signed *M. B. Drapier*, on Irish manufactures, and especially those in opposition to Wood's monopoly of copper coinage, in 1724, wrought upon the people, producing such a spirit of resistance that the project of a debased coinage failed; and so influential did Swift become, that he was able to say to the Archbishop of Dublin, "Had I raised my finger, the mob would have torn you to pieces." This popularity was increased by the fact that a reward of £300 was offered by Lord Carteret and the privy council for the discovery of the authorship of the fourth letter; but although it was commonly known that Swift was the author, proof could not be obtained. Carteret, the Lord Lieutenant, afterwards said, "When people ask me how I governed Ireland, I said that I pleased Doctor Swift."

Thus far Swift's literary labors are manifest history: we come now to consider that great work, *Gulliver's Travels*, — the most successful of its kind ever written, — in which, with all the charm of fiction in plot, incident, and description, he pictures the great men and the political parties of the day.

GULLIVER'S TRAVELS. — Lemuel Gulliver, a surgeon's mate, finds himself shipwrecked on the shore of the country of Lilliput, the people of which are only six inches in height. His adventures are so vividly described that our charmed fancy places us among them as we read, and we, for a time, abandon ourselves to a belief in their reality. It was, however, begun as a political satire; in the insignificance of the court of pigmies, he attacks the feebleness and folly of the new reign. *Flimnap*, the prime minister of Lilliput, is a caricature of Walpole; the *Big Indians* and *Little Indians* represent the Protestants and Roman Catholics; the *High Heels* and *Low Heels* stand for the Whigs and Tories; and the heir-apparent, who wears one heel high and the other low, is the Prince of Wales, afterwards George II., who favored both parties in order to gain both to his purpose.

In his second voyage, that to Brobdignag, his satirical imagination took a wider range — European politics as they appear to a superior intelligence, illustrated by a man of *sixty* feet in comparison with one of *six*. As Gulliver had looked with curious contempt upon the united efforts of the Lilliputians, he now found himself in great jeopardy and fear when in the hands of a giant of Brobdignag. As the pigmy metropolis, five hundred yards square, was to London, so were London and other European capitals to the giants' city, two thousand miles in circumference. And what are the armies of Europe, when compared with that magnificent cavalry manœuvring on a parade-ground twenty miles square, each mounted trooper ninety feet high, and all, as they draw their swords at command, representing ten thousand flashes of lightning?

The third part contains the voyage of Gulliver — no less improbable than the former ones — to *Laputa*, the flying island of projectors and visionaries. This is a varied satire upon the Royal Society, the eccentricities of the savans, empirics of all kinds, mathematical magic, and the like. In this, political schemes to restore the pretender are aimed at. The Mississippi Scheme and the South Sea bubble are denounced. Here, too, in his journey to Luggnagg, he introduces the sad and revolting picture of the Struldbrugs, those human beings who live on, losing all their power and becoming hideously old.

In his last voyage — to the land of the *Houyhnhnms* — his misanthropy is painfully manifest. This is the country where horses are masters, and men a servile and degraded race; and he has painted the men so brutish and filthy that the satire loses its point. The power of satire lies in contrast; we must compare the evil in men with the good: when the whole race is included in one sweeping condemnation, and an inferior being exalted, in opposition to all possibility, the standard is absurd, and the satirist loses his pains.

The horses are the *Houyhnhnms*, (the name is an attempt to imitate a neigh,) a noble race, who are amazed and disgusted at the Yahoos, — the degraded men, — upon whom Swift, in his sweeping misanthropy, has exhausted his bitterness and his filth.

Stella and Vanessa. — While Swift's mysterious associations with Stella and Vanessa have but little to do with the course of English Literature, they largely affect his personality, and no sketch of him would be complete without introducing them to the reader. We cannot conjure up the tall, burly form, the heavy-browed, scowling, contemptuous face, the sharp blue eye, and the bushy black hair of the dean, without seeing on one side and the other the two pale, meek-eyed, devoted women, who watch his every look, shrink from his sudden bursts of wrath, receive for their infatuation a few fair words without sentiment, and earnestly crave a little love as a return for their whole hearts. It is a wonderful, touching, baffling story.

Stella he had known and taught in her young maidenhood at Sir William Temple's. As has been said, she was called the daughter of his steward and housekeeper, but conjectures are rife that she was Sir William's own child. When Swift removed to Ireland, she came, at Swift's request, with a matron friend, Mrs. Dingley, to live near him. Why he did not at once marry her, and why, at last, he married her secretly, in 1716, are questions over which curious readers have puzzled themselves in vain, and upon which, in default of evidence, some perhaps uncharitable conclusions have been reached. The story of their association may be found in the *Journal to Stella.*

With Miss Hester Vanhomrigh (Vanessa) he became acquainted in London, in 1712: he was also her instructor; and when with her he seems to have forgotten his allegiance to Stella. Cadenus, as he calls himself, was too tender and fond: Vanessa became infatuated; and when she heard of Swift's private marriage with Stella, she died of chagrin or of a broken heart. She had cancelled the will which she had made in Swift's favor, and left it in charge to her executors to publish their correspondence. Both sides of the history of this connection are fully displayed in the poem of *Cadenus and Vanessa*, and in the *Correspondence of Swift and Vanessa.*

CHARACTER AND DEATH. — Pride overbearing and uncontrollable, misanthropy, excessive dogmatism, a singular pleasure in giving others pain, were among his personal faults or misfortunes. He abused his companions and servants; he never forgave his sister for marrying a tradesman; he could attract with winning words and repel with furious invective; and he was always anxiously desiring the day of his death, and cursing that of his birth. His common farewell was "Good-bye; I hope we may never meet again." There is a painful levity in his verses *On the Death of Doctor Swift*, in which he gives an epitome of his life:

From Dublin soon to London spread,
'T is told at court the dean is dead!
And Lady Suffolk, in the spleen,
Runs laughing up to tell the queen:
The queen, so gracious, mild, and good,
Cries, "Is he gone? it's time he should."

At last the end came. While a young man, he had suffered from a painful attack of vertigo, brought on by a surfeit of fruit; "eating," he says, in a letter to Mrs. Howard, "an hundred golden pippins at a time." This had occasioned a deafness; and both giddiness and deafness had recurred at intervals, and at last manifestly affected his mind. Once, when walking with some friends, he had pointed to an elm-tree, blasted by lightning, and had said, "I shall be like that tree: I shall die first at the top." And thus at last the doom fell. Struck on the brain, he lingered for nine years in that valley of spectral horrors, of whose only gates idiocy and madness are the hideous wardens. From this bondage he was released by death on the 19th of October, 1745.

Many have called it a fearful retribution for his sins, and especially for his treatment of Stella and Vanessa. A far more reasonable and charitable verdict is that the evil in his conduct through life had its origin in congenital disorder;

and in his days of apparent sanity, the character of his eccentric actions is to be palliated, if not entirely excused, on the plea of insanity. Additional force is given to this judgment by the fact that, when he died, it was found that he had left his money to found a hospital for the insane, illustrating the line,—

A fellow-feeling makes us wondrous kind.

In that day of great classical scholars, Swift will hardly rank among the most profound; but he possessed a creative power, a ready and versatile fancy, a clear and pleasing but plain style. He has been unjustly accused by Lady Montagu of having stolen plot and humor from Cervantes and Rabelais: he drew from the same source as they; and those suggestions which came to him from them owe all their merit to his application of them. As a critic, he was heartless and rude; but as a polemic and a delineator of his age, he stands prominently forth as an historian, whose works alone would make us familiar with the period.

Other Writers of the Age.

Sir William Temple, 1628–1698: he was a statesman and a political writer; rather a man of mark in his own day than of special interest to the present time. After having been engaged in several important diplomatic affairs, he retired to his seat of Moor Park, and employed himself in study and with his pen. His *Essays and Observations on Government* are valuable as a clue to the history. In his controversy with Bentley on the *Epistles of Phalaris*, and the relative merits of ancient and modern authors, he was overmatched in scholarship. In a literary point of view, Temple deserves praise for the ease and beauty of his style. Dr. Johnson says he "was the first writer who gave cadence to English prose." "What can be more pleasant," says Charles Lamb, "than the way in which the retired statesman peeps out in his essays, penned in his delightful retreat at Shene?" He is perhaps better known in literary history as the early patron of Swift, than for his own works.

Sir Isaac Newton, 1642–1727: the chief glory of Newton is not connected with literary effort: he ranks among the most profound and original philosophers, and was one of the purest and most unselfish of men.

The son of a farmer, he was born at Woolsthorpe, in Lincolnshire, after his father's death,—a feeble, sickly child. The year of his birth was that in which Galileo died. At the age of fifteen he was employed on his mother's farm, but had already displayed such an ardor for learning that he was sent first to school and then to Cambridge, where he was soon conspicuous for his talents and his genius. In due time he was made a professor. His discoveries in astronomy, mechanics, and optics are of world-wide renown. The law of gravitation was established by him, and set forth in his paper *De Motu Corporum*. His treatise on *Fluxions* prepared the way for that wonderful mathematical, labor-saving instrument—the differential calculus. In 1687 he published his *Philosophiæ Naturalis Principia Mathematica*, in which all his mathematical theories are propounded. In 1696 he was made Warden of the Mint, and in 1699 Master of the Mint. Long a member of the Royal Society, he was its president for the last twenty-four years of his life. In 1688 he was elected member of parliament for the university of Cambridge. Of purely literary works he left two, entitled respectively, *Observations upon the Prophecies of Daniel and the Apocalypse of St. John*, and a *Chronology of Ancient Kingdoms Amended;* both of which are of little present value except as the curious remains of so great a man.

Viscount Bolingbroke (Henry St. John), 1678–1751: as an erratic statesman, a notorious free-thinker, a dissipated lord, a clever political writer, and an eloquent speaker, Lord Bolingbroke was a centre of attraction in his day, and demands observation in literary history. During the reign of Queen Anne he was a plotter in favor of the pretender, and when she died, he fled the realm to avoid impeachment for treason. In France he joined the pretender as Secretary of State, but was dismissed for intrigue; and on being pardoned by the English king, he returned to England. His writings are brilliant but specious. His influence was felt in the literary society he drew around him,—Swift, Pope, and others,—and, as has been already said, his opinions are to be found in that *Essay on Man* which Pope dedicated to him. In his meteoric political career he represents and typifies one phase of the time in which he lived.

George Berkeley, 1684–1753: he was educated at Trinity College, Dublin, and soon engaged in metaphysical controversy. In 1724 he was made Dean of Derry, and in 1734, Bishop of Cloyne. A man of great philanthropy, he set forth a scheme for the founding of the *Bermudas College*, to train missionaries for the colonies and to labor among the North American Indians. As a metaphysician, he was an *absolute idealist*. This is no place to discuss his theory. In the words of Dr. Reid, "He maintains . . . that there is no such thing as matter in the universe; that the sun and moon, earth and sea, our own bodies and those of our friends, are nothing but ideas in the minds of those who think of them, and that they have no existence when they are not objects of thought; that all that is in the universe may be reduced to two categories, to wit, *minds* and *ideas in the mind*." The reader is referred, for a full discussion of this question, to Sir William Hamilton's *Metaphysics*. Berkeley's chief writings are: *New Theory of Vision*, *Treatise Concerning the Principles of Human Knowledge*, and *Dialogues Between Hylas and Philonous*. His name and memory are especially dear to the American people; for, although his scheme of the training-college failed, he lived for two years and a half in Newport, where his house still stands, and where one of his children is buried. He presented to Yale College his library and his estate in Rhode Island, and he wrote that beautiful poem with its kindly prophecy:

Westward the course of empire takes its way:
  The four first acts already past,
A fifth shall close the drama with the day;
  Time's noblest offspring is the last.

CHAPTER XXVII.

THE RISE AND PROGRESS OF MODERN FICTION.

The New Age. | Daniel Defoe. | Robinson Crusoe. | Richardson. | Pamela, and Other Novels. | Fielding. | Joseph Andrews. | Tom Jones. | Its Moral. | Smollett. | Roderick Random. | Peregrine Pickle

THE NEW AGE.

WE have now reached a new topic in the course of English Literature — contemporaneous, indeed, with the subjects just named, but marked by new and distinct development. It was a period when numerous and distinctive forms appeared; when genius began to segregate into schools and divisions; when the progress of letters and the demands of popular curiosity gave rise to works which would have been impossible, because uncalled for, in any former period. English enterprise was extending commerce and scattering useful arts in all quarters of the globe, and thus giving new and rich materials to English letters. Clive was making himself a lord in India; Braddock was losing his army and his life in America. This spirit of English enterprise in foreign lands was evoking literary activity at home: there was no exploit of English valor, no extension of English dominion and influence, which did not find its literary reproduction. Thus, while it was an age of historical research, it was also that of actual delineations of curious novelties at home and abroad.

Poetry was in a transition state; it was taking its leave of the unhealthy satire and the technical wit of Queen Anne's reign, and attempting, on the one hand, the impostures of Macpherson and Chatterton, — to which we shall hereafter refer, — and, on the other, the restoration of the pastoral from the theatrical to the real, in Thomson's song of the Rolling Year, and Cowper's pleasant Task, so full of life and nature. Swallow-like, English poetry had hung about the eaves or skimmed the surface of town and court; but now, like the lark, it soared into freer air —

> Cœtusque vulgares et udam
> Spernit humum fugiente penna.

In short, it was a day of general awakening. The intestine troubles excited by the Jacobites were brought to an end by the disaster of Culloden, in 1745. The German campaigns culminating at Minden, in 1759, opened a door to the study of German literature, and of the Teutonic dialects as elements of the English language.

It is, therefore, not astonishing that in this period Literature should begin to arrange itself into its present great divisions. As in an earlier age the drama had been born to cater to a popular taste, so in this, to satisfy the public demand, arose English *prose fiction* in its peculiar and enduring form. There had been grand and desultory works preceding this, such as *Robinson Crusoe*, *The Pilgrim's Progress*, and Swift's inimitable story of *Gulliver;* but the modern novel, unlike these, owes its origin to a general desire for delineations of private life and manners. "Show us ourselves!" was the cry.

A novel may be defined as a fictitious story of modern life describing the management and mastery of the human passions, and especially the universal passion of love. Its power consists in the creation of ideal characters, which leave a real impress upon the reader's mind; it must be a prose *epic* in that there is always a hero, or, at least, a heroine, generally both, and a *drama* in its presentation of scenes and supplementary personages. Thackeray calls his *Vanity Fair* a novel without a hero: it is impossible to conceive a novel without a heroine. There must also be a *dénouement*, or consummation; in short, it must have, in the words of Aristotle, a beginning, middle, and ending, in logical connection and consecutive interest.

DANIEL DEFOE. — Before, however, proceeding to consider the modern novel, we must make mention of one author, distinctly of his own age as a political pamphleteer, but who, in his chief and inimitable work, stands alone, without antecedent or consequent. *Robinson Crusoe* has had a host of imitators, but no rival.

Daniel Foe, or, as he afterwards called himself, De Foe, was born in London, in the year 1661. He was the son of a butcher, but such was his early aptitude for learning, that he was educated to become a dissenting minister. His own views, however, were different: he became instead a political author, and wrote with great force against the government of James II. and the Established Church, and in favor of the dissenters. When the Duke of Monmouth landed to make his fatal campaign, Defoe joined his standard; but does not seem to have suffered with the greater number of the duke's adherents.

He was a warm supporter of William III.; and his famous poem, *The True-Born Englishman*, was written in answer to an attack upon the king and the Dutch, called *The Foreigners*. Of his own poem he says, in the preface, "When I see the town full of lampoons and invectives against the Dutch, only because they are foreigners, and the king reproached and insulted by insolent pedants and ballad-making poets for employing foreigners and being a foreigner himself, I confess myself moved by it to remind our nation of their own original, thereby to let them see what a banter they put upon themselves, since — speaking of Englishmen *ab origine* — we are really all foreigners ourselves:"

The Pict and painted Briton, treach'rous Scot,
By hunger, theft, and rapine hither brought;
Norwegian pirates, buccaneering Danes,
Whose red-haired offspring everywhere remains;
Who, joined with Norman-French, compound the breed
From whence your true-born Englishmen proceed.

In 1702, just after the death of King William, Defoe published his severely ironical pamphlet, *The Shortest Way with the Dissenters.* Assuming the character of a High Churchman, he says: "'T is vain to trifle in the matter. The light, foolish handling of them by fines is their glory and advantage. If the gallows instead of the compter, and the galleys instead of the fines, were the reward of going to a conventicle, there would not be so many sufferers." His irony was at first misunderstood: the High Churchmen hailed him as a champion, and the Dissenters hated him as an enemy. But when his true meaning became apparent, a reward of £50 was offered by the government for his discovery. His so-called "scandalous and seditious pamphlet" was burnt by the common hangman: he was tried, and sentenced to pay two hundred marks, to stand three times in the pillory, and to be imprisoned during the queen's pleasure. He bore his sentence bravely, and during his two years' residence in prison he published a periodical called *The Review.* In 1709 he wrote a *History of the Union* between England and Scotland.

Robinson Crusoe. — But none of these things, nor all combined, would have given to Defoe that immortality which is his as the author of *Robinson Crusoe.* Of the groundwork of the story not much need be said.

Alexander Selkirk, the sailing-master of an English privateer, was set ashore, in 1704, at his own request, on the uninhabited island Juan Fernandez, which lies several hundred miles from the coast of Chili, in the Pacific Ocean. He was supplied with clothing and arms, and remained there alone for four years and four months. It is supposed that his adventures suggested the work. It is also likely that Defoe had read the journal of Peter Serrano, who, in the sixteenth century, had been *marooned* in like manner on a desolate island lying off the mouth of the Oroonoque (Orinoco). The latter locality was adopted by Defoe. But it is not the fact or the adventures which give power to *Robinson Crusoe.* It is the manner of treating what might occur to any fancy, even the dullest. The charm consists in the simplicity and the verisimilitude of the narrative, the rare adaptation of the common man to his circumstances, his projects and failures, the birth of religion in his soul, his conflicting hopes and fears, his occasional despair. We see in him a brother, and a suffering one. We live his life on the island; we share his terrible fear at the discovery of the footprint, his courage in destroying the cannibal savages and rescuing the victim. Where is there in fiction another man Friday? From the beginning of his misfortunes until he is again sailing for England, after nearly thirty years of captivity, he holds us spellbound by the reality, the simplicity, and the pathos of his narrative; but, far beyond the temporary illusion of the modern novel, everything remains real: the shipwrecked mariner spins his yarns in sailor fashion, and we believe and feel every word he says. The book, although wonderfully good throughout, is unequal: the prime interest only lasts until he is rescued, and ends with his embarkation for England. The remainder of his travels becomes, as a narrative, comparatively tiresome and tame; and we feel, besides, that, after his unrivalled experience, he should have remained in England, "the observed of all observers." Yet it must be said that we are indebted to his later journey in Spain and France, his adventures in the Eastern Seas, his caravan ride overland from China to Europe, for much which illustrates the manners and customs of navigation and travel in that day.

Robinson Crusoe stands alone among English books, a perennial fountain of instruction and pleasure. It aids in educating each new generation: children read it for its incident; men to renew their youth; literary scholars to discover what it teaches of its time and of its author's genius. Its influence continues unabated; it incites boys to maritime adventure, and shows them how to use in emergency whatever they find at hand. It does more: it tends to reclaim the erring by its simple homilies; it illustrates the ruder navigation of its day; shows us the habits and morals of the merchant marine, and the need and means of reforming what was so very bad.

Defoe's style is clear, simple, and natural. He wrote several other works, of which few are now read. Among these are the *Account of the Plague*, *The Life and Piracies of Captain Singleton*, and *The Fortunes and Misfortunes of Moll Flanders*. He died on the 24th of April, 1731.

RICHARDSON. — Samuel Richardson, who, notwithstanding the peculiar merits of Defoe, must be called the *Father of Modern Prose Fiction*, was born in Derbyshire, in 1689. The personal events of his life are few and uninteresting. A carpenter's son, he had but little schooling, and owed everything to his own exertions. Apprenticed to a printer in London, at the age of fifteen, he labored assiduously at his trade, and it rewarded him with fortune: he became, in turn, printer of the Journals of the House of Commons, Master of the Stationers' Company, and Printer to the King. While young, he had been the confidant of three young women, and had written or corrected their love-letters for them. He seems to have had great fluency in letter-writing; and being solicited by a publisher to write a series of familiar letters on the principal concerns of life, which might be used as models, — a sort of "Easy Letter-Writer," — he began the task, but, changing his plan, he wrote a story in a series of letters. The first volume was published in 1741, and was no less a work than *Pamela*. The author was then fifty years old;

and he presents in this work a matured judgment concerning the people and customs of the day,—the printer's notions of the social condition of England,—shrewd, clever, and defective.

Wearied as the world had been by what Sir Walter Scott calls the "huge folios of inanity" which had preceded him, the work was hailed with delight. There was a little affectation; but the sentiment was moral and natural. Ladies carried *Pamela* about in their rides and walks. Pope, near his end, said it was a better moral teacher than sermons: Sherlock recommended it from the pulpit.

PAMELA, AND OTHER NOVELS.—*Pamela* is represented as a poor servant-maid, but beautiful and chaste, whose honor resists the attack of her dissolute master, and whose modesty and virtue overcome his evil nature. Subdued and reclaimed by her chastity and her charms, he reforms, and marries her. Some pictures which are rather warmly colored and indelicate in our day were quite in keeping with the taste of that time, and gave greater effect to the moral lesson assigned to be taught.

In his next work, *Clarissa Harlowe*, which appeared in 1749, he has drawn the picture of a perfect woman preserving her purity amid seductive gayeties, and suffering sorrows to which those of the Virgin Martyr are light. We have, too, an excellent portraiture of a bold and wicked, but clever and gifted man—Lovelace.

His third and last novel, *Sir Charles Grandison*, appeared in 1753. The hero, *Sir Charles*, is the model of a Christian gentleman; but is, perhaps, too faultless for popular appreciation.

In his delineations of humbler natures,—country girls like *Pamela*,—Richardson is happiest: in his descriptions of high life he has failed from ignorance. He was not acquainted with the best society, and all his grandees are stilted, artificial, and affected; but even in this fault he is of value, for he shows us how men of his class at that time regarded the society of those above them.

These works, which, notwithstanding their length, were devoured eagerly as soon as they appeared, are little read at present, and exist rather as historical interpreters of an age that is past, than as present light literature: they have been driven from our shelves by Scott, Dickens, Thackeray, and a host of charming novelists since his day.

Richardson lived the admired of a circle of ladies,—to whose sex he had paid so noble a tribute,—the hero of tea-drinkings at his house on Parson's Green; his books gave him fame, but his shop—in the back office of which he wrote his novels, when not pressed by business—gave him money and its comforts. He died at the age of seventy-two, on the 4th of July, 1761.

He was an unconscious actor in a great movement which had begun in France. The brilliant theories of Voltaire, Rousseau, Montesquieu, and Dalembert—containing much truth and many heresies—were felt in England, and had given a new impetus to English intellect; indeed, it is not strange, when we come to consider, that while Richardson's works were praised in English pulpits, Voltaire and the French atheists declared that they saw in them an advance towards human perfectibility and self-redemption, of which, if true, Richardson himself was unconscious. From the amours of men and women of fashion, aided by intriguing maid-servants and lying valets, Richardson turned away to do honor to untitled merit, to exalt the humble, and to defy gilded vice. Whatever were the charms of rank, he has elevated our humanity; thus far, and thus far only, has he sympathized with the Frenchmen who attacked the corruptions of the age, but who assaulted also its faith and its reverence.

Henry Fielding. — The path of prose fiction, so handsomely opened by Richardson, was immediately entered and pursued by a genius of higher order, and as unlike him as it was possible to be. Richardson still clung to romantic sentiment, Fielding eschewed it; Richardson was a teacher of morality, Fielding shielded immorality; Richardson described artificial manners in a society which he did not frequent, Fielding, in the words of Coleridge, "was like an open lawn on a breezy day in May;" Richardson was a plebeian, a carpenter's son, a successful printer; Fielding was a gentleman, the son of General Fielding, and grandson of the Earl of Denbigh; Richardson steadily rose, by his honest exertions, to independent fortune, Fielding passed from the high estate of his ancestors into poverty and loose company; the one has given us mistaken views of high life, the other has been enabled, by his sad experience, to give us truthful pictures of every grade of English society in his day from the lord, the squire, and the fop to the thief-taker, the prostitute, and the thief.

Henry Fielding was born on the 22d of April, 1707, at Sharpham Park, Somersetshire. While yet a young man, he had read *Pamela;* and to ridicule what he considered its prudery and over-righteousness, he hastily commenced his novel of *Joseph Andrews.* This Joseph is represented as the brother of Pamela, — a simple country lad, who comes to town and finds a place as Lady Booby's footman. As Pamela had resisted her master's seductions, he is called upon to oppose the vile attempts of his mistress upon his virtue.

In that novel, as well as in its successors, *Tom Jones* and *Amelia,* Fielding has given us rare pictures of English life, and satires upon English institutions, which present the social history of England a century ago: in this view our sympathies are not lost upon purely ideal creations.

In him, too, the French *illuminati* claimed a co-laborer; and their influence is more distinctly seen than in Richardson's works: great social problems are discussed almost in the manner of a Greek chorus; mechanical forms of religion are denounced. The French philosophers attacked errors so intertwined with truth, that the violent stabs at the former have cut the latter almost to death; Richardson attacked the errors without injuring the truth: he is the champion of purity. If *Joseph Andrews* was to rival *Pamela* in chastity, *Tom Jones* was to be contrasted with both in the same particular.

TOM JONES. — Fielding has received the highest commendations from literary men. Byron calls him the "prose Homer of human nature;" and Gibbon, in noticing that the Lords of Denbigh were descended, like Charles V., from Rudolph of Hapsburg, says: "The successors of Charles V. may despise their brethren of England, but the romance of *Tom Jones* — that exquisite picture of human manners — will outlive the Palace of the Escurial and the Imperial Eagle of Austria." We cannot go so far; we quote the praise, but doubt the prophecy. The work is historically valuable, but technically imperfect and unequal. The plot is rambling, without method: most of the scenes lie in the country or in obscure English towns; the meetings are as theatrical as stage encounters; the episodes are awkwardly introduced, and disfigure the unity; the classical introductions and invocations are absurd. His heroes are men of generous impulses but dissolute lives, and his women are either vile, or the puppets of circumstance.

ITS TRUE VALUE. — What can redeem his works from such a category of condemnation? Their rare portraiture of character and their real glimpses of nature: they form an album of photographs of life as it was — odd, grotesque, but true. They have no mysterious Gothic castles like that of Otranto, nor enchanted forests like that of Mrs. Radcliffe. They present homely English life and people, — *Partridge*, barber, schoolmaster, and coward; *Mrs. Honor*, the type of maid-servants, devoted to her mistress, and yet artful; *Squire Western*, the foul and drunken country gentleman; *Squire Allworthy*, a noble specimen of human nature; *Parson Adams*, who is regarded by the critics as the best portrait among all his characters.

And even if we can neither commend nor recommend heroes like *Tom Jones*, such young men really existed, and the likeness is speakingly drawn: we bear with his faults because of his reality. Perhaps our verdict may be best given in the words of Thackeray. "I am angry," he says, "with Jones. Too much of the plum-cake and the rewards of life fall to that boisterous, swaggering young scapegrace. Sophia actually surrenders without a proper sense of decorum; the fond, foolish, palpitating little creature. 'Indeed, Mr. Jones,' she says, 'it rests with you to name the day.' . . . And yet many a young fellow, no better than Mr. Thomas Jones, has carried by a *coup-de-main* the heart of many a kind girl who was a great deal too good for him."

When *Joseph Andrews* appeared, and Richardson found that so profane a person as Fielding had dared to burlesque his *Pamela*, he was angry; and his little tea-drinking coterie was warm in his defence; but Fielding's party was then, and has remained, the stronger.

In his novel of *Amelia*, we have a general autobiography of Fielding. Amelia, his wife, is lovely, chaste, and constant. Captain Booth — Fielding himself — is errant, guilty, generous, and repentant. We have besides in it many varieties of English life, — lords, clergymen, officers; Vauxhall and the masquerade; the sponging-house and its inmates, debtors and criminals, — all as Fielding saw and knew them.

The condition of the clergy is more clearly set forth in Fielding's novels than in the pages of Echard, Oldham, Wood, Macaulay, or Churchill Babington. So changed was their estate since the Reformation, that few high-born youths, except the weak or lame, took holy orders. Many clergymen worked during the week. One, says South, was a cobbler on weekdays, and preached on Sundays. Wilmot says: "We are struck by the phenomenon of a learned man sitting down to prove, with the help of logic, that a priest or a chaplain in a family is not a servant." —Jeremy Collier: *Essays on Pride and the Office of a Chaplain.*

Fielding drew them and their condition from the life. Parson Adams is the most excellent of men. His cassock is ten years old; over it he dons a coarse white overcoat, and travels on foot to London to sell nine volumes of sermons, wherewithal to buy food for his family. He engages the innkeeper in serious talk; he does desperate battle to defend a young woman who has fallen into the hands of ruffians on the highway; and when he is arrested, his manuscript Eschylus is mistaken for a book of ciphers unfolding a dreadful plot against the government. This is a hit against the ignorance and want of education among the people; for it is some time before some one in the company thinks he saw such characters many years ago when he was young, and that it may be Greek. The incident of Parson Trulliber mistaking his fellow-priest for a pork-merchant, on account of his coarse garments, is excellent, but will not bear abbreviation. Adams is splattered by the huge, overfed swine, and ejaculates, "*Nil habeo cum porcis;* I am a clergyman, sir, and am not come to buy hogs!" The condition of a curate and the theology of the publican are set forth in the conversation between Parson Adams and the innkeeper.

The works of Fielding may be justly accused of describing immoral scenes and using lewd language; but even in this they are delineative of the manners and conversation of an age in which such men lived, such scenes occurred, such language was used. I liken the great realm of English prose fiction to some famous museum of art. The instructor of the young may carefully select what pictures to show them; but the student of English literature moves through the rooms and galleries, gazing, judging, approving, condemning, comparing. Genius may have soiled its canvas with what is prurient and vile; lascivious groups may stand side by side with pictures of saints and madonnas. To leave the figure, it is wise counsel to read on principle, and, armed with principle, to accept and imitate the good, and to reject the evil. Conscience gives the rule, and for every bane will give the antidote.

Of this school and period, Fielding is the greatest figure. One word as to his career. Passing through all social conditions, — first a country gentleman, living on or rather squandering his first wife's little fortune in following the hounds and entertaining the county; then a playwright, vegetating very seedily on the proceeds of his comedies; justice of the peace, and encountering, in his vocation, such characters as *Jonathan Wild;* drunken, licentious, unfaithful to his wife, but always — strange paradox of poor human nature — generous as the day; mourning with bitter tears the loss of his first wife, and then marrying her faithful maid-servant, that they may mourn for her together, — he seems to have been a rare mechanism without a *governor.* "Poor Harry Fielding!" And yet to this irregular, sinful character, we owe the inimitable portraitures of English life as it was, in *Joseph Andrews, Tom Jones,* and *Amelia.*

Fielding's habits, acting upon a naturally weak constitution, wore him out. He left England, and wandered to the English factory at Lisbon, where he died, in 1754, in the forty-eighth year of his age.

Tobias George Smollett. — Smollett, the third in order and in rank of the novelists of his age, was born at Cardross, Dumbartonshire, in 1721, of a good family; but he had small means. After some schooling at Dumbarton and a university career at Glasgow, he was, from necessity, apprenticed to a surgeon. But as his grandfather, Sir James Smollett, on whom he depended, died, he left his master, at the age of eighteen, and, taking in his pocket a manuscript play he had thus early written, — *The Regicides,* — he made his way to London, the El Dorado of all youths with literary aspirations. The play was not accepted; but, through the knowledge obtained in the surgery, he received an appointment as surgeon's mate, and went out with Admiral Vernon's fated expedition to Carthagena in that capacity, and thus acquired a knowledge of the sea and of sailors which he was to use with great effect in his later writings. For a time he remained in the West Indies, where he fell in love with Miss Anne Lascelles, whom he afterwards married. In 1746 he returned to London, and, after an unsuccessful attempt to practise medicine, he threw himself with great vigor into the field of literature. He was a man of strange and antagonistic features, just and generous in theory, quarrelsome and overbearing in practice. From the year 1746 his pen seems to have been always busy. He first tried his hand on some satires, which gained for him numerous enemies; and in 1748 he produced his first novel, *Roderick Random,* which, in spite of its indecency, the world at once acknowledged to be a work of genius: the verisimilitude was perfect; every one recognized in the hero the type of many a young North countryman going out to seek his fortune. The variety is great, the scenes are more varied and real than those in Richardson and Fielding, the characters are numerous and vividly painted, and the keen sense of ridicule pervading the book makes it a broad jest from beginning to end. Historically, his delineations are valuable; for he describes a period in the annals of the British marine which has happily passed away, — a hard life in little stifling holds or forecastles, with hard fare, — a base life, for the sailor, oppressed on shipboard, was the prey of vile women and land-sharks when on shore. What pictures of prostitution and indecency! what obscenity of language! what drunken infernal orgies! We may shun the book as we would shun the company, and yet the one is the exact portraiture of the other.

Roderick Random was followed, in 1751, by *Peregrine Pickle*, a book in similar taste, but the characters in which are even more striking. The forms of Commodore Trunnion, Lieutenant Hatchway, Pipes the boatswain, and Ap Morgan the choleric Welsh surgeon, are as familiar to us now as at the first.

Smollett had now retired to Chelsea, where his facile pen was still hard at work. In 1753 appeared his *Ferdinand Count Fathom*, the portraiture of a complete villain, corresponding in character with Fielding's *Jonathan Wild*, but with a better moral.

About this time he translated *Don Quixote;* and although his version is still published, it is by no means true to the idiom of the language, nor to the higher purpose of Cervantes.

Passing by his *Complete History of Authentic and Entertaining Voyages*, we come to his *History of England from the Descent of Julius Cæsar to the Treaty of Aix-la-Chapelle, in* 1748. It is not a profound work; but it is so currently written, that, in lieu of better, the latter portion was taken to supplement Hume; as a work of less merit than either, that of Bissett was added in the later editions to supplement Smollett and Hume. For this history he is said to have received £2000.

In 1762 he issued *The Adventures of Sir Launcelot Greaves*, who, with his attendant, *Captain Crowe*, goes forth, in the style of Don Quixote and Sancho, to *do* the world. Smollett's forte was in the broadly humorous, and this is all that redeems this work from utter absurdity.

HUMPHREY CLINKER. — His last work of any importance, and perhaps his best, is *The Expedition of Humphrey Clinker*, described in a series of letters descriptive of this amusing imaginative journey. Mrs. Winifred, Tabitha, and, best of all, Lismahago, are rare characters, and in all respects, except its vulgarity, it was the prototype of Hood's exquisite *Up the Rhine*.

From the year 1756, Smollett edited, at intervals, various periodicals, and wrote what he thought very good poetry, now forgotten, — an *Ode to Independence*, after the Greek manner of strophe and antistrophe, not wanting in a noble spirit; and *The Tears of Scotland*, written on the occasion of the Duke of Cumberland's barbarities, in 1746, after the battle of Culloden:

Mourn, hapless Caledonia, mourn
Thy banished peace, thy laurels torn!
Thy sons, for valor long renowned,
Lie slaughtered on thy native ground.

Smollett died abroad on the 21st of October, 1771. His health entirely broken, he had gone to Italy, and taken a cottage near Leghorn: a slight resuscitation was the consequence, and he had something in prospect to live for: he was the heir-at-law to the estate of Bonhill, worth £1000 per annum; but the remorseless archer would not wait for his fortune.

CHAPTER XXVIII.

STERNE, GOLDSMITH, AND MACKENZIE.

THE SUBJECTIVE SCHOOL.

IN the same age, and inspired by similar influences, there sprang up a widely-different school of novelists, which has been variously named as the Sentimental and the Subjective School. Richardson and Fielding depicted what they saw around them objectively, rather than the impressions made upon their individual sensitiveness. Both Sterne and Goldsmith were eminently subjective. They stand as a transparent medium between their works and the reader. The medium through which we see *Tristram Shandy* is a double lens, — one part of which is the distorted mind of the author, and the other the nondescript philosophy which he pilfered from Rabelais and Burton. The glass through which the *Vicar of Wakefield* is shown us is the good-nature and loving heart of Goldsmith, which brighten and gladden every creation of his pen. Thus it is that two men, otherwise essentially unlike, appear together as representatives of a school which was at once sentimental and subjective.

STERNE. — Lawrence Sterne was the son of an officer in the British army, and was born, in 1713, at Clonmel, in Ireland, where his father was stationed.

His father died not long afterwards, at Gibraltar, from the

effect of a wound which he had received in a duel; and it is indicative of the *code of honor* in that day, that the duel was about a goose at the mess-table! What little Lawrence learned in his brief military experience was put to good use afterwards in his army reminiscences and portraitures in *Tristram Shandy*. No doubt My Uncle Toby and Corporal Trim are sketches from his early recollections. Aided by his mother's relations, he studied at Cambridge, and afterwards, without an inward call, but in accordance with the custom of the day, he entered into holy orders, and was presented to a living, of which he stood very much in need.

HIS SERMONS. — With no spirit for parochial work, it must be said that he published very forcible and devout sermons, and set before his people and the English world a pious standard of life, by which, however, he did not choose to measure his own: he preached, but did not practise. In a letter to Mr. Foley, he says: "I have made a good campaign in the field of the literati: . . . two volumes of sermons which I shall print very soon will bring me a considerable sum. . . . 'T is but a crown for sixteen sermons — dog cheap; but I am in quest of honor, not money."

These discourses abound in excellent instruction and in pithy expressions; but it is painful to see how often his pointed rebukes are undesignedly aimed at his own conduct. In one of them he says: "When such a man tells you that a thing goes against his conscience, always believe he means exactly the same thing as when he tells you it goes against his stomach — a present want of appetite being generally the true cause of both." In his discourse on *The Forgiveness of Injuries*, we have the following striking sentiment: "The brave only know how to forgive: it is the most refined and generous pitch of virtue human nature can arrive at. Cowards have done good and kind actions; cowards have even fought, nay, sometimes even conquered; but a coward never forgave." All readers of *Tristram Shandy* will recall his sermon on the text, "For we trust we have a good conscience," so affecting to Corporal Trim and so overwhelming to Dr. Slop.

But if his sermons are so pious and good, we look in vain into his entertaining *Letters* for a corresponding piety in his life. They are witty, jolly, occasionally licentious. They touch and adorn every topic except religion; and so it may be feared that all his religion was written, printed, bound, and sold by subscription, in those famous sermons, sixteen for a crown—"dog cheap!"

TRISTRAM SHANDY.—In 1759 appeared the first part of *Tristram Shandy*—a strange, desultory work, in which many of the curious bits of philosophy are taken from Montaigne, Burton, Rabelais, and others; but which has, besides, great originality in the handling and in the portraiture of characters. Much of what Sterne borrowed from these writers passed for his own in that day, when there were comparatively few readers of the authors mentioned. As to the charge of plagiarism, we may say that Sterne's hero is like the *Gargantua* of Rabelais in many particulars; but he is a man instead of a monster; while the chapter on *Hobby-Horses* is a reproduction, in a new form of crystallization, of *Gargantua's wooden horses*.

So, too, the entire theological cast of *Tristram Shandy* is that of the sixteenth century;—questions before the Sorbonne, the use of excommunication, and the like. Dr. Slop, the Roman Catholic surgeon of the family, is but a weak mouthpiece of his Church in the polemics of the story; for Sterne was a violent opponent of the Church of Rome in story as well as in sermon; and Obadiah, the stupid man-servant, is the lay figure who receives the curses which Dr. Slop reads,—"cursed in house and stable, garden and field and highway, in path or in wood, in the water or in the church." Whether the doctor was in earnest or not, Obadiah paid him fully by upsetting him and his pony with the coach-horse.

But in spite of the resemblance to Rabelais and a former age, it must be allowed that *Tristram Shandy* contains many of the richest pictures and fairest characters of the age in which it was written. Rural England is truthfully presented, and the political cast of the day is shown in his references to the war in Flanders. Among the sterling original portraits are those of Mr. Shandy, the country gentleman, controversial and consequential; Mrs. Shandy, the nonentity, — the Amelia Osborne and Mrs. Nickleby of her day; Yorick, the lukewarm, time-serving priest — Sterne himself: and these are only supplementary characters.

The sieges of towns in the Low Countries, then going on, are pleasantly connected with that most exquisite of characters, *my Uncle Toby*, who has a fortification in his garden, — sentry-box, cannon, and all, — and who follows the great movement on this petty scale from day to day, as the bulletins come in from the seat of war.

The *Widow Wadman*, with her artless wiles, and the "something in her eye," makes my Uncle Toby — who protests he can see nothing in the white — look, not without peril, "with might and main into the pupil." Ah, that sentry-box and the widow's tactics might have conquered many a more wary man than my Uncle Toby! and yet my Uncle Toby escaped.

Now, all these are real English characters, sketched from life by the hand of genius, and they become our friends and acquaintances forever. It seems as though Sterne, after a long and close study of Rabelais and Burton, had fancied that, with their aid, he might write a money-making book; but his own genius, rising superior to the plagiarism, took the project out of his venal hands; and from the antique learning and the incongruities which he had heaped together, bright and beautiful forms sprang forth like genii from the mine, to subsidize the tears and laughter of all future time. What an exquisite creation is my Uncle Toby! — a soldier in the van of battle, a man of honor and high tone in every-day life, a kind brother, a good master to Corporal Trim, simple as a child, benevolent as an angel. "Go, poor devil," quoth he to the fly which buzzed about his nose all dinner-time, "get thee gone; why should I hurt thee? This world is surely wide enough to hold both thee and me!"

And as for Corporal Trim, he is a host in himself. There is in the English literary portrait-gallery no other Uncle Toby, there is no other Corporal Trim. Hazlitt has not exaggerated in saying that the *Story of Le Fevre* is perhaps the finest in the English language. My Uncle Toby's conduct to the dying officer is the perfection of loving-kindness and charity.

THE SENTIMENTAL JOURNEY. — Sterne's *Sentimental Journey*, although charmingly written, — and this is said in spite of the preference of such a critic as Horace Walpole, — will not compare with *Tristram Shandy*: it is left unfinished, and is constantly suggestive of licentiousness.

Sterne's English is excellent and idiomatic, and has commended his works to the ordinary reader, who shrinks from the hyperlatinism of the time represented so strongly by Dr. Johnson and his followers. His wit, if sometimes artificial, is always acute; his sentiment is entirely artificial; "he is always protruding his sensibility, trying to play upon you as upon an instrument; more concerned that you should acknowledge his power than have any depth of feeling." Thackeray, whose opinion is just quoted, calls him "a great jester, not a great humorist." He had lived a careless, self-indulgent life, and was no honor to his profession. His death was like a retribution. In a mean lodging, with no friends but his bookseller, he died suddenly from hemorrhage. His funeral was hasty, and only attended by two persons; his burial was in an obscure graveyard; and his body was taken up by corpse-snatchers for the dissecting-room of the professor of anatomy at Cambridge, — alas, poor Yorick!

OLIVER GOLDSMITH. — We have placed Goldsmith in immediate connection with Sterne as, like him, of the Subjective School, in his story of the *Vicar of Wakefield* and his numerous biographical and prose sketches; but he belongs to more than one literary school of his period. He was a poet, an essayist, a dramatist, and an historian; a writer who, in the words of his epitaph, — written by Dr. Johnson, and with no extravagant eulogium, — touched all subjects, and touched none that he did not adorn, — *nullum quod tetigit non ornavit*. His life was a strange melodrama, so varied with laughter and tears, so checkered with fame and misfortune, so resounding with songs pathetic and comic, that, were he an unknown hero, his adventures would be read with pleasure by all persons of sensibility. There is no better illustration of the *subjective* in literature. It is the man who is presented to us in his works, and who can no more be disjoined from them than the light from the vase, the beauties of which it discloses. As an essayist, he was of the school of Addison and Steele; but he has more ease of style and more humor than his teachers. As a dramatist, he had many and superior competitors in his own vein; and yet his plays still occupy the stage. As an historian, he was fluent but superficial; and yet the charm of his style and the easy flow of his narrative, have given his books currency as manuals of instruction. And although as a writer of fiction, or of truth gracefully veiled in the garments of fiction, he stands unrivalled in his beautiful and touching story of the incorruptible *Vicar*, yet this is his only complete story, and presents but one side of his literary character. Considering him first as a poet, we shall find that he is one of the Transition School, but that he has a beautiful originality: his poems appeal not to the initiated alone, but to human nature in all its conditions and guises; they are elevated and harmonious enough for the most fastidious taste, and simple and artless enough to please the rustic and the child. To say that he is the most popular writer in the whole course of

English Literature thus far, is hardly to overstate his claims; and the principal reason is that, with a blundering and improvident nature, a want of dignity, a lack of coherence, he had a great heart, alive to human suffering; he was generous to a fault, true to the right, and ever seeking, if constantly failing, to direct and improve his own life, and these good characteristics are everywhere manifest in his works. A brief recital of the principal events in his career will throw light upon his works, and will do the best justice to his peculiar character.

Oliver Goldsmith was born at the little village of Pallas, in Ireland, where his father was a poor curate, on the 10th of November, 1728. There were nine children, of whom he was the fifth. His father afterwards moved to Lissoy, which the poet described, in his *Deserted Village*, as

> Sweet Auburn, loveliest village of the plain,
> Where health and plenty cheered the laboring swain.

As his father was entirely unable to educate so numerous a family, Goldsmith owed his education partly to his uncle, the Rev. Thomas Contarini, and in part to his brother, the Rev. Henry Goldsmith, whom he cherished with the sincerest affection. An attack of the small-pox while he was a boy marked his face, and he was to most persons an unprepossessing child. He was ill-treated at school by larger boys, and afterwards at Trinity College, Dublin, which he entered as a sizar, by his tutor. He was idle, careless, and improvident: he left college without permission, but was taken back by his brother, and was finally graduated with a bachelor's degree, in 1749. His later professional studies were spasmodic and desultory: he tried law and medicine, and more than once gained a scanty support by teaching. Seized with a rambling spirit, he went to the Continent, and visited Holland, France, Germany, Switzerland, and Italy; sometimes gaining a scanty livelihood by teaching English, and sometimes wandering without money, depending upon his flute to win a supper and bed from the rustics who lived on the highway. He obtained, it is said, the degree of Doctor of Medicine at Padua; and on his return to England, he went before a board of examiners to obtain the position of surgeon's mate in the army or navy. He was at this time so poor that he was obliged to borrow a suit of clothes to make a proper appearance before the examiners. He failed in his examination, and then, in despair, he pawned the borrowed clothes, to the great anger of the publisher who had lent them. This failure in his medical examination, unfortunate as it then seemed, secured him to literature. From that time his pen was constantly busy for the reviews and magazines. His first work was *An Inquiry into the Present State of Polite Learning in Europe*, which, at least, prepared the way for his future efforts. This appeared in 1759, and is characterized by general knowledge and polish of style.

HIS POEMS. — In 1764 he published *The Traveller*, a moralizing poem upon the condition of the people under the European governments. It was at once and entirely successful; philosophical, elegant, and harmonious, it is pitched in a key suited to the capacity of the world at large; and as, in the general comparison of nations, he found abundant reason for lauding England, it was esteemed patriotic, and was on that account popular. Many of its lines have been constantly quoted since.

In 1770 appeared his *Deserted Village*, which was even more popular than *The Traveller;* nor has this popularity flagged from that time down to the present day. It is full of exquisite pictures of rural life and manners. It is what it claims to be, — not an attempt at high art or epic, but a gallery of cabinet pictures of rare finish and detail, painted by the poet's heart and appealing to the sensibility of every reader. The world knows it by heart, — the portraiture of the village schoolmaster and his school; the beautiful picture of the country parson:

A man he was to all the country dear,
And passing rich with forty pounds a year.

This latter is a worthy companion-piece to Chaucer's "poor persoune," and is, besides, a filial tribute to Goldsmith's father. So real are the characters and scenes, that the poem has been a popular subject for the artist. If in *The Traveller* he has been philosophical and didactic, in the *Deserted Village* he is only descriptive and tender. In no work is there a finer spirit of true charity, the love of man for God's sake, — like God himself, "no respecter of persons."

While in form and versification he is like Pope and the Artificial School, he has the sensibility to nature of Thomson, and the simplicity of feeling and thought of Wordsworth; and thus he stands between the two great poetic periods, partaking of the better nature of both.

THE VICAR OF WAKEFIELD. — Between the appearance of these two poems, in 1766, came forth that nonpareil of charming stories, *The Vicar of Wakefield*. It is so well known that we need not enter into an analysis of it. It is the story of a good vicar, of like passions with ourselves; not wanting in vanity and impetuosity, but shining in his Christian virtue like a star in the midst of accumulating misfortunes, — a man of immaculate honor and undying faith, preaching to his fellow-prisoners in the jail, surveying death without fear, and at last, like Job, restored to happiness, and yet maintaining his humility. It does not seem to have been constructed according to artificial rules, but rather to have been told extemporaneously, without effort and without ambition; and while this very fact has been the cause of some artistic faults and some improbabilities, it has also given it a peculiar charm, by contrast with such purely artificial constructions as the *Rasselas* of Johnson.

So doubtful was the publisher, who had bought the manuscript for £60, that he held it back for two years, until the name of the author had become known through *The Traveller*, and was thus a guarantee for its success. The *Vicar of Wakefield* has also an additional value in its delineation of manners, persons, and conditions in that day, and in its strictures upon the English penal law, in such terms and with such suggestions as seem a prophecy of the changes which have since taken place.

HISTORIES, AND OTHER WORKS.—Of Goldsmith's various histories it may be said that they are of value for the clear, if superficial, presentation of facts, and for their charm of style.

The best is, without doubt, *The History of England;* but the *Histories of Greece and Rome,* re-edited, are still used as text-books in many schools. The *Vicar* has been translated into most of the modern languages, and imitated by many writers since.

As an essayist, Goldsmith has been a great enricher of English history. His Chinese letters — for the idea of which he was indebted to the *Lettres Persanes* of Montesquieu — describe England in his day with the same *vraisemblance* which we have noticed in *The Spectator.* These were afterwards collected and published in a volume entitled *The Citizen of the World.* And besides the pleasure of biography, and the humor of the presentment, his *Life of Beau Nash* introduces us to Bath and its frequenters with historical power. The life at the Spring is one and a very valuable phase of English society.

As a dramatist, he was more than equalled by Sheridan; but his two plays, *The Good-Natured Man* and *She Stoops to Conquer,* are still favorites upon the stage.

The irregularities of Goldsmith's private life seem to have been rather defects in his character than intentional wrongdoings. Generous to a fault, squandering without thought what was due to his creditors, losing at play, he lived in continual pecuniary embarrassment, and died unhappy, with a debt of £1000, the existence of which led Johnson to ejaculate, "Was ever poet so trusted before?" He lived a bachelor; and the conclusion seems forced upon us that had he married a woman who could have controlled him, he would have been a happier and more respectable man, but perhaps have done less for literature than he did.

While Goldsmith was a type and presenter of his age, and while he took no high flights in the intellectual realms, he so handled what the age presented that he must be allowed the claim of originality, both in his poems and in the *Vicar;* and he has had, even to the present day, hosts of imitators. Poems on college gala-days were for a long time faint reflections of his *Traveller,* and simple, causal stories of quiet life are the teeming progeny of the *Vicar,* in spite of the Whistonian controversy, and the epitaph of his living wife.

A few of his ballads and songs display great lyric power, but the most of his poetry is not lyric; it is rather a blending of the pastoral and epic with rare success. His minor poems are few, but favorites. Among these is the beautiful ballad entitled *Edwin and Angelina,* or *The Hermit,* which first appeared in *The Vicar of Wakefield,* but which has since been printed separately among his poems. Of its kind and class it has no superior. *Retaliation* is a humorous epitaph upon his friends and co-literati, hitting off their characteristics with truth and point; and *The Haunch of Venison* — upon which he did not dine — is an amusing incident which might have happened to any Londoner like himself, but which no one could have related so well as he.

He died in 1774, at the age of forty-five; but his fame — his better life — is more vigorous than ever. Washington Irving, whose writings are similar in style to those of Goldsmith, has extended and perpetuated his reputation in America by writing his Biography; a charming work, many touches of which seem almost autobiographical, as displaying the resemblance between the writer and his subject.

MACKENZIE. — From Sterne and Goldsmith we pass to Mackenzie, who, if not a conscious imitator of the former, is, at least, unconsciously formed upon the model of Sterne, without his genius, but also without his coarseness: in the management of his narrative, he is a medium between Sterne and Walter Scott; indeed, from his long life, he saw the period of both these authors, and his writings partake of the characteristics of both.

Henry Mackenzie was born at Edinburgh, in August, 1745, and lived until 1831, to the ripe age of eighty-six. He was educated at the University of Edinburgh, and afterwards studied law. He wrote some strong political pamphlets in favor of the Pitt government, for which he was rewarded with the office of comptroller of the taxes, which he held to the day of his death.

THE MAN OF FEELING. — In 1771 the world was equally astonished and delighted by the appearance of his first novel, *The Man of Feeling*. In this there are manifest tokens of his debt to Sterne's *Sentimental Journey*, in the journey of Harley, in the story of the beggar and his dog, and in somewhat of the same forced sensibility in the account of Harley's death.

In 1773 appeared his *Man of the World*, which was in some sort a sequel to the *Man of Feeling*, but which wearies by the monotony of the plot.

In 1777 he published *Julia de Roubigné*, which, in the opinion of many, shares the palm with his first novel: the plot is more varied than that of the second, and the language is exceedingly harmonious — elegiac prose. The story is plaintive and painful: virtue is extolled, but made to suffer, in a domestic tragedy, which all readers would be glad to see ending differently.

At different times Mackenzie edited *The Mirror* and *The Lounger*, and he has been called the restorer of the Essay.

His story of the venerable *La Roche*, contributed to *The Mirror*, is perhaps the best specimen of his powers as a sentimentalist: it portrays the influence of Christianity, as exhibited in the very face of infidelity, to support the soul in the sorest of trials — the death of an only and peerless daughter.

His contributions to the above-named periodicals were very numerous and popular.

The name of his first novel was applied to himself as a man. He was known as the *man of feeling* to the whole community. This was a misnomer: he was kind and affable; his evening parties were delightful; but he had nothing of the pathetic or sentimental about him. On the contrary, he was humorous, practical, and worldly-wise; very fond of field sports and athletic exercises. His sentiment — which has been variously criticized, by some as the perfection of moral pathos, and by others as lackadaisical and canting — may be said to have sprung rather from his observations of life and manners than to have welled spontaneously from any source within his own heart.

Sterne and Goldsmith will be read as long as the English language lasts, and their representative characters will be quoted as models and standards everywhere: Mackenzie is fast falling into an oblivion from which he will only be resuscitated by the historian of English Literature.

CHAPTER XXIX.

THE HISTORICAL TRIAD IN THE SCEPTICAL AGE.

The Sceptical Age.	Metaphysics.	Histories.
David Hume.	Essay on Miracles.	Gibbon.
History of England.	Robertson.	The Decline and Fall.

THE SCEPTICAL AGE.

HISTORY presents itself to the student in two forms: The first is *chronicle*, or a simple relation of facts and statistics; and the second, *philosophical history*, in which we use these facts and statistics in the consideration of cause and effect, and endeavor to extract a moral from the actions and events recorded. From pregnant causes the philosophic historian traces, at long distances, the important results; or, conversely, from the present condition of things — the good and evil around him — he runs back, sometimes remotely, to the causes from which they have sprung. Chronicle is very pleasing to read, and the reader may be, to some extent, his own philosopher; but the importance of history as a study is found in its philosophy.

As far down as the eighteenth century, almost everything in history partakes of the nature of chronicle. In that century, in obedience to the law of human progress, there sprang up in England and on the Continent the men who first made chronicle material for philosophy, and used philosophy to teach by example what to imitate and what to shun.

What were the circumstances which led, in the eighteenth century, to the simultaneous appearance of Hume, Gibbon, and Robertson, as the originators of a new school of history?

Some of them have been already mentioned in treating of the antiquarian age. We have endeavored to show how the English literati — novelists, essayists, and poets — have been in part unconscious historians. It will also appear that the professed historians themselves have been, in a great measure, the creatures of English history. The *fifteenth* century was the period when the revival of letters took place, and a great spur was given to mental activity; but the world, like a child, was again learning rudiments, and finding out what it was, and what it possessed at that present time: it received the new classical culture presented to it at the fall of the lower empire, and was content to learn the existing, without endeavoring to create the new, or even to recompose the scattered fragments of the past. The *eighteenth* century saw a new revival: the world had become a man; great progress was reported in arts, in inventions, and in discoveries; science began to labor at the arduous but important task of classification; new theories of government and laws were propounded; the past was consulted that its experience might be applied; the partisan chronicles needed to be united and compared that truth might be elicited; the philosophic historian was required, and the people were ready to learn, and to criticize, what he produced.

I have ventured to call this the Sceptical Age. It had other characteristics: this was one. We use the word sceptical in its etymological sense: it was an age of inquiry, of doubt to be resolved. Voltaire, Montesquieu, Rousseau, D'Alembert, and Diderot had founded a new school of universal inquiry, and from their bold investigations and startling theories sprang the society of the *illuminati*, and the race of thinkers. They went too far: they stabbed the truth as it lay in the grasp of error. From thinkers they became free-thinkers: from philosophers they became infidels, and some of them atheists. This was the age which produced "the triumvirate of British historians who," in the words of Montgomery, "exemplified in their very dissimilar styles the triple contrast of simplicity, elegance, and splendor."

Imbued with this spirit of the time, Hume undertook to write a *History of England*, which, with all its errors and faults, still ranks among the best efforts of English historians. Like the French philosophers, Hume was an infidel, and his scepticism appears in his writings; but, unlike them — for they were stanch reformers in government as well as infidels in faith — he who was an infidel was also an aristocrat in sentiment, and a consistent Tory his life long. In his history, with all the artifices of a philosopher, he takes the Jacobite side in the civil war.

HUME. — David Hume was born in Edinburgh on the 26th of April (O. S.), 1711. His life was without many vicissitudes of interest, but his efforts to achieve an enduring reputation on the most solid grounds, mark him as a notable example of patient industry, study, and economy. He led a studious, systematic, and consistent life.

Although of good family, — being a descendant of the Earl of Home, — he was in poor circumstances, and after some study of the law, and some unsuccessful literary ventures, he was obliged to seek employment as a means of livelihood. Thus he became tutor or keeper to the young Marquis of Annandale, who was insane. Abandoning this position in disgust, he was appointed secretary to General St. Clair in various embassies, — to Paris, Vienna, and Turin; everywhere hoarding his pay, until he became independent, "though," he says, "most of my friends were inclined to smile when I said so; in short, I was master of a thousand pounds."

His earliest work was a *Treatise on Human Nature*, published in 1738, which met with no success. Nothing discouraged thereat, in 1741 he issued a volume of *Essays Moral and Political*, the success of which emboldened him to publish, in 1748, his *Inquiry Concerning the Human Understanding*.

These and other works were preparing his pen for its greater task, the material for which he was soon to find.

In 1752 he was appointed librarian to the Faculty of Advocates, not for the emolument, but with the real purpose of having entire control of the books and material in the library; and then he determined to write the *History of England*.

History of England. — He began with the accession of the Stuarts, in 1603, the period when the popular element, so long kept tranquil by the power and sex of Queen Elizabeth, was ready first to break out into open assertion. Hume's self-deception must have been rudely discovered to him; for he tells us, in an autobiography fortunately preserved, that he expected so dispassionately to steer clear of all existent parties, or, rather, to be so just to all, that he should gain universal approbation. "Miserable," he adds, "was my disappointment. I was assailed by one cry of reproach, disapprobation, and even detestation. English, Scotch, Irish, Whig and Tory, churchman and sectary, free-thinker and religionist, patriot and courtier, united, in their rage, against the man who had presumed to shed a generous tear for the fate of Charles I. and the Earl of Strafford." How far, too, this was ignorant invective, may be judged from the fact that in twelve months only forty-five copies of his work were sold.

However, he patiently continued his labor. The first volume, containing the reigns of James I. and Charles I., had been issued in 1754; his second, published in 1756, and containing the later history of the Commonwealth, of Charles II., and James II., and concluding with the revolution of 1688, was received with more favor, and "helped to buoy up its unfortunate brother." Then he worked backward: in 1759 he produced the reigns of the house of Tudor; and in 1761, the earlier history, completing his work, from the earliest times to 1688. The tide had now turned in his favor; the sales were large, and his pecuniary rewards greater than any historian had yet received.

The Tory character of his work is very decided: he not only sheds a generous tear for the fate of Charles I., but conceals or glosses the villanies of Stuarts far worse than Charles. The liberties of England consist, in his eyes, of wise concessions made by the sovereign, rather than as the inalienable birthright of the English man.

He has also been charged with want of industry and honesty in the use of his materials — taking things at second-hand, without consulting original authorities which were within his reach, and thus falling into many mistakes, while placing in his marginal notes the names of the original authors. This charge is particularly just with reference to the Anglo-Saxon period, since so picturesquely described by Sharon Turner.

The first in order of the philosophical historians, he is rather a collector of facts than a skilful diviner with them. His style is sonorous and fluent, but not idiomatic. Dr. Johnson said, "His style is not English; the structure of his sentences is French," —an opinion concurred in by the eminent critic, Lord Jeffrey.

But whatever the criticism, the *History* of Hume is a great work. He did what was never done before. For a long time his work stood alone; and even now it has the charm of a clear, connected narrative, which is still largely consulted by many who are forewarned of its errors and faults. And however unidiomatic his style, it is very graceful and flowing, and lends a peculiar charm to his narrative.

METAPHYSICS.—Of Hume as a philosopher, we need not here say much. He was acute, intelligent, and subtle; he was, in metaphysical language, "a sceptical nihilist." And here a distinction must be made between his religious tenets and his philosophical views, — a distinction so happily stated by Sir William Hamilton, that we present it in his words: "Though decidedly opposed to one and all of Hume's theological conclusions, I have no hesitation in asserting of his philosophical scepticism, that this was not only beneficial in its results, but, in the circumstances of the period, even a necessary step in the progress of Philosophy towards Truth." And again he says, "To Hume we owe the philosophy of Kant, and therefore also, in general, the later philosophy of Germany." "To Hume, in like manner, we owe the philosophy of Reid, and, consequently, what is now distinctively known in Europe as the Philosophy of the Scottish School." Great praise this from one of the greatest Christian philosophers of this century, and it shows Hume to have been more original as a philosopher than as an historian.

He is also greatly commended by Lord Brougham as a political economist. "His *Political Discourses*," says his lordship, "combine almost every excellence which can belong to such a performance. . . . Their great merit is their originality, and the new system of politics and political economy which they unfold."

MIRACLES. — The work in which is most fairly set forth his religious scepticism is his *Essay on Miracles*. In it he adopts the position of Locke, who had declared "that men should not believe any proposition that is contrary to reason, on the authority either of inspiration or of miracle; for the reality of the inspiration or of the miracle can only be established by reason." Before Hume, assaults on the miracles recorded in Scripture were numerous and varied. Spinoza and the Pantheistic School had started the question, "Are miracles possible?" and had taken the negative. Hume's question is, "Are miracles credible?" And as they are contrary to human experience, his answer is essentially that it must be always more probable that a miracle is false than that it is true; since it is not contrary to experience that witnesses are false or deceived. With him it is, therefore, a question of the preponderance of evidence, which he declares to be always against the miracle. This is not the place to discuss these topics. Archbishop Whately has practically illustrated the fallacy of Hume's reasoning, in a little book called *Historic Doubts relative to Napoleon Bonaparte,* in which, with Hume's logic, he has proved that the great emperor never lived; and Whately's successor in the archbishopric of Dublin, Dr. Trench, has given us some thoughtful words on the subject: "So long as we abide in the region of nature, miraculous and improbable, miraculous and incredible may be allowed to remain convertible terms; but once lift up the whole discussion into a higher region, once acknowledge aught higher than nature — *a kingdom of God,* and men the intended denizens of it — and the whole argument loses its strength and the force of its conclusions."

Hume's death occurred on the 25th of August, 1776. His scepticism, or philosophy as he called it, remained with him to the end. He even diverted himself with the prospect of the excuses he would make to Charon as he reached the fatal river, and is among the few doubters who have calmly approached the grave without that concern which the Christian's hope alone is generally able to dispel.

William Robertson — the second of the great historians of the eighteenth century, although very different from the others in his personal life and in his creed, — was, like them, a representative and creature of the age. They form, indeed, a trio in literary character as well as in period; and we have letters from each to the others on the appearance of their works, showing that they form also what in the present day is called a "Mutual Admiration Society." They were above common envy: they recognized each other's excellence, and forbore to speak of each other's faults. As a philosopher, Hume was the greatest of the three; as an historian, the palm must be awarded to Gibbon. But Robertson surprises us most from the fact that a quiet Scotch pastor, who never travelled, should have attempted, and so gracefully treated, subjects of such general interest as those he handled.

William Robertson was the son of a Scottish minister, and was born at Borthwick, in Scotland, on September 19th, in the year 1721. He was a precocious child, and, after attending school at Dalkeith, he entered the University of Edinburgh at the age of twelve. At the age of twenty he was licensed to preach. He published, in 1755, a sermon on *The Situation of the World at the Time of Christ's Appearance*, which attracted attention; but he astonished the world by issuing, in 1759, his *History of Scotland During the Reigns of Queen Mary, and of James VI. until his Accession to the Crown of England.* This is undoubtedly his best work, but not of such general interest as his others. His materials were scanty, and he did not consult such as were in his reach with much assiduity. The invaluable records of the archives of Simancas were not then opened to the world, but he lived among the scenes of his narrative, and had the advantage of knowing all the traditions and of hearing all the vehement opinions *pro* and *con* upon the subjects of which he treated. The character of Queen Mary is drawn with a just but sympathetic hand, and his verdict is not so utterly denunciatory as that of Mr. Froude. Such was the popularity of this work, that in 1764 its author was appointed to the honorable office of Historiographer to His Majesty for Scotland. In 1769 he published his *History of Charles V.* Here was a new surprise. Whatever its faults, as afterwards discerned by the critics, it opened a new and brilliant page to the uninitiated reader, and increased his reputation very greatly. The history is preceded by a *View of the Progress of Society in Europe from the Subversion of the Roman Empire to the Beginning of the Sixteenth Century.* The best praise that can be given to this *View* is, that students have since used it as the most excellent summary of that kind existing. Of the history itself it may be said that, while it is greatly wanting in historic material in the interest of the narrative and the splendor of the pageantry of the imperial court, it marked a new era in historical delineations.

HISTORY OF AMERICA. — In 1777 appeared the first eight books of his *History of America*, to which, in 1778, he appended additions and corrections. The concluding books, the ninth and tenth, did not appear until 1796, when, three years after his death, they were issued by his son. As a connected narrative of so great an event in the world's history as the discovery of America, it stood quite alone. If, since that time, far better and fuller histories have appeared, we should not withhold our meed of praise from this excellent forerunner of them all. One great defect of this and the preceding work was his want of knowledge of the German and Spanish historians, and of the original papers then locked up in the archives of Simancas; later access to which has given such great value to the researches of Irving and Prescott and Sterling. Besides, Robertson lacked the life-giving power which is the property of true genius. His characters are automata gorgeously arrayed, but without breath; his style is fluent and sometimes sparkling, but in all respects he has been superseded, and his works remain only as curious representatives of the age to the literary student. One other work remains to be mentioned, and that is his *Historical Disquisition Concerning the Knowledge which the Ancients had of India, and the Progress of Trade with that Country Prior to the Discovery of the Passage to it by the Cape of Good Hope.* This is chiefly of value as it indicates the interest felt in England at the rise of the English Empire in India; but for real facts it has no value at all.

GIBBON. — Last in order of time, though far superior as an historian to Hume and Robertson, stands Edward Gibbon, the greatest historian England has produced, whether we regard the dignity of his style — antithetic and sonorous; the range of his subject — the history of a thousand years; the astonishing fidelity of his research in every department which contains historic materials; or the symmetry and completeness of his colossal work.

Like Hume, he has left us a sketch of his own life and labors, simple and dispassionate, from which it appears that he was born in London on the 27th of April, 1737; and, being of a good family, he had every advantage of education. Passing a short time at the University of Oxford, he stands in a small minority of those who can find no good in their *Alma Mater*. "To the University of Oxford," he says, "I acknowledge no obligation, and she will as cheerfully renounce me for a son as I am willing to disclaim her for a mother. I spent fourteen months at Magdalen College. They proved to be fourteen of the most idle and unprofitable months of my whole life." This singular experience may be contrasted with that of hundreds, but may be most fittingly illustrated by stating that of Dr. Lowth, a venerable contemporary of the historian. He speaks enthusiastically of the place where the student is able "to breathe the same atmosphere that had been breathed by Hooker and Chillingworth and Locke; to revel in its grand and well-ordered libraries; to form part of that academic society where emulation without envy, ambition without jealousy, contention without animosity, incited industry and awakened genius."

Gibbon, while still in his boyhood, had read with avidity ancient and modern history, and had written a juvenile paper on *The Age of Sesostris*, which was, at least, suggested by Voltaire's *Siècle de Louis XIV.*

Early interested, too, in the history of Christianity, his studies led him to become a Roman Catholic; but his belief was by no means stable. Sent by his father to Lausanne, in Switzerland, to be under the religious training of a Protestant minister, he changed his opinions, and became again a Protestant. His convictions, however, were once more shaken, and, at the last, he became a man of no creed, a sceptic of the school of Voltaire, a creature of the age of illumination.

Many passages of his history display a sneering unbelief, which moves some persons more powerfully than the subtlest argument. This modern Platonist, beginning with sensation, evolves his philosophy from within, — from the finite mind; whereas human history can only be explained in the light of revelation, which gives to humanity faith, but which educes all science from the infinite — the mind of God.

The history written by Gibbon, called *The Decline and Fall of the Roman Empire*, begins with that empire in its best days, under Hadrian, and extends to the taking of Constantinople by the Turks, under Mohammed II., in 1453.

And this marvellous scope he has treated with a wonderful equality of research and power; — the world-absorbing empire, the origin and movements of the northern tribes and the Scythian marauders, the fall of the Western Empire, the history of the civil law, the establishment of the Gothic monarchies, the rise and spread of Mohammedanism, the obscurity of the middle age deepening into gloom, the crusades, the dawning of letters, and the inauguration of the modern era after the fall of Constantinople, — the detailed history of a thousand years. It is difficult to conceive that any one should suggest such a task to himself; it is astonishing to think that, with a dignified, self-reliant tenacity of purpose, it should have been completely achieved. It was an historic period, in which, in the words of Corneille, "*Un grand destin commence un grand destin s'achève.*" In many respects Gibbon's work stands alone; the general student must refer to Gibbon, because there is no other work to which he can refer. It was translated by Guizot into French, the first volume by Wenck into German (he died before completing it); and it was edited by Dean Milman in England.

The style of Gibbon is elegant and powerful; at first it is singularly pleasing, but as one reads it becomes too sonorous, and fatigues, as the crashing notes of a grand march tire the ear. His periods are antithetic; each contains a surprise and a witty point. His first two volumes have less of this stately magnificence, but in his later ones, in seeking to vindicate popular applause, he aims to shine, and perpetually labors for effect. Although not such a philosopher as Hume, his work is quite as philosophical as Hume's history, and he has been more faithful in the use of his materials. Guizot, while pointing out his errors, says he was struck, after "a second and attentive perusal," with "the immensity of his researches, the variety of his knowledge, and, above all, with that truly philosophical discrimination which judges the past as it would judge the present."

The danger to the unwary reader is from the sceptical bias of the author, which, while he states every important fact, leads him, by its manner of presentation, to warp it, or put it in a false light. Thus, for example, he has praise for paganism, and easy absolution for its sins; Mohammed walks the stage with a stately stride; Alaric overruns Europe to a grand quickstep; but Christianity awakens no enthusiasm, and receives no eulogium, although he describes its early struggles, its martyrdoms, its triumphs under Constantine, its gentle radiance during the dark ages, and its powerful awakening. Because he cannot believe, he cannot even be just.

In his special chapter on the rise and spread of Christianity, he gives a valuable summary of its history, and of the claims of the papacy, with perhaps a leaning towards the Latin Church. Gibbon finished his work at Lausanne on the 27th of June, 1787.

Its conception had come to his mind as he sat one evening amid the ruins of the Capitol at Rome, and heard the barefooted friars singing vespers in the Temple of Jupiter. He had then thought of writing the decline and fall of the city of Rome, but soon expanded his view to the empire. This was in 1764. Nearly thirteen years afterwards, he wrote the last line of the last page in his garden-house at Lausanne, and reflected joyfully upon his recovered freedom and his permanent fame.

His second thought, however, will fitly close this notice with a moral from his own lips: "My pride was soon humbled, and a sober melancholy was spread over my mind by the idea that I had taken an everlasting leave of an old and agreeable companion, and that whatever might be the future fate of my history, the life of the historian must be short and precarious."

OTHER CONTRIBUTORS TO HISTORY.

James Boswell, 1740–1795: he was the son of a Scottish judge called Lord Auchinleck, from his estate. He studied law, and travelled, publishing, on his return, *Journal of a Tour in Corsica*. He appears to us a simple-hearted and amiable man, inquisitive, and exact in details. He became acquainted with Dr. Johnson in 1763, and conceived an immense admiration for him. In numerous visits to London, and in their tour to the Hebrides together, he noted Johnson's speech and actions, and, in 1791, published his life, which has already been characterized as the greatest biography ever written. Its value is manifold; not only is it a faithful portrait of the great writer, but, in the detailed record of his life, we have the wit, dogmatism, and learning of his hero, as expressing and illustrating the history of the age, quite as fully as the published works of Johnson. In return for this most valuable contribution to history and literature, the critics, one and all, have taxed their ingenuity to find strong words of ridicule and contempt for Boswell, and have done him great injustice. Because he bowed before the genius of Johnson, he was not a toady, nor a fool; at the worst, he was a fanatic, and a not always wise champion. Johnson was his king, and his loyalty was unqualified.

Horace Walpole, the Right Honorable, and afterwards Earl of Orford, 1717–1797: he was a wit, a satirist, and a most accomplished writer, who, notwithstanding, affected to despise literary fame. His paternity was doubted; but he enjoyed wealth and honors, and, by the possession of three sinecures, he lived a life of elegant leisure. He transformed a small house on the bank of the Thames, at Twickenham, into a miniature castle, called *Strawberry Hill*, which he filled with curiosities. He held a very versatile pen, and wrote much on many subjects. Among his desultory works are: *Anecdotes of Painting in England*, and *Ædes Walpolianæ*, a description of the pictures at Houghton Hall, the seat of Sir Robert Walpole. He also ranks among the novelists, as the author of *The Castle of Otranto*, in which he deviates from the path of preceding writers of fiction — a sort of individual reaction from their portraitures of existing society to the marvellous and sensational. This work has been variously criticized; by some it has been considered a great flight of the imagination, but by most it is regarded as unnatural and full of "pasteboard machinery." He had immediate followers in this vein, among whom are Mrs. Aphra Behn, in her *Old English Baron;* and Ann Radcliffe, in *The Romance of the Forest*, and *The Mysteries of Udolpho.* Walpole also wrote a work entitled *Historic Doubts on the Life and Reign of Richard III.* But his great value as a writer is to be found in his *Memoirs* and varied *Correspondence*, in which he presents photographs of the society in which he lives. Scott calls him "the best letter-writer in the language." Among the series of his letters, those of the greatest historical importance are those addressed to Sir Horace Mann, between 1760 and 1785. Of this series, Macaulay, who is his severest critic, says: "It forms a connected whole — a regular journal of what appeared to Walpole the most important transactions of the last twenty years of George II.'s reign. It contains much new information concerning the history of that time, the portion of English history of which common readers know the least."

John Lord Hervey, 1696–1743: he is known for his attempts in poetry, and for a large correspondence, since published; but his chief title to rank among the contributors to history is found in his *Memoirs of the Court of George II. and Queen Caroline*, which were not published until 1848. They give an unrivalled view of the court and of the royal household; and the variety of the topics, combined with the excellence of description, render them admirable as aids to understanding the history.

Sir William Blackstone, 1723–1780: a distinguished lawyer, he was an unwearied student of the history of the English statute law, and was on that account made Professor of Law in the University of Oxford. Some time a member of Parliament, he was afterwards appointed a judge. He edited *Magna Charta* and *The Forest Charter* of King John and Henry III. But his great work, one that has made his name famous, is *The Commentaries on the Laws of England.* Notwithstanding much envious criticism, it has maintained its place as a standard work. It has been again and again edited, and perhaps never better than by the Hon. George Sharswood, one of the Judges of the Supreme Court of Pennsylvania.

Adam Smith, 1723–1790: this distinguished writer on political economy, the intelligent precursor of a system based upon the modern usage of nations, was educated at Glasgow and Oxford, and became in turn Professor of Logic and of Moral Philosophy in the University of Glasgow. His lecture courses in Moral Science contain the germs of his two principal works: 1. *The Theory of Moral Sentiments*, and 2. *An Enquiry into the Nature and Causes of the Wealth of Nations.* The theory of the first has been superseded by the sounder views of later writers; but the second has conferred upon him enduring honor. In it he establishes as a principle that *labor* is the source of national wealth, and displays the value of division of labor. This work — written in clear, simple language, with copious illustrations — has had a wonderful influence upon the legislation and the commercial system of all civilized states since its issue, and has greatly conduced to the happiness of the human race. He wrote it in retirement, during a period of ten years. He astonished and instructed his period by presenting it with a new and necessary science.

CHAPTER XXX.

SAMUEL JOHNSON AND HIS TIMES.

Early Life and Career.	The Dictionary.	Person and Character.
London.	Other Works.	Style.
Rambler and Idler.	Lives of the Poets.	Junius.

Early Life and Career.

DOCTOR SAMUEL JOHNSON was poet, dramatist, essayist, lexicographer, dogmatist, and critic, and, in this array of professional characters, played so distinguished a part in his day that he was long regarded as a prodigy in English literature. His influence has waned since his personality has grown dim, and his learning been superseded or overshadowed; but he still remains, and must always remain, the most prominent literary figure of his age; and this is in no small measure due to his good fortune in having such a champion and biographer as James Boswell. Johnson's Life by Boswell is without a rival among biographies: in the words of Macaulay: "Homer is not more decidedly the first of heroic poets; Shakspeare is not more decidedly the first of dramatists; Demosthenes is not more decidedly the first of orators, than Boswell is the first of biographers;" and Burke has said that Johnson appears far greater in Boswell's book than in his own. We thus know everything about Johnson, as we do not know about any other literary man, and this knowledge, due to his biographer, is at least one of the elements of Johnson's immense reputation.

He was born at Lichfield on the 18th of September, 1709. His father was a bookseller; and after having had a certain amount of knowledge "well beaten into him" by Mr. Hunter, young Johnson was for two years an assistant in his father's shop. But such was his aptitude for learning, that he was sent in 1728 to Pembroke College, Oxford. His youth was not a happy one: he was afflicted with scrofula, "which disfigured a countenance naturally well formed, and hurt his visual nerves so much that he did not see at all with one of his eyes." He had a morbid melancholy,—fits of dejection which made his life miserable. He was poor; and when, in 1731, his father died insolvent, he was obliged to leave the university without a degree. After fruitless attempts to establish a school, he married, in 1736, Mrs. Porter, a widow, who had £800. Rude and unprepossessing to others, she was sincerely loved by her husband, and deeply lamented when she died. In 1737 Johnson went to London in company with young Garrick, who had been one of his few pupils, and who was soon to fill the English world with his theatrical fame.

LONDON.—Johnson soon began to write for Cave's *Gentleman's Magazine*, and in 1738 he astonished Pope and the artificial poets by producing, in their best vein, his imitation of the third Satire of Juvenal, which he called *London*. This was his usher into the realm of literature. But he did not become prominent until he had reached his fiftieth year; he continued to struggle with gloom and poverty, too proud to seek patronage in an age when popular remuneration had not taken its place. In 1740 he was a reporter of the debates in parliament for Cave; and it is said that many of the indifferent speakers were astonished to read the next day the fine things which the reporter had placed in their mouths, which they had never uttered.

In 1749 he published his *Vanity of Human Wishes*, an imitation of the tenth Satire of Juvenal, which was as heartily welcomed as *London* had been. It is Juvenal applied to English and European history. It contains many lines familiar to us all; among them are the following:

> Let observation with extended view
> Survey mankind from China to Peru.

In speaking of Charles XII., he says:

> His fall was destined to a barren strand,
> A petty fortress and a dubious hand;
> He left a name at which the world grew pale,
> To point a moral or adorn a tale.
>
> From Marlborough's eyes the streams of dotage flow,
> And Swift expires a driveller and a show.

In the same year he published his tragedy of *Irene*, which, notwithstanding the friendly efforts of Garrick, who was now manager of Drury Lane Theatre, was not successful. As a poet, Johnson was the perfection of the artificial school; and this very technical perfection was one of the causes of the reaction which was already beginning to sweep it away.

RAMBLER AND IDLER.—In 1750 he commenced *The Rambler*, a periodical like *The Spectator*, of which he wrote nearly all the articles, and which lived for two years. Solemn, didactic, and sonorous, it lacked the variety and genial humor which had characterized Addison and Steele. In 1758 he started *The Idler*, in the same vein, which also ran its respectable course for two years. In 1759 his mother died, and, in order to defray the expenses of her funeral, he wrote his story of *Rasselas* in the evenings of one week, for two editions of which he received £125. Full of moral aphorisms and instruction, this "Abyssinian tale" is entirely English in philosophy and fancy, and has not even the slight illusion of other Eastern tales in French and English, which were written about the same time, and which are very similar in form and matter.

Of *Rasselas*, Hazlitt says: "It is the most melancholy and debilitating moral speculation that was ever put forth."

THE DICTIONARY.—As early as 1747 he had begun to write his English Dictionary, which, after eight years of incessant and unassisted labor, appeared in 1755. It was a noble thought, and produced a noble work—a work which filled an original vacancy. In France, a National Academy had undertaken a similar work; but this English giant had accomplished his labors alone. The amount of reading necessary to fix and illustrate his definitions was enormous, and the book is especially valuable from the apt and varied quotations from English authors. He established the language, as he found it, on a firm basis in signification and orthography. He laid the foundation upon which future lexicographers were to build; but he was ignorant of the Teutonic languages, from which so much of the structure and words of the English are taken, and thus is signally wanting in the scientific treatment of his subject. This is not to his discredit, for the science of language has had its origin in a later and modern time.

Perhaps nothing displays more fully the proud, sturdy, and self-reliant character of the man, than the eight years of incessant and unassisted labor upon this work.

His letter to Lord Chesterfield, declining his tardy patronage, after experiencing his earlier neglect, is a model of severe and yet respectful rebuke, and is to be regarded as one of the most significant events in his history. In it he says: "The notice you have been pleased to take of my labors, had it been early, had been kind; but it has been delayed till I am indifferent, and cannot enjoy it; till I am solitary, and cannot impart it; till I am known, and do not want it. I hope it is no very cynical asperity not to confess obligation when no benefit has been received, or to be unwilling that the public should consider me as owing that to a patron which Providence has enabled me to do for myself." Living as he did in an age when the patronage of the great was wearing out, and public appreciation beginning to reward an author's toils, this manly letter gave another stab to the former, and hastened the progress of the latter.

OTHER WORKS. — The fame of Johnson was now fully established, and his labors were rewarded, in 1762, by the receipt of a pension of £300 from the government, which made him quite independent. It was then, in the very heyday of his reputation, that, in 1763, he became acquainted with James Boswell, to whom he at once became a Grand Lama; who took down the words as they dropped from his lips, and embalmed his fame.

In 1764 he issued his edition of Shakspeare, in eight octavo volumes, of which the best that can be said is, that it is not valuable as a commentary. A commentator must have something in common with his author; there was nothing congenial between Shakspeare and Johnson.

It was in 1773, that, urged by Boswell, he made his famous *Journey to the Hebrides*, or Western Islands of Scotland, of which he gave delightful descriptions in a series of letters to his friend Mrs. Thrale, which he afterwards wrote out in more pompous style for publication. The letters are current, witty, and simple; the published work is stilted and grandiloquent.

It is well known that he had no sympathy with the American colonies in their struggle against British oppression. When, in 1775, the Congress published their *Resolutions* and *Address*, he answered them in a prejudiced and illogical paper entitled *Taxation no Tyranny*. Notwithstanding its want of argument, it had the weight of his name and of a large party; but history has construed it by the *animus* of the writer, who had not long before declared of the colonists that they were "a race of convicts, and ought to be thankful for anything we allow them short of hanging."

As early as 1744 he had published a Life of the gifted but

unhappy Savage, whom in his days of penury he had known, and with whom he had sympathized; but in 1781 appeared his *Lives of the English Poets, with Critical Observations on their Works*, and *Lives of Sundry Eminent Persons.*

LIVES OF THE POETS. — These comprise fifty-two poets, most of them little known at the present day, and thirteen *eminent persons*. Of historical value, as showing us the estimate of an age in which Johnson was an usher to the temple of Fame, they are now of little other value; those of his own school and coterie he could undeistand and eulogize. To Milton he accorded carefully measured praise, but could not do him full justice, from entire want of sympathy; the majesty of blank verse pentameters he could not appreciate, and from Milton's puritanism he recoiled with disgust.

Johnson died on the 13th of December, 1784, and was buried in Westminster Abbey; a flat stone with an inscription was placed over his grave: it was also designed to erect his monument there, but St. Paul's Cathedral was afterwards chosen as the place. There, a colossal figure represents the distinguished author, and a Latin epitaph, written by Dr. Parr, records his virtues and his achievements in literature.

PERSON AND CHARACTER. — A few words must suffice to give a summary of his character, and will exhibit some singular contrarieties. He had varied but not very profound learning; was earnest, self-satisfied, overbearing in argument, or, as Sir Walter Scott styles it, *despotic*. As distinguished for his powers of conversation as for his writings, he always talked *ex cathedra*, and was exceedingly impatient of opposition. Brutal in his word attacks, he concealed by tone and manner a generous heart. Grandiloquent in ordinary matters, he "made little fishes talk like whales."

Always swayed by religious influences, he was intolerant of the sects around him; habitually pious, he was not without superstition; he was not an unbeliever in ghostly apparitions, and had a great fear of death; he also had the touching mania — touching every post as he walked along the street, thereby to avoid some unknown evil.

Although of rural origin, he became a thorough London cockney, and his hatred of Scotchmen and dissenters is at once pitiful and ludicrous. His manners and gestures were uncouth and disagreeable. He devoured rather than eat his food, and was a remarkable tea-drinker; on one occasion, perhaps for bravado, taking twenty-five cups at a sitting.

Massive in figure, seamed with scrofulous scars and marks, seeing with but one eye, he had convulsive motions and twitches, and his slovenly dress added to the uncouthness and oddity of his appearance. In all respects he was an original, and even his defects and peculiarities seemed to conduce to make him famous.

Considered the first among the critics of his own day, later judgments have reversed his decisions; many of those whom he praised have sunk into obscurity, and those whom he failed to appreciate have been elevated to the highest pedestals in the literary House of Fame.

STYLE. — His style is full-sounding and antithetic, his periods are carefully balanced, his manner eminently respectable and good; but his words, very many of them of Latin derivation, constitute what the later critics have named *Johnsonese*, which is certainly capable of translation into plainer Saxon English, with good results. Thus, in speaking of Addison's style, he says: "It is pure without scrupulosity, and exact without apparent elaboration; . . . he seeks no ambitious ornaments, and tries no hazardous innovations; his page is always luminous, but never blazes in unexpected splendor." Very numerous examples might be given of sentences most of the words in which might be replaced by simpler expressions with great advantage to the sound and to the sense.

As a critic, his word was law: his opinion was clearly and often severely expressed on literary men and literary subjects, and no great writer of his own or a past age escaped either his praise or his censure. Authors wrote with the fear of his criticism before their eyes; and his pompous diction was long imitated by men who, without this influence, would have written far better English. But, on the other hand, his honesty, his scholarship, his piety, and his championship of what was good and true, as depicted in his writings, made him a blessing to his time, and an honored and notable character in the noble line of English authors.

JUNIUS.—Among the most significant and instructive writings to the student of English history, in the earlier part of the reign of George III., is a series of letters written by a person, or by several persons in combination, whose *nom de plume* was Junius. These letters specified the errors and abuses of the government, were exceedingly bold in denunciation and bitter in invective. The letters of Junius were forty-four in number, and were addressed to Mr. Woodfall, the proprietor of *The Public Advertiser*, a London newspaper, in which they were published. Fifteen others in the same vein were signed Philo-Junius; and there are besides sixty-two notes addressed by Junius to his publisher.

The principal letters signed Junius were addressed to ministers directly, and the first, on the *State of the Nation*, was a manifesto of the grounds of his writing and his purpose. It was evident that a bold censor had sprung forth; one acquainted with the secret movements of the government, and with the foibles and faults of the principal statesmen: they writhed under his lash. Some of the more gifted attempted to answer him, and, as in the case of Sir William Draper, met with signal discomfiture. Vigorous efforts were made to discover the offender, but without success; and as to his first patriotic intentions he soon added personal spite, the writer found that his life would not be safe if his secret were discovered. The rage of parties has long since died away, and the writer or writers have long been in their graves, but the curious secret still remains, and has puzzled the brains of students to the present day. Allibone gives a list of forty-two persons to whom the letters were in whole or in part ascribed, among whom are Colonel Barré, Burke, Lord Chatham, General Charles Lee, Horne Tooke, Wilkes, Horace Walpole, Lord Lyttleton, Lord George Sackville, and Sir Philip Francis. Pamphlets and books have been written by hundreds upon this question of authorship, and it is not yet by any means definitely settled. The concurrence of the most intelligent investigators is in favor of Sir Philip Francis, because of the handwriting being like his, but slightly disguised; because he and Junius were alike intimate with the government workings in the state department and in the war department, and took notes of speeches in the House of Lords; because the letters came to an end just before Francis was sent to India; and because, indecisive as these claims are, they are stronger than those of any other suspected author. Macaulay adds to these: "One of the strongest reasons for believing that Francis was Junius is the *moral* resemblance between the two men."

It is interesting to notice that the ministry engaged Dr. Johnson to answer the *forty-second* letter, in which the king is especially arraigned. Johnson's answer, published in 1771, is entitled *Thoughts on the Late Transactions respecting Falkland's Islands*. Of Junius he says: "He cries havoc without reserve, and endeavors to let slip the dogs of foreign and civil war, ignorant whither they are going, and careless what may be their prey." "It is not hard to be sarcastic in a mask; while he walks like Jack the giant-killer, in a coat of darkness, he may do much mischief with little strength." "Junius is an unusual phenomenon, on which some have gazed with wonder and some with terror; but wonder and terror are transitory passions. He will soon be more closely viewed, or more attentively examined, and what folly has taken for a comet, that from its flaming hair shook pestilence and war, inquiry will find to be only a meteor formed by the vapors of putrefying democracy, and kindled into flame by the effervescence of interest struggling with conviction, which, after having plunged its followers into a bog, will leave us inquiring why we regarded it."

Whatever the moral effect of the writings of Junius, as exhibited by silent influence in the lapse of years, the schemes he proposed and the party he championed alike failed of success. His farewell letter to Woodfall bears date the 19th of January, 1773. In that letter he declared that "he must be an idiot to write again; that he had meant well by the cause and the public; that both were given up; that there were not ten men who would act steadily together on any question."[1] But one thing is sure: he has enriched the literature with public letters of rare sagacity, extreme elegance of rhetoric and great logical force, and has presented a problem always curious and interesting for future students,—not yet solved, in spite of Mr. Chabot's recent book,[2] and every day becoming more difficult of solution,—*Who was Junius?*

[1] Macaulay: Art. on Warren Hastings.

[2] The handwriting of Junius professionally investigated by Mr. Charles P. Chabot. London, 1871.

CHAPTER XXXI.

THE LITERARY FORGERS IN THE ANTIQUARIAN AGE.

The Eighteenth Century.

THE middle of the eighteenth century is marked as a period in which, while other forms of literature flourished, there arose a taste for historic research. Not content with the *actual* in poetry and essay and pamphlet, there was a looking back to gather up a record of what England had done and had been in the past, and to connect, in logical relation, her former with her latter glory. It was, as we have seen, the era of her great historians, Hume, Gibbon, and Robertson, who, upon the chronicles, and the abundant but scattered material, endeavored to construct philosophic history; it was the day of her greatest moralists, Adam Smith, Tucker, and Paley, and of research in metaphysics and political economy. In this period Bishop Percy collected the ancient English ballads, and also historic poems from the Chinese and the Runic; in it Warton wrote his history of poetry. Dr. Johnson, self-reliant and laborious, was producing his dictionary, and giving limits and coherence to the language. Mind was on the alert, not only subsidizing the present, but looking curiously into the past. I have ventured to call it the antiquarian age. In 1751, the Antiquarian Society of London was firmly established; men began to collect armor and relics: in this period grew up such an antiquary as Mr. Oldbuck, who curiously sought out every relic of the Roman times, — armor, fosses, and *prætoria,* — and found, with much that was real, many a fraud or delusion. It was an age which, in the words of old Walter Charleton, "despised the present as an innovation, and slighted the future, like the madman who fell in love with Cleopatra."

There was manifestly a great temptation to adventurous men — with sufficient learning, and with no high notion of honor — to creep into the distant past; to enact, in mask and domino, its literary parts, and endeavor to deceive an age already enthusiastic for antiquity.

Thus, in the third century, if we may believe the Scotch and Irish traditions, there existed in Scotland a great chieftain named Fion na Gael — modernized into Fingal — who fought with Cuthullin and the Irish warriors, and whose exploits were, as late as the time of which we have been speaking, the theme of rude ballads among the highlands and islands of Scotland. To find and translate these ballads was charming and legitimate work for the antiquarian; to counterfeit them, and call them by the name of a bard of that period, was the great temptation to the literary forger. Of such a bard, too, there was a tradition. As brave as were the deeds of Fingal, their fame was not so great as that of his son Ossian, who struck a lofty harp as he recounted his father's glory. Could the real poems be found, they would verify the lines:

> From the barred visor of antiquity
> Reflected shines the eternal light of Truth
> As from a mirror.

And if they could not be found, they might be counterfeited. This was undertaken by Doctor James Macpherson. Catering to the spirit of the age, he reproduced the songs of Ossian and the lofty deeds of Fingal.

Again, we have referred, in an early part of this work, to the almost barren expanse in the highway of English literature from the death of Chaucer to the middle of the sixteenth century; this barrenness was due, as we saw, to the turbulence of those years — civil war, misgovernment, a time of bloody action rather than peaceful authorship. Here, too, was a great temptation for some gifted but oblique mind to supply a partial literature for that bare period; a literature which, entirely fabricated, should yet bear all the characteristics of the history, language, customs, manners, and religion of that time.

This attempt was made by Thomas Chatterton, an obscure, ill-educated lad, without means or friends, but who had a master-mind, and would have accomplished some great feat in letters, had he not died, while still very young, by his own hand.

Let us examine these frauds in succession: we shall find them of double historic value, as literary efforts in one age designed to represent the literature of a former age.

James Macpherson. — James Macpherson was born at Ruthven, a village in Inverness-shire, in 1738. Being intended for the ministry, he received a good preliminary education, and became early interested in the ancient Gaelic ballads and poetic fragments still floating about the Highlands of Scotland. By the aid of Mr. John Home, the author of *Douglas*, and his friends Blair and Ferguson, he published, in 1760, a small volume of sixty pages entitled, *Fragments of Ancient Poetry translated from the Gaelic or Erse Language.* They were heroic and harmonious, and were very well received: he had catered to the very spirit of the age. At first, there seemed to be no doubt as to their genuineness. It was known to tradition that this northern Fingal had fought with Sevérus and Caracalla, on the banks of the Carun, and that blind Ossian had poured forth a flood of song after the fight, and made the deeds immortal. And now these songs and deeds were echoing in English ears, — the thrumming of the harp which told of "the stream of those olden years, where they have so long hid, in their mist, their many-colored sides." (*Cathloda*, Duan III.)

So enthusiastically were these poems received, that a subscription was raised to enable Macpherson to travel in the Highlands, and collect more of this lingering and beautiful poetry.

Gray the poet, writing to William Mason, in 1760, says: "These poems are in everybody's mouth in the Highlands; have been handed down from father to son. We have therefore set on foot a subscription of a guinea or two apiece, in order to enable Mr. Macpherson to recover this poem (Fingal), and other fragments of antiquity."

FINGAL. — On his return, in 1762, he published *Fingal*, and, in the same volume, some smaller poems. This Fingal, which he calls "an ancient epic poem" in six duans or books, recounts the deliverance of Erin from the King of Lochlin. The next year, 1763, he published *Temora*. Among the earlier poems, in all which Fingal is the hero, are passages of great beauty and touching pathos. Such, too, are found in *Carricthura and Carthon, the War of Inis-thona*, and the *Songs of Selma*. After reading these, we are pleasantly haunted with dim but beautiful pictures of that Northern coast where "the blue waters rolled in light," "when morning rose in the east;" and again with ghostly moonlit scenes, when "night came down on the sea, and Rotha's Bay received the ship." "The wan, cold moon rose in the east; sleep descended upon the youths; their blue helmets glitter to the beam; the fading fire decays; but sleep did not rest on the king; he rode in the midst of his arms, and slowly ascended the hill to behold the flame of Sarno's tower. The flame was dim and distant; the moon hid her red face in the east. A blast came from the mountain; on its wings was the spirit of

Loda." In *Carthon* occurs that beautiful address to the Sun, which we are fortunate in knowing, from other sources than Macpherson, is a tolerably correct translation of a real original. If we had that alone, it would be a revelation of the power of Ossian, and of the aptitudes of a people who could enjoy it. It is not within our scope to quote from the veritable Ossian, or to expose the bombast and fustian, tumid diction and swelling sound of Macpherson, of which the poems contain so much.

As soon as a stir was made touching the authenticity of the poems, a number of champions sprang up on both sides: among those who favored Macpherson, was Dr. Hugh Blair, who wrote the critical dissertation usually prefixed to the editions of Ossian, and who compares him favorably to Homer. First among the incredulous, as might be expected, was Dr. Samuel Johnson, who, in his *Journey to the Hebrides*, lashes Macpherson for his imposture, and his insolence in refusing to show the original. Johnson was threatened by Macpherson with a beating, and he answered: "I hope I shall never be deterred from detecting what I think a cheat by the menaces of a ruffian. . . I thought your book an imposture; I think it an imposture still. . . Your rage I defy. . . You may print this if you will."

Proofs of the imposture were little by little discovered by the critics. There were some real fragments in his first volume; but even these he had altered, and made symmetrical, so as to disguise their original character. Ossian would not have known them. As for Fingal, in its six duans, with captional arguments, it was made up from a few fragments, and no such poem ever existed. It was Macpherson's from beginning to end.

The final establishment of the forgery was not simply by recourse to scholars versed in the Celtic tongues, but the Highland Society appointed a committee in 1767, whose duty it was to send to the Highland pastors a circular, inquiring whether they had heard in the original the poems of Ossian, said to be translated by Macpherson; if so, where and by whom they had been written out or repeated: whether similar fragments still existed, and whether there were persons living who could repeat them; whether, to their knowledge, Macpherson had obtained such poems in the Highlands; and for any information concerning the personality of Fingal and Ossian.

CRITICISM. — The result was as follows: Certain Ossianic poems did exist, and some manuscripts of ancient ballads and bardic songs. A few of these had formed the foundation of Macpherson's so-called translations of the earlier pieces; but he had altered and added to them, and joined them with his own fancies in an arbitrary manner.

Fingal and *Temora* were also made out of a few fragments; but in their epic and connected form not only did not exist, but lack the bardic character and construction entirely.

Now that the critics had the direction of the chase made known, they discovered that Macpherson had taken his imagery from the Bible, of which Ossian was ignorant; from classic authors, of whom he had never heard; and from modern sources down to his own day.

Then Macpherson's Ossian — which had been read with avidity and translated into many languages, while it was considered an antique gem only reset in English — fell into disrepute, and was unduly despised when known to be a forgery.

It is difficult to conceive why he did not produce the work as his own, with a true story of its foundation: it is not so difficult to understand why, when he was detected, he persisted in the falsehood. For what it really is, it must be partially praised; and it will remain not only as a literary curiosity, but as a work of unequal but real merit. It was greatly admired by Napoleon and Madame de Staël, and, in endeavoring to consign it to oblivion, the critics are greatly in the wrong.

Macpherson resented any allusion to the forgery, and any leading question concerning it. He refused, at first, to produce the originals; and when he did say where they might be found, the world had decided so strongly against him, that there was no curiosity to examine them. He at last maintained a sullen silence; and, dying suddenly, in 1796, left no papers which throw light upon the controversy. The subject is, however, still agitated. Later writers have endeavored to reverse the decision of his age, without, however, any decided success. For much information concerning the Highland poetry, the reader is referred to *A Summer in Skye*, by Alexander Smith.

OTHER WORKS. — His other principal work was a *Translation of the Iliad of Homer* in the Ossianic style, which was received with execration and contempt. He also wrote *A History of Great Britain from the Restoration to the Accession of the House of Hanover*, which Fox — who was, however, prejudiced — declared to be full of impudent falsehoods.

Of his career little more need be said: he was too shrewd a man to need sympathy; he took care of himself. He was successful in his pecuniary schemes; as agent of the Nabob of Arcot, he had a seat in parliament for ten years, and was quite unconcerned what the world thought of his literary performances. He had achieved notoriety, and enjoyed it.

But, unfortunately, his forgery did fatal injury by its example; it inspired Chatterton, the precocious boy, to make another attempt on public credulity. It opened a seductive path for one who, inspired by the adventure and warned by the causes of exposure, might make a better forgery, escape detection, and gain great praise in the antiquarian world.

THOMAS CHATTERTON. — With this name, we accost the

most wonderful story of its kind in any literature; so strange, indeed, that we never take it up without trying to discover some new meaning in it. We hope, against hope, that the forgery is not proved.

Chatterton was born in Bristol, on the Avon, in 1752, of poor parents, but early gave signs of remarkable genius, combined with a prurient ambition. A friend who wished to present him with an earthen-ware cup, asked him what device he would have upon it. "Paint me," he answered, "an angel with wings and a trumpet, to trumpet my name over the world." He learned his alphabet from an old music-book; at eight years of age he was sent to a charity-school, and he spent his little pocket-money at a circulating library, the books of which he literally devoured.

At the early age of eleven he wrote a piece of poetry, and published it in the *Bristol Journal* of January 8, 1763; it was entitled *On the last Epiphany, or Christ coming to Judgment*, and the next year, probably, a *Hymn to Christmas-day*, of which the following lines will give an idea:

How shall we celebrate his name,
Who groaned beneath a life of shame,
  In all afflictions tried?
The soul is raptured to conceive
A truth which being must believe;
  The God eternal died.

My soul, exert thy powers, adore;
Upon Devotion's plumage soar
  To celebrate the day.
The God from whom creation sprung
Shall animate my grateful tongue,
  From Him I'll catch the lay.

Some member of the Chatterton family had, for one hundred and fifty years, held the post of sexton in the church of St. Mary Redcliffe at Bristol; and at the time of which we write his uncle was sexton. In the muniment-room of the church were several coffers, containing old papers and parchments in black letter, some of which were supposed to be of value. The chests were examined by order of the vestry; the valuable papers were removed, and of the rest, as perquisites of the sexton, some fell into the hands of Chatterton's father. The boy, who had been, upon leaving school, articled to an attorney, and had thus become familiar with the old English text, caught sight of these, and seemed then to have first formed the plan of turning them to account, as *The Rowlie papers.*

Old Manuscripts. — If he could be believed, he found a variety of material in this old collection. To a credulous and weak acquaintance, Mr. Burgum, he went, beaming with joy, to present the pedigree and illuminated arms of the de Bergham family — tracing the honest mechanic's descent to a noble house which crossed the Channel with William the Conqueror. The delighted Burgum gave him a crown, and Chatterton, pocketing the money, lampooned his credulity thus:

> Gods! what would Burgum give to get a name,
> And snatch his blundering dialect from shame?
> What would he give to hand his memory down
> To time's remotest boundary? a crown!
> Would you ask more, his swelling face looks blue —
> Futurity he rates at two pound two!

In September, 1768, the inauguration or opening of the new bridge across the Avon took place; and, taking advantage of the temporary interest it excited, Chatterton, then sixteen, produced in the *Bristol Journal* a full description of the opening of the old bridge two hundred years before, which he said he found among the old papers: "A description of the Fryers first passing over the old bridge, taken from an ancient manuscript," with details of the procession, and the Latin sermon preached on the occasion by Ralph de Blundeville;

ending with the dinner, the sports, and the illumination on Kynwulph Hill.

This paper, which attracted general interest, was traced to Chatterton, and when he was asked to show the original, it was soon manifest that there was none, but that the whole was a creation of his fancy. The question arises, — How did the statements made by Chatterton compare with the known facts of local history?

There was in the olden time in Bristol a great merchant named William Canynge, who was remembered for his philanthropy; he had altered and improved the church of St. Mary, and had built the muniment-room: the reputed poems, some of which were said to have been written by himself, and others by the monk Rowlie, Chatterton declared he had found in the coffers. Thomas Rowlie, "the gode preeste," appears as a holy and learned man, poet, artist, and architect. Canynge and Rowlie were strong friends, and the latter was supposed to have addressed many of the poems to the former, who was his good patron.

The principal of the Rowlie poems is the *Bristowe* (Bristol) *Tragedy*, or *Death of Sir Charles Bawdin*. This Bawdin, or Baldwin, a real character, had been attainted by Edward IV. of high treason, and brought to the block. The poem is in the finest style of the old English ballad, and is wonderfully dramatic. King Edward sends to inform Bawdin of his fate:

> Then with a jug of nappy ale
> His knights did on him waite;
> "Go tell the traitor that to daie
> He leaves this mortal state."

Sir Charles receives the tidings with bold defiance. Good Master Canynge goes to the king to ask the prisoner's life as a boon.

> "My noble liege," good Canynge saide,
> "Leave justice to our God;
> And lay the iron rule aside,
> Be thine the olyve rodde."

The king is inexorable, and Sir Charles dies amid tears and loud weeping around the scaffold.

Among the other Rowlie poems are the *Tragical Interlude of Ella,* "plaied before Master Canynge, and also before Johan Howard, Duke of Norfolk;" *Godwin,* a short drama; a long poem on *The Battle of Hastings,* and *The Romaunt of the Knight,* modernized from the original of John de Bergham.

THE VERDICT. — These poems at once became famous, and the critics began to investigate the question of their authenticity. From this investigation Chatterton did not shrink. He sent some of them with letters to Horace Walpole, and, as Walpole did not immediately answer, he wrote to him quite impertinently. Then they were submitted to Mason and Gray. The opinion of those who examined them was almost unanimous that they were forgeries: he could produce no originals; the language is in many cases not that of the period, and the spelling and idioms are evidently factitious. A few there were who seemed to have committed themselves, at first, to their authenticity; but Walpole, the Wartons, Dr. Johnson, Gibbon the historian, Sheridan, and most other literary men, were clear as to their forgery. The forged manuscripts which he had the hardihood afterwards to present, were totally unlike those of Edward the Fourth's time; he was entirely at fault in his heraldry; words were used out of their meaning; and, in his poem on *The Battle of Hastings*, he had introduced the modern discoveries concerning Stone Henge. He uses the possessive case *yttes,* which did not come into use until long after the Rowlie period. Add to these that Chatterton's reputation for veracity was bad.

The truth was, that he had found some curious scraps, which had set his fancy to work, and the example of Macpherson had led to the cheat he was practising upon the public. To some friends he confessed the deception, denying it again, violently, soon after; and he had been seen smoking parchment to make it look old. The lad was crazy.

HIS SUICIDE. — Keeping up appearances, he went to London, and tried to get work. At one time he was in high spirits, sending presents to his mother and sisters, and promising them better days; at another, he was in want, in the lowest depression, no hope in the world. He only asks for work; he is entirely unconcerned for whom he writes or what party he eulogizes; he wants money and a name, and when these seem unattainable, he takes refuge from "the whips and scorns of time," the burning fever of pride, the gnawings of hunger, in suicide. He goes to his little garret room, — refusing, as he goes, a dinner from his landlady, although he is gaunt with famine, — mixes a large dose of arsenic in water, and — "jumps the life to come." He was just seventeen years and nine months old! When his room was forced open, it was found that he had torn up most of his papers, and had left nothing to throw light upon his deception.

The verdict of literary criticism is that of the medical art — he was insane; and to what extent this mania acted as a monomania, that is, how far he was himself deceived, the world can never know. One thing, at least; it redeems all his faults. Precocious beyond any other known instance of precocity; intensely haughty; bold in falsehood; working best when the moon was at the full, he stands in English literature as the most singular of its curiosities. His will is an awful jest; his declaration of his religious opinions a tissue of contradictions and absurdities: he bequeathes to a clergyman his humility; to Mr. Burgum his prosody and grammar, with half his modesty — the other half to any young lady that needs it; his abstinence — a fearful legacy — to the aldermen of Bristol at their annual feast! to a friend, a mourning ring — "provided he pays for it himself" — with the motto, "Alas, poor Chatterton!" Fittest ending to his biography — "Alas, poor Chatterton!"

And yet it is evident that the crazy Bristol boy and the astute Scotchman were alike the creatures of the age and the peculiar circumstances in which they lived. No other age of English history could have produced them. In an earlier period, they would have found no curiosity in the people to warrant their attempts; and in a later time, the increase in antiquarian studies would have made these efforts too easy of detection.

CHAPTER XXXII.

POETRY OF THE TRANSITION SCHOOL.

The Transition Period.	Mark Akenside.	William Cowper.
James Thomson.	Pleasures of the Imagination.	The Task.
The Seasons.	Thomas Gray.	Translation of Homer.
The Castle of Indolence.	The Elegy. The Bard.	Other Writers.

THE TRANSITION PERIOD.

THE poetical standards of Dryden and Pope, as poetic examples and arbiters, exercised tyrannical sway to the middle of the eighteenth century, and continued to be felt, with relaxing influence, however, to a much later period. Poetry became impatient of too close a captivity to technical rules in rhythm and in subjects, and began once again to seek its inspiration from the worlds of nature and of feeling. While seeking this change, it passed through what has been properly called the period of transition,—a period the writers of which are distinctly marked as belonging neither to the artificial classicism of Pope, nor to the simple naturalism of Wordsworth and the Lake school; partaking, indeed, in some degree of the former, and preparing the way for the latter.

The excited condition of public feeling during the earlier period, incident to the accession of the house of Hanover and the last struggles of the Jacobites, had given a political character to every author, and a political significance to almost every literary work. At the close of this abnormal condition of things, the poets of the transition school began their labors; untrammelled by the court and the town, they invoked the muse in green fields and by babbling brooks;

from materialistic philosophy in verse they appealed through the senses to the hearts of men; and appreciation and popularity rewarded and encouraged them.

James Thomson. — The first distinguished writer of this school was Thomson, the son of a Scottish minister. He was born on the 11th of September, 1700, at Ednam in Roxburghshire. While a boy at school in Jedburgh, he displayed poetical talent: at the University of Edinburgh he completed his scholastic course, and studied divinity; which, however, he did not pursue as a profession. Being left, by his father's death, without means, he resolved to go to the great metropolis to try his fortunes. He arrived in London in sorry plight, without money, and with ragged shoes; but through the assistance of some persons of station, he procured occupation as tutor to a lord's son, and thus earned a livelihood until the publication of his first poem in 1726. That poem was *Winter*, the first of the series called *The Seasons*: it was received with unusual favor. The first edition was speedily exhausted, and with the publication of the second, his position as a poet was assured. In 1727 he produced the second poem of the series, *Summer*, and, with it, a proposal for issuing the *Four Seasons*, with a *Hymn* on their succession. In 1728 his *Spring* appeared, and in the next year an unsuccessful tragedy called *Sophonisba*, which owed its immediate failure to the laughter occasioned by the line,

O Sophonisba, Sophonisba O!

This was parodied by some wag in these words:

O Jemmie Thomson, Jemmie Thomson O!

and the ridicule was so potent that the play was ruined.

The last of the seasons, *Autumn*, and the *Hymn*, were first printed in a complete edition of *The Seasons*, in 1730. It was at once conceded that he had gratified the cravings of the day, in producing a real and beautiful English pastoral. The reputation which he thus gained caused him to be selected as the mentor and companion of the son of Sir Charles Tálbot in a tour through France and Italy in 1730 and 1731.

In 1734 he published the first part of a poem called *Liberty*, the conclusion of which appeared in 1736. It is designed to trace the progress of Liberty through Italy, Greece, and Rome, down to her excellent establishment in Great Britain, and was dedicated to Frederick, Prince of Wales.

His tragedies *Agamemnon* and *Edward and Eleanora* are in the then prevailing taste. They were issued in 1738–39. The latter is of political significance, in that Edward was like Frederick the Prince of Wales — heir apparent to the crown; and some of the passages are designed to strengthen the prince in the favor of the people.

The personal life of Thomson is not of much interest. From his first residence in London, he supported, with his slender means, a brother, who died young of consumption, and aided two maiden sisters, who kept a small milliner-shop in Edinburgh. This is greatly to his praise, as he was at one time so poor that he was arrested for debt and committed to prison. As his reputation increased, his fortunes were ameliorated. In 1745 his play *Tancred and Sigismunda* was performed. It was founded upon a story universally popular, — the same which appears in the episode of *The Fatal Marriage* in Gil Blas, and in one of the stories of Boccaccio. He enjoyed for a short time a pension from the Prince of Wales, of which, however, he was deprived without apparent cause; but he received the office of Surveyor-General of the Leeward Islands, the duties of which he could perform by deputy; after that he lived a lazy life at his cottage near Richmond, which, if otherwise reprehensible, at least gave him the power to write his most beautiful poem, *The Castle of Indolence*. It appeared in 1748, and was universally admired; it has a rhetorical harmony similar and quite equal

30

to that of the *Lotos Eaters* of Tennyson. The poet, who had become quite plethoric, was heated by a walk from London, and, from a check of perspiration, was thrown into a high fever, a relapse of which caused his death on the 27th of August, 1748. His friend Lord Lyttleton wrote the prologue to his play of *Coriolanus*, which was acted after the poet's death, in which he says:

> "—— His chaste Muse employed her heaven-taught lyre
> None but the noblest passions to inspire,
> Not one immoral, one corrupted thought,
> *One line which, dying, he could wish to blot.*"

The praise accorded him in this much-quoted line is justly his due: it is greater praise that he was opening a new pathway in English Literature, and supplying better food than the preceding age had given. His *Seasons* supplied a want of the age: it was a series of beautiful pastorals. The descriptions of nature will always be read and quoted with pleasure; the little episodes, if they affect the unity, relieve the monotony of the subject, and, like figures introduced by the painter into his landscape, take away the sense of loneliness, and give us a standard at once of judgment, of measurement, and of sympathetic enjoyment; they display, too, at once the workings of his own mind in his production, and the manners and sentiments of the age in which he wrote. It was fitting that he who had portrayed for us such beautiful gardens of English nature, should people them instead of leaving them solitary.

THE CASTLE OF INDOLENCE. — This is an allegory, written after the manner of Spenser, and in the Spenserian stanza. He also employs archaic words, as Spenser did, to give it greater resemblance to Spenser's poem. The allegorical characters are well described, and the sumptuous adornings and lazy luxuries of the castle are set forth *con amore*. The spell that enchants the castle is broken by the stalwart knight *Industry;* but the glamour of the poem remains, and makes the reader in love with *Indolence*.

MARK AKENSIDE. — Thomson had restored or reproduced the pastoral from Nature's self; Akenside followed in his steps. Thomson had invested blank verse with a new power and beauty; Akenside produced it quite as excellent. But Thomson was the original, and Akenside the copy. The one is natural, the other artificial.

Akenside was the son of a butcher, and was born at New Castle, in 1721. Educated at the University of Edinburgh, he studied medicine, and received, at different periods, lucrative and honorable professional appointments. His great work, and the only one to which we need refer, is his *Pleasures of the Imagination.* Whether his view of the imagination is always correct or not, his sentiments are always elevated; his language high sounding but frequently redundant, and his versification correct and pleasing. His descriptions of nature are cold but correct; his standard of humanity is high but mortal. Grand and sonorous, he constructs his periods with the manner of a declaimer; his ascriptions and apostrophes are like those of a high-priest. The title of his poem, if nothing more, suggested *The Pleasures of Hope* to Campbell, and *The Pleasures of Memory* to Rogers. As a man, Akenside was overbearing and dictatorial; as a hospital surgeon, harsh in his treatment of poor patients. His hymn to the Naiads has been considered the most thoroughly and correctly classical of anything in English. He died on the 23d of June, 1770.

THOMAS GRAY. — Among those who form a link between the school of Pope and that of the modern poets, Gray occupies a distinguished place, both from the excellence of his writings, and from the fact that, while he unconsciously conduced to the modern, he instinctively resisted its progress. He was in taste and intention an extreme classicist. Thomas Gray was born in London on the 26th December, 1716. His father was a money scrivener, and, to his family at least, a bad man; his mother, forced to support herself, kept a linen-draper shop; and to her the poet owed his entire education. He was entered at Eton College, and afterwards at Cambridge, and found in early life such friendships as were of great importance to him later in his career. Among his college friends were Horace Walpole, West, the son of the Lord Chancellor of Ireland, and William Mason, who afterwards wrote the poet's life. After completing his college course, he travelled on the continent with Walpole; but, on account of incompatibility of temper, they quarrelled and parted, and Gray returned home. Although Walpole took the blame upon himself, it would appear that Gray was a somewhat captious person, whose serious tastes interfered with the gayer pleasures of his friend. On his return, Gray went to Cambridge, where he led the life of a retired student, devoting himself to the ancient authors, to poetry, botany, architecture, and heraldry. He was fastidious as to his own productions, which were very few, and which he kept by him, pruning, altering, and polishing, for a long time before he would let them see the light. His lines entitled *A Distant Prospect of Eton College* appeared in 1742, and were received with great applause.

It was at this time that he also began his *Elegy in a Country Churchyard;* which, however, did not appear until seven or eight years later, and which has made him immortal. The grandeur of its language, the elevation of its sentiments, and the sympathy of its pathos, commend it to all classes and all hearts; and of its kind of composition it stands alone in English literature.

The ode on the progress of poetry appeared in 1755. Like the *Elegy*, his poem of *The Bard* was for several years on the literary easel, and he was accidentally led to finish it by hearing a blind harper performing on a Welsh harp.

On the death of Cibber, Gray was offered the laureate's crown, which he declined, to avoid its conspicuousness and the envy of his brother poets. In 1762, he applied for the professorship of modern history at Cambridge, but failed to obtain the position. He was more fortunate in 1768, when it again became vacant; but he held it as a sinecure, doing none of its duties. He died in 1770, on the 3d of July, of gout in the stomach. His habits were those of a recluse; and whether we agree or not, with Adam Smith, in saying that nothing is wanting to render him perhaps the first poet in the English language, but to have written a little more, it is astonishing that so great and permanent a reputation should have been founded on so very little as he wrote. Gray has been properly called the finest lyric poet in the language; and his lyric power strikes us as intuitive and original; yet he himself, adhering strongly to the artificial school, declared, if there was any excellence in his own numbers, he had learned it wholly from Dryden. His archæological tastes are further shown by his enthusiastic study of heraldry, and by his surrounding himself with old armor and other curious relics of the past. Mr. Mitford, in a curious dissection of the *Elegy*, has found numerous errors of rhetoric, and even of grammar.

His *Bard* is founded on a tradition that Edward I., when he conquered Wales, ordered all the bards to be put to death, that they might not, by their songs, excite the Welsh people to revolt. The last one who figures in his story, sings a lament for his brethren, prophesies the downfall of the usurper, and then throws himself over the cliff:

> "Be thine despair and sceptered care,
> To triumph and to die are mine!"
> He spoke, and headlong from the mountain's height,
> Deep in the roaring tide, he plunged to endless night.

WILLIAM COWPER. — Next in the catalogue of the transition school occurs the name of one who, like Gray, was a recluse, but with a better reason and a sadder one. He was a gentle hypochondriac, and, at intervals, a maniac, who literally turned to poetry, like Saul to the harper, for relief from his sufferings. William Cowper, the eldest son of the Rector of Berkhampsted in Hertfordshire, was born on the 15th of November, 1731. He was a delicate and sensitive child, and was seriously affected by the loss of his mother when he was six years old. At school, he was cruelly treated by an older boy, which led to his decided views against public schools, expressed in his poem called *Tirocinium*. His morbid sensitiveness increased upon him as he grew older, and interfered with his legal studies and advancement. His depression of spirits took a religious turn; and we are glad to think that religion itself brought the balm which gave him twelve years of unclouded mind, devoted to friendship and to poetry. He was offered, by powerful friends, eligible positions connected with the House of Lords, in 1762; but as the one of these which he accepted was threatened with a public examination, he abandoned it in horror; not, however, before the fearful suspense had unsettled his brain, so that he was obliged to be placed, for a short time, in an asylum for the insane. When he left this asylum, he went to Huntingdon, where he became acquainted with the Rev. William Unwin, who, with his wife and son, seem to have been congenial companions to his desolate heart. On the death of Mr. Unwin, in 1767, he removed with the widow to Olney, and there formed an intimate acquaintance with another clergyman, the Rev. William Newton. Here, and in this society, the remainder of the poet's life was passed in writing letters, which have been considered the best ever written in England; in making hymns, in conjunction with Mr. Newton, which have ever since been universal favorites; and in varied poetic attempts, which give him high rank in the literature of the day. The first of his larger pieces was a poem entitled, *The Progress of Error*, which appeared in 1783, when the author had reached the advanced age of 52. Then followed *Truth* and *Expostulation*, which, according to the poet himself, did much towards diverting his melancholy thoughts. These poems would not have fixed his fame; but Lady Austen, an accomplished woman with whom he became acquainted in 1781, deserves our gratitude for having proposed to him the subjects of those poems which have really made him famous, namely, *The Task*, *John Gilpin*, and the translation of *Homer*. Before, however, undertaking these, he wrote poems on *Hope*, *Charity*, *Conversation*, and *Retirement*. The story of *John Gilpin* — a real one as told him by Lady Austen — made such an impression upon him, that he dashed off the ballad at a sitting.

THE TASK. — The origin of *The Task* is well known. In 1783, Lady Austen suggested to him to write a poem in blank verse: he said he would, if she would suggest the subject. Her answer was, "Write on *this sofa*." The poem thus begun was speedily expanded into those beautiful delineations of varied nature, domestic life, and religious sentiment which rivalled the best efforts of Thomson. The title that connects them is *The Task*. *Tirocinium*, or *the Review of Schools*, appeared soon after, and excited considerable attention in a country where public education has been the rule of the higher social life. Cowper began the translation of Homer in 1785, from a feeling of the necessity of employment for his mind. His translations of both Iliad and Odyssey, which occupied him for five years, and which did not entirely keep off his old enemy, were published in 1791. They are correct in scholarship and idiom, but lack the nature and the fire of the old Grecian bard.

The rest of his life was busy, but sad — a constant effort to drive away madness by incessant labor. The loss of his friend, Mrs. Unwin, in 1796, affected him deeply, and the clouds settled thicker and thicker upon his soul. In the year before his death, he published that painfully touching poem, *The Castaway*, which gives an epitome of his own sufferings in the similitude of a wretch clinging to a spar in a stormy night upon the Atlantic

His minor and fugitive poems are very numerous; and as they were generally inspired by persons and scenes around him, they are truly literary types of the age in which he lived. In his *Task,* he resembles Thomson and Akenside; in his didactic poems, he reminds us of the essays of Pope; in his hymns he catered successfully to the returning piety of the age; in his translations of Homer and of Ovid, he presented the ancients to moderns in a new and acceptable dress; and in his Letters he sets up an epistolary model, which may be profitably studied by all who desire to express themselves with energy, simplicity, and delicate taste.

Other Writers of the Transition School.

James Beattie, 1735–1803: he was the son of a farmer, and was educated at Marischal College, Aberdeen, where he was afterwards professor of natural philosophy. For four years he taught a village school. His first poem, *Retirement,* was not much esteemed; but in 1771 appeared the first part of *The Minstrel,* a poem at once descriptive, didactic, and romantic. This was enthusiastically received, and gained for him the favor of the king, a pension of £200 per annum, and a degree from Oxford. The second part was published in 1774. *The Minstrel* is written in the Spenserian stanza, and abounds in beautiful descriptions of nature, marking a very decided progress from the artificial to the natural school. The character of Edwin, the young minstrel, ardent in search for the beautiful and the true, is admirably portrayed; as is also that of the hermit who instructs the youth. The opening lines are very familiar:

> Ah, who can tell how hard it is to climb
> The steep where Fame's proud temple shines afar;

and the description of the morning landscape has no superior in the language:

> But who the melodies of morn can tell?
> The wild brook babbling down the mountain side;
> The lowing herd; the sheepfold's simple bell;
> The pipe of early shepherd dim descried
> In the lone valley.

Beattie wrote numerous prose dissertations and essays, one of which was in answer to the infidel views of Hume — *Essay on the Nature and Immutability of Truth, in Opposition to Sophistry and Scepticism.* Beattie was of an excitable and sensitive nature, and his polemical papers are valued rather for the beauty of their language, than for acuteness of logic.

William Falconer, 1730–1769: first a sailor in the merchant service, he afterwards entered the navy. He is chiefly known by his poem *The Shipwreck*, and for its astonishing connection with his own fortunes and fate. He was wrecked off Cape Colonna, on the coast of Greece, before he was eighteen; and this misfortune is the subject of his poem. Again, in 1760, he was cast away in the Channel. In 1769, the Aurora frigate, of which he was the purser, foundered in Mozambique Channels, and he, with all others on board, went down with her. The excellence of his nautical directions and the vigor of his descriptions establish the claims of his poem; but it has the additional interest attaching to his curious experience — it is his autobiography and his enduring monument. The picture of the storm is very fine; but in the handling of his verse there is more of the artificial than of the romantic school.

William Shenstone, 1714–1763: his principal work is *The Schoolmistress*, a poem in the stanza of Spenser, which is pleasing from its simple and sympathizing description of the village school, kept by a dame; with the tricks and punishment of the children, and many little traits of rural life and character. It is pitched in so low a key that it commends itself to the world at large. Shenstone is equally known for his mania in landscape gardening, upon which he spent all his means. His place, *The Leasowes* in Shropshire, has gained the greater notoriety through the descriptions of Dodsley and Goldsmith. The natural simplicity of *The Schoolmistress* allies it strongly to the romantic school, which was now about to appear.

William Collins, 1720–1756: this unfortunate poet, who died at the early age of thirty-six, deserves particular mention for the delicacy of his fancy and the beauty of his diction. His *Ode on the Passions* is universally esteemed for its sudden and effective changes from the bewilderment of Fear, the violence of Anger, and the wildness of Despair to the rapt visions of Hope, the gentle dejection of Pity, and the sprightliness of Mirth and Cheerfulness. His *Ode on the Death of Thomson* is an exquisite bit of pathos, as is also the *Dirge on Cymbeline.* Everybody knows and admires the short ode beginning

> How sleep the brave who sink to rest
> By all their country's wishes blest!

His *Oriental Eclogues* please by the simplicity of the colloquies, the choice figures of speech, and the fine descriptions of nature. But of all his poems, the most finished and charming is the *Ode to Evening.* It contains thirteen four-lined stanzas of varied metre, and in blank verse so full of harmony that rhyme would spoil it. It presents a series of soft, dissolving views, and stands alone in English poetry, with claims sufficient to immortalize the poet, had he written nothing else. The latter part of his life was clouded by mental disorders, not unsuggested to the reader by the pathos of many of his poems. Like Gray, he wrote little, but every line is of great merit.

Henry Kirke White, 1785–1806: the son of a butcher, this gifted youth displayed, in his brief life, such devotion to study, and such powers of mind, that his friends could not but predict a brilliant future for him, had he lived. Nothing that he produced is of the highest order of poetic merit, but everything was full of promise. Of a weak constitution, he could not bear the rigorous study which he prescribed to himself, and which hastened his death. With the kind assistance of Mr. Capel Lofft and the poet Southey, he was enabled to leave the trade to which he had been apprenticed and go to Cambridge. His poems have most of them a strongly devotional cast. Among them are *Gondoline, Clifton Grove,* and the *Christiad,* in the last of which, like the swan, he chants his own death-song. His memory has been kept green by Southey's edition of his *Remains,* and by the beautiful allusion of Byron to his genius and his fate in *The English Bards and Scotch Reviewers.* His sacred piece called *The Star of Bethlehem* has been a special favorite:

When marshalled on the nightly plain
The glittering host bestud the sky,
One star alone of all the train
Can fix the sinner's wandering eye.

Bishop Percy, 1728–1811: Dr. Thomas Percy, Bishop of Dromore, deserves particular notice in a sketch of English Literature not so much for his own works, — although he was a poet, — as for his collection of ballads, made with great research and care, and published in 1765. By bringing before the world these remains of English songs and idyls, which lay scattered through the ages from the birth of the language, he showed England the true wealth of her romantic history, and influenced the writers of the day to abandon the artificial and reproduce the natural, the simple, and the romantic. He gave the impulse which produced the minstrelsy of Scott and the simple stories of Wordsworth.

Many of these ballads are descriptive of the border wars between England and Scotland; among the greatest favorites are *Chevy Chase*, *The Battle of Otterburne*, *The Death of Douglas*, and the story of *Sir Patrick Spens*.

Anne Letitia Barbauld, 1743–1825: the hymns and poems of Mrs. Barbauld are marked by an adherence to the artificial school in form and manner; but something of feminine tenderness redeems them from the charge of being purely mechanical. Her *Hymns in Prose for Children* have been of value in an educational point of view; and the tales comprised in *Evenings at Home* are entertaining and instructive. Her *Ode to Spring*, which is an imitation of Collins's *Ode to Evening*, in the same measure and comprising the same number of stanzas, is her best poetic effort, and compares with Collins's piece as an excellent copy compares with the picture of a great master.

CHAPTER XXXIII.

THE LATER DRAMA.

The Progress of the Drama.	Cumberland.	George Colman, the Younger.
Garrick.	Sheridan.	Other Dramatists and Humorists.
Foote.	George Colman.	Other Writers on Various Subjects.

The Progress of the Drama.

THE latter half of the eighteenth century, so marked, as we have seen, for manifold literary activity, is, in one phase of its history, distinctly represented by the drama. It was a very peculiar epoch in English annals. The accession of George III., in 1760, gave promise, from the character of the king and of his consort, of an exemplary reign. George III. was the first monarch of the house of Hanover who may be justly called an English king in interest and taste. He and his queen were virtuous and honest; and their influence was at once felt by a people in whom virtue and honesty are inherent, and whose consciences and tastes had been violated by the evil examples of the former reigns.

In 1762 George Augustus Frederick, Prince of Wales, was born; and as soon as he approached manhood, he displayed the worst features of his ancestral house: he was extravagant and debauched; he threw himself into a violent opposition to his father: with this view he was at first a Whig, but afterwards became a Tory. He had also peculiar opportunities for exerting authority during the temporary fits of insanity which attacked the king in 1764, in 1788, and in 1804. At last, in 1810, the king was so disabled from attending to his duties, that the prince became regent, and assumed the reins of government, not to resign them again during his life.

In speaking of the drama of this period, we should hardly, therefore, be wrong in calling it the Drama of the Regency. It held, however, by historic links, following the order of historic events, to the earlier drama. Shakspeare and his contemporaries had established the dramatic art on a firm basis. The frown of puritanism, in the polemic period, had checked its progress: with the restoration of Charles II., it had returned to rival the French stage in wicked plots and prurient scenes. With the better morals of the Revolution, and the popular progress which was made at the accession of the house of Hanover, the drama was modified: the older plays were revived in their original freshness; a new and better taste was to be catered to; and what of immorality remained was chiefly due to the influence of the Prince of Wales. Actors, so long despised, rose to importance as great artists. Garrick and Foote, and, later, Kemble, Kean, and Mrs. Siddons, were social personages in England. Peers married actresses, and enduring reputation was won by those who could display the passions and the affections to the life, giving flesh and blood and mind and heart to the inimitable creations of Shakspeare.

It must be allowed that this power of presentment marks the age more powerfully than any claims of dramatic authorship. The new play-writers did not approach Shakspeare; but they represented their age, and repudiated the vices, in part at least, of their immediate predecessors. In them, too, is to be observed the change from the artificial to the romantic and natural. The scenes and persons in their plays are taken from the life around them, and appealed to the very models from which they were drawn.

DAVID GARRICK. — First among these purifiers of the drama is David Garrick, who was born in Lichfield, in 1716.

He was a pupil of Dr. Johnson, and came up with that distinguished man to London, in 1735. The son of a captain in the Royal army, but thrown upon his own exertions, he first tried to gain a livelihood as a wine merchant; but his fondness for the stage led him to become an actor, and in taking this step he found his true position. A man of respectable parts and scholarship, he wrote many agreeable pieces for the stage; which, however, owed their success more to his accurate knowledge of the *mise en scene*, and to his own representation of the principal characters, than to their intrinsic merits. His mimetic powers were great: he acted splendidly in all casts, excelling, perhaps, in tragedy; and he, more than any actor before or since, has made the world thoroughly acquainted with Shakspeare. Dramatic authors courted him; for his appearance in any new piece was almost an assurance of its success.

Besides many graceful prologues, epigrams, and songs, he wrote, or altered, forty plays. Among these the following have the greatest merit: *The Lying Valet*, a farce founded on an old English comedy; *The Clandestine Marriage*, in which he was aided by the elder Colman; (the character of *Lord Ogleby* he wrote for himself to personate;) *Miss in her Teens*, a very clever and amusing farce. He was charmingly natural in his acting; but he was accused of being theatrical when off the stage. In the words of Goldsmith:

On the stage he was natural, simple, affecting;
'Twas only that when he was off, he was acting.

Garrick married a dancer, who made him an excellent wife. By his own exertions he won a highly respectable social position, and an easy fortune of £140,000, upon which he retired from the stage. He died in London in 1779.

In 1831–2 his *Private Correspondence with the Most Celebrated Persons of his Time* was published, and opened a rich field to the social historian. Among his correspondents were

Dr. Johnson, Boswell, Goldsmith, Cibber, Sheridan, Burke, Wilkes, Junius, and Dr. Franklin. Thus Garrick catered largely to the history of his period, as an actor and dramatic author, illustrating the stage; as a reviver of Shakspeare, and as a correspondent of history.

Samuel Foote. — Among the many English actors who have been distinguished for great powers of versatility in voice, feature, and manner, there is none superior to Foote. Bold and self-reliant, he was a comedian in every-day life; and his ready wit and humor subdued Dr. Johnson, who had determined to dislike him. He was born in 1722, at Truro, and educated at Oxford: he studied law, but his peculiar aptitudes soon led him to the stage, where he became famous as a comic actor. Among his original pieces are *The Patron*, *The Devil on Two Stilts*, *The Diversions of the Morning*, *Lindamira*, and *The Slanderer*. But his best play, which is a popular burlesque on parliamentary elections, is *The Mayor of Garrat*. He died in 1777, at Dover, while on his way to France for the benefit of his health. His plays present the comic phase of English history in his day.

Richard Cumberland. — This accomplished man, who, in the words of Walter Scott, has given us "many powerful sketches of the age which has passed away," was born in 1732, and lived to the ripe age of seventy-nine, dying in 1811. After receiving his education at Cambridge, he became secretary to Lord Halifax. His versatile pen produced, besides dramatic pieces, novels and theological treatises, illustrating the principal topics of the time. In his plays there is less of immorality than in those of his contemporaries. *The West Indian*, which was first put upon the stage in 1771, and which is still occasionally presented, is chiefly noticeable in that an Irishman and a West Indian are the principal characters, and that he has not brought them into ridicule, as was common at the time, but has exalted them by their merits. The best of his other plays are *The Jew*, *The Wheel of Fortune*, and *The Fashionable Lover*. Goldsmith, in his poem *Retaliation*, says of Cumberland, referring to his greater morality and his human sympathy,

> Here Cumberland lies, having acted his parts,
> The Terence of England, the mender of hearts;
> A flattering painter, who made it his care
> To draw men as they ought to be, not as they are.

RICHARD BRINSLEY SHERIDAN. — No man represents the Regency so completely as Sheridan. He was a statesman, a legislator, an orator, and a dramatist; and in social life a wit, a gamester, a spendthrift, and a debauchee. His manifold nature seemed to be always in violent ebullition. He was born in September, 1751, and was the son of Thomas Sheridan, the actor and lexicographer. His mother, Frances Sheridan, was also a writer of plays and novels. Educated at Harrow, he was there considered a dunce; and when he grew to manhood, he plunged into dissipation, and soon made a stir in the London world by making a runaway match with Miss Linley, a singer, who was noted as one of the handsomest women of the day. A duel with one of her former admirers was the result.

As a dramatist, he began by presenting *A Trip to Scarborough*, which was altered from Vanbrugh's *Relapse;* but his fame was at once assured by his production, in 1775, of *The Duenna* and *The Rivals*. The former is called an opera, but is really a comedy containing many songs: the plot is varied and entertaining; but it is far inferior to *The Rivals*, which is based upon his own adventures, and is brimming with wit and humor. Mrs. Malaprop, Bob Acres, Sir Lucius O'Trigger, and the Absolutes, father and son, have been prime favorites upon the stage ever since.

In 1777 he produced *The School for Scandal*, a caustic

satire on London society, which has no superior in genteel comedy. It has been said that the characters of Charles and Joseph Surface were suggested by the Tom Jones and Blifil of Fielding; but, if this be true, the handling is so original and natural, that they are in no sense a plagiarism. Without the rippling brilliancy of *The Rivals*, *The School for Scandal* is better sustained in scene and colloquy; and in spite of some indelicacy, which is due to the age, the moral lesson is far more valuable. The satire is strong and instructive, and marks the great advance in social decorum over the former age.

In 1779 appeared *The Critic*, a literary satire, in which the chief character is that of Sir Fretful Plagiary.

Sheridan sat in parliament as member for Stafford. His first effort in oratory was a failure; but by study he became one of the most effective popular orators of his day. His speeches lose by reading: he abounded in gaudy figures, and is not without bombast; but his wonderful flow of words and his impassioned action dazzled his audience and kept it spell-bound. His oratory, whatever its faults, gained also the unstinted praise of his colleagues and rivals in the art. Of his great speech in the trial of Warren Hastings, in 1788, Fox declared that "all he had ever heard, all he had ever read, when compared with it, dwindled into nothing, and vanished like vapor before the sun." Burke called it "the most astonishing effort of eloquence, argument, and wit united, of which there was any record or tradition;" and Pitt said "that it surpassed all the eloquence of ancient or modern times."

Sheridan was for some time the friend and comrade of the Prince Regent, in wild courses which were to the taste of both; but this friendship was dissolved, and the famous dramatist and orator sank gradually in the social scale, until he had sounded the depths of human misery. He was deeply in debt; he obtained money under mean and false pretences;

he was drunken and debauched; and even death did not bring rest. He died in July, 1816. His corpse was arrested for debt, and could not be buried until the debt was paid. In his varied brilliancy and in his fatal debauchery, his character stands forth as the completest type of the period of the Regency. Many memoirs have been written, among which those of his friend Moore, and his granddaughter the Hon. Mrs. Norton, although they unduly palliate his faults, are the best.

George Colman. — Among the respectable dramatists of this period who exerted an influence in leading the public taste away from the witty and artificial schools of the Restoration, the two Colmans deserve mention. George Colman, the elder, was born in Florence in 1733, but began his education at Westminster School, from which he was removed to Oxford. After receiving his degree he studied law; but soon abandoned graver study to court the comic muse. His first piece, *Polly Honeycomb*, was produced in 1760; but his reputation was established by *The Jealous Wife*, suggested by a scene in Fielding's *Tom Jones*. Besides many humorous miscellanies, most of which appeared in *The St. James' Chronicle*, — a magazine of which he was the proprietor, — he translated Terence, and produced more than thirty dramatic pieces, some of which are still presented upon the stage. The best of these is *The Clandestine Marriage*, which was the joint production of Garrick and himself. Of this play, Davies says "that no dramatic piece, since the days of Beaumont and Fletcher, had been written by two authors, in which wit, fancy, and humor were so happily blended." In 1768 he became one of the proprietors of the Covent Garden Theatre: in 1789 his mind became affected, and he remained a mental invalid until his death in 1794.

George Colman, the Younger. — This writer was the

son of George Colman, and was born in 1762. Like his father, he was educated at Westminster and Oxford; but he was removed from the university before receiving his degree, and was graduated at King's College, Aberdeen. He inherited an enthusiasm for the drama and considerable skill as a dramatic author. In 1787 he produced *Inkle and Yarico,* founded upon the pathetic story of Addison, in *The Spectator.* In 1796 appeared *The Iron Chest;* this was followed, in 1797, by *The Heir at Law* and *John Bull.* To him the world is indebted for a large number of stock pieces which still appear at our theatres. In 1802 he published a volume entitled *Broad Grins,* which was an expansion of a previous volume of comic scraps. This is full of frolic and humor: among the verses in the style of Peter Pindar are the well-known sketches *The Newcastle Apothecary,* (who gave the direction with his medicine, "When taken, to be well shaken,") and *Lodgings for Single Gentlemen.*

The author's fault is his tendency to farce, which robs his comedies of dignity. He assumed the cognomen *the younger* because, he said, he did not wish his father's memory to suffer for his faults. He died in 1836.

Other Humorists and Dramatists of the Period.

John Wolcot, 1738–1819: his pseudonym was *Peter Pindar.* He was a satirist as well as a humorist, and was bold in lampooning the prominent men of his time, not even sparing the king. The world of literature knows him best by his humorous poetical sketches, *The Apple-Dumplings and the King, The Razor-Seller, The Pilgrims and the Peas,* and many others.

Hannah More, 1745–1833: this lady had a flowing, agreeable style, but produced no great work. She wrote for her age and pleased it; but posterity disregards what she has written. Her principal plays are: *Percy,* presented in 1777, and a tragedy entitled *The Fatal Falsehood.* She was a poet and a novelist also; but in neither part did she rise above mediocrity. In 1782 appeared her volume of *Sacred Dramas.* Her best novel is entitled *Cœlebs in Search of a Wife, comprehending*

Observations on Domestic Habits and Manners, Religion and Morals. Her greatest merit is that she always inculcated pure morals and religion, and thus aided in improving the society of her age. Something of her fame is also due to the rare appearance, up to this time, of women in the fields of literature; so that her merits are indulgently exaggerated.

Joanna Baillie, 1762–1851: this lady, the daughter of a Presbyterian divine, wrote graceful verses, but is principally known by her numerous plays. Among these, which include thirteen *Plays on the Passions*, and thirteen *Miscellaneous Plays*, those best known are *De Montfort* and *Basil*—both tragedies, which have received high praise from Sir Walter Scott. Her *Ballads* and *Metrical Legends* are all spirited and excellent; and her *Hymns* breathe the very spirit of devotion. Very popular during her life, and still highly estimated by literary critics, her works have given place to newer and more favorite authors, and have already lost interest with the great world of readers.

Other Writers on Various Subjects.

Thomas Warton, 1728–1790: he was Professor of Poetry and of Ancient History at Oxford, and, for the last five years of his life, poet-laureate. The student of English Literature is greatly indebted to him for his *History of English Poetry*, which he brings down to the early part of the seventeenth century. No one before him had attempted such a task; and, although his work is rather a rare mass of valuable materials than a well articulated history, it is of great value for its collected facts, and for its suggestions as to where the scholar may pursue his studies farther.

Joseph Warton, 1722–1800: a brother of Thomas Warton; he published translations and essays and poems. Among the translations was that of the *Eclogues and Georgics of Virgil*, which is valued for its exactness and perspicuity.

Frances Burney, (Madame D'Arblay,) 1752–1840: the daughter of Dr. Burney, a musical composer. While yet a young girl, she astonished herself and the world by her novel of *Evelina*, which at once took rank among the standard fictions of the day. It is in the style of Richardson, but more truthful in the delineation of existing manners, and in the expression of sentiment. She afterwards published *Cecilia* and several other tales, which, although excellent, were not as good as the first. She led an almost menial life, as one of the ladies in waiting upon Queen Charlotte; but the genuine fame achieved by her writings in some degree relieved the sense of thraldom, from which she happily escaped with a pension. The novels of Madame D'Arblay are the intermediate step between the novels of Richardson, Fielding, and Smollett, and the Waverly novels of Walter Scott. They are entirely free from any taint of immorality; and they were among the first feminine efforts that were received with enthusiasm: thus it is that, without being of the first order of merit, they mark a distinct era in English letters.

Edmund Burke, 1730–1797: he was born in Dublin, and educated at Trinity College. He studied law, but soon found his proper sphere in public life. He had brilliant literary gifts; but his fame is more that of a statesman and an orator, than an author. Prominent in parliament, he took noble ground in favor of American liberty in our contest with the mother country, and uttered speeches which have remained as models of forensic eloquence. His greatest oratorical efforts were his famous speeches as one of the committee of impeachment in the case of Warren Hastings, Governor-General of India. Whatever may be thought of Hastings and his administration, the famous trial has given to English oratory some of its noblest specimens; and the people of England learned more of their empire in India from the learned, brilliant, and exhaustive speeches of Burke, than they could have learned in any other way. The greatest of his written works is: *Reflections on the Revolution in France*, written to warn England to avoid the causes of such colossal evil. In 1756 he had published his *Inquiry into the Origin of our Ideas of the Sublime and Beautiful.* This has been variously criticized; and, although written with vigor of thought and brilliancy of style, has now taken its place among the speculations of theory, and not as establishing permanent canons of æsthetical science. His work entitled *The Vindication of Natural Society, by a late noble writer*, is a successful attempt to overthrow the infidel system of Lord Bolingbroke, by applying it to civil society, and thus showing that it proved too much — "that if the abuses of or evils sometimes connected with religion invalidate its authority, then every institution, however beneficial, must be abandoned." Burke's style is peculiar, and, in another writer, would be considered pompous and pedantic; but it so expresses the grandeur and dignity of the man, that it escapes this criticism. His learning, his private worth, his high aims and incorruptible faith in public station, the dignity of his statesmanship, and the power of his oratory, constitute Mr. Burke as one of the noblest characters of any English period; and, although his literary reputation is not equal to his political fame, his accomplishments in the field of letters are worthy of admiration and honorable mention.

Hugh Blair, 1718–1800: a Presbyterian divine in Edinburgh, Dr. Blair deserves special mention for his lectures on *Rhetoric and Belles-Lettres*, which for a long time constituted the principal text-book on those subjects in our schools and colleges. A better understanding of the true scope of rhetoric as a science has caused this work to be superseded by later text-books. Blair's lectures treat principally of style and literary criticism, and are excellent for their analysis of some of the best authors, and for happy illustrations from their works. Blair wrote many eloquent sermons, which were published, and was one of the strong champions of Macpherson, in the controversy concerning the poems of Ossian. He occupied a high place as a literary critic during his life.

William Paley, 1743–1805: a clergyman of the Established Church, he rose to the dignity of Archdeacon and Chancellor of Carlisle. At first thoughtless and idle, he was roused from his unprofitable life by the earnest warnings of a companion, and became a severe student and a vigorous writer on moral and religious subjects. Among his numerous writings, those principally valuable are: *Horæ Paulinæ*, and *A View of the Evidences of Christianity* — the former setting forth the life and character of St. Paul, and the latter being a clear exposition of the truth of Christianity, which has long served as a manual of academic instruction. His treatise on *Natural Theology* is, in the words of Sir James Mackintosh, "the wonderful work of a man who, after sixty, had studied anatomy in order to write it." Later investigations of science have discarded some of his *facts*; but the handling of the subject and the array of arguments are the work of a skilful and powerful hand. He wrote, besides, a work on *Moral and Political Philosophy*, and numerous sermons. His theory of morals is, that whatever is expedient is right; and thus he bases our sense of duty upon the ground of the production of the greatest amount of happiness. This low view has been successfully refuted by later writers on moral science.

CHAPTER XXXIV.

THE NEW ROMANTIC POETRY: SCOTT.

THE transition school, as we have seen, in returning to nature, had redeemed the pastoral, and had cultivated sentiment at the expense of the epic. As a slight reaction, and yet a progress, and as influenced by the tales of modern fiction, and also as subsidizing the antiquarian lore and taste of the age, there arose a school of poetry which is best represented by its *Tales in verse;* — some treating subjects of the olden time, some laying their scenes in distant countries, and some describing home incidents of the simplest kind. They were all minor epics: such were the poetic stories of Scott, the *Lalla Rookh* of Moore, *The Bride* and *The Giaour* of Byron, and *The Village* and *The Borough* of Crabbe; all of which mark the taste and the demand of the period.

WALTER SCOTT. — First in order of the new romantic poets was Scott, alike renowned for his *Lays* and for his wonderful prose fictions; at once the most equable and the most prolific of English authors.

Walter Scott was born in Edinburgh, on the 15th of August, 1771. His father was a writer to the signet; his mother was Anne Rutherford, the daughter of a medical professor in the University of Edinburgh. His father's family belonged to the clan Buccleugh. Lame from his early childhood, and thus debarred the more active pleasures of children, his imagination was unusually vigorous; and he took special pleasure in the many stories, current at the time, of predatory warfare, border forays, bogles, warlocks, and second sight. He spent some of his early days in the country, and thus became robust and healthy; although his lameness remained throughout life. He was educated in Edinburgh, at the High School and the university; and, although not noted for excellence as a scholar, he exhibited precocity in verse, and delighted his companions by his readiness in reproducing old stories or improving new ones. After leaving the university he studied law, and ranged himself in politics as a Conservative or Tory.

Although never an accurate classical scholar, he had a superficial knowledge of several languages, and was an industrious collector of old ballads and relics of the antiquities of his country. He was, however, better than a scholar; — he had genius, enthusiasm, and industry: he could create character, adapt incident, and, in picturesque description, he was without a rival.

During the rumors of the invasion of Scotland by the French, which he has treated with such comical humor in *The Antiquary*, his lameness did not prevent his taking part with the volunteers, as quartermaster — a post given him to spare him the fatigue and rough service of the ranks. The French did not come; and Scott returned to his studies with a budget of incident for future use.

TRANSLATIONS AND MINSTRELSY. — The study of the German language was then almost a new thing, even among educated people in England; and Scott made his first public essay in the form of translations from the German. Among these were versions of the *Erl König* of Gœthe, and the *Lenore* and *The Wild Huntsman* of Bürger, which appeared in 1796. In 1797 he rendered into English *Otho of Wittels-*

bach by Steinburg, and in 1799 Gœthe's tragedy, *Götz von Berlichingen*. These were the trial efforts of his "'prentice hand," which predicted a coming master.

On the 24th of December, 1797, he married Miss Carpenter, or Charpentier, a lady of French parentage, and retired to a cottage at Lasswade, where he began his studies, and cherished his literary aspirations in earnest and for life.

In 1799 he was so fortunate as to receive the appointment of Sheriff of Selkirkshire, with a salary of £300 per annum. His duties were not onerous: he had ample time to scour the country, ostensibly in search of game, and really in seeking for the songs and traditions of Scotland, border ballads, and tales, and in storing his fancy with those picturesque views which he was afterwards to describe so well in verse and prose. In 1802 he was thus enabled to present to the world his first considerable work, *The Minstrelsy of the Scottish Border*, containing many new ballads which he had collected, with very valuable local and historical notes. This was followed, in 1804, by the metrical romance of *Sir Tristrem*, the original of which was by Thomas of Ercildoune, of the thirteenth century, known as *Thomas the Rhymer:* it was he who dreamed on Huntley bank that he met the Queen of Elfland,

> And, till seven years were gone and past,
> True Thomas on earth was never seen.

The reputation acquired by these productions led the world to expect something distinctly original and brilliant from his pen; a hope which was at once realized.

THE LAY OF THE LAST MINSTREL. — In 1805 appeared his first great poem, *The Lay of the Last Minstrel*, which immediately established his fame: it was a charming presentation of the olden time to the new. It originated in a request of the Countess of Dalkeith that he would write a ballad on the legend of Gilpin Horner. The picture of the last minstrel, "infirm and old," fired by remembrance as he begins to tell an old-time story of Scottish valor, is vividly drawn. The bard is supposed to be the last of his fraternity, and to have lived down to 1690. The tale, mixed of truth and fable, is exceedingly interesting. The octo-syllabic measure, with an occasional line of three feet, to break the monotony, is purely minstrelic, and reproduces the effect of the *troubadours and trouvères*. The wizard agency of Gilpin Horner's brood, and the miracle at the tomb of Michael Scott, are by no means out of keeping with the minstrel and the age of which he sings. The dramatic effects are good, and the descriptions very vivid. The poem was received with great enthusiasm, and rapidly passed through several editions. One element of its success is modestly and justly stated by the author in his introduction to a later edition: "The attempt to return to a more simple and natural style of poetry was likely to be welcomed at a time when the public had become tired of heroic hexameters, with all the buckram and binding that belong to them in modern days."

With an annual income of £1000, and an honorable ambition, Scott worked his new literary mine with great vigor. He saw not only fame but wealth within his reach. He entered into a silent partnership with the publisher, James Ballantyne, which was for a long time lucrative, by reason of the unprecedented sums he received for his works. In 1806 he was appointed to the reversion — on the death of the incumbent — of the clerkship of the Court of Sessions, a place worth £1300 per annum.

Other Poems. — In 1808, before *The Lay* had lost its freshness, *Marmion* appeared: it was kindred in subject and form, and was received with equal favor. *The Lady of the Lake*, the most popular of these poems, was published in 1810; and with it his poetical talent culminated. The later poems were not equal to any of those mentioned, although they were not without many beauties and individual excellences.

The Vision of Don Roderick, which appeared in 1811, is founded upon the legend of a visit made by one of the Gothic kings of Spain to an enchanted cavern near Toledo. *Rokeby* was published in 1812; *The Bridal of Triermain* in 1813; *The Lord of the Isles*, founded upon incidents in the life of Bruce, in 1815; and *Harold the Dauntless* in 1817. With the decline of his poetic power, manifest to himself, he retired from the field of poetry, but only to appear upon another and a grander field with astonishing brilliancy: it was the domain of the historical romance. Such, however, was the popular estimate of his poetry, that in 1813 the Prince Regent offered him the position of poet-laureate, which was gratefully and wisely declined.

Just at this time the new poets came forth, in his own style, and actuated by his example and success. He recognized in Byron, Moore, Crabbe, and others, genius and talent; and, with his generous spirit, exaggerated their merits by depreciating his own, which he compared to cairngorms beside the real jewels of his competitors. The mystics, following the lead of the Lake poets, were ready to increase the depreciation. It soon became fashionable to speak of *The Lay,* and *Marmion,* and *The Lady of the Lake* as spirited little stories, not equal to Byron's, and not to be mentioned beside the occult philosophy of *Thalaba* and gentle egotism of *The Prelude.* That day is passed: even the critical world returns to its first fancies. In the words of Carlyle, a great balance-striker of literary fame, speaking in 1838: "It were late in the day to write criticisms on those metrical romances; at the same time, the great popularity they had seems natural enough. In the first place, there was the indisputable impress of worth, of genuine human force in them. . . Pictures were actually painted and presented; human emotions conceived and sympathized with. Considering that wretched Dellacruscan and other vamping up of wornout tattlers was the staple article then, it may be granted that Scott's excellence was superior and supreme." Without preferring any claim to epic grandeur, or to a rank among the few great poets of the first class, Scott is entitled to the highest eminence in minstrelic power. He is the great modern troubadour. His descriptions of nature are simple and exquisite. There is nothing in this respect more beautiful than the opening of *The Lady of the Lake.* His battle-pieces live and resound again: what can be finer than Flodden field in *Marmion,* and The Battle of Beal and Duine in *The Lady of the Lake?*

His love scenes are at once chaste, impassioned, and tender; and his harp songs and battle lyrics are unrivalled in harmony. And, besides these merits, he gives us everywhere glimpses of history, which, before his day, were covered by the clouds of ignorance, and which his breath was to sweep away.

Such are his claims as the first of the new romantic poets. We might here leave him, to consider his prose works in another connection; but it seems juster to his fame to continue and complete a sketch of his life, because all its parts are of connected interest. The poems were a grand proem to the novels.

While he was achieving fame by his poetry, and reaping golden rewards as well as golden opinions, he was also ambitious to establish a family name and estate. To this end, he bought a hundred acres of land on the banks of the Tweed, near Melrose Abbey, and added to these from time to time by the purchase of adjoining properties. Here he built a great mansion, which became famous as Abbotsford: he called it one of his air-castles reduced to solid stone and mortar. Here he played the part of a feudal proprietor, and did the honors for Scotland to distinguished men from all quarters: his hospitality was generous and unbounded.

The Waverley Novels. — As early as 1805, while producing his beautiful poems, he had tried his hand upon a story in prose, based upon the stirring events in 1745, resulting in the fatal battle of Culloden, which gave a death-blow to the cause of the Stuarts, and to their attempts to regain the crown. Dissatisfied with the effort, and considering it at that time less promising than poetry, he had thrown the manuscript aside in a desk with some old fishing-tackle. There it remained undisturbed for eight years. With the decline of his poetic powers, he returned to the former notion of writing historical fiction; and so, exhuming his manuscript, he modified and finished it, and presented it anonymously to the world in 1814. He had at first proposed the title of *Waverley, or 'Tis Fifty Years Since*, which was afterwards altered to *'Tis Sixty Years Since*. This, the first of his splendid series of fictions, which has given a name to the whole series, is by no means the best; but it was good and novel enough to strike a chord in the popular heart at once. Its delineations of personal characters already known to history were masterly; its historical pictures were in a new and striking style of art. There were men yet living to whom he could appeal — men who had *been out* in the '45, who had seen Charles Edward and many of the originals of the author's heroes and heroines. In his researches and wanderings, he had imbibed the very spirit of Scottish life and history; and the Waverley novels are among the most striking literary types and expounders of history.

Particular Mention. — In 1815, before half the reading world had delighted themselves with *Waverley*, his rapid pen had produced *Guy Mannering*, a story of English and Scottish life, superior to Waverley in its original descriptions and more general interest. He is said to have written it in six weeks at Christmas time. The scope of this volume will not permit a critical examination of the Waverley novels. The world knows them almost by heart. In *The Antiquary*, which appeared in 1816, we have a rare delineation of local manners, the creation of distinct characters, and a humorous description of the sudden arming of volunteers in fear of invasion by the French. *The Antiquary* was a free portrait or sketch of Mr. George Constable, filled in perhaps unconsciously from the author's own life; for he, no less than his friend, delighted in collecting relics, and in studying out the lines, prætoria, and general castrametation of the Roman armies. Andrew Gemmels was the original of that Ëdie Ochiltree who was bold enough to dispute the antiquary's more learned assertions.

In the same year, 1816, was published the first series of *The Tales of my Landlord*, containing *The Black Dwarf* and *Old Mortality*, both valuable as contributions to Scottish history. The former is not of much literary merit; and the author was so little pleased with it, that he brought it to a hasty conclusion: the latter is an extremely animated sketch of the sufferings of the Covenanters at the hands of Grahame of Claverhouse, with a fairer picture of that redoubted commander than the Covenanters have drawn. *Rob Roy*, the best existing presentation of Highland life and manners, appeared in 1817. Thus Scott's prolific pen, like nature, produced annuals. In 1818 appeared *The Heart of Mid-Lothian*, that touching story of Jeanie and Effie Deans, which awakens the warmest sympathy of every reader, and teaches to successive generations a moral lesson of great significance and power.

In 1819 he wrote *The Bride of Lammermoor*, the story of a domestic tragedy, which warns the world that outraged nature will sometimes assert herself in fury; a story so popular that it has been since arranged as an Italian opera. With that came *The Legend of Montrose*, another historic sketch of great power, and especially famous for the character of Major Dugald Dalgetty, soldier of fortune and pedant of Marischal

College, Aberdeen. The year 1819 also beheld the appearance of *Ivanhoe*, which many consider the best of the series. It describes rural England during the regency of John, the romantic return of Richard Lion-heart, the glowing embers of Norman and Saxon strife, and the story of the Templars. His portraiture of the Jewess Rebecca is one of the finest in the Waverley Gallery.

The next year, 1820, brought forth *The Monastery*, the least popular of the novels thus far produced; and, as Scott tells us, on the principle of sending a second arrow to find one that was lost, he wrote *The Abbot*, a sequel, to which we are indebted for a masterly portrait of Mary Stuart in her prison of Lochleven. The *Abbot*, to some extent, redeemed and sustained its weaker brother. In this same year Scott was created a baronet, in recognition of his great services to English Literature and history. The next five years added worthy companion-novels to the marvellous series. *Kenilworth* is founded upon the visit of Queen Elizabeth to her favorite Leicester, in that picturesque palace in Warwickshire, and contains that beautiful and touching picture of Amy Robsart. *The Pirate* is a story the scene of which is laid in Shetland, and the material for which he gathered in a pleasure tour among those islands. In *The Fortunes of Nigel*, London life during the reign of James I. is described; and it contains life-like portraits of that monarch, of his unfortunate son, Prince Charles, and of Buckingham. *Peveril of the Peak* is a story of the time of Charles II., which is not of equal merit with the other novels. *Quentin Durward*, one of the very best, describes the strife between Louis XI. of France and Charles the Bold of Burgundy, and gives full-length historic portraits of these princes. The scene of *St. Ronan's Well* is among the English lakes in Cumberland, and the story describes the manners of the day at a retired watering-place. *Red Gauntlet* is a curious narrative connected with one of the latest attempts of Charles Edward — abortive at the outset — to effect a rising in Scotland. In 1825 appeared his *Tales of the Crusaders*, comprising *The Betrothed* and *The Talisman*, of which the latter is the more popular, as it describes with romantic power the deeds of Richard and his comrades in the second crusade.

A glance at this almost tabular statement will show the scope and versatility of his mind, the historic range of his studies, the fertility of his fancy, and the rapidity of his pen. He had attained the height of fame and happiness; his success had partaken of the miraculous; but misfortune came to mar it all, for a time.

PECUNIARY TROUBLES. — In the financial crash of 1825–6, he was largely involved. As a silent partner in the publishing house of the Ballantynes, and as connected with them in the affairs of Constable & Co., he found himself, by the failure of these houses, legally liable to the amount of £117,000. To relieve himself, he might have taken the benefit of the *bankrupt law;* or, such was his popularity, that his friends desired to raise a subscription to cover the amount of his indebtedness; but he was now to show by his conduct that, if the author was great, the man was greater. He refused all assistance, and even rejected general sympathy. He determined to relieve himself, to pay his debts, or die in the effort. He left Abbotsford, and took frugal lodgings in Edinburgh; curtailed all his expenses, and went to work — which was over-work — not for fame, but for guineas; and he gained both.

His first novel after this, and the one which was to test the practicability of his plan, was *Woodstock*, a tale of the troublous times of the Civil War, in the last chapter of which he draws the picture of the restored Charles coming in peaceful procession to his throne. This he wrote in three months; and for it he received upwards of £8000. With this and the proceeds of his succeeding works, he was enabled to pay over to his creditors the large sum of £70,000; a feat unparalleled in the history of literature. But the anxiety and the labor were too much even for his powerful constitution: he died in his heroic attempt.

HIS MANLY PURPOSE. — More for money than for reputation, he compiled hastily, and from partial and incomplete material, a *Life of Napoleon Bonaparte*, which appeared in 1827. The style is charming and the work eminently readable; but it contains many faults, is by no means unprejudiced, and, as far as pure truth is concerned, is, in parts, almost as much of a romance as any of the Waverley novels; but, for the first two editions, he received the enormous sum of £18,000. The work was accomplished in the space of one year. Among the other *task-work* books were the two series of *The Chronicles of the Canongate* (1827 and 1828), the latter of which contains the beautiful story of *St. Valentine's Day*, or *The Fair Maid of Perth*. It is written in his finest vein, especially in those chapters which describe the famous Battle of the Clans. In 1829 appeared *Anne of Geierstein*, another story presenting the figure of Charles of Burgundy, and his defeat and death in the battle with the Swiss at Nancy.

POWERS OVERTASKED. — And now new misfortunes were to come upon him. In 1826 he had lost his wife: his sorrows weighed upon him, and his superhuman exertions were too much for his strength. In 1829 he was seized with a nervous attack, accompanied by hemorrhages of a peculiar kind. In February, 1830, a slight paralysis occurred, from which he speedily recovered; this was soon succeeded by another; and it was manifest that his mind was giving way. His last novel, *Count Robert of Paris*, was begun in 1830, as one of a fourth series of *The Tales of My Landlord*: it bears manifest marks of his failing powers, but is of value for the historic stores which it draws from the Byzantine historians, and especially from the unique work of Anna Comnena: "I almost wish," he said, "I had named it Anna Comnena." A slight attack of apoplexy in November, 1830, was followed by a severer one in the spring of 1831. Even then he tried to write, and was able to produce *Castle Dangerous*. With that the powerful pen ended its marvellous work. The manly spirit still chafed that his debts were not paid, and could not be, by the labor of his hands.

FRUITLESS JOURNEY. — In order to divert his mind, and, as a last chance for health, a trip to the Mediterranean was projected. The Barham frigate was placed by the government at his disposal; and he wandered with a party of friends to Malta, Naples, Pompeii, Paestum, and Rome. But feeling the end approaching, he exclaimed, "Let us to Abbotsford:" for the final hour he craved the *grata quies patriæ;* to which an admiring world has added the remainder of the verse — *sed et omnis terra sepulchrum.* It was not a moment too soon: he travelled northward to the Rhine, down that river by boat, and reached London "totally exhausted;" thence, as soon as he could be moved, he was taken to Abbotsford.

RETURN AND DEATH. — There he lingered from July to September, and died peacefully on the 21st of the latter month, surrounded by his family and lulled to repose by the rippling of the Tweed. Among the noted dead of 1832, including Gœthe, Cuvier, Crabbe, and Mackintosh, he was the most distinguished; and all Scotland and all the civilized world mourned his loss.

HIS FAME. — At Edinburgh a colossal monument has been erected to his memory, within which sits his marble figure. Numerous other memorial columns are found in other cities, but all Scotland is his true monument, every province and town of which he has touched with his magic pen. Indeed, Scotland may be said to owe to him a new existence. In the words of Lord Meadowbank,— who presided at the Theatrical Fund dinner in 1827, and who there made the first public announcement of the authorship of the Waverley novels, — Scott was "the mighty magician who rolled back the current of time, and conjured up before our living senses the men and manners of days which have long since passed away. . . It is he who has conferred a new reputation on our national character, and bestowed on Scotland an imperishable name."

Besides his poetry and novels, he wrote very much of a miscellaneous character for the reviews, and edited the works of the poets with valuable introductions and congenial biographies. Most of his fictions are historical in plot and personages; and those which deal with Scottish subjects are enriched by those types of character, those descriptions of manners — national and local — and those peculiarities of language, which give them additional and more useful historical value. It has been justly said that, by his masterly handling of historical subjects, he has taught the later historians how to write, how to give vivid and pictorial effects to what was before a detail of chronology or a dry schedule of philosophy. His critical powers may be doubted: he was too kind and genial for a critic; and in reading contemporary authors seems to have endued their inferior works with something of his own fancy.

The *Life of Scott*, by his son-in-law, J. G. Lockhart, is one of the most complete and interesting biographies in the language. In it the student will find a list of all his works, with the dates of their production; and will wonder that an author who was so rapid and so prolific could write so much that was of the highest excellence. If not the greatest genius of his age, he was its greatest literary benefactor; and it is for this reason that we have given so much space to the record of his life and works.

CHAPTER XXXV.

THE NEW ROMANTIC POETRY: BYRON AND MOORE.

IN immediate succession after Scott comes the name of Byron. They were both great lights of their age; but the former may be compared to a planet revolving in regulated and beneficent beauty through an unclouded sky; while the latter is more like a comet whose lurid light came flashing upon the sight in wild and threatening career.

Like Scott, Byron was a prolific poet; and he owes to Scott the general suggestion and much of the success of his tales in verse. His powers of description were original and great: he adopted the new romantic tone, while in his more studied works he was an imitator and a champion of a former age, and a contemner of his own.

Early Life of Byron. — The Honorable George Gordon Byron, afterwards Lord Byron, was born in London on the 22d of January, 1788. While he was yet an infant, his father — Captain Byron — a dissipated man, deserted his mother; and she went with her child to live upon a slender pittance at Aberdeen. She was a woman of peculiar disposition, and was unfortunate in the training of her son. She alternately petted and quarrelled with him, and taught him to emulate her irregularities of temper. On account of an accident at his birth, he had a malformation in one of his feet, which, producing a slight limp in his gait through life, rendered his sensitive nature quite unhappy, the signs of which are to be discerned in his drama, *The Deformed Transformed.* From the age of five years he went to school at Aberdeen, and very early began to exhibit traits of generosity, manliness, and an imperious nature: he also displayed great quickness in those studies which pleased his fancy.

In 1798, when he was eleven years old, his grand-uncle, William, the fifth Lord Byron, died, and was succeeded in the title and estates by the young Gordon Byron, who was at once removed with his mother to Newstead Abbey. In 1801 he was sent to Harrow, where he was well esteemed by his comrades, but was not considered forward in his studies.

He seems to have been of a susceptible nature, for, while still a boy, he fell in love several times. His third experience in this way was undoubtedly the strongest of his whole life. The lady was Miss Mary Chaworth, who did not return his affection. His last interview with her he has powerfully described in his poem called *The Dream.* From Harrow he went to Trinity College, Cambridge, where he lived an idle and self-indulgent life, reading discursively, but not studying the prescribed course. As early as November, 1806, before he was nineteen, he published his first volume, *Poems on Various Occasions*, for private distribution, which was soon after enlarged and altered, and presented to the public as *Hours of Idleness, a Series of Poems Original and Translated, by George Gordon, Lord Byron, A Minor.* These productions, although by no means equal to his later poems, are not without merit, and did not deserve the exceedingly severe criticism they met with from the *Edinburgh Review.* The critics soon found that they had bearded a young lion: in his rage, he sprang out upon the whole literary craft in a satire, imitated from Juvenal, called *The English Bards and Scotch Reviewers*, in which he ridicules and denounces the very best poets of the day furiously but most uncritically. That his conduct was absurd and unjust, he himself allowed afterwards; and he attempted to call in and destroy all the copies of this work.

Childe Harold and Eastern Tales. — In March, 1809, he took his seat in the House of Lords, where he did not accomplish much. He took up his residence at Newstead Abbey, his ancestral seat, most of which was in a ruinous condition; and after a somewhat disorderly life there, he set out on his continental tour, spending some time at Lisbon, Cadiz, Gibraltar, Malta, and in Greece. On his return, after two years' absence, he brought a summary of his travels in poetical form, — the first part of *Childe Harold;* and also a more elaborated poem entitled *Hints from Horace.* Upon the former he set little value; but he thought the latter a noble work. The world at once reversed his decision. The satire in the Latin vein is scarcely read; while to the first cantos of *Childe Harold* it was due that, in his own words, "he woke up one morning and found himself famous." As fruits of the eastern portion of his travels, we have the romantic tale, *The Giaour*, published in 1811, and *The Bride of Abydos*, which appeared in 1813. The popularity of these oriental stories was mainly due to their having been conceived on the spots they describe. In 1814 he issued *The Corsair*, perhaps the best of these sensational stories; and with singular versatility, in the same year, inspired by the beauty of the Jewish history, he produced *The Hebrew Melodies*, some of which are fervent, touching, and melodious. Late in the same year *Lara* was published, in the same volume with Mr. Rogers's *Jacqueline*, which it threw completely into the shade. Thus closed one distinct period of his life and of his authorship. A change came over the spirit of his dream.

Unhappy Marriage. — In 1815, urged by his friends, and thinking it due to his position, he married Miss Milbanke; but the union was without affection on either side, and both were unhappy. One child, a daughter, was born to them; and a year had hardly passed when they were separated, by mutual consent and for reasons never truly divulged; and which, in spite of modern investigations, must remain mysterious. He was licentious, extravagant, of a violent temper: his wife was of severe morals, cold, and unsympathetic. We need not advance farther into the horrors recently suggested to the world. The blame has rested on Byron; and, at the time, the popular feeling was so strong, that it may be said to have driven him from England. It awoke in him a dark misanthropy which returned English scorn with an unnatural hatred. He sojourned at various places on the continent. At Geneva he wrote a third canto of *Childe Harold*, and the touching story of Bonnivard, entitled *The Prisoner of Chillon*, and other short poems.

In 1817 he was at Venice, where he formed a connection with the Countess Guiccioli, to the disgrace of both. In Venice he wrote a fourth canto of *Childe Harold*, the story of *Mazeppa*, the first two cantos of *Don Juan*, and two dramas, *Marino Faliero* and *The Two Foscari*.

For two years he lived at Ravenna, where he wrote some of his other dramas, and several cantos of *Don Juan*. In 1821 he removed to Pisa; thence, after a short stay, to Genoa, still writing dramas and working at *Don Juan*.

PHILHELLENISM: HIS DEATH. — The end of his misanthropy and his debaucheries was near; but his story was to have a ray of sunset glory — his death was to be connected with a noble effort and an exhibition of philanthropic spirit which seem in some degree to palliate his faults. Unlike some writers who find in his conduct only a selfish whim, we think that it casts a beautiful radiance upon the early evening of a stormy life. The Greeks were struggling for independence from Turkish tyranny: Byron threw himself heart and soul into the movement, received a commission from the Greek government, recruited a band of Suliotes, and set forth gallantly to do or die in the cause of Grecian freedom: he died, but not in battle. He caught a fever of a virulent type, from his exposure, and after very few days expired, on the 19th of April, 1824, amid the mourning of the nation. Of this event, Macaulay — no mean or uncertain critic — could say, in his epigrammatical style: "Two men have died within our recollection, who, at a time of life at which few people have completed their education, had raised themselves, each in his own department, to the height of glory. One of them died at Longwood; the other at Missolonghi."

ESTIMATE OF HIS POETRY. — In giving a brief estimate of his character and of his works, we may begin by saying that he represents, in clear lineaments, the nobleman, the traveller, the poet, and the debauchee, of the beginning of the nineteenth century. In all his works he unconsciously depicts himself. He is in turn Childe Harold, Lara, the Corsair, and Don Juan. He affected to despise the world's opinion so completely that he has made himself appear worse than he really was — more profane, more intemperate, more licentious. It is equally true that this tendency, added to the fact that he was a handsome peer, had much to do with the immediate popularity of his poems. There was also a paradoxical vanity, which does not seem easily reconcilable with his misanthropy, that thus led him to reproduce himself in a new dress in his dramas and tales. He paraded himself as if, after all, he did value the world's opinion.

That he was one of the new romantic poets, with, however, a considerable tincture of the transition school, may be readily discerned in his works: his earlier poems are full of the conceits of the artificial age. His *English Bards and Scotch Reviewers* reminds one of the *MacFlecknoe* of Dryden and *The Dunciad* of Pope, without being as good as either. When he began that original and splendid portrait of himself, and transcript of his travels, *Childe Harold*, he imitated Spenser in form and in archaism. But he was possessed by the muse: the man wrote as the spirit within dictated, as the Pythian priestess is fabled to have uttered her oracles. *Childe Harold* is a stream of intuitive, irrepressible poetry; not art, but overflowing nature: the sentiments good and bad came welling forth from his heart. His descriptive powers are great but peculiar. Travellers find in *Childe Harold* lightning glimpses of European scenery, art, and nature, needing no illustrations, almost defying them. National conditions, manners, customs, and costumes, are photographed in his verses: — the rapid rush to Waterloo; a bull-fight in Spain; the women of Cadiz or Saragossa; the Lion of St. Mark; the eloquent statue of the Dying Gladiator; "Fair Greece, sad relic of departed worth;" the address to the ocean; touches of love and hate; pictures of sorrow, of torture, of death. Everywhere thought and glance are powerfully concentrated, and we find the poem to be journal, history, epic, and autobiography. His felicity of expression is so great, that, as we come upon the happy conceptions exquisitely rendered, we are inclined to say of each, as he has said of the Egeria of Muna:

> . . . whatsoe'er thy birth,
> Thou wert a beautiful thought and softly bodied forth.

Of his dramas which are founded upon history, we cannot say so much; they are dramatic only in form: some of them are spectacular, like *Sardanapalus*, which is still presented upon the stage on account of its scenic effects. In *Manfred* we have a rare insight into his nature, and *Cain* is the vehicle for his peculiar, dark sentiments on the subject of religion.

Don Juan is illustrative not only of the poet, but of the age; there was a generation of such men and women. But quite apart from its moral, or rather immoral, character, the poem is one of the finest in our literature: it is full of wonderful descriptions, and exhibits a splendid mastery of language, rhythm, and rhyme: a glorious epic with an inglorious hero, and that hero Byron himself.

As a man he was an enigma to the world, and doubtless to himself: he was bad, but he was bold. If he was vindictive, he was generous; if he was misanthropic and sceptical, it was partly because he despised shams: in all his actions, we see that implicit working out of his own nature, which not only conceals nothing, but even exaggerates his own faults. His antecedents were bad;—his father was a villain; his grand-uncle a murderer; his mother a woman of violent temper; and himself, with all this legacy, a man of powerful passions. If evil is in any degree to be palliated because it is hereditary, those who most condemn it in the abstract, may still look with compassionate leniency upon the career of Lord Byron.

THOMAS MOORE. — Emphatically the creature of his age, Moore wrote sentimental songs in melodious language to the old airs of Ireland, and used them as an instrument to excite the Irish people in the struggle they were engaged in against English misgovernment. But his songs were true neither to tradition nor to nature; they placed before the ardent Celtic fancy an Irish glory and grandeur entirely different from the reality. Nor had he in any degree caught the bardic spirit. His lyre was attuned to reach the ear rather than the heart; his scenes are in enchanted lands; his *dramatis personæ* tread theatrical boards; his thunder is a melo-dramatic roll; his lightning is pyrotechny; his tears are either hypocritical or maudlin; and his laughter is the perfection of genteel comedy.

Thomas Moore was born in Dublin, on the 28th of May, 1779: he was a diminutive but precocious child, and was paraded by his father and mother, who were people in humble life, as a reciter of verse, and as an early rhymer also.

His first poem was printed in a Dublin magazine, when he was fourteen years old. In 1794 he entered Trinity College, Dublin; and, although never considered a good scholar, he was graduated in 1798, when he was nineteen years old.

ANACREON. — The first work which brought him into notice, and which manifests at once the precocity of his powers and the peculiarity of his taste, was his translation of the *Odes of Anacreon*. He had begun this work while at college, but it was finished and published in London, whither he had gone after leaving college, to enter the Middle Temple, in order to study law. With equal acuteness and adaptation to character, he dedicated the poems to the Prince of Wales, an anacreontic hero. As might be expected, with such a patron, the volume was a success. In 1801 he published another series of erotic poems, under the title *The Poetical Works of the late Thomas Little*. This gained for him, in Byron's line, the name of "the young Catullus of his day;" and, at the instance of Lord Moira, he was appointed poet-laureate, a post he filled only long enough to write one birthday ode. What seemed a better fortune came in the shape of an appointment as Registrar of the Admiralty Court of Bermuda. He went to the island; remained but a short time; and turned over the uncongenial duties of the post to a deputy, who subsequently became a defaulter, and involved Moore to a large amount. Returning from Bermuda, he travelled in the United States and Canada; not without some poetical record of his movements. In 1806 he published his *Epistles, Odes, and Other Poems*, which called down the righteous wrath of the Edinburgh Review: Jeffrey denounced the book as "a public nuisance," and "a corrupter of public morals." For this harsh judgment, Moore challenged him; but the duel was stopped by the police. This hostile meeting was turned to ridicule by Byron in the lines:

When Little's leadless pistols met his eye,
And Bow-street myrmidons stood laughing by.

Later Fortunes. — Moore was now the favorite — the poet and the dependent of the nobility; and his versatile pen was principally employed to amuse and to please. He soon began that series of *Irish Melodies* which he continued to augment with new pieces for nearly thirty years.

Always of a theatrical turn, he acted well in private drama, in which the gentlemen were amateurs, and the female parts were personated by professional actresses. Thus playing in a cast with Miss Dyke, the daughter of an Irish actor, Moore fell in love with her, and married her on the 25th of March, 1811.

With a foolish lack of judgment, he lost his hopes of preferment, by writing satires against the regent; but as a means of livelihood, he engaged to write songs for Powers, at a salary of £500 per annum, for seven years.

Lalla Rookh. — The most acceptable offering to fame, and the most successful pecuniary venture, was his *Lalla Rookh.* The East was becoming known to the English; and the fancy of the poet could convert the glimpses of oriental things into charming pictures. Long possessed with the purpose to write an Eastern story in verse, Moore set to work with laudable industry to read books of travels and history, in order to form a strong and sensible basis for his poetical superstructure. The work is a collection of beautiful poems, in a delicate setting of beautiful prose. The princess Lalla Rookh journeys, with great pomp, to become the bride of the youthful king of Bokkara, and finds among her attendants a handsome young poet, who beguiles the journey by singing to her these tales in verse. The dangers of the process became manifest — the king of Bokkara is forgotten, and the heart of the unfortunate princess is won by the beauty and the minstrelsy of the youthful poet. What is her relief and her joy to find on her arrival the unknown poet seated upon the throne as the king, who had won her heart as an humble bard!

This beautiful and popular work was published in 1817; and for it Moore received from his publishers, the Longmans, £3000.

In the same year Moore took a small cottage at Sloperton, on the estate of the Marquis of Lansdowne, which, with some interruptions of travel, and a short residence in Paris, continued to be his residence during his life. Improvident in money matters, he was greatly troubled by his affairs in Bermuda;—the amount for which he became responsible by the defalcation of his deputy was £6000; which, however, by legal cleverness, was compromised for a thousand guineas.

HIS DIARY.—It is very fortunate, for a proper understanding of Moore's life, that we have from this time a diary which is invaluable to the biographer. In 1820 he went to Paris, where he wasted his time and money in fashionable dissipation, and produced nothing of enduring value. Here he sketched an Egyptian story, versified in *Alciphron*, but enlarged in the prose romance called *The Epicurean.*

On a short tour he visited Venice, where he received, as a gift from Lord Byron, his autobiographical memoirs, which contained so much that was compromising to others, that they were never published—at least in that form. They were withdrawn from the Murrays, in whose hands he had placed them, upon the death of Byron in 1824, and destroyed. A short visit to Ireland led to his writing the *Memoirs of Captain Rock*, a work which attained an unprecedented popularity in Ireland.

In 1825 he published his *Life of Sheridan*, which is rather a friendly panegyric than a truthful biography.

During three years—from 1827 to 1830—he was engaged upon the *Life of Byron*, which concealed more truth than it divulged. But in all these years, his chief dependence for daily bread was upon his songs and glees, squibs for newspapers and magazines, and review articles.

In 1831 he made another successful hit in his *Life of Lord Edward Fitzgerald*, a rebel of '98, which was followed in 1833 by *The Travels of an Irish Gentleman in Search of a Religion*.

In 1835, through the agency of Lord John Russel, the improvident poet received a pension of £300. It came in a time of need; for he was getting old, and his mind moved more sluggishly. His infirmities made him more domestic; but his greater trials were still before him. His sons were frivolous spendthrifts; one for whom he had secured a commission in the army behaved ill, and drew upon his impoverished father again and again for money: both died young. This cumulation of troubles broke him down; he had a cerebral attack in December, 1849, and lived helpless and broken until the 26th of February, 1852, when he expired without suffering.

His Poetry. — In most cases, the concurrence of what an author has written will present to us the mental and moral features of the man. It is particularly true in the case of Moore. He appears to us in Protean shapes, indeed, but not without an affinity between them. Small in stature, of jovial appearance; devoted to the gayest society; not very earnest in politics; a Roman Catholic in name, with but little practical religion, he pandered at first to a frivolous public taste, and was even more corrupt than the public morals.

Not so apparently as Pope an artificial poet, he had few touches of nature. Of lyric sentiment he has but little; but we must differ from those who deny to him rare lyrical expression, and happy musical adaptations. His songs one can hardly *read;* we feel that they must be sung. He has been accused, too violently, by Maginn of plagiarism: this, of course, means of phrases and ideas. In our estimate of Moore, it counts but little; his rare rhythm and exquisite cadences are not plagiarized; they are his own, and his chief merit.

He abounds in imagery of oriental gorgeousness; and if, in personality, he may be compared to his own Peri, or one of "the beautiful blue damsel flies" of that poem, he has given to his unfriendly critics a judgment of his own style, in a criticism made by Fadladeen of the young poet's story to Lalla Rookh;—"it resembles one of those Maldivian boats—a slight, gilded thing, sent adrift without rudder or ballast, and with nothing but vapid sweets and faded flowers on board." "The effect of the whole," says one of his biographers, speaking of Lalla Rookh, "is much the same as that of a magnificent ballet, on which all the resources of the theatre have been lavished, and no expense spared in golden clouds, ethereal light, gauze-clad sylphs, and splendid tableaux."

Moore has been felicitously called "the poet of all circles," a phrase which shows that he reflected the general features of his age. At no time could the license of *Anacreon*, or the poems of Little, have been so well received as when "the first gentleman in Europe" set the example of systematic impurity. At no time could *Irish Melodies* have had such a *furore* of adoption and applause, as when *Repeal* was the cry, and the Irish were firing their minds by remembering "the glories of Brian the Brave;" that Brian Boroimhe who died in the eleventh century, after defeating the Danes in twenty-five battles.

Moore's *Biographies*, with all their faults, are important social histories. *Lalla Rookh* has a double historical significance: it is a reflection—like *Anastasius* and *Vathek*, like *Thalaba* and *The Curse of Kehama*, like *The Giaour* and *The Bride of Abydos*—of English conquest, travel, and adventure in the East. It is so true to nature in oriental descriptions and allusions, that one traveller declared that to read it was like riding on a camel; but it is far more important to observe that the relative conditions of England and the Irish Roman Catholics are symbolized in the Moslem rule over the Ghebers, as delineated in *The Fire Worshippers.* In his preface to that poem, Moore himself says: "The cause of tolerance was again my inspiring theme; and the spirit that had spoken in the melodies of Ireland soon found itself at home in the East."

In an historic view of English Literature, the works of Moore, touching almost every subject, must always be of great value to the student of his period: there he will always have his prominent place. But he is already losing his niche in public favor as a poet proper; better taste, purer morals, truer heart-songs, and more practical views will steadily supplant him, until, with no power to influence the present, he shall stand only as a charming relic of the past.

CHAPTER XXXVI.

THE NEW ROMANTIC POETRY (CONTINUED).

Robert Burns.	George Crabbe.	P. B. Shelley.
His Poems.	Thomas Campbell.	John Keats.
His Career.	Samuel Rogers.	Other Writers.

ROBERT BURNS.

IF Moore was, in the opinion of his age, an Irish prodigy, Burns is, for all time, a Scottish marvel. The one was polished and musical, but artificial and insidiously immoral; the other homely and simple, but powerful and effective to men of all classes in society. The one was the poet of the aristocracy; the other the genius whose sympathies were with the poor. One was most at home in the palaces of the great; and the other, in the rude Ayrshire cottage, or in the little sitting-room of the landlord in company with Souter John and Tam O'Shanter. As to most of his poems, Burns was really of no distinct school, but seems to stand alone, — the creature of circumstance rather than of the age, in an unnatural and false position, compared by himself to the daisy he uprooted with his ploughshare:

Even thou who mourn'st the daisy's fate,
That fate is thine — no distant date;
Stern Ruin's ploughshare drives elate,
Full on thy bloom,
Till crushed beneath the furrow's weight
Shall be thy doom!

His life was uneventful. He was the son of a very poor

man who was gardener to a gentleman at Ayr. He was born in Alloway on the 25th of January, 1759. His early education was scanty; but he read with avidity the few books on which he could lay his hands, among which he particularly mentions, in his short autobiography, *The Spectator*, the poems of Pope, and the writings of Sterne and Thomson. But the work which he was to do needed not even that training: he drew his simple subjects from surrounding nature, and his ideas came from his heart rather than his head. Like Moore, he found the old tunes or airs of the country, and set them to new words — words full of sentiment and sense.

His Poems. — Most of his poems are quite short, and of the kind called fugitive, except that they will not fly away. *The Cotter's Saturday Night* is for men of all creeds, a pastoral full of divine philosophy. His *Address to the Deil* is a tender thought even for the Prince of Darkness, whom, says Carlyle, his kind nature could not hate with right orthodoxy. His poems on *The Louse*, *The Field-Mouse's Nest*, and *The Mountain Daisy*, are homely meditations and moral lessons, and contain counsels for all hearts. In *The Twa Dogs* he contrasts, in fable, the relative happiness of rich and poor. In the beautiful song

Ye banks and braes of bonnie Doun,

he expresses that hearty sympathy with nature which is one of the most attractive features of his character. His *Bruce's Address* stirs the blood, and makes one start up into an attitude of martial advance. But his most famous poem — drama, comedy, epic, and pastoral — is *Tam o' Shanter:* it is a universal favorite; and few travellers leave Scotland without standing at the window of "Alloway's auld haunted kirk," walking over the road upon which Meg galloped, pausing over "the keystane of the brigg" where she lost her tail; and then returning, full of the spirit of the poem, to sit in Tam's chair, and drink ale out of the same silver-bound wooden bicker, in the very room of the inn where Tam and the poet used to get "unco fou," while praising "inspiring bold John Barley-corn." Indeed, in the words of the poor Scotch carpenter, met by Washington Irving at Kirk Alloway, "it seems as if the country had grown more beautiful since Burns had written his bonnie little songs about it."

HIS CAREER. — The poet's career was sad. Gifted but poor, and doomed to hard work, he was given a place in the excise. He went to Edinburgh, and for a while was a great social lion; but he acquired a horrid thirst for drink, which shortened his life. He died in Dumfries, at the early age of thirty-seven. His allusions to his excesses are frequent, and many of them touching. In his praise of *Scotch Drink* he sings *con amore*. In a letter to Mr. Ainslie, he epitomizes his failing: "Can you, amid the horrors of penitence, regret, headache, nausea, and all the rest of the hounds of hell that beset a poor wretch who has been guilty of the sin of drunkenness, — can you speak peace to a troubled soul."

Burns was a great letter-writer, and thought he excelled in that art; but, valuable as his letters are, in presenting certain phases of his literary and personal character, they display none of the power of his poetry, and would not alone have raised him to eminence. They are in vigorous and somewhat pedantic English; while most of his poems are in that Lowland Scottish language or dialect which attracts by its homeliness and pleases by its *couleur locale*. It should be stated, in conclusion, that Burns is original in thought and presentation; and to this gift must be added a large share of humor, and an intense patriotism. Poverty was his grim horror. He declared that it killed his father, and was pursuing him to the grave. He rose above the drudgery of a farmer's toil, and he found no other work which would sustain him; and yet this needy poet stands to-day among the most distinguished Scotchmen who have contributed to English Literature.

George Crabbe. — Also of the transition school; in form and diction adhering to the classicism of Pope, but, with Thomson, restoring the pastoral to nature, the poet of the humble poor;—in the words of Byron, "Pope in worsted stockings," Crabbe was the delight of his time; and Sir Walter Scott, returning to die at Abbotsford, paid him the following tribute: he asked that they would read him something amusing, "Read me a bit of Crabbe." As it was read, he exclaimed, "Capital — excellent — very good; Crabbe has lost nothing."

George Crabbe was born on December 24th, 1754, at Aldborough, Suffolk. His father was a poor man; and Crabbe, with little early education, was apprenticed to a surgeon, and afterwards practised; but his aspirations were such that he went to London, with three pounds in his pocket, for a literary venture. He would have been in great straits, had it not been for the disinterested generosity of Burke, to whom, although an utter stranger, he applied for assistance. Burke aided him by introducing him to distinguished literary men; and his fortune was made. In 1781 he published *The Library*, which was well received. Crabbe then took orders, and was for a little time curate at Aldborough, his native place, while other preferment awaited him. In 1783 he appeared under still more favorable auspices, by publishing *The Village*, which had a decided success. Two livings were then given him; and he, much to his credit, married his early love, a young girl of Suffolk. In *The Village* he describes homely scenes with great power, in pentameter verse. The poor are the heroes of his humble epic; and he knew them well, as having been of them. In 1807 appeared *The Parish Register*, in 1810 *The Borough*, and in 1812 his *Tales in Verse*,— the precursor, in the former style, however, of Wordsworth's lyrical stories. All these were excellent and very popular, because they were real, and from his own experience. *The Tales of the Hall*, referring chiefly to the higher classes of society, are more artificial, and not so good. His pen was most at home in describing smugglers, gipsies, and humble villagers, and in delineating poverty and wretchedness; and thus opening to the rich and titled, doors through which they might exercise their philanthropy and munificence. In this way Crabbe was a reformer, and did great good; although his scenes are sometimes revolting, and his pathos too exacting. As a painter of nature, he is true and felicitous; especially in marine and coast views, where he is a pre-Raphaelite in his minuteness. Byron called him "Nature's sternest painter, but the best." He does not seem to write for effect, and he is without pretension; so that the critics were quite at fault; for what they mainly attack is not the poet's work so much as the consideration whether his works come up to his manifesto. Crabbe died in 1832, on the 3d of February, being one of the famous dead of that fatal year.

Crabbe's poems mark his age. At an earlier time, when literature was for the fashionable few, his subjects would have been beneath interest; but the times had changed; education had been more diffused, and readers were multiplied. Goldsmith's *Deserted Village* had struck a new chord, upon which Crabbe continued to play. Of his treatment of these subjects it must be said, that while he holds a powerful pen, and portrays truth vividly, he had an eye only for the sadder conditions of life, and gives pain rather than excites sympathy in the reader. Our meaning will be best illustrated by a comparison of *The Village* of Crabbe with *The Deserted Village* of Goldsmith, and the pleasure with which we pass from the squalid scenes of the former to the gentler sorrows and sympathies of the latter.

THOMAS CAMPBELL. — More identified with his age than

any other poet, and yet forming a link between the old and the new, was Campbell. Classical and correct in versification, and smothering nature with sonorous prosody, he still had the poetic fire, and an excellent power of poetic criticism. He was the son of a merchant, and was born at Glasgow on the 27th of July, 1777. He thus grew up with the French revolution, and with the great progress of the English nation in the wars incident to it. He was carefully educated, and was six years at the University of Glasgow, where he received prizes for composition. He went later to Germany, after being graduated, to study Greek literature with Heyne. After some preliminary essays in verse, he published the *Pleasures of Hope* in 1799, before he was twenty-two years old. It was one of the greatest successes of the age, and has always since been popular. His subject was one of universal interest; his verse was high-sounding; and his illustrations modern — such as the fall of Poland — *Finis Poloniæ;* and although there is some turgidity, and some want of unity, making the work a series of poems rather than a connected one, it was most remarkable for a youth of his age. It was perhaps unfortunate for his future fame; for it led the world to expect other and better things, which were not forthcoming. Travelling on the continent in the next year, 1800, he witnessed the battle of Hohenlinden from the monastery of St. Jacob, and wrote that splendid, ringing battle-piece, which has been so often recited and parodied. From that time he wrote nothing in poetry worthy of note, except songs and battle odes, with one exception. Among his battle-pieces which have never been equalled are *Ye Mariners of England*, *The Battle of the Baltic*, and *Lochiel's Warning*. His *Exile of Erin* has been greatly admired, and was suspected at the time of being treasonable; the author, however, being entirely innocent of such an intention, as he clearly showed.

Besides reviews and other miscellanies, Campbell wrote

The Annals of Great Britain, from the Accession of George III. to the Peace of Amiens, which is a graceful but not valuable work. In 1805 he received a pension of £200 per annum.

In 1809 he published his *Gertrude of Wyoming* — the exception referred to — a touching story, written with exquisite grace, but not true to the nature of the country or the Indian character. Like *Rasselas*, it is a conventional-English tale with foreign names and localities; but as an English poem it has great merit; and it turned public attention to the beautiful Valley of Wyoming, and the noble river which flows through it.

As a critic, Campbell had great acquirements and gifts. These were displayed in his elaborate *Specimens of the British Poets*, published in 1819, and in his *Lectures on Poetry* before the Surrey Institution in 1820. In 1827 he was elected Lord Rector of the University of Glasgow; but afterwards his literary efforts were by no means worthy of his reputation. Few have read his *Pilgrim of Glencoe;* and all who have, are pained by its manifestation of his failing powers. In fact, his was an unfinished fame — a brilliant beginning, but no continuance. Sir Walter Scott has touched it with a needle, when he says, "Campbell is in a manner a bugbear to himself; the brightness of his early success is a detriment to all his after efforts. He is afraid of the shadow which his own fame casts before him." Byron placed him in the second category of the greatest living English poets; but Byron was no critic.

He also published a *Life of Petrarch*, and a *Life of Frederick the Great;* and, in 1830, he edited the *New Monthly Magazine*. He died at Boulogne, June 15th, 1844, after a long period of decay in mental power.

SAMUEL ROGERS. — Rogers was a companion or consort to Campbell, although the two men were very different person ally. As Campbell had borrowed from Akenside and written *The Pleasures of Hope*, Rogers enriched our literature with *The Pleasures of Memory*, a poem of exquisite versification, more finished and unified than its pendent picture; containing neither passion nor declamation, but polish, taste, and tenderness.

Rogers was born in a suburb of London, in 1762. His father was a banker; and, although well educated, the poet was designed to succeed him, as he did, being until his death a partner in the same banking-house. Early enamored of poetry by reading Beattie's *Minstrel*, Rogers devoted all his spare time to its cultivation, and with great and merited success.

In 1786 he produced his *Ode to Superstition*, after the manner of Gray, and in 1792 his *Pleasures of Memory*, which was enthusiastically received, and which is polished to the extreme. In 1812 appeared a fragment, *The Voyage of Columbus*, and in 1814 *Jacqueline*, in the same volume with Byron's *Lara*. *Human Life* was published in 1819. It is a poem in the old style, (most of his poems are in the rhymed pentameter couplet;) but in 1822 appeared his poem of *Italy*, in blank verse, which has the charm of originality in presentation, freshness of personal experience, picturesqueness in description, novelty in incident and story, scholarship, and taste in art criticism. In short, it is not only the best of his poems, but it has great merit besides that of the poetry. The story of Ginevra is a masterpiece of cabinet art, and is universally appreciated. With these works Rogers contented himself. Rich and distinguished, his house became a place of resort to men of distinction and taste in art: it was filled with articles of *vertu;* and Rogers the poet lived long as Rogers the *virtuoso*. His breakfast parties were particularly noted. His long, prosperous, and happy life was ended on the 18th December, 1855, at the age of ninety-two.

The position of Rogers may be best illustrated in the words

of Sir J. Mackintosh, in which he says: "He appeared at the commencement of this literary revolution, without paying court to the revolutionary tastes, or seeking distinction by resistance to them." His works are not destined to live freshly in the course of literature, but to the historical student they mark in a very pleasing manner the characteristics of his age.

PERCY B. SHELLEY. — Revolutions never go backward; and one of the greatest characters in this forward movement was a gifted, irregular, splendid, unbalanced mind, who, while taking part in it, unconsciously, as one of many, stands out also in a very singular individuality.

Percy Bysshe Shelley was born on the 4th of August, 1792, at Fieldplace, in Sussex, England. He was the eldest son of Sir Timothy Shelley, and of an ancient family, traced back, it is said, to Sir Philip Sidney. When thirteen years old he was sent to Eton, where he began to display his revolutionary tendencies by his resistance to the fagging system; and where he also gave some earnest in writing of his future powers. At the age of sixteen he entered University College, Oxford, and appeared as a radical in most social, political, and religious questions. On account of a paper entitled *The Necessity of Atheism,* he was expelled from the university and went to London. In 1811 he made a runaway match with Miss Harriet Westbrook, the daughter of the keeper of a coffee-house, which brought down on him the wrath of his father. After the birth of two children, a separation followed; and he eloped with Miss Godwin in 1814. His wife committed suicide in 1816; and then the law took away from him the control of his children, on the ground that he was an atheist.

After some time of residence in England, he returned to Italy, where soon after he met with a tragical end. Going in an open boat from Leghorn to Spezzia, he was lost in a storm on the Mediterranean: his body was washed on shore near the town of Via Reggio, where his remains were burned in the presence of Lord Byron, Leigh Hunt, and others. The ashes were afterwards buried in the Protestant cemetery at Rome in July, 1822.

Shelley's principles were irrational and dangerous. He was a transcendentalist of the extreme order, and a believer in the perfectability of human nature. His works are full of his principles. The earliest was *Queen Mab,* in which his profanity and atheism are clearly set forth. It was first privately printed, and afterwards published in 1821. This was followed by *Alastor, or the Spirit of Solitude,* in 1816. In this he gives his own experience in the tragical career of the hero. His longest and most pretentious poem was *The Revolt of Islam,* published in 1819. It is in the Spenserian stanza. Also, in the same year, he published *The Cenci,* a tragedy, a dark and gloomy story on what should be a forbidden subject, but very powerfully written. In 1820 he also published *The Prometheus Unbound,* which is full of his irreligious views. His remaining works were smaller poems, among which may be noted *Adonais,* and the odes *To the Skylark* and *The Cloud.*

In considering his character, we must first observe the power of his imagination; it was so strong and all-absorbing, that it shut out the real and the true. He was a man of extreme sensibility; and that sensibility, hurt by common contact with things and persons around him, made him morbid in morality and metaphysics. He was a polemic of the fiercest type; and while he had an honest desire for reform of the evils that he saw about him, it is manifest that he attacked existing institutions for the very love of controversy. Bold, retired, and proud, without a spice of vanity, if he has received harsh judgment from one half the critical world, who had at least the claim that they were supporting pure morals and true religion, his character has been unduly exalted by the other half, who have mistaken reckless dogmatism for true nobility of soul. The most charitable judgment is that of Moir, who says: "It is needless to disguise the fact — and it accounts for all — his mind was diseased; he never knew, even from boyhood, what it was to breathe the atmosphere of healthy life — to have the *mens sana in corpore sano.*"

But of his poetical powers we must speak in a different manner. What he has left, gives token that, had he lived, he would have been one of the greatest modern poets. Thoroughly imbued with the Greek poetry, his verse-power was wonderful, his language stately and learned without pedantry, his inspiration was that of nature in her grandest moods, his fancy always exalted; and he presents the air of one who produces what is within him from an intense love of his art, without regard to the opinion of the world around him,— which, indeed, he seems to have despised more thoroughly than any other poet has ever done. Byron affected to despise it; Shelley really did.

We cannot help thinking that, had he lived after passing through the fiery trial of youthful passions and disordered imagination, he might have astonished the world with the grand spectacle of a convert to the good and true, and an apostle in the cause of both. Of him an honest thinker has said, — and there is much truth in the apparent paradox, — "No man who was not a fanatic, had ever more natural piety than he; and his supposed atheism is a mere metaphysical crotchet in which he was kept by the affected scorn and malignity of dunces." [1]

JOHN KEATS. — Another singular illustration of eccentricity and abnormal power in verse is found in the brief career of John Keats, the son of the keeper of a livery-stable in London, who was born on the 29th October, 1795.

Keats was a sensitive and pugnacious youth; and in 1810,

[1] H. C. Robinson, Diary II., 79.

after a very moderate education, he was apprenticed to a surgeon; but the love of poetry soon interfered with the surgery, and he began to read, not without the spirit of emulation, the works of the great poets — Chaucer, Spenser, Shakspeare, and Milton. After the issue of a small volume which attracted little or no attention, he published his *Endymion* in 1818, which, with some similarity in temperament, he inscribed to the memory of Thomas Chatterton. It is founded upon the Greek mythology, and is written in a varied measure. Its opening line has been a familiar quotation since:

A thing of beauty is a joy forever.

It was assailed by all the critics; but particularly, although not unfairly, by Jeffrey, in the *Edinburgh Review.* An article in *Blackwood,* breathing the spirit of British caste, had the bad taste to tell the young apothecary to go back to his galley-pots. The excessive sensibility of Keats received a great shock from this treatment; but we cannot help thinking that too much stress has been laid upon this in saying that he was killed by it. This was more romantic than true. He was by inheritance consumptive, and had lost a brother by that disease. Add to this that his peculiar passions and longings took the form of fierce hypochondria.

With a decided originality, he was so impressible that there are in his writings traces of the authors whom he was reading, if he did not mean to make them models of style.

In 1820 he published a volume containing *Lamia*, *Isabella*, and *The Eve of St. Agnes*, and *Hyperion*, a fragment, which was received with far greater favor by the reviewers. Keats was self-reliant, and seems to have had something of that magnificent egotism which is not infrequently displayed by great minds.

The judicious verdict at last pronounced upon him may be thus epitomized: he was a poet with fine fancy, original ideas, felicity of expression, but full of faults due to his individuality and his youth; and his life was not spared to correct these. In 1820 a hemorrhage of brilliant arterial blood heralded the end. He himself said, "Bring me a candle; let me see this blood;" and when it was brought, added, "I cannot be deceived in that color; that drop is my death-warrant: I must die." By advice he went to Italy, where he grew rapidly worse, and died on the 23d of February, 1821, having left this for his epitaph: "Here lies one whose name was writ in water." Thus dying at the age of twenty-four, he must be judged less for what he was, than as an earnest of what he would have been. *The Eve of St. Agnes* is one of the most exquisite poems in any language, and is as essentially allied to the simplicity and nature of the modern school of poetry as his *Endymion* is to the older school. Keats took part in what a certain writer has called "the reaction against the barrel-organ style, which had been reigning by a kind of sleepy, divine right for half a century."

OTHER WRITERS OF THE PERIOD.

In consonance with the Romantic school of Poetry, and as contributors to the prose fiction of the period of Scott, Byron, and Moore, a number of gifted women have made good their claim to the favor of the reading world, and have left to us productions of no mean value. First among these we mention Mrs. FELICIA DOROTHEA HEMANS, 1794–1835: early married to Captain Hemans, of the army, she was not happy in the conjugal state, and lived most of her after-life in retirement, separated from her husband. Her style is harmonious, and her lyrical power excellent; she makes melody of common-places; and the low key in which her poetry is pitched made her a favorite with the multitude. There is special fervor in her religious poems. Most of her writings are fugitive and occasional pieces. Among the longer poems are *The Forest Sanctuary*, *Dartmoor*, (a lyric poem,) and *The Restoration of the works of Art to Italy*. *The Siege of Valencia* and *The Vespers of Palermo* are plays on historical subjects. There is a sameness in her poetry which tires; but few persons can be found who do not value highly such a descriptive poem as *Bernardo del Carpio*, conceived in the very spirit of the Spanish Ballads, and such a sad and tender moralizing as that found in *The Hour of Death:*

Leaves have their time to fall,
  And flowers to wither, at the north-wind's breath,
And stars to set — but all,
  Thou hast all seasons for thine own, O Death!

Such poems as these will live when the greater part of what she has written has been forgotten, because its ministry has been accomplished.

Mrs. Caroline Elizabeth Norton, (born in 1808, still living:) she is the daughter of Thomas Sheridan, and the grand-daughter of the famous R. B. Sheridan. She married the Hon. Mr. Norton, and, like Mrs. Hemans, was unhappy in her union. As a poet, she has masculine gifts combined with feminine grace and tenderness. Her principal poems are *The Sorrows of Rosalie*, *The Undying One*, (founded on the legend of *The Wandering Jew*,) and *The Dream*. Besides these her facile pen has produced a multitude of shorter pieces, which have been at once popular. Her claims to enduring fame are not great, and she must be content with a present popularity.

Letitia Elizabeth Landon, 1802–1839: more gifted, and yet not as well trained as either of the preceding, Miss Landon (L. E. L.) has given vent to impassioned sentiment in poetry and prose. Besides many smaller pieces, she wrote *The Improvisatrice*, *The Troubadour*, *The Golden Violet*, and several prose romances, among which the best are *Romance and Reality*, and *Ethel Churchill*. She wrote too rapidly to finish with elegance; and her earlier pieces are disfigured by this want of finish, and by a lack of cool judgment; but her later writings are better matured and more correct. She married Captain Maclean, the governor of Cape Coast Castle, in Africa, and died there suddenly, from an overdose of strong medicine which she was accustomed to take for a nervous affection.

Maria Edgeworth, 1767–1849: she was English born, but resided most of her life in Ireland. Without remarkable genius, she may be said to have exercised a greater influence over her period than any other woman who lived in it. There is an aptitude and a practical utility in her stories which are felt in all circles. Her works for children are delightful and formative. Every one has read and re-read with pleasure the interesting and instructive stories contained in *The Parents' Assistant*. And what these are to the children, her novels are to those of larger growth. They are eighteen in number, and are illustrative of the society, fashion, and morals of the day; and always inculcate a good moral. Among them we may particularize *Forester*, *The Absentee*, and *The Modern Griselda*. All critics, even those who deny her great genius, agree in their estimate of the moral value of her stories, every one of which is at once a portraiture of her age and an instructive lesson to it. The feminine delicacy with which she offers counsel and administers reproof gives a great charm to, and will insure the permanent popularity of, her productions.

Jane Austen, 1775–1817: as a novelist she occupied a high place in her day, but her stories are gradually sinking into an historic repose, from which the coming generations will not care to disturb them. *Pride and Prejudice* and *Sense and Sensibility* are perhaps the best of her productions, and are valuable as displaying the society and the nature around her with delicacy and tact.

Mary Ferrier, 1782–1855: like Miss Austen, she wrote novels of existing society, of which *The Marriage* and *The Inheritance* are the best known. They were great favorites with Sir Walter Scott, who esteemed Miss Ferrier's genius highly: they are little read at the present time.

Robert Pollok, 1799–1827: a Scottish minister, who is chiefly known by his long poem, cast in a Miltonic mould, entitled *The Course of Time*. It is singularly significant of religious fervor, delicate health, youthful immaturity, and poetic yearnings. It abounds in startling effects, which please at first from their novelty, but will not bear a calm, critical analysis. On its first appearance, *The Course of Time* was immensely popular; but it has steadily lost favor, and its highest flights are "unearthly flutterings" when compared with the powerful soarings of Milton's imagination and the gentle harmonies of Cowper's religious muse. Pollok died early of consumption: his youth and his disease account for the faults and defects of his poem.

Leigh Hunt, 1784–1859: a novelist, a poet, an editor, a critic, a companion of literary men, Hunt occupies a distinct position among the authors of his day. Wielding a sensible and graceful rather than a powerful pen, he has touched almost every subject in the range of our literature, and has been the champion and biographer of numerous literary friends. He was the companion of Byron, Shelley, Keats, Lamb, Coleridge, and many other authors. He edited at various times several radical papers — *The Examiner*, *The Reflector*, *The Indicator*, and *The Liberal*: for a satire upon the regent, published in the first, he was imprisoned for two years. Among his poems *The Story of Rimini* is the best. His *Legend of Florence* is a beautiful drama. There are few pieces containing so small a number of lines, and yet enshrining a full story, which have been as popular as his *Abou Ben Adhem*. Always cheerful, refined and delicate in style, appreciative of others, Hunt's place in English literature is enviable, if not very exalted; like the atmosphere, his writings circulate healthfully and quietly around the efforts of greater poets than himself.

James Hogg, 1770–1835: a self-taught rustic, with little early schooling, except what the shepherd-boy could draw from nature, he wrote from his own head and heart without the canons and the graces of the Schools. With something of the homely nature of Burns, and the Scottish romance of Walter Scott, he produced numerous poems which are stamped with true genius. He catered to Scottish feeling, and began his fame by the stirring lines beginning:

> My name is Donald McDonald,
> I live in the Highlands so grand.

His best known poetical works are *The Queen's Wake*, containing seventeen stories in verse, of which the most striking is that of *Bonny Kilmeny.* He was always called "The Ettrick Shepherd." Wilson says of *The Queen's Wake* that "it is a garland of fresh flowers bound with a band of rushes from the moor;" a very fitting and just view of the work of one who was at once poet and rustic.

Allan Cunningham, 1785–1842: like Hogg, in that as a writer he felt the influence of both Burns and Scott, Cunningham was the son of a gardener, and a self-made man. In early life he was apprenticed to a mason. He wrote much fugitive poetry, among which the most popular pieces are, *A Wet Sheet and a Flowing Sea, Gentle Hugh Herries,* and *It's Hame and it's Hame.* Among his stories are *Traditional Tales of the Peasantry, Lord Roldan,* and *The Maid of Elwar.* His position for a time, as clerk and overseer of Chantrey's establishment, gave him the idea of writing *The Lives of Eminent British Painters, Sculptors, and Architects.* He was a voluminous author; his poetry is of a high lyrical order, and true to nature; but his prose will not retain its place in public favor: it is at once diffuse and obscure.

Thomas Hope, 1770–1831: an Amsterdam merchant, who afterwards resided in London, and who illustrated the progress of knowledge concerning the East by his work entitled, *Anastasius, or Memoirs of a Modern Greek.* Published anonymously, it excited a great interest, and was ascribed by the public to Lord Byron. The intrigues and adventures of the hero are numerous and varied, and the book has great literary merit; but it is chiefly of historical value in that it describes persons and scenes in Greece and Turkey, countries in which Hope travelled at a time when few Englishmen visited them.

William Beckford, 1760–1844: he was the son of an alderman, who became Lord Mayor of London. After a careful education, he found himself the possessor of a colossal fortune. He travelled extensively, and wrote sketches of his travels. His only work of importance is that called *Vathek,* in which he describes the gifts, the career, and the fate of the Caliph of that name, who was the grandson of the celebrated Haroun al Raschid. His palaces are described in a style of Oriental gorgeousness; his temptations, his lapses from virtue, his downward progress, are presented with dramatic power; and there is nothing in our literature more horribly real and terror-striking than the *Hall of Eblis,* — that hell where every heart was on fire, where "the Caliph Vathek, who, for the sake of empty pomp and forbidden power, had sullied himself with a thousand crimes, became a prey to grief without end and remorse without mitigation." Many of Beckford's other writings are blamed for their voluptuous character; the last scene in *Vathek* is, on the other hand, a most powerful and influential sermon. Beckford was eccentric and unsocial: he lived for some time in Portugal, but returned to England, and built a luxurious palace at Bath.

William Roscoe, 1753–1831: a merchant and banker of Liverpool. He is chiefly known by his *Life of Lorenzo de Medici,* and *The Life and Pontificate of Leo X.,* both of which contained new and valuable information. They are written in a pleasing style, and with a liberal and charitable spirit as to religious opinions. Since they appeared, history has developed new material and established more exacting canons, and the studies of later writers have already superseded these pleasing works.

CHAPTER XXXVII.

WORDSWORTH, AND THE LAKE SCHOOL.

The New School.

IN the beginning of the year 1820 George III. died, after a very long — but in part nominal — reign of fifty-nine years, during a large portion of which he was the victim of insanity, while his son, afterwards George IV., administered the regency of the kingdom.

George III. did little, either by example or by generosity, to foster literary culture: his son, while nominally encouraging authors, did much to injure the tone of letters in his day. But literature was now becoming independent and self-sustaining: it needed to look no longer wistfully for a monarch's smile: it cared comparatively little for the court: it issued its periods and numbers directly to the English people: it wrote for them and of them; and when, in 1830, the last of the Georges died, after an ill-spent life, in which his personal pleasures had concerned him far more than the welfare of his people, former prescriptions and prejudices rapidly passed away; and the new epoch in general improvement and literary culture, which had already begun its course, received a marvellous impulsion.

The great movement, in part unconscious, from the artificial rhetoric of the former age towards the simplicity of nature, was now to receive its strongest propulsion: it was to be preached like a crusade; to be reduced to a system, and set forth for the acceptance of the poetical world: it was to meet with criticism, and even opprobrium, because it had the arrogance to declare that old things had entirely passed away, and that all things must conform themselves to the new doctrine. The high-priest of this new poetical creed was Wordsworth: he proposed and expounded it; he wrote according to its tenets; he defended his illustrations against the critics by elaborate prefaces and essays. He boldly faced the clamor of a world in arms; and what there was real and valuable in his works has survived the fierce battle, and gathered around him an army of proselytes, champions, and imitators.

WORDSWORTH. — William Wordsworth was the son of the law-agent to the Earl of Lonsdale; he was born at Cockermouth, Cumberland, in 1770. It was a gifted family. His brother, Dr. Christopher Wordsworth, was Master of Trinity College. Another, the captain of an East Indiaman, was lost at sea in his own ship. He had also a clever sister, who was the poet's friend and companion as long as she lived.

Wordsworth and his companions have been called the Lake Poets, because they resided among the English lakes. Perhaps too much has been claimed for the Lake country, as giving inspiration to the poets who lived there: it is beautiful, but not so surpassingly so as to create poets as its children. The name is at once arbitrary and convenient.

Wordsworth was educated at St. John's College, Cambridge, which he entered in 1787; but whenever he could escape from academic restraints, he indulged his taste for pedestrian excursions: during these his ardent mind became intimate and intensely sympathetic with nature, as may be seen in his *Evening Walk*, in the sketch of the skater, and in the large proportion of description in all his poems.

It is truer of him than perhaps of any other author, that the life of the man is the best history of the poet. All that is eventful and interesting in his life may be found translated in his poetry. Milton had said that the poet's life should be a grand poem. Wordsworth echoed the thought:

> If thou indeed derive thy light from Heaven,
> Then to the measure of that Heaven-born light,
> Shine, Poet! in thy place, and be content.

He was not distinguished at college; the record of his days there may be found in *The Prelude,* which he calls *The Growth of a Poet's Mind.* He was graduated in 1791, with the degree of B. A., and went over to France, where he, among others, was carried away with enthusiasm for the French Revolution, and became a thorough Radical. That he afterwards changed his political views, should not be advanced in his disfavor; for many ardent and virtuous minds were hoping to see the fulfilment of recent predictions in greater freedom to man. Wordsworth erred in a great company, and from noble sympathies. He returned to England in 1792, with his illusions thoroughly dissipated. The workings of his mind are presented in *The Prelude.*

In the same year he published *Descriptive Sketches,* and *An Evening Walk,* which attracted little attention. A legacy of £900 left him by his friend Calvert, in 1795, enabled the frugal poet to devote his life to poetry, and particularly to what he deemed the emancipation of poetry from the fetters of the mythic and from the smothering ornaments of rhetoric.

In Nov., 1797, he went to London, taking with him a play called *The Borderers:* it was rejected by the manager. In the autumn of 1798, he published his *Lyrical Ballads,* which contained, besides his own verses, a poem by an anonymous friend.. The poem was *The Ancient Mariner;* the friend, Coleridge. In the joint operation, Wordsworth took the part based on nature; Coleridge illustrated the supernatural. The *Ballads* were received with undisguised contempt; nor, by reason of its company, did *The Ancient Mariner* have a much better hearing. Wordsworth preserved his equanimity, and an implicit faith in himself.

After a visit to Germany, he settled in 1799 at Grasmere, in the Lake country, and the next year republished the *Lyrical Ballads* with a new volume, both of which passed to another edition in 1802. With this edition, Wordsworth ran up his revolutionary flag and nailed it to the mast.

POETICAL CANONS. — It would be impossible as well as unnecessary to attempt an analysis of even the principal poems of so voluminous a writer; but it is important to state in substance the poetical canons he laid down. They may be found in the prefaces to the various editions of his *Ballads*, and may be thus epitomized:

I. He purposely chose his incidents and situations from common life, because in it our elementary feelings coexist in a state of simplicity.

II. He adopts the *language* of common life, because men hourly communicate with the best objects from which the best part of language is originally derived; and because, being less under the influence of social vanity, they convey their feelings and notions in simple and unelaborated expressions.

III. He asserts that the language of poetry is in no way different, except in respect to metre, from that of good prose. Poetry can boast of no celestial *ichor* that distinguishes her vital juices from those of prose: the same human blood circulates through the veins of them both. In works of imagination and sentiment, in proportion as ideas and feelings are valuable, whether the composition be in prose or verse, they require and exact one and the same language.

Such are the principal changes proposed by Wordsworth; and we find Herder, the German poet and metaphysician, agreeing with him in his estimate of poetic language. Having thus propounded his tenets, he wrote his earlier poems as illustrations of his views, affecting a simplicity in subject and diction that was sometimes simply ludicrous. It was an affected simplicity: he was simple with a purpose; he wrote his poems to suit his canons, and in that way his simplicity became artifice.

Jeffrey and other critics rose furiously against the poems which inculcated such doctrines. "This will never do" were the opening words of an article in the *Edinburgh Review*. One of the *Rejected Addresses*, called *The Baby's Début, by W. W.*, (spoken in the character of Nancy Lake, eight years old, who is drawn upon the stage in a go-cart,) parodies the ballads thus:

> What a large floor! 'tis like a town;
> The carpet, when they lay it down,
> Won't hide it, I 'll be bound:
> And there 's a row of lamps, my eye!
> How they do blaze: I wonder why
> They keep them on the ground?

And this, Jeffrey declares, is a flattering imitation of Wordsworth's style.

The day for depreciating Wordsworth has gone by; but calmer critics must still object to his poetical views in their entireness. In binding all poetry to his *dicta*, he ignores that *mythus* in every human mind, that longing after the heroic, which will not be satisfied with the simple and commonplace. One realm in which Poetry rules with an enchanted sceptre is the land of reverie and day-dream, — a land of fancy, in which genius builds for itself castles at once radiant and, for the time, real; in which the beggar is a king, the poor man a Crœsus, the timid man a hero: this is the fairy-land of the imagination. Among Wordsworth's poems are a number called *Poems of the Imagination*. He wrote learnedly about the imagination and fancy; but the truth is, that of all the great poets, — and, in spite of his faults, he is a great poet, — there is none so entirely devoid of imagination. What has been said of the heroic may be applied to wit, so important an element in many kinds of poetry; he ignores it because he was without it totally. If only humble life and commonplace incidents and unfigured rhetoric and bald language are the proper materials for the poetry, what shall be said of all literature, ancient and modern, until Wordsworth's day?

THE EXCURSION AND SONNETS. — With his growing fame and riper powers, he had deviated from his own principles, especially of language; and his peaceful epic, *The Excursion*, is full of difficult theology, exalted philosophy, and glowing rhetoric. His only attempt to adhere to his system presents the incongruity of putting these subjects into the lips of men, some of whom, the Scotch pedler for example, are not supposed to be equal to their discussion. In his language, too, he became far more polished and melodious. The young writer of the *Lyrical Ballads* would have been shocked to know that the more famous Wordsworth could write

> A golden lustre slept upon the hills;

or speak of

> A pupil in the many-chambered school,
> Where superstition weaves her airy dreams.

The Excursion, although long, is unfinished, and is only a portion of what was meant to be his great poem — *The Recluse*. It contains poetry of the highest order, apart from its mannerism and its improbable narrative; but the author is to all intents a different man from that of the *Ballads*: as different as the conservative Wordsworth of later years was from the radical youth who praised the French Revolution of 1791. As a whole, *The Excursion* is accurate, philosophic, and very dull, so that few readers have the patience to complete its perusal, while many enjoy its beautiful passages.

To return to the events of his life. In 1802 he married; and, after several changes of residence, he finally purchased a place called Rydal-mount in 1813, where he spent the remainder of his long, learned, and pure life. Long-standing dues from the Earl of Lonsdale to his father were paid; and he received the appointment of collector at Whitehaven and stamp distributor for Cumberland. Thus he had an ample income, which was increased in 1842 by a pension of £300 per annum. In 1843 he was made poet-laureate. He died in 1850, a famous poet, his reputation being due much more to his own clever individuality than to the poetic principles he asserted.

His ecclesiastical sonnets compare favorably with any that have been written in English. Landor, no friend of the poet, says: "Wordsworth has written more fine sonnets than are to be met with in the language besides."

AN ESTIMATE. — The great amount of verse Wordsworth has written is due to his estimate of the proper uses of poetry. Where other men would have written letters, journals, or prose sketches, his ready metrical pen wrote in verse: an excursion to England or Scotland, *Yarrow Visited and Revisited*, journeys in Germany and Italy, are all in verse. He exhibits in them all great humanity and benevolence, and is emphatically and without cant the poet of religion and morality. Coleridge — a poet and an attached friend, perhaps a partisan — claims for him, in his *Biographia Literaria*, "purity of language, freshness, strength, *curiosa felicitas* of diction, truth to nature in his imagery, imagination in the highest degree, but faulty fancy." We have already ventured to deny him the possession of imagination: the rest of his friend's eulogium is not undeserved. He had and has many ardent admirers, but none more ardent than himself. He constantly praised his own verses, and declared that they would ultimately conquer all prejudices and become universally popular — an opinion that the literary world does not seem disposed to adopt.

ROBERT SOUTHEY. — Next to Wordsworth, and, with certain characteristic differences, of the same school, but far beneath him in poetical power, is Robert Southey, who was born at Bristol, August 12, 1774. He was the son of a linen-draper in that town. He entered Balliol College, Oxford, in 1792, but left without taking his degree. In 1794 he published a radical poem on the subject of *Wat Tyler*, the sentiments of which he was afterwards very willing to repudiate. With the enthusiastic instinct of a poet, he joined with Wordsworth and Coleridge in a scheme called *Pantisocrasy;* that is, they were to go together to the banks of the Susquehanna, in a new country of which they knew nothing except by description; and there they were to realize a dream of nature in the golden age — a Platonic republic, where everything was to be in common, and from which vice and selfishness were to be forever excluded. But these young neo-platonists had no money, and so the scheme was given up.

In 1795 he married Miss Fricker, a milliner of Bristol, and made a voyage to Lisbon, where his uncle was chaplain to the British Factory. He led an unsettled life until 1804, when he established himself at Keswick in the Lake country, where he spent his life. He was a literary man and nothing else, and perhaps one of the most industrious writers that ever held a literary pen. Much of the time, indeed, he wrote for magazines and reviews, upon whatever subject was suggested to him, to win his daily bread.

HIS WRITINGS. — After the publication of *Wat Tyler* he wrote an epic poem called *Joan of Arc*, in 1796, which was crude and severely criticized. After some other unimportant essays, he inaugurated his purpose of illustrating the various oriental mythologies, by the publication of *Thalaba the Destroyer*, which was received with great disfavor at the time, and which first coupled his name with that of Wordsworth as of the school of Lake poets. It is in irregular metre, which at first has the charm of variety, but which afterwards loses its effect, on account of its broken, disjointed versification. In 1805 appeared *Madoc* — a poem based upon the subject of early Welsh discoveries in America. It is a long poem in two parts: the one descriptive of *Madoc in Wales* and the other of *Madoc in Aztlan*. Besides many miscellaneous works in prose, we notice the issue, in 1810, of *The Curse of Kehama* — the second of the great mythological poems referred to.

Among his prose works must be mentioned *The Chronicle of the Cid*, *The History of Brazil*, *The Life of Nelson*, and *The History of the Peninsular War*. A little work called *The Doctor* has been greatly liked in America.

Southey wrote innumerable reviews and magazine articles; and, indeed, tried his pen at every sort of literary work. His diction — in prose, at least — is almost perfect, and his poetical style not unpleasing. His industry, his learning, and his care in production must be acknowledged; but his poems are very little read, and, in spite of his own prophecies, are doomed to the shelf rather than retained upon the table. Like Wordsworth, he was one of the most egotistical of men; he had no greater admirer than Robert Southey; and had his exertions not been equal to his self-laudation, he would have been intolerable.

The most singular instance of perverted taste and unmerited eulogy is to be found in his *Vision of Judgment*, which, as poet-laureate, he produced to the memory of George the Third. The severest criticism upon it is Lord Byron's *Vision of Judgment* — reckless, but clever and trenchant. The consistency and industry of Southey's life caused him to be appointed poet-laureate upon the death of Pye; and in 1835, having declined a baronetcy, he received an annual pension of £300. Having lost his first wife in 1837, he married Miss Bowles, the poetess, in 1839; but soon after his mind began to fail, and he had reached a state of imbecility which ended in death on the 21st of March, 1843. In 1837, at the age of sixty-three, he collected and edited his complete poetical works, with copious and valuable historical notes.

Historical Value. — It is easy to see in what manner Southey, as a literary man, has reflected the spirit of the age. Politically, he exhibits partisanship from Radical to Tory, which may be clearly discerned by comparing his *Wat Tyler* with his *Vision of Judgment* and his *Odes*. As to literary and poetic canons, his varied metre, and his stories in the style of Wordsworth, show that he had abandoned all former schools. In his histories and biographies he is professedly historical; and in his epics he shows that greater range of learned investigation which is so characteristic of that age. The *Curse of Kehama* and *Thalaba* would have been impossible in a former age. He himself objected to be ranked with the Lakers; but Wordsworth, Southey, and Coleridge have too much in common, notwithstanding much individual difference, not to be classed together as innovators and asserters, whether we call them Lakers or something else.

It was on the occasion of his publishing *Thalaba*, that his name was first coupled with that of Wordsworth. His own words are, "I happened to be residing at Keswick when Mr. Wordsworth and I began to be acquainted. Mr. Coleridge also had resided there; and this was reason enough for classing us together as a school of poets." There is not much external resemblance, it is true, between *Thalaba* and the *Excursion;* but the same poetical motives will cause both to remain unread by the multitude — unnatural comparisons, recondite theology, and a great lack of common humanity,

That there was a mutual admiration is found in Southey's declaration that Wordsworth's sonnets contain the profoundest poetical wisdom, and that the *Preface* is the quintessence of the philosophy of poetry.

SAMUEL TAYLOR COLERIDGE. — More individual, more eccentric, less commonplace, in short, a far greater genius than either of his fellows, Coleridge accomplished less, had less system, was more visionary and fragmentary than they: he had an amorphous mind of vast proportions. The man, in his life and conversation, was great; the author has left little of value which will last when the memory of his person has disappeared. He was born on the 21st of October, 1772, at Ottery St. Mary. His father was a clergyman and vicar of the parish. He received his education at Christ's Hospital in London, where, among others, he had Charles Lamb as a comrade, and formed with him a friendship which lasted as long as they both lived.

EARLY LIFE. — There he was an erratic student, but always a great reader; and while he was yet a lad, at the age of fourteen, he might have been called a learned man.

He had little self-respect, and from stress of poverty he intended to apprentice himself to a shoemaker; but friends who admired his learning interfered to prevent this, and he was sent with a scholarship to Jesus College, Cambridge, in 1791. Like Wordsworth and Southey, he was an intense Radical at first; and on this account left college without his degree in 1793. He then enlisted as a private in the 15th Light Dragoons; but, although he was a favorite with his comrades, whose letters he wrote, he made a very poor soldier. Having written a Latin sentence under his saddle on the stable wall, his superior education was recognized; and he was discharged from the service after only four months' duty. Eager for adventure, he joined Southey and Lloyd in their scheme of pantisocracy, to which we have already referred; and when that failed for want of money, he married the sister-in-law of Southey — Miss Fricker, of Bristol. He was at this time a Unitarian as well as a Radical, and officiated frequently as a Unitarian minister. His sermons were extremely eloquent. He had already published some juvenile poems, and a drama on the fall of Robespierre, and had endeavored to establish a periodical called *The Watchman.* He was always erratic, and dependent upon the patronage of his friends; in short, he always presented the sad spectacle of a man who could not take care of himself.

HIS WRITINGS. — After a residence at Stowey, in Somersetshire, where he wrote some of his finest poems, among which were the first part of *Christabel*, *The Ancient Mariner*, and *Remorse*, a tragedy, he was enabled, through the kindness of friends, to go, in 1798, to Germany, where he spent fourteen months in the study of literature and metaphysics. In the year 1800 he returned to the Lake country, where he for some time resided with Southey at Keswick; Wordsworth being then at Grasmere. Then was established as a fixed fact in English literature the Lake school of poetry. These three poets acted and reacted upon each other. From having been great Radicals they became Royalists, and Coleridge's Unitarian belief was changed into orthodox churchmanship. His translation of Schiller's *Wallenstein* should rather be called an expansion of that drama, and is full of his own poetic fancies. After writing for some time for the *Morning Post,* he went to Malta as the Secretary to the Governor in 1804, at a salary of £800 per annum. But his restless spirit soon drove him back to Grasmere, and to desultory efforts to make a livelihood.

In 1816 he published the two parts of *Christabel*, an unfinished poem, which, for the wildness of the conceit, exquisite imagery, and charming poetic diction, stands quite alone in English literature. In a periodical called *The Friend*, which he issued, are found many of his original ideas; but it was discontinued after twenty-seven numbers. His *Biographia Literaria*, published in 1817, contains valuable sketches of literary men, living and dead, written with rare critical power.

In his *Aids to Reflection*, published in 1825, are found his metaphysical tenets; his *Table-Talk* is also of great literary value; but his lectures on Shakspeare show him to have been the most remarkable critic of the great dramatist whom the world has produced.

It has already been mentioned that when the first volume of Wordsworth's *Lyrical Ballads* was published, *The Ancient Mariner* was included in it, as a poem by an anonymous friend. It had been the intention of Coleridge to publish another poem in the second volume; but it was considered incongruous, and excluded. That poem was the exquisite ballad entitled *Love*, or *Genevieve*.

His Helplessness. — With no home of his own, he lived by visiting his friends; left his wife and children to the support of others, and seemed incapable of any other than this shifting and shiftless existence. This natural imbecility was greatly increased during a long period by his constant use of opium, which kept him, a greater portion of his life, in a world of dreams. He was fortunate in having a sincere and appreciative friend in Mr. Gilman, surgeon, near London, to whose house he went in 1816; and where, with the exception of occasional visits elsewhere, he resided until his death in 1834. If the Gilmans needed compensation for their kindness, they found it in the celebrity of their visitor; even strangers made pilgrimages to the house at Highgate to hear the rhapsodies of "the old man eloquent." Coleridge once asked Charles Lamb if he had ever heard him preach, referring to the early days when he was a Unitarian preacher.

"I never heard you do anything else," was the answer he received. He was the prince of talkers, and talked more coherently and connectedly than he wrote: drawing with ease from the vast stores of his learning, he delighted men of every degree. While of the Lake school of poetry, and while in some sort the creature of his age and his surroundings, his eccentricities gave him a rare independence and individuality. A giant in conception, he was a dwarf in execution; and something of the interest which attaches to a *lusus naturæ* is the chief claim to future reputation which belongs to S. T. C.

HARTLEY COLERIDGE, his son, (1796–1849,) inherited much of his father's talents; but was an eccentric, deformed, and, for a time, an intemperate being. His principal writings were monographs on various subjects, and articles for Blackwood. HENRY NELSON COLERIDGE, (1800–1843,) a nephew and son-in-law of the poet, was also a gifted man, and a profound classical scholar. His introduction to the study of the great classic poets, containing his analysis of Homer's epics, is a work of great merit.

CHAPTER XXXVIII.

THE REACTION IN POETRY.

Alfred Tennyson.	Idyls of the King.	Her Faults.
Early Works.	Elizabeth B. Browning.	Robert Browning.
The Princess.	Aurora Leigh.	Other Poets.

TENNYSON AND THE BROWNINGS.

ALFRED TENNYSON. — It is the certain fate of all extravagant movements, social or literary, to invite criticism and opposition, and to be followed by reaction. The school of Wordsworth was the violent protest against what remained of the artificial in poetry; but it had gone, as we have seen, to the other extreme. The affected simplicity, and the bald diction which it inculcated, while they raised up an army of feeble imitators, also produced in the ranks of poetry a vindication of what was good in the old; new theories, and a very different estimate of poetical subjects and expression. The first poet who may be looked upon as leading the reactionary party is Alfred Tennyson. He endeavored out of all the schools to synthesize a new one. In many of his descriptive pieces he followed Wordsworth: in his idyls, he adheres to the romantic school; in his treatment and diction, he stands alone.

EARLY EFFORTS. — He was the son of a clergyman of Lincolnshire, and was born at Somersby, in 1810. After a few early and almost unknown efforts in verse, the first volume bearing his name was issued in 1830, while he was yet an under-graduate at Cambridge: it had the simple title —

Poems, chiefly Lyrical. In their judgment of this new poet, the critics were almost as much at fault as they had been when the first efforts of Wordsworth appeared; but for very different reasons. Wordsworth was simple and intensely realistic. Tennyson was mystic and ideal: his diction was unusual; his little sketches conveyed an almost hidden moral; he seemed to inform the reader that, in order to understand his poetry, it must be studied; the meaning does not sparkle upon the surface; the language ripples, the sense flows in an undercurrent. His first essays exhibit a mania for finding strange words, or coining new ones, which should give melody to his verse. Whether this was a process of development or not, he has in his later works gotten rid of much of this apparent mannerism, while he has retained, and even improved, his harmony. He exhibits a rare power of concentration, as opposed to the diffusiveness of his contemporaries. Each of his smaller poems is a thought, briefly, but forcibly and harmoniously, expressed. If it requires some exertion to comprehend it, when completely understood it becomes a valued possession.

It is difficult to believe that such poems as *Mariana* and *Recollections of the Arabian Nights* were the production of a young man of twenty.

In 1833 he published his second volume, containing additional poems, among which were *Enone, The May Queen, The Lotos-Eaters*, and *A Dream of Fair Women. The May Queen* became at once a favorite, because every one could understand it: it touched a chord in every heart; but his rarest power of dreamy fancy is displayed in such pieces as *The Arabian Nights* and the *Lotos-Eaters.* No greater triumph has been achieved in the realm of fancy than that in the court of good Haroun al Raschid, and amid the Lotos dreams of the Nepenthe coast. These productions were not received with the favor which they merited, and so he let the critics alone for nine years. In 1842 he again appeared in print, with, among other poems, the exquisite fragment of the *Morte d'Arthur*, *Godiva*, *St. Agnes*, *Sir Galahad*, *Lady Clara Vere de Vere*, *The Talking Oak*, and chief, perhaps, of all, *Locksley Hall*. In these poems he is not only a poet, but a philosopher. Each of these is an extended apothegm, presenting not only rules of life, but mottoes and maxims for daily use. They are soliloquies of the nineteenth century, and representations of its men and conditions.

THE PRINCESS. — In 1847 he published *The Princess, a Medley* — a pleasant and suggestive poem on woman's rights, in which exquisite songs are introduced, which break the monotony of the blank verse, and display his rare lyric power. The *Bugle Song* is among the finest examples of the adaptation of sound to sense in the language; and there is nothing more truthful and touching than the short verses beginning,

Home they brought her warrior dead.

Arthur Hallam, a gifted son of the distinguished historian, who was betrothed to Tennyson's sister, died young; and the poet has mourned and eulogized him in a long poem entitled *In Memoriam*. It contains one hundred and twenty-nine four-lined stanzas, and is certainly very musical and finished; but it is rather the language of calm philosophy elaborately studied, than that of a poignant grief. It is not, in our judgment, to be compared with his shorter poems, and is generally read and overpraised only by his more ardent admirers, who discover a crystal tear of genuine emotion in every stanza.

IDYLS OF THE KING. — The fragment on the death of Arthur, already mentioned, foreshadowed a purpose of the poet's mind to make the legends of that almost fabulous monarch a vehicle for modern philosophy in English verse.

In 1859 appeared a volume containing the *Idyls of the King*. They are rather minor epics than idyls. The simple materials are taken from the Welsh and French chronicles, and are chiefly of importance in that they cater to that English taste which finds national greatness typified in Arthur. It had been a successful stratagem with Spenser in *The Fairy Queen*, and has served Tennyson equally well in the *Idyls*. It unites the ages of fable and of chivalry; it gives a noble lineage to heroic deeds. The best is the last — *Guinevere* — almost the perfection of pathos in poetry. The picturesqueness of his descriptions is evinced by the fact that Gustave Doré has chosen these *Idyls* as a subject for illustration, and has been eminently successful in his labor.

Maud, which appeared in 1855, notwithstanding some charming lyrical passages, may be considered Tennyson's failure. In 1869 he completed *The Idyls* by publishing *The Coming of Arthur*, *The Holy Grail*, and *Pelleas and Etteare*. He also finished the *Morte d'Arthur*, and put it in its proper place as *The Passing of Arthur*.

Tennyson was appointed poet-laureate upon the death of Wordsworth, in 1850, and receives besides a pension of £200. He lived for a long time in great retirement at Farringford, on the Isle of Wight; but has lately removed to Petersfield, in Hampshire. It may be reasonably doubted whether this hermit-life has not injured his poetical powers; whether, great as he really is, a little inhalation of the air of busy every-day life would not have infused more of nature and freshness into his verse. Among his few *Odes* are that on the death of the Duke of Wellington, the dedication of his poems to the Queen, and his welcome to Alexandra, Princess of Wales, all of which are of great excellence. His *Charge of the Light Brigade*, at Balaclava, while it gave undue currency to that stupid military blunder, must rank as one of the finest battle-lyrics in the language.

The poetry of Tennyson is eminently representative of the

Victorian age. He has written little; but that little marks a distinct era in versification — great harmony untrammelled by artificial *correctness;* and in language, a search for novelty to supply the wants and correct the faults of the poetic vocabulary. He is national in the *Idyls;* philosophic in *The Two Voices*, and similar poems. The *Princess* is a gentle satire on the age; and though, in striving for the reputation of originality, he sometimes mistakes the original for the beautiful, he is really the laurelled poet of England in merit as well as in title.

Elizabeth Barrett Browning. — The literary usher is now called upon to cry with the herald of the days of chivalry — *Place aux dames.* A few ladies, as we have seen, have already asserted for themselves respectable positions in the literary ranks. Without a question as to the relative gifts of mind in man and woman, we have now reached a name which must rank among those of the first poets of the present century — one which represents the Victorian age as fully and forcibly as Tennyson, and with more of novelty than he. Nervous in style, elevated in diction, bold in expression, learned and original, Mrs. Browning divides the poetic renown of the period with Tennyson. If he is the laureate, she was the acknowledged queen of poetry until her untimely death.

Miss Elizabeth Barrett was born in London, in 1809. She was educated with great care, and began to write at a very early age. A volume, entitled *Essays on Mind, with Other Poems*, was published when she was only seventeen. In 1833 she produced *Prometheus Bound*, a translation of the drama of Æschylus from the original Greek, which exhibited rare classical attainments; but which she considered so faulty that she afterwards retranslated it. In 1838 appeared *The Seraphim, and other Poems;* and in 1839, *The Romaunt of the Page.* Not long after, the rupture of a blood-vessel brought her to the verge of the grave; and while she was still in a precarious state of health, her favorite brother was drowned. For several years she lived secluded, studying and composing when her health permitted; and especially drawing her inspiration from original sources in Greek and Hebrew. In 1844 she published her collected poems in two volumes. Among these was *Lady Geraldine's Courtship*: an exquisite story, the perusal of which is said to have induced Robert Browning to seek her acquaintance. Her health was now partially restored; and they were married in 1846. For some time they resided at Florence, in a congenial and happy union. The power of passionate love is displayed in her *Sonnets from the Portuguese*, which are among the finest in the language. Differing in many respects from those of Shakspeare, they are like his in being connected by one impassioned thought, and being, without doubt, the record of a heart experience.

Thoroughly interested in the social and political conditions of struggling Italy, she gave vent to her views and sympathies in a volume of poems, entitled *Casa Guidi Windows*. Casa Guidi was the name of their residence in Florence, and the poems vividly describe what she saw from its windows — divers forms of suffering, injustice, and oppression, which touched the heart of a tender woman and a gifted poet, and compelled it to burst forth in song.

AURORA LEIGH. — But by far the most important work of Mrs. Browning is *Aurora Leigh*: a long poem in nine books, which appeared in 1856, in which the great questions of the age, social and moral, are handled with great boldness. It is neither an epic, nor an idyl, nor a tale in verse: it combines features of them all. It presents her clear convictions of life and art, and is full of philosophy, largely expressed in the language of irony and sarcasm. She is an inspired advocate of the intellectual claims of woman; and the poem is, in some degree, an autobiography: the identity of the poet and the heroine gives a great charm to the narrative. There are few finer pieces of poetical inspiration than the closing scene, where the friend and lover returns blind and helpless, and the woman's heart, unconquered before, surrenders to the claims of misfortune as the champion of love.

After a happy life with her husband and an only child, sent for her solace, this gifted woman died in 1863.

HER FAULTS. — It is as easy to criticize Mrs. Browning's works as to admire them; but our admiration is great in spite of her faults: in part because of them, for they are faults of a bold and striking individuality. There is sometimes an obscurity in her fancies, and a turgidity in her language. She seems to transcend the poet's license with a knowledge that she is doing so. For example:

> We will sit on the throne of a purple sublimity,
> And grind down men's bones to a pale unanimity.

And again, in speaking of Gœthe, she says:

> His soul reached out from far and high,
> And fell from inner entity.

Her rhymes are frequently and arrogantly faulty: she seems to scorn the critics; she writes more for herself than for others, and infuses all she writes with her own fervent spirit: there is nothing commonplace or lukewarm. She is so strong that she would be masculine; but so tender that she is entirely feminine: at once one of the most vigorous of poets and one of the best of women. She has attained the first rank among the English poets.

ROBERT BROWNING. — As a poet of decided individuality, which has gained for him many admirers, Browning claims particular mention. His happy marriage has for his fame the disadvantage that he gave his name to a greater poet; and it is never mentioned without an instinctive thought of her superiority. Many who are familiar with her verses have never read a line of her husband. This is in part due to a mysticism and an intense subjectivity, which are not adapted to the popular comprehension. He has chosen subjects unknown or uninteresting to the multitude of readers, and treats them with such novelty of construction and such an affectation of originality, that few persons have patience to read his poems.

Robert Browning was born, in 1812, at Camberwell; and after a careful education, not at either of the universities, (for he was a dissenter,) he went at the age of twenty to Italy, where he eagerly studied the history and antiquity to be found in the monasteries and in the remains of the mediæval period. He also made a study of the Italian people. In 1835 he published a drama called *Paracelsus,* founded upon the history of that celebrated alchemist and physician, and delineating the conditions of philosophy in the fifteenth century. It is novel, antique, and metaphysical: it exhibits the varied emotions of human sympathy; but it is eccentric and obscure, and cannot be popular. He has been called the poet for poets; and this statement seems to imply that he is not the poet for the great world.

In 1837 he published a tragedy called *Strafford;* but his Italian culture seems to have spoiled his powers for portraying English character, and he has presented a stilted Strafford and a theatrical Charles I.

In 1840 appeared *Sordello,* founded upon incidents in the history of that Mantuan poet Sordello, whom Dante and Virgil met in purgatory; and who, deserting the language of Italy, wrote his principal poems in the Provençal. The critics were so dissatisfied with this work, that Browning afterwards omitted it in the later editions of his poems. In 1843 he published a tragedy entitled *A Blot on the 'Scutcheon,* and a play called *The Dutchess of Cleves*. In 1850 appeared *Christmas Eve* and *Easter Day*. Concerning all these, it may be said that it is singular and sad that a real poetic gift, like that of Browning, should be so shrouded with faults of conception and expression. What leads us to think that many of these are an affectation, is that he has produced, almost with the simplicity of Wordsworth, those charming sketches, *The Good News from Ghent to Aix*, and *An Incident at Ratisbon*.

Among his later poems we specially commend *A Death in the Desert*, and *Pippa Passes*, as less obscure and more interesting than any, except the lyrical pieces just mentioned. It is difficult to show in what manner Browning represents his age. His works are only so far of a modern character that they use the language of to-day without subsidizing its simplicity, and abandon the old musical couplet without presenting the intelligible if commonplace thought which it used to convey.

Other Poets of the Latest Period.

Reginald Heber, 1783–1826: a godly Bishop of Calcutta. He is most generally known by one effort, a little poem, which is a universal favorite, and has preached, from the day it appeared, eloquent sermons in the cause of missions — *From Greenland's Icy Mountains*. Among his other hymns are *Brightest and Best of the Sons of the Morning*, and *The Son of God goes forth to War*.

Barry Cornwall, born 1790: this is a *nom de plume* of *Bryan Proctor*, a pleasing, but not great poet. His principal works are *Dramatic Scenes*, *Mirandola*, a tragedy, and *Marcian Colonna*. His minor poems are characterized by grace and fluency. Among these are *The Return of the Admiral; The Sea, the Sea, the Open Sea;* and *A Petition to Time*. He also wrote essays and tales in prose — a *Life of Edmund Keane*, and a *Memoir of Charles Lamb*. His daughter, *Adelaide Anne Proctor*, is a gifted poetess, and has written, among other poems, *Legends and Lyrics*, and *A Chaplet of Verses*.

James Sheridan Knowles, 1784–1862: an actor and dramatist. He left the stage and became a Baptist minister. His plays were very successful upon the stage. Among them, those of chief merit are *The Hunch-*

back, Virginius and Caius Gracchus, and *The Wife, a Tale of Mantua.*

Jean Ingelow, born 1830: one of the most popular of the later English poets. *The Song of Seven,* and *My Son's Wife Elizabeth,* are extremely pathetic, and of such general application that they touch all hearts. The latter is the refrain of *High Tide on the Coast of Lancashire.* She has published, besides, several volumes of stories for children, and one entitled *Studies for Stories.*

Algernon Charles Swinburne, born 1843: he is principally and very favorably known by his charming poem *Atalanta in Calydon.* He has also written a somewhat heterodox and licentious poem entitled *Laus Veneris, Chastelard,* and *The Song of Italy;* besides numerous minor poems and articles for magazines. He is among the most notable and prolific poets of the age; and we may hope for many and better works from his pen.

Richard Harris Barham, 1788–1845: a clergyman of the Church of England, and yet one of the most humorous of writers. He is chiefly known by his *Ingoldsby Legends,* which were contributed to the magazines. They are humorous tales in prose and verse; the latter in the vein of Peter Pindar, but better than those of Wolcot, or any writer of that school. Combined with the humorous and often forcible, there are touches of pathos and terror which are extremely effective. He also wrote a novel called *My Cousin Nicholas.*

Philip James Bailey, born 1816: he published, in 1839, *Festus,* a poem in dramatic form, having, for its *dramatis personæ,* God in his three persons, Lucifer, angels, and man. Full of rare poetic fancy, it repels many by the boldness of its flight in the consideration of the incomprehensible, which many minds think the forbidden. *The Angel World* and *The Mystic* are of a similar kind; but his last work, *The Age, a Colloquial Satire,* is on a mundane subject and in a simpler style.

Charles Mackay, born 1812: principally known by his fugitive pieces, which contain simple thoughts on pleasant language. His poetical collections are called *Town Lyrics* and *Egeria.*

John Keble, 1792–1866: the modern George Herbert; a distinguished clergyman. He was Professor of Poetry at Oxford, and produced, besides *Tracts for the Times,* and other theological writings, *The Christian Year,* containing a poem for every Sunday and holiday in the ecclesiastical year. They are devout breathings in beautiful verse, and are known and loved by great numbers out of his own communion. Many of them have been adopted as hymns in many collections.

Martin Farquhar Tupper, born 1810: his principal work is *Proverbial*

Philosophy, in two series. It was unwontedly popular; and Tupper's name was on every tongue. Suddenly, the world reversed its decision and discarded its favorite; so that, without having done anything to warrant the desertion, Tupper finds himself with but very few admirers, or even readers: so capricious is the *vox populi.* The poetry is not without merit; but the world cannot forgive itself for having rated it too high.

Matthew Arnold, born 1822: the son of Doctor Arnold of Rugby. He has written numerous critical papers, and was for some time Professor of Poetry at Oxford. *Sorab and Rustam* is an Eastern tale in verse, of great beauty. His other works are *The Strayed Reveller*, and *Empedocles on Etna.* More lately, an Inspector of Schools, he has produced several works on education, among which are *Popular Education in France* and *The Schools and Universities of the Continent.*

CHAPTER XXXIX.

THE LATER HISTORIANS.

New Materials. George Grote. History of Greece.	Lord Macaulay History of England. Its Faults.	Thomas Carlyle. Life of Frederick II. Other Historians.

NEW MATERIALS.

NOTHING more decidedly marks the nineteenth century than the progress of history as a branch of literature. A wealth of material, not known before, was brought to light, increasing our knowledge and reversing time-honored decisions upon historic points. Countries were explored and their annals discovered. Expeditions to Egypt found a key to hieroglyphs; State papers were arranged to the hand of the scholar; archives, like those of Simancas, were thrown open. The progress of Truth, through the extension of education, unmasked ancient prescriptions and prejudices: thus, where the chronicle remained, philosophy was transformed; and it became evident that the history of man in all times must be written anew, with far greater light to guide the writer than the preceding century had enjoyed. Besides, the world of readers became almost as learned as the historian himself, and he wrote to supply a craving and a demand such as had never before existed. A glance at the labors of the following historians will show that they were not only annalists, but reformers in the full sense of the word: they re-wrote what had been written before, supplying defects and correcting errors.

George Grote. — This distinguished writer was born near London, in 1794. He was the son of a banker, and received his education at the Charter House. Instead of entering one of the universities, he became a clerk in his father's banking-house. Early imbued with a taste for Greek literature, he continued his studies with great zeal; and was for many years collecting the material for a history of Greece. The subject was quietly and thoroughly digested in his mind before he began to write. A member of Parliament from 1832 to 1841, he was always a strong Whig, and was specially noted for his championship of the vote by ballot. There was no department of wholesome reform which he did not sustain. He opposed the corn laws, which had become oppressive; he favored the political rights of the Jews, and denounced prescriptive evils of every kind.

History of Greece. — In 1846 he published the first volume of his *History of Greece from the Earliest Period to the Death of Alexander the Great:* the remaining volumes appeared between that time and 1856. The work was well received by critics of all political opinions; and the world was astonished that such a labor should have been performed by any writer who was not a university man. It was a luminous ancient history, in a fresh and racy modern style: the review of the mythology is grand; the political conditions, the manners and customs of the people, the military art, the progress of law, the schools of philosophy, are treated with remarkable learning and clearness. But he as clearly exhibits the political condition of his own age, by the sympathy which he displays towards the democracy of Athens in their struggles against the tenets and actions of the aristocracy. The historian writes from his own political point of view; and Grote's history exhibits his own views of reform as plainly as that of Mitford sets forth his aristocratic proclivities. Thus the English politics of the age play a part in the Grecian history.

There were several histories of Greece written not long before that of Grote, which may be considered as now set aside by his greater accuracy and better style. Among these the principal are that of JOHN GILLIES, 1747–1836, which is learned, but statistical and dry; that of CONNOP THIRLWALL, born 1797, Bishop of St. David's, which was greatly esteemed by Grote himself; and that of WILLIAM MITFORD, 1744–1827, to correct the errors and supply the deficiencies of which, Grote's work was written.

LORD MACAULAY.—Thomas Babington Macaulay was born at Rothley, in Leicestershire, on the 25th of October, 1800. His father, Zachary Macaulay, a successful West Indian merchant, devoted his later life to philanthropy. His mother was Miss Selina Mills, the daughter of a bookseller of Bristol. After an early education, chiefly conducted at home, he was entered at Trinity College, Cambridge, in 1818, where he distinguished himself as a debater, and gained two prize poems and a scholarship. He was graduated in 1822, and afterwards continued his studies; producing, during the next four years, several of his stirring ballads. He began to write for the Edinburgh Review in 1825. In 1830 he entered Parliament, and was immediately noted for his brilliant oratory in advocating liberal principles. In 1834 he was sent to India, as a member of the Supreme Council; and took a prominent part in preparing an Indian code of laws. This code was published on his return to England, in 1838; but it was so kind and considerate to the natives, that the martinets in India defeated its adoption. From his return until 1847, he had a seat in Parliament as member for Edinburgh; but in the latter year his support of the grant to the Maynooth (Roman Catholic) College so displeased his constituents, that in the next election he lost his seat.

During all these busy years he had been astonishing and delighting the reading world by his truly brilliant papers in the *Edinburgh Review*, which have been collected and published as *Miscellanies*. The subjects were of general interest; their treatment novel and bold; the learning displayed was accurate and varied; and the style pointed, vigorous, and harmonious. The papers upon *Clive* and *Hastings* are enriched by his intimate knowledge of Indian affairs, acquired during his residence in that country. His critical papers are severe and satirical, such as the articles on *Croker's Boswell*, and on *Mr. Robert Montgomery's Poems*. His unusual self-reliance as a youth led him to great vehemence in the expression of his opinions, as well as into errors of judgment, which he afterwards regretted. The radicalism which is displayed in his essay on *Milton* was greatly modified when he came to treat of kindred subjects in his History.

THE HISTORY OF ENGLAND. — He had long cherished the intention of writing the history of England, "from the accession of James II. down to a time which is within the memory of men still living." The loss of his election at Edinburgh gave him the leisure necessary for carrying out this purpose. In 1848 he published the first and second volumes, which at once achieved an unprecedented popularity. His style had lost none of its brilliancy; his reading had been immense; his examination of localities was careful and minute. It was due, perhaps, to this growing fame, that the electors of Edinburgh, without any exertion on his part, returned him to Parliament in 1852. In 1855 the third and fourth volumes of his History appeared, bringing the work down to the peace of Ryswick, in 1697. All England applauded the crown when he was elevated to the peerage, in 1857, as Baron Macaulay of Rothley.

It was now evident that Macaulay had deceived himself as to the magnitude of his subject; at least, he was never to finish it. He died suddenly of disease of the heart, on the 28th of December, 1859; and all that remained of his History was a fragmentary volume, published after his death by his sister, Lady Trevelyan, which reaches the death of William III., in 1702.

Its Faults. — The faults of Macaulay's History spring from the character of the man: he is always a partisan or a bitter enemy. His heroes are angels; those whom he dislikes are devils; and he pursues them with the ardor of a crusader or the vendetta of a Corsican. The Stuarts are painted in the darkest colors; while his eulogy of William III. is fulsome and false. He blackens the character of Marlborough for real faults indeed; but for such as Marlborough had in common with thousands of his contemporaries. If, as has been said, that great captain deserved the greatest censure as a statesman and warrior, it is equally true, paradoxical as it may seem, that he deserved also the greatest praise in both capacities. Macaulay has fulminated the censure and withheld the praise.

What is of more interest to Americans, he loses no opportunity of attacking and defaming William Penn; making statements which have been proved false, and attributing motives without reason or justice.

His style is what the French call the *style coupé*, — short sentences, like those of Tacitus, which ensure the interest by their recurring shocks. He writes history with the pen of a reviewer, and gives verdicts with the authority of a judge. He seems to say, Believe the autocrat; do not venture to philosophize.

His poetry displays tact and talent, but no genius; it is pageantry in verse. His *Lays of Ancient Rome* are scholarly, of course, and pictorial in description, but there is little of nature, and they are theatrical rather than dramatic; they are to be declaimed rather than to be read or sung.

In society, Macaulay was a great talker — he harangued his friends; and there was more than wit in the saying of Sidney

Smith, that his conversation would have been improved by a few "brilliant flashes of silence."

But in spite of his faults, if we consider the profoundness of his learning, the industry of his studies, and the splendor of his style, we must acknowledge him as the most distinguished of English historians. No one has yet appeared who is worthy to complete the magnificent work which he left unfinished.

THOMAS CARLYLE. — A literary brother of a very different type, but of a more distinct individuality, is Carlyle, who was born in Dumfries-shire, Scotland, in 1795. He was the eldest son of a farmer. After a partial education at home, he entered the University of Edinburgh, where he was noted for his attainments in mathematics, and for his omnivorous reading. After leaving the university he became a teacher in a private family, and began to study for the ministry, a plan which he soon gave up.

His first literary effort was a *Life of Schiller*, issued in numbers of the *London Magazine*, in 1823–4. He turned his attention to German literature, in the knowledge of which he has surpassed all other Englishmen. He became as German as the Germans.

In 1826 he married, and removed to Craigen-Puttoch, on a farm, where, in isolation and amid the wildness of nature, he studied, and wrote articles for the *Edinburgh Review*, the *Foreign Quarterly*, and some of the monthly magazines. His study of the German, acting upon an innate peculiarity, began to affect his style very sensibly, as is clearly seen in the singular, introverted, parenthetical mode of expression which pervades all his later works. His earlier writings are in ordinary English, but specimens of *Carlylese* may be found in his *Sartor Resartus*, which at first appalled the publishers and repelled the general reader. Taking man's clothing as a nominal subject, he plunges into philosophical speculations with which clothes have nothing to do, but which informed the world that an original thinker and a novel and curious writer had appeared.

In 1834 he removed to Chelsea, near London, where he has since resided. In 1837, he published his *French Revolution*, in three volumes, — *The Bastile*, *The Constitution*, *The Guillotine*. It is a fiery, historical drama rather than a history; full of rhapsodies, startling rhetoric, disconnected pictures. It has been fitly called "a history in flashes of lightning." No one could learn from it the history of that momentous period; but one who has read the history elsewhere, will find great interest in Carlyle's wild and vivid pictures of its stormy scenes.

In 1839 he wrote, in his dashing style, upon *Chartism*, and about the same time read a course of lectures upon *Heroes, Hero-Worship, and the Heroic in History*, in which he is an admirer of will and impulse, and palliates evil when found in combination with these.

In 1845 he edited *The Letters and Speeches of Oliver Cromwell*, and in his extravagant eulogies worships the hero rather than the truth.

FREDERICK II. — In 1858 appeared the first two volumes of *The Life of Frederick the Great*, and since that time he has completed the work. This is doubtless his greatest effort. It is full of erudition, and contains details not to be found in any other biography of the Prussian monarch; but so singularly has he reasoned and commented upon his facts, that the enlightened reader often draws conclusions different from those which the author has been laboring to establish. While the history shows that, for genius and success, Frederick deserved to be called the Great, Carlyle cannot make us believe that he was not grasping, selfish, a dissembler, and an immoral man.

The author's style has its admirers, and is a not unpleasing novelty and variety to lovers of plain English; but it wearies in continuance, and one turns to French or German with relief. The Essays upon *German Literature*, *Richter*, and *The Niebelungen Lied* are of great value to the young student. Such tracts as *Past and Present*, and *The Latter-Day Pamphlets*, have caused him to be called the "Censor of the Age." He is too eccentric and prejudiced to deserve the name in its best meaning. If he fights shams, he sometimes mistakes windmills and wine-skins for monsters, and, what is worse, if he accost a shepherd or a milkmaid, they at once become *Amadis de Gaul* and *Dulcinea del Toboso*. In spite of these prejudices and peculiarities, Carlyle will always be esteemed for his arduous labors, his honest intentions, and his boldness in expressing his opinions. His likes and dislikes find ready vent in his written judgments, and he cares for neither friend nor foe, in setting forth his views of men and events. On many subjects it must be said his views are just. There are fields in which his word must be received with authority.

Other Historians of the Latest Period.

John Lingard, 1771–1851: a Roman Catholic priest. He was a man of great probity and worth. His chief work is *A History of England*, from the first invasion of the Romans to the accession of William and Mary. With a natural leaning to his own religious side in the great political questions, he displays great industry in collecting material, beauty of diction, and honesty of purpose. His history is of particular value, in that it stands among the many Protestant histories as the champion of the Roman Catholics, and gives an opportunity to "hear the other side," which could not have had a more respectable advocate. In all the great controversies, the student of English history must consult Lingard, and collate his facts and opinions with those of the other historians. He wrote, besides, numerous theological and controversial works.

Patrick Fraser Tytler, 1791–1849: the author of *A History of Scotland from Alexander III. to James VI.* (*James I. of England*), and *A History of England during the reigns of Edward VI. and Mary*. His *Universal History* has been used as a text-book, and in style and construction has great merit, although he does not rise to the dignity of a philosophic historian.

Sir William Francis Patrick Napier, 1785–1866: a distinguished soldier, and, like Cæsar, a historian of the war in which he took part. His *History of the War in the Peninsula* stands quite alone. It is clear in its strategy and tactics, just to the enemy, and peculiar but effective in style. It was assailed by several military men, but he defended all his positions in bold replies to their strictures, and the work remains as authority upon the great struggle which he relates.

Lord Mahon, Earl of Stanhope, born 1805: his principal work is a *History of England from the Peace of Utrecht to the Peace of Versailles.* He had access to much new material, and from the Stuart papers has drawn much of interest with reference to that unfortunate family. His view of the conduct of Washington towards Major André has been shown to be quite untenable. He also wrote a *History of the War of Succession in Spain.*

Henry Thomas Buckle, 1822–1862: he was the author of a *History of Civilization*, of which he published two volumes, the work remaining unfinished at the time of his death. For bold assumptions, vigorous style, and great reading, this work must be greatly admired; but all his theories are based on second principles, and Christianity, as a divine institution, is ignored. It startled the world into admiration, but has not retained the place in popular esteem which it appeared at first to make for itself. He is the English *Comte*, without the eccentricity of his model.

Sir Archibald Alison, 1792–1867: he is the author of *The History of Europe from the Commencement of the French Revolution to the Restoration of the Bourbons*, and a continuation from 1815 to 1852. It may be doubted whether even the most dispassionate scholar can write the history of contemporary events. We may be thankful for the great mass of facts he has collated, but his work is tinctured with his high Tory principles; his material is not well digested, and his style is clumsy.

Agnes Strickland, born 1806: after several early attempts Miss Strickland began her great task, which she executed nobly — *The Queens of England.* Accurate, philosophic, anecdotal, and entertaining, this work ranks among the most valuable histories in English. If the style is not so nervous as that of masculine writers, there is a ready intuition as to the rights and the motives of the queens, and a great delicacy combined with entire lack of prudery in her treatment of their crimes. The library of English history would be singularly incomplete without Miss Strickland's work. She also wrote *The Queens of Scotland*, and *The Bachelor Kings of England.*

Henry Hallam, 1778–1859: the principal works of this judicious and learned writer are *A View of Europe during the Middle Ages*, *The Constitutional History of England*, and *An Introduction to the Literature of Europe* in the fifteenth, sixteenth, and seventeenth centuries. With the skill of an advocate he combines the calmness of a judge; and he has been justly called "the accurate Hallam," because his facts are in all cases to be depended on. By his clear and illustrative treatment of dry subjects, he has made them interesting; and his works have done as much to instruct his age as those of any writer. Later researches in literature and constitutional history may discover more than he has presented, but he taught the new explorers the way, and will always be consulted with profit, as the representative of this varied learning during the first half of the nineteenth century.

James Anthony Froude, born 1818: an Oxford graduate, Mr. Froude represents the Low Church party in a respectable minority. His chief work is *A History of England from the Fall of Wolsey to the Death of Elizabeth*. With great industry, and the style of a successful novelist in making his groups and painting his characters, he has written one of the most readable books published in this period. He claimed to take his authorities from unpublished papers, and from the statute-books, and has endeavored to show that Henry VIII. was by no means a bad king, and that Elizabeth had very few faults. His treatment of Anne Boleyn and Mary Queen of Scots is unjust and ignoble. Not content with publishing what has been written in their disfavor, with the omniscience of a romancer, he asserts their motives, and produces thoughts which they never uttered. A race of powerful critics has sprung forth in defence of Mary, and Mr. Froude's inaccuracies and injustice have been clearly shown. To novel readers who are fond of the sensational, we commend his work: to those who desire historic facts and philosophies, we proclaim it to be inaccurate, illogical, and unjust in the highest degree.

Sharon Turner, 1768–1847: among many historical efforts, principally concerning England in different periods, his *History of the Anglo-Saxons* stands out prominently as a great work. He was an eccentric scholar, and an antiquarian, and he found just the place to delve in when he undertook that history. The style is not good — too epigrammatic and broken; but his research is great, his speculations bold, and his information concerning the numbers, manners, arts, learning, and other characters of the Anglo-Saxons, immense. The student of English history must read Turner for a knowledge of the Saxon period.

Thomas Arnold, 1795–1832: widely known and revered as the Great Schoolmaster. He was head-master at Rugby, and influenced his pupils more than any modern English instructor. Accepting the views of Niebuhr, he wrote a work on *Roman History* up to the close of the second Punic war. But he is more generally known by his historical lectures delivered at Oxford, where he was Professor of Modern History. A man of original views and great honesty of purpose, his influence in England has been strengthened by the excellent biography written by his friend Dean Stanley.

William Hepworth Dixon, born 1821: he was for some time editor of *The Athenæum.* In historic biography he appears as a champion of men who have been maligned by former writers. He vindicates *William Penn* from the aspersions of Lord Macaulay, and *Bacon* from the charges of meanness and corruption.

Charles Merivale, born 1808: he is a clergyman, and a late Fellow of Cambridge, and is favorably known by his admirable work entitled, *The History of the Romans under the Empire.* It forms an introduction to Gibbon, and displays a thorough grasp of the great epoch, varied scholarship, and excellent taste. His analyses of Roman literature are very valuable, and his pictures of social life so vivid that we seem to live in the times of the Cæsars as we read.

CHAPTER XL.

THE LATER NOVELISTS AS SOCIAL REFORMERS.

Bulwer.	His Varied Powers.	Henry Esmond.
Changes in Writing.	Second Visit to America.	The Newcomes.
Dickens's Novels.	Thackeray.	The Georges.
American Notes.	Vanity Fair.	Estimate of his Powers.

THE great feature in the realm of prose fiction, since the appearance of the works of Richardson, Fielding, and Smollett, had been the Waverley novels of Sir Walter Scott; but these apart, the prose romance had not played a brilliant part in literature until the appearance of Bulwer, who began, in his youth, to write novels in the old style; but who underwent several organic changes in modes of thought and expression, and at last stood confessed as the founder of a new school.

BULWER. — Edward George Earle Lytton Bulwer was a younger son of General Bulwer of Heydon Hall, Norfolk, England. He was born, in 1806, to wealth and ease, but was early and always a student. Educated at Cambridge, he took the Chancellor's prize for a poem on *Sculpture*. His first public effort was a volume of fugitive poems, called *Weeds and Wild Flowers*, of more promise than merit. In 1827 he published *Falkland*, and very soon after *Pelham, or the Adventures of a Gentleman*. The first was not received favorably; but *Pelham* was at once popular, neither for the skill of the plot nor for its morality, but because it describes the character, dissipations, and good qualities of a fashionable young man, which are always interesting to an English public. Those novels that immediately followed are so alike in general features that they may be called the Pelham series. Of these the principal are *The Disowned*, *Devereux*, and *Paul Clifford* — the last of which throws a sentimental, rosy light upon the person and adventures of a highwayman; but it is too unreal to have done as much injury as the *Pirate's Own Book*, or the *Adventures of Jack Sheppard*. It may be safely asserted that *Paul Clifford* never produced a highwayman. Of the same period is *Eugene Aram*, founded upon the true story of a scholar who was a murderer — a painful subject powerfully handled.

In 1831 Bulwer entered Parliament, and seems to have at once commenced a new life. With his public duties he combined severe historical study; and the novels he now produced gave witness of his riper and better learning. Chief among these were *Rienzi*, and *The Last Days of Pompeii*. The former is based upon the history of that wonderful and unfortunate man who, in the fourteenth century, attempted to restore the Roman republic, and govern it like an ancient tribune. The latter is a noble production: he has caught the very spirit of the day in which Pompeii was submerged by the lava-flood; his characters are masterpieces of historic delineation; he handles like an adept the conflicting theologies, Christian, Roman, and Egyptian; and his natural scenes — Vesuvius in fury, the Bay of Naples in the lurid light, the crowded amphitheatre, and the terror which fell on man and beast, gladiator and lion — are *chef-d'œuvres* of Romantic art.

CHANGES IN WRITING. — For a time he edited *The New Monthly Magazine*, and a change came over the spirit of his novels. This was first noticed in his *Ernest Maltravers*, and the sequel, *Alice, or the Mysteries*, which are marked by sentimental passion and mystic ideas. In *Night and Morning* he is still mysterious: a blind fate seems to preside over his characters, robbing the good of its free merit and condoning the evil.

In 1838 he was made a baronet. His versatile pen now turned to the drama; and although he produced nothing great, his *Lady of Lyons*, *Richelieu*, *Money*, and *The Sea Captain* have always since been favorites upon the stage, subsidizing the talents of actors like Macready, Kean, and Edwin Booth.

We must now chronicle another change, from the mystic to the supernatural, as displayed in *Zanoni* and *Lucretia*, and especially in *A Strange Story*, which is the strangest of all. It was at the same period that he wrote *The Last of the Barons*, or the story of Warwick the king-maker, and *Harold, the Last of the Saxon Kings*. Both are valuable to the student of English history as presenting the fruits of his own historic research.

The last and most decided, and, we may add, most beneficial, change in Bulwer as a writer, was manifested in his publication of the *Caxtons*, the chief merit of which is as an usher of the novels which were to follow. Pisistratus Caxton is the modern Tristram Shandy, and becomes the putative editor of the later novels. First of these is *My Novel, or Varieties of English Life*. It is an admirable work: it inculcates a better morality, and a sense of Christian duty, at which Pelham would have laughed in scorn. Like it, but inferior to it, is *What Will He do with It?* which has an interesting plot, an elevated style, and a rare human sympathy.

Among other works, which we cannot mention, he wrote *The New Timon*, and *King Arthur*, in poetry, and a prose history entitled *Athens, its Rise and Fall*.

Without the highest genius, but with uncommon scholarship and great versatility, Bulwer has used the materials of many kinds lying about him, to make marvellous mosaics, which imitate very closely the finest efforts of word-painting of the great geniuses of prose fiction.

CHARLES DICKENS. — Another remarkable development of

the age was the use of prose fiction, instead of poetry, as the vehicle of satire in the cause of social reform. The world consents readily to be amused, and it likes to be amused at the expense of others; but it soon tires of what is simply amusing or satirical unless some noble purpose be disclosed. The novels of former periods had interested by the creation of character and scenes; and there had been numerous satires prompted by personal pique. It is the glory of this latest age that it demands what shall so satirize the evil around it in men, in classes, in public institutions, that the evil shall recoil before the attack, and eventually disappear. Chief among such reformers are Dickens and Thackeray.

Charles Dickens, the prince of modern novelists, was born at Landsport, Portsmouth, England, in 1812. His father was at the time a clerk in the Pay Department of the Navy, but afterwards became a reporter of debates in Parliament. After a very hard early life and an only tolerable education, young Dickens made some progress in the study of law; but soon undertook his father's business as reporter, in which he struggled as he has made David Copperfield to do in becoming proficient.

His first systematic literary efforts were as a daily writer and reporter for *The True Sun;* he then contributed his sketches of life and character, drawn from personal observation, to the *Morning Chronicle:* these were an earnest of his future powers. They were collected as *Sketches by Boz,* in two volumes, and published in 1836.

PICKWICK. — In 1837 he was asked by a publisher to prepare a series of comic sketches of cockney sportsmen, to illustrate, as well as to be illustrated by, etchings by Seymour. This yoking of two geniuses was a trammel to both; but the suicide of Seymour dissolved the connection, and Dickens had free play to produce the *Pickwick Papers,* by Boz, which were illustrated, as he proceeded, by H. K. Browne (Phiz).

The work met and has retained an unprecedented popularity. Caricature as it was, it caricatured real, existent oddities; everything was probable; the humor was sympathetic if farcical, the assertion of humanity bold, and the philosophy of universal application. He had touched our common nature in all ranks and conditions; he had exhibited men and women of all types; he had exposed the tricks of politics and the absurdity of elections; the snobs of society were severely handled. He was the censor of law courts, the exposer of swindlers, the dread of cockneys, the friend of rustics and of the poor; and he has displayed in the principal character, that of the immortal Pickwick, the power of a generous, simple-hearted, easily deceived, but always philanthropic man, who comes through all his trials without bating a jot of his love for humanity and his faith in human nature. But the master-work of his plastic hand was Sam Weller, whose wit and wisdom pervaded both hemispheres, and is as potent to excite laughter to-day as at the first.

In this work he began that assault, not so much on shams as upon prominent, unblushing evil, which he carried on in some form or other in all his later works; and which was to make him prominent among the reformers and benefactors of his age. He was at once famous, and his pen was in demand to amuse the idle and to aid the philanthropic.

NICHOLAS NICKLEBY.— The *Pickwick Papers* were in their intention a series of sketches somewhat desultory and loosely connected. His next work was *Nicholas Nickleby*, a complete story, in which he was entirely successful. Wonderful in the variety and reality of his characters, his powerful satire was here principally directed against the private boarding-schools in England, where unloved children, exiled and forgotten, were ill fed, scantily clothed, untaught, and beaten. Do-the-boys' Hall was his type, and many a school prison under that name was fearfully exposed and scourged.

The people read with wonder and applause; these haunts of cruelty were scrutinized, some of them were suppressed; and since Nicholas Nickleby appeared no such school can live, because Squeers and Smike are on every lip, and punishment awaits the tyrant.

Our scope will not permit a review of his numerous novels. In *Oliver Twist* he denounces the parish system in its care of orphans, and throws a Drummond light upon the haunts of crime in London.

The Old Curiosity Shop exposes the mania of gaming, and seems to have been a device for presenting the pathetic pictures of *Little Nell* and her grandfather, the wonderful and rapid learning of the marchioness, and the uncommon vitality of Mr. Richard Swiveller; and also the compound of will and hideousness in Quilp.

He affected to find in the receptacle of Master Humphrey's clock, his *Barnaby Rudge*, a very dramatic picture of the great riot incited by Lord George Gordon in 1780, which, in its gathering, its fury, and its easy dispersion, was not unlike that of Wat Tyler. Dickens's delineations are eminently historic, and present a better notion of the period than the general history itself.

AMERICAN NOTES. — In 1841 Dickens visited America, where he was received by the public with great enthusiasm, and annoyed, as the author of his biography says, by many individuals. On his return to England, he produced his *American Notes for General Circulation.* They were sarcastic, superficial, and depreciatory, and astonished many whose hospitalities he had received. But, in 1843, he published *Martin Chuzzlewit*, in which American peculiarities are treated with the broadest caricature. The *Notes* might have been forgiven; but the novel excited a great and just anger in America. His statements were not true; his pictures were not just; his prejudice led him to malign a people who had received him with a foolish hospitality. He had eaten and drunk at the hands of the men whom he abused, and his character suffered more than that of his intended victims. In taking a few foibles for his caricature, he had left our merits untold, and had been guilty of the implication that we had none, although he knew that there were as elegant gentlemen, as refined ladies, and as cultivated society in America as the best in England. But a truce to reproaches; he has been fully forgiven.

His next novel was *Dombey and Son*, in which he attacks British pomp and pride of state in the haughty merchant. It is full of character and of pathos. Every one knows, as if they had appeared among us, the proud and rigid Dombey, J. B. the sly, the unhappy Floy, the exquisite Toots, the inimitable Nipper, Sol Gills the simple, and Captain Cuttle with his hook and his notes.

This was followed by *David Copperfield*, which is, to some extent, an autobiography describing the struggles of his youth, his experience in acquiring short-hand to become a reporter, and other vicissitudes of his own life. In it there is an attack upon the system of model prisons; but the chief interest is found in his wonderful portraitures of varied and opposite characters: the Peggottys, Steerforth, the inimitable Micawber, Betsy Trotwood; Agnes, the lovely and lovable; Mr. Dick, with such noble method in his madness; Dora, the child-wife; the simple Traddles, and Uriah Heep, the 'umble intriguer and villain.

Bleak House is a tremendous onslaught upon the Chancery system, and is said to have caused a modification of it; his knowledge of law gave him the power of an expert in detailing and dissecting its enormities.

Little Dorrit presents the heartlessness of society, and is besides a full and fearful picture of the system of imprisonment for debt. For variety, power, and pathos, it is one of his best efforts.

A Tale of Two Cities is a gloomy but vivid story of the French Revolution, which has by no means the popularity of his other works.

In *Hard Times*, a shorter story, he has shown the evil consequences of a hard, statistical, cramming education, in which the sympathies are repressed, and the mind made a practical machine. The failure of Gradgrind has warned many a parent from imitating him.

Great Expectations failed to fulfil the promise of the name; but Joe Gargery is as original a character as any he had drawn.

His last completed story is *Our Mutual Friend*, which, although unequal to his best novels, has still original characters and striking scenes. The rage for rising in the social scale ruins the Veneerings, and Podsnappery is a well-chosen name for the heartless dogmatism which rules in English society.

Besides these splendid works, we must mention the delight he has given, and the good he has done in expanding individual and public charity, by his exquisite Christmas stories, of which *The Chimes*, *The Christmas Carol*, and *The Cricket on the Hearth* are the best.

His dramatic power has been fully illustrated by the ready adaptations of his novels to the stage; they are, indeed, in scenes, personages, costume, and interlocution, dramas in all except the form; and he himself was an admirable actor.

HIS VARIED POWERS. — His tenderness is touching, and his pathos at once excites our sympathy. He does not tell us to feel or to weep, but he shows us scenes like those in the life of Smike, and in the sufferings and death of Little Nell, which so simply appeal to the heart that we are for the time forgetful of the wand which conjures them before us.

Dickens is bold in the advocacy of truth and in denouncing error; he is the champion of honest poverty; he is the foe of class pretension and oppression; he is the friend of friendless children; the reformer of those whom society has made vagrants. Without many clear assertions of Christian doctrine, but with no negation of it, he believes in doing good for its own sake,—in self-denial, in the rewards which virtue gives herself. His faults are few and venial. His merry life smacks too much of the practical joke and the punch-bowl; he denounces cant in the self-appointed ministers of the gospel, but he is not careful to draw contrasted pictures of good pastors. His opinion seems to be based upon a human perfectibility. But for rare pictures of real life he has never been surpassed; and he has instructed an age, concerning itself, wisely, originally, and usefully. He has the simplicity of Goldsmith, and the truth to nature of Fielding and Smollett, without a spice of sentimentalism or of impurity; he has brought the art of prose fiction to its highest point, and he has left no worthy successor. He lived for years separated from his wife on the ground of incompatibility, and, during his later years at Gadshill, twenty miles from London, to avoid the dissipations and draughts upon his time in that city.

SECOND VISIT TO AMERICA.—In 1868 he again visited America, to read portions of his own works. He was well received by the public; but society had learned its lesson on his former visit, and he was not overwhelmed with a hospitality he had so signally failed to appreciate. And if we had learned better, he had vastly improved; the genius had become a gentleman. His readings were a great pecuniary success, and at their close he made an amend which was graceful and proper; so that when he departed from our shores his former errors were fully condoned, and he left an admiring hemisphere behind him.

In the glow of health, and while writing, in serial numbers, a very promising novel entitled *The Mystery of Edwin Drood*, he was struck by apoplexy, in June, 1870, and in a few hours was dead. England has hardly experienced a greater loss. All classes of men mourned when he was buried in Westminster Abbey, in the poets' corner, among illustrious writers, — a prose-poet, none of whom has a larger fame than he; a historian of his time of greater value to society than any who distinctively bear the title. His characters are drawn from life; his own experience is found in *Nicholas Nickleby* and *David Copperfield; Micawber* is a caricature of his own father. *Traddles* is said to represent his friend Talfourd. *Skimpole* is supposed to be an original likeness of Leigh Hunt, and William and Daniel Grant, of Manchester, were the originals of the *Brothers Cheeryble.*

WILLIAM MAKEPEACE THACKERAY. — Dickens gives us real characters in the garb of fiction; but Thackeray uses fiction as the vehicle of social philosophy. Great name, second only to Dickens; he is not a story-teller, but an eastern Cadi administering justice in the form of apologue. Dickens is eminently dramatic; Thackeray has nothing dramatic, neither scene nor personage. He is Democritus the laughing philosopher, or Jupiter the thunderer; he arraigns vice, pats virtue on the shoulder, shouts for muscular Christianity, uncovers shams, — his personages are only names. Dickens describes individuals; Thackeray only classes: his men and women are representatives, and, with but few exceptions, they excite our sense of justice, but not our sympathy; the principal exception is *Colonel Newcome*, a real individual creation upon whom Thackeray exhausted his genius, and he stands alone.

Thackeray was born in Calcutta, of an old Yorkshire family, in 1811. His father was in the civil service, and he was sent home, when a child of seven, for his education at the Charter House in London. Thence he was entered at Cambridge, but left without being graduated. An easy fortune of £20,000 led him to take life easily; he studied painting with somewhat of the desultory devotion he has ascribed to Clive Newcome, and, like that worthy, travelled on the Continent. Partly by unsuccessful investments, and partly by careless living, his means were spent, and he took up writing as a profession. The comic was his forte, and his early pieces, written under the pseudonym of Michael Angelo Fitzmarsh and George Fitz Boodle, are broadly humorous, but by no means in his later finished style. *The Great Hoggarty Diamond* (1841) did not disclose his full powers.

In 1841, *Punch*, a weekly comic illustrated sheet, was begun, and it opened to Thackeray a field which exactly suited him. Short scraps of comedy, slightly connected sketches, and the weekly tale of brick, chimed with his humor, and made him at once a favorite. The best of these serial contributions were *The Snob Papers:* they are as fine specimens of humorous satire as exist in the language. But these would not have made him famous, as they did not disclose his power as a novelist.

VANITY FAIR. — This was done by his *Vanity Fair*, which was published, in monthly numbers, between 1846 and 1848. It was at once popular, and is the most artistic of all his works. He called it a novel without a hero, and he is right; the mind repudiates all aspirants for the post, and settles upon poor Major Sugar-Plums as the best man in it. He could not have said *without a heroine*, for does not the world since ring with the fame of Becky Sharpe, the cleverest and wickedest little woman in England? The virtuous reader even is sorry that Becky must come to grief, as, with a propei respect to morality, the novelist makes her.

Never had the Vanity Fair of European society received so scathing a dissection; and its author was immediately recognized as one of the greatest living satirists and novelists. If he adheres more to the old school of Fielding, who was his model, in his plots and handling of the story, he was evidently original in his satire.

In 1847, upon the completion of this work, he began his *History of Pendennis*, in serial numbers, in which he presents the hero, Arthur Pendennis, as an average youth of the day, full of faults and foibles, but likewise generous and repentant. Here he enlists the sympathies which one never feels for perfection; and here, too, he portrays female loveliness and endurance in his Mrs. Pendennis and Laura. Arthur is a purer Tom Jones and Laura a superior Sophia Western.

In 1851 he gave a course of lectures, repeated in America the next year, on "the English Humorists of the Eighteenth Century." There was no one better fitted to write such a course; he felt with them and was of them. But if this enabled him to present them sympathetically, it also caused him to overrate them, and in some cases to descend to the standpoint of their own partial views. He is wrong in his estimate of Swift, and too eulogistic of Addison; but he is thoroughly English in both.

HENRY ESMOND. — The study of history necessary to prepare these led to his undertaking a novel on the time of Queen Anne, entitled *The History of Henry Esmond, Esq., written by himself.* His appreciation of the age is excellent; but the book, leaving for the most part the comic field in which he was most at home, is drier and less read than his others; as an historical presentation a great success, with rare touches of pathos; as a work of fiction not equal to his other stories. The comic muse assumes a tragic, or at least a very sombre, dress. We have a portraiture of Queen Anne in her last days, and a sad picture of him who, to the Protestant succession, was the pretender, and to the hopeful Jacobites, James III. The character of Marlborough is given with but little of what was really meritorious in that great captain.

His novel of *Pendennis* gave him, after the manner of Bulwer's *Caxton*, an editor in *Arthur Pendennis*, who presents us *The Newcomes, Memoirs of a Most Respectable Family*, which he published in a serial form, completing it in 1855.

THE NEWCOMES. — In that work we have the richest culture, the finest satire, and the rarest social philosophy. The character — the hero by pre-eminence — is Colonel Newcome, a nobleman of nature's creation, generous, simple, a yearningly affectionate father, a friend to all the poor and afflicted, one of the best men ever delineated by a novelist; few hearts are so hard as not to be touched by the story of his death in his final retirement at the Charter House. When, surrounded by weeping friends, he heard the bell, "a peculiar sweet smile shone over his face, and he lifted up his head a little, and quickly said 'Adsum,' and fell back: it was the word we used at school when names were called; and, lo! he, whose heart was that of a little child, had answered to his name, and stood in the presence of the Master."

THE GEORGES. — While he was writing *The Newcomes*, he had prepared a course of four lectures on the *Four Georges*, kings of England, with which he made his second visit to the United States, and which he delivered in the principal cities, to make a fund for his daughters and for his old age. It was entirely successful, and he afterwards read them in England and Scotland. They are very valuable historically, as they give us the truth with regard to men whose reigns were brilliant and on the whole prosperous, but who themselves, with the exception of the third of the name, were as bad men as ever wore crowns. George III. was continent and honest, but a maniac, and Mr. Thackeray has treated him with due forbearance and eulogy.

In 1857, Mr. Thackeray was a candidate for Parliament

from Oxford, but was defeated by a small majority; his conduct in the election was so magnanimous, that his defeat may be regarded as an advantage to his reputation.

In the same year he began *The Virginians,* which may be considered his failure; it is historically a continuation of *Esmond,* — some of the English characters, the Esmonds in Virginia, being the same as in that work. But his presentation and estimate of Washington are a caricature, and his sketch of General James Wolfe, the hero of Quebec, is tame and untrue to life. His descriptions of Virginia colonial life are unlike the reality; but where he is on his own ground, describing English scenes and customs in that day, he is more successful. To paint historical characters is beyond the power of his pencil, and his Doctor Johnson is not the man whom Boswell has so successfully presented.

In 1860 he originated the *Cornhill Magazine,* to which his name gave unusual popularity: it attained a circulation of one hundred thousand — unprecedented in England. In that he published *Lovel the Widower,* which was not much liked, and a charming reproduction of the Newcomes,—for it is nothing more,—entitled *The Adventures of Philip on His Way through the World.* Philip is a more than average Englishman, with a wicked father and rather a stupid wife; but "the little sister" is a star — there is no finer character in any of his works. *Philip,* in spite of its likeness to *The Newcomes,* is a delightful book.

With an achieved fame, a high position, a home which he had just built at Kensington, a large income, he seemed to have before him as prosperous an old age as any one could desire, when, such are the mysteries of Providence, he was found dead in his room on the morning of December 24, 1863.

ESTIMATE OF HIS POWERS. — Thackeray's excellences are manifest: he was the master of idiomatic English, a great moralist and reformer, and the king of satire, all the weapons of which he managed with perfect skill. He had a rapier for aristocratic immunities of evil, arrows to transfix prescriptions and shams; and with snobs (we must change the figure) he played as a cat does with a mouse, torturing and then devouring. In the words of Miss Bronté, "he was the first social regenerator of the day, the very master of that working corps who would restore to rectitude the warped system of things." But this was his chief and glorious strength: in the truest sense, he was a satirist and a humorist, but not a novelist; he could not create character. His dramatic persons do not speak for themselves; he tells us what they are and do. His mission seems to have been to arraign and demolish evil rather than to applaud good, and thus he enlists our sinless anger as crusaders rather than our sympathy as philanthropists. In Dickens we are sometimes disposed to skip a little, in our ardor, to follow the plot and find the denouement. In Thackeray we read every word, for it is the philosophy we want; the plot and personages are secondary, as indeed he considered them; for he often tells us, in the time of greatest depression of his hero, that it will all come out right at the end,—that Philip will marry Charlotte, and have a good income, while the poor soul is wrestling with the *res augusta domi*. Dickens and Thackeray seemed to draw from each other in their later works; the former philosophizing more in his *Little Dorrit* and *Our Mutual Friend*, and the latter attempting more of the descriptive in *The Newcomes* and *Philip*. Of minor pieces we may mention his *Rebecca* and *Rowena*, and his *Kickleburys on the Rhine;* his *Essay on Thunder* and *Small Beer;* his *Notes on a Journey from Cornhill to Grand Cairo*, in 1846, and his published collection of smaller sketches called *The Roundabout Papers*. That Thackeray was fully conscious of the dignity of his functions may be gathered from his own words in *Henry Esmond*. "I would have history familiar rather than heroic, and think

Mr. Hogarth and Mr. Fielding [and, we may add, Mr. Thackeray,] will give our children a much better idea of the manners of that age in England than the *Court Gazette* and the newspapers which we get thence." At his death he left an unfinished novel, entitled *Dennis Duval.* A gifted daughter, who was his kind amanuensis, Miss ANNE E. THACKERAY, has written several interesting tales, among which are *The Village on the Cliff* and *The Story of Elizabeth.*

CHAPTER XLI.

THE LATER WRITERS.

Charles Lamb.	Thomas de Quincey.	Writers on Science and
Thomas Hood.	Other Novelists.	Philosophy.

Charles Lamb. — This distinguished writer, although not a novelist like Dickens and Thackeray, in the sense of having produced extensive works of fiction, was, like them, a humorist and a satirist, and has left miscellaneous works of rare merit. He was born in London, and was the son of a servant to one of the Benches of the Inner Temple; he was educated at Christ's Hospital, where he became the warm friend of Coleridge. In 1792 he received an appointment as clerk in the South Sea House, which he retained until 1825, when, owing to the distinction he had obtained in the world of letters, he was permitted to retire with a pension of £450. He describes his feelings on this happy release from business, in his essay on *The Superannuated Man.* He was an eccentric man, a serio-comic character, whose sad life is singularly contrasted with his irrepressible humor. His sister, whom he has so tenderly described as Bridget Elia, in a fit of insanity killed their mother with a carving-knife, and Lamb devoted himself to her care.

He was a poet, and left quaint and beautiful album verses and minor pieces. As a dramatist, he is known by his tragedy *John Woodvil,* and the farce *Mr. H——,* neither of which was a success. But he has given us in his *Specimens of Old English Dramatists* the result of great reading and rare criticism.

But it is chiefly as a writer of essays and short stories that he is distinguished. The *Essays of Elia,* in their vein, mark an era in the literature; they are light, racy, seemingly dashed off, but really full of his reading of the older English authors. Indeed, he is so quaint in thought and style, that he seems an anachronism—a writer of the Elizabethan period returned to life in this century. He bubbles over with puns, jests, and repartees; and although not popular in the sense of reaching the multitude, he is the friend and companion of congenial readers. Among his essays, we may mention the stories of *Rosamund Gray* and *Old Blind Margaret. Dream Children* and *The Child Angel* are those of greatest power; but every one he has written is charming. His sly hits at existing abuses are designed to laugh them away. He was the favorite of his literary circle, and as a talker had no superior. After a life of care, not unmingled with pleasures, he died in 1834. Lamb's letters are racy, witty, idiomatic, and unlabored; and, as most of them are to colleagues in literature and on subjects of social and literary interest, they are important aids in studying the history of his period.

THOMAS HOOD. — The greatest humorist, the best punster, and the ablest satirist of his age, Hood attacked the social evils around him with such skill and power that he stands forth as a philanthropist. He was born in London in 1798, and, after a limited education, he began to learn the art of engraving; but his pen was more powerful than his burin. He soon began to contribute to the *London Magazine* his *Whims and Oddities;* and, in irregular verse, satirized the would-be great men of the time, and the eccentric legislation they proposed in Parliament. These short poems are full of puns and happy *jeux de mots,* and had a decided effect in frustrating the foolish plans. After this he published *National Tales,* in the same comic vein; but also produced his exquisite serious pieces, *The Plea of the Midsummer Fairies, Hero and Leander*, and others, all of which are striking and tasteful. In 1838 he commenced *The Comic Annual*, which appeared for several years, brimful of mirth and fun. He was editor of various magazines,— *The New Monthly*, and *Hood's Magazine*. For *Punch* he wrote *The Song of the Shirt*, and *The Bridge of Sighs*. No one can compute the good done by both; the hearts touched; the pockets opened. The sewing women were better paid, more cared for, elevated in the social scale; and many of them saved from that fate which is so touchingly chronicled in *The Bridge of Sighs*. Hood was a true poet and a great poet. *Miss Kilmansegg and her Precious Leg* is satire, story, epic, comedy, in one.

If he owed to Smollett's *Humphrey Clinker* the form of his *Up the Rhine*, he has equalled Smollett in the narrative, in the variety of character, and in the admirable cacography of Martha Penny. His caricatures fasten facts in the memory, and every tourist up the Rhine recognizes Hood's personages wherever he lands.

After a life of ill-health and pecuniary struggle, Hood died, greatly lamented, on the 3d of May, 1845, and left no successor to wield his subtle pen.

THOMAS DE QUINCEY (1785–1859).— This singular author, and very learned and original thinker, owes much of his reputation to the evil habit of opium-eating, which affected his personal life and authorship. His most popular work is *The Confessions of an English Opium-Eater*, which interests the reader by its curious pictures of the abnormal conditions in which he lived and wrote. He abandoned this noxious practice in the year 1820. He produced much which he did not publish; and his writings all contain a suggestion of strength and scholarship, a surplus beyond what he has given to the world. There are numerous essays and narratives, among which his paper entitled *Murder considered as One of the Fine Arts* is especially notable. His prose is considered a model of good English.

The death of Dickens and Thackeray left England without a novelist of equal fame and power, but with a host of scholarly and respectable pens, whose productions delight the popular taste, and who are still in the tide of busy authorship.

Our purpose is already accomplished, and we might rest without the proceeding beyond the middle of the century; but it will be proper to make brief mention of those, some of whom have already departed, but many of whom still remain, and are producing new works, who best illustrate the historical value and teachings of English literature, and whose writings will be read in the future for their delineations of the habits and conditions of the present period.

Other Novelists.

Captain Frederick Marryat, of the Royal Navy, 1792–1848: in his sea novels depicts naval life with rare fidelity, and with a roystering joviality which makes them extremely entertaining. The principal of these are *Frank Mildmay*, *Newton Forster*, *Peter Simple*, and *Midshipman Easy*. His works constitute a truthful portrait of the British Navy in the beginning of the eighteenth century, and have influenced many high-spirited youths to choose a maritime profession.

George P. R. James, 1806–1860: is the author of nearly two hundred novels, chiefly historical, which have been, in their day, popular. It was soon found, however, that he repeated himself, and the sameness of handling began to tire his readers. His "two travellers," with whom he opens his stories, have become proverbially ridiculous. But he has depicted scenes in modern history with skill, and especially in French history. His *Richelieu* is a favorite; and in his *Life of Charlemagne* he has brought together the principal events in the career of that distinguished monarch with logical force and historical accuracy.

Benjamin d'Israeli, born 1805: is far more famous as a persevering, acute, and able statesman than as a novelist. In proof of this, having surmounted unusual difficulties, he has been twice Chancellor of the Exchequer and once Prime Minister of England. Among his earlier novels, which are pictures of existing society, are: *Vivian Gray*, *Contarini Fleming*, *Coningsby*, and *Henrietta Temple*. In *The Wondrous Tale of Alroy* he has described the career of that singular claimant to the Jewish Messiahship. *Lothair*, which was published in 1869, is the story of a young nobleman who was almost enticed to enter the Roman Catholic Church. The descriptions of society are either very much overwrought or ironical; but his knowledge of State craft and Church craft renders the book of great value to the history of religious polemics. His father, *Isaac d'Israeli*, is favorably known as the author of *The Curiosities of Literature*, *The Amenities of Literature*, and *The Quarrels of Authors*.

Charles Lever, 1806–1872: he was born in Dublin, and, after a partial University career, studied medicine. He has embodied his experience of military life in several striking but exaggerated works, — among these are: *The Confessions of Harry Lorrequer*, *Charles O'Malley*, and *Jack Hinton*. He excels in humor and in picturesque battle-scenes, and he has painted the age in caricature. Of its kind, *Charles O'Malley* stands pre-eminent: the variety of character is great; all classes of military men figure in the scenes, from the Duke of Wellington to the inimitable Mickey Free. He was for some time editor of the *Dublin University Magazine*, and has written numerous other novels, among which are: *Roland Cashel*, *The Knight of Gwynne*, and *The Dodd Family Abroad;* and, last of all, *Lord Kilgobbin*.

Charles Kingsley, born 1809: this accomplished clergyman, who is a canon of Chester, is among the most popular English writers, — a poet, a novelist, and a philosopher. He was first favorably known by a poetical drama on the story of St. Elizabeth of Hungary, entitled *The Saint's Tragedy*. Among his other works are: *Alton Locke, Tailor and Poet; Hypatia, the Story of a Virgin Martyr; Andromeda; Westward Ho! or the Adventures of Sir Amyas Leigh; Two Years Ago;* and *Hereward, the Last of the English*. This last is a very vivid historical picture of the way in which the man of the fens, under the lead of this powerful outlaw, held out against William the Conqueror. The busy pen of Kingsley has produced numerous lectures, poems, reviews, essays, and some plain and useful sermons. He is now Professor of Modern History at Cambridge.

Charlotte Brontë, 1816–1855: if of an earlier period, this gifted woman would demand a far fuller mention and a more critical notice than can be with justice given of a contemporary. She certainly wrote from the depths of her own consciousness. *Jane Eyre*, her first great work, was received with intense interest, and was variously criticized. The daughter of a poor clergyman at Haworth, and afterwards a teacher in a school at Brussels, with little knowledge of the world, she produced a powerful book containing much curious philosophy, and took rank at once among the first novelists of the age. Her other works, if not equal to *Jane Eyre*, are still of great merit, and deal profoundly with the springs of human action. They are: *The Professor*, *Villette*, and *Shirley*. Her characters are portraits of the men and women around her, painted from life; and she speaks boldly of motives and customs which other novelists have touched very delicately. She had two gifted sisters, who were also successful novelists; but who died young. Miss Brontë died a short time after her marriage to Mr. Nichol, her father's curate. *Mrs. Elizabeth Gaskell*, her near friend, and the author of a successful novel called *Mary Barton*, has written an interesting biography of Mrs. Nichol.

George Eliot, born 1820: under this pseudonym, Miss Evans has written several works of great interest. Among these are: *Adam Bede; The Mill on the Floss; Romola*, an Italian story; *Felix Holt;* and *Silas Marner*. Simple, and yet eminently dramatic in scene, character, and interlocution, George Eliot has painted pictures from middle and common life, and is thus the exponent of a large humanity. She is now the wife of the popular author, G. H. Lewes.

Dinah Maria Muloch (Mrs. Craik), born 1826: a versatile writer. She is best known by her novels entitled *John Halifax* and *The Ogilvies*.

Wilkie Collins, born 1824: he is the son of a landscape-painter, and is renowned for his curious and well-concealed plots, phantom-like characters, and striking effects. Among his novels the best known are: *Antonina, The Dead Secret, The Woman in White, No Name, Armadale, The Moonstone*, and *Man and Wife*. There is a sameness in these works; and yet it is evident that the author has put his invention on the rack to create new intrigues, and to mystify his reader from the beginning to the end of each story.

Charles Reade, born 1814: he is one of the most prolific writers of the day, as well as one of the most readable in all that he has written. He draws many impassioned scenes, and is as sensuous in literature as Rubens in art Among his principal works are: *White Lies, Love Me Little, Love Me Long; The Cloister and The Hearth; Hard Cash*, and *Griffith Gaunt*, which convey little, if any, practical instruction. His *Never Too Late to Mend* is of great value in displaying the abuses of the prison system in England; and his *Put Yourself in His Place* is a very powerful attack upon the Trades' Unions. A singular epigrammatic style keeps up the interest apart from the story.

Mary Russell Mitford, 1786–1855: she was a poet and a dramatist, but is chiefly known by her stories. In the collection called *Our Vil-*

lage, she has presented beautiful and simple pictures of English country life which are at once touching and instructive.

Charlotte Mary Yonge, born 1823: among the many interesting works of this author, *The Heir of Redclyff* is the first and best. This was followed by *Daisy Chain*, *Heartsease*, *The Clever Woman of the Family*, and numerous other works of romance and of history,—all of which are valuable for their high tone of moral instruction and social manners.

Anthony Trollope, born 1815: he and his brother, Thomas Adolphus Trollope, are sons of that Mrs. Frances Trollope who abused our country in her work entitled *The Domestic Manners of the Americans*, in terms that were distasteful even to English critics. Anthony Trollope is a successful writer of society-novels, which, without being of the highest order, are faithful in their portraitures. Among those which have been very popular are: *Barchester Towers*, *Framley Parsonage*, *Doctor Thorne*, and *Orley Farm*. He travelled in the United States, and has published a work of discernment entitled *North America*. His brother Thomas is best known by his *History of Florence to the Fall of the Republic*.

Thomas Hughes, born 1823: the popular author of *Tom Brown's School-Days at Rugby*, and *Tom Brown at Oxford*,—books which display the workings of these institutions, and set up a standard for English youth. The first is the best, and has made him famous.

Writers on Science and Philosophy.

Although these do not come strictly within the scope of English literature, they are so connected with it in the composition of general culture, and give such a complexion to the age, that it is well to mention the principal names.

Sir William Hamilton, 1788–1856: for twenty years Professor of Logic and Metaphysics in the University of Edinburgh. His voluminous lectures on both these subjects were edited, after his death, by Mansel and Veitch, and have been since of the highest authority.

William Whewell, 1795–1866: for some time Master of Trinity College, Cambridge. He has written learnedly on many subjects: his most valuable works are: *A History of the Inductive Sciences*, *The Elements of Morality*, and *The Plurality of Worlds*. Of Whewell it has been pithily said, that "science was his forte, and omniscience his foible."

Richard Whately, D.D., 1787–1863: he was appointed in 1831 Archbishop of Dublin and Kildare, in Ireland. His chief works are: *Elements of Logic*, *Elements of Rhetoric*, and *Lectures on Political Economy*. He gave a new impetus to the study of Logic and Rhetoric, and presented the formal logic of Aristotle anew to the world; thus marking a distinct epoch in the history of that much controverted science.

John Ruskin, born 1819: he ranks among the most original critics in art; but is eccentric in his opinions. His powers were first displayed in his *Modern Painters*. In his *Seven Lamps of Architecture* he has laid down the great fundamental principles of that art, among the forms of which the Gothic claims the pre-eminence. These are further carried out in *The Stones of Venice*. He is a transcendentalist and a pre-Raphaelite, and exceedingly dogmatic in stating his views. His descriptive powers are very great.

Hugh Miller, 1802–1856: an uneducated mechanic, he was a brilliant genius and an observant philosopher. His best works are: *The Old Red Sandstone*, *Footprints of the Creator*, and *The Testimonies of the Rocks*. He shot himself in a fit of insanity.

John Stuart Mill, born 1806: the son of James Mill, the historian of India. He was carefully educated, and has written on many subjects. He is best known by his *System of Logic;* his work on *Political Economy;* and his *Treatise on Liberty*. Each of these topics being questions of controversy, Mr. Mill states his views strongly in respect to opposing systems, and is very clear in the expression of his own dogmas.

Thomas Chalmers, D. D., 1780–1847: this distinguished divine won his greatest reputation as an eloquent preacher. He was for some time Professor of Moral Philosophy in the University of St. Andrew's, and wrote on *Natural Theology*, *The Evidences of Christianity*, and some lectures on *Astronomy*. But all his works are glowing sermons rather than philosophical treatises.

Richard Chevenix Trench, D. D., born 1807: the present Archbishop of Dublin. He has written numerous theological works of popular value, among which are *Notes on the Parables, and on Miracles*. He has also published two series of charming lectures on English philology, entitled *The Study of Words* and *English Past and Present*. They are suggestive and discursive rather than philosophical, but have incited many persons to pursue this delightful study.

Arthur Penrhyn Stanley, D.D., born 1815: Dean of Westminster. He was first known by his excellent biography of Dr. Arnold of Rugby; but has since enriched biblical literature by his lectures on *The Eastern Church* and on *The Jewish Church*. He accompanied the Prince of

40*

Wales on his visit to Palestine, and was not only eager in collecting statistics, but has reproduced them with poetic power.

Nicholas Wiseman, D.D., 1802–1865: the head of the Roman Catholic Church in England. Cardinal Wiseman has written much on theological and ecclesiastical questions; but he is best known to the literary world by his able lectures on *The Connection between Science and Revealed Religion*, which are additionally valuable because they have no sectarian character.

Charles Darwin, born 1809: although he began his career at an early age, his principal works are so immediately of the present time, and his speculations are so involved in serious controversies, that they are not within the scope of this work. His principal works are: *The Origin of Species by means of Natural Selection*, and *The Descent of Man*. His facts are curious and very carefully selected; but his conclusions have been severely criticized.

Frederick Max Müller, born 1823: a German by birth. He is a professional Oxford, and has done more to popularize the Science of Language than any other writer. He has written largely on Oriental linguistics, and has given two courses of lectures on *The Science of Language*, which have been published, and are used as text-books. His *Chips from a German Workshop* is a charming book, containing his miscellaneous articles in reviews and magazines.

CHAPTER XLII.

ENGLISH JOURNALISM.

ROMAN NEWS LETTERS. —English serials and periodicals, from the very time of their origin, display, in a remarkable manner, the progress both of English literature and of English history, and form the most striking illustration that the literature interprets the history. In using the caption, "journalism," we include all forms of periodical literature—reviews, magazines, weekly and daily papers. The word journalism is, in respect to many of them, a misnomer, etymologically considered: it is a French corruption of *diurnal*, which, from the Latin *dies*, should mean a daily paper; but it is now generally used to include all periodicals. The origin of newspapers is quite curious, and antedates the invention of printing. The *acta diurna*, or journals of public events, were the daily manuscript reports of the Roman Government during the later commonwealth. In these, among other matters of public interest, every birth, marriage, and divorce was entered. As an illustration of the character of these brief entries, we have the satire of Petronius, which he puts in the mouth of the freedman Trimalchio: "The seventh of the Kalends of Sextilis, on the estate at Cumæ, were born thirty boys, twenty girls; were carried from the floor to the barn, 500,000 bushels of wheat; were broke 500 oxen. The same day the slave Mithridates was crucified for blasphemy against the Emperor's genius; the same day was placed in the chest the sum of ten millions sesterces, which could not be put out to use." Similar in character were the *Acta Urbana*, or city register, the *Acta Publica*, and the *Acta Senatus*, whose names indicate their contents. They were brief, almost tabular, and not infrequently sensational.

THE GAZETTE. — After the downfall of Rome, and during the Dark Ages, there are few traces of journalism. When Venice was still in her palmy days, in 1563, during a war with the Turks, printed bulletins were issued from time to time, the price for reading which was a coin of about three farthings' value called a *gazetta;* and so the paper soon came to be called a gazette. Old files, to the amount of thirty volumes, of great historical value, may be found in the Magliabecchian Library at Florence.

Next in order, we find in France *Affiches*, or *placards*, which were soon succeeded by regular sheets of advertisement, exhibited at certain offices.

As early as the time of the intended invasion of England by the Spanish Armada, about the year 1588, we find an account of its defeat and dispersion in the *Mercurie*, issued by Queen Elizabeth's own printer. In another number is the news of a plot for killing the queen, and a statement that instruments of torture were on board the vessels, to set up the Inquisition in London. Whether true or not, the newspaper said it; and the English people believed it implicitly.

About 1600, with the awakening spirit of the people, there began to appear periodical papers containing specifically news from Germany, from Italy, &c. And during the Thirty Years' War there was issued a weekly paper called *The Certain News of the Present Week.* Although the word *news* is significant enough, many persons considered it as made up of the initial letters representing the cardinal points of the compass, *N.E.W.S.*, from which the curious people looked for satisfying intelligence.

THE CIVIL WAR. — The progress of English journalism received a great additional impetus when the civil war broke out between Charles I. and his Parliament, in 1642. To meet the demands of both parties for intelligence, numbers of small sheets were issued : *Truths from York* told of the rising in the king's favor there. There were : *Tidings from Ireland, News from Hull,* telling of the siege of that place in 1643; *The Dutch Spy; The Parliament Kite; The Secret Owl; The Scot's Dove,* with the olive-branch. Then flourished the *Weekly Discoverer,* and *The Weekly Discoverer Stripped Naked.* But these were only bare and partial statements, which excited rancor without conveying intelligence. "Had there been better vehicles for the expression of public opinion," says the author of the Student's history of England, "the Stuarts might have been saved from some of those schemes which proved so fatal to themselves."

In the session of Parliament held in 1695, there occurred a revolution of great moment. There had been an act, enforced for a limited time, to restrain unlicensed printing, and under it censors had been appointed; but, in this year, the Parliament refused to re-enact or continue it, and thus the press found itself comparatively free.

We have already referred to the powerful influence of the essayists in *The Tatler, Spectator, Guardian,* and *Rambler,* which may be called the real origin of the present English press.

LATER DIVISIONS. — Coming down to the close of the eighteenth century, we find the following division of English periodical literature: *Quarterlies,* usually called *Reviews; Monthlies,* generally entitled *Magazines; Weeklies,* containing digests of news; and *Dailies,* in which are found the intelligence and facts of the present moment; and in this order, too, were the intellectual strength and learning of the time at first employed. The *Quarterlies* contained the articles of the great men — the acknowledged critics in politics, literature, and art; the *Magazines*, a current literature of poetry and fiction; the *Weeklies* and *Dailies*, reporters' facts and statistics; the latter requiring activity rather than cleverness, and beginning to be a vehicle for extensive advertisements.

This general division has been since maintained; but if the order has not been reversed, there can be no doubt that the great dailies have steadily risen; on most questions of popular interest in all departments, long and carefully written articles in the dailies, from distinguished pens, anticipate the quarterlies, or force them to seek new grounds and forms of presentation after forestalling their critical opinions. Not many years ago, the quarterlies subsidized the best talent; now the men of that class write for *The Times*, *Standard*, *Telegraph*, &c.

Let us look, in the order we have mentioned, at some representatives of the press in its various forms.

Each of the principal reviews represents a political party, and at the same time, in most cases, a religious denomination; and they owe much of their interest to the controversial spirit thus engendered.

Reviews. — First among these, in point of origin, is the *Edinburgh Review*, which was produced by the joint efforts of several young, and comparatively unknown, gentlemen, among whom were Francis (afterwards) Lord Jeffrey, Lord Murray, Mr. (since Lord) Brougham, and the Rev. Sydney Smith. The latter gentleman was appointed first editor, and remained long enough in Edinburgh to edit the first number. Thereafter Jeffrey conducted it. The men were clever, witty, studious, fearless; and the Review was not only from the first a success, but its fiat was looked for by authors with fear and trembling. It became a vehicle for the efforts of the best minds. Macaulay wrote for it those brilliant miscellanies which at once established his fame, and gave it much of its popularity. In it Jeffrey attacked the Lake poetry, and incurred the hatred of Byron. Its establishment, in 1803, was an era in the world of English letters. The papers were not merely reviews, but monographs on interesting subjects — a new anatomy of history; it was in a general way an exponent, but quite an independent one, of the Whig party, or those who would liberally construe the Constitution, — putting Churchmen and Dissenters on the same platform; although published in Edinburgh, it was neither Scotch nor Presbyterian. It attacked ancient prescriptions and customs; agitated questions long considered settled both of present custom and former history; and thus imitated the champion knights who challenged all comers, and sustained no defeats.

Occupying opposite ground to this is the great English review called the *London Quarterly:* it was established in 1809; is an uncompromising Tory,—entirely conservative as to monarchy, aristocracy, and Established Church. Its first editor was William Gifford; but it attained its best celebrity under the charge of John Gibson Lockhart, the son-in-law of Sir Walter Scott, a man of singular critical power. Among its distinguished contributors were Southey, Scott, Canning, Croker, and Wordsworth.

The *North British Review,* which never attained the celebrity of either of these, and which has at length, in 1871, been discontinued, occupied strong Scottish and Presbyterian ground, and had its respectable supporters.

But besides the parties mentioned, there is a floating one, growing by slow but sure accretion, know as the *Radical.* It includes men of many stamps, mainly utilitarian, — radical in politics, innovators, radical in religion, destructive as to systems of science and arts, a learned and inquisitive class, — rational, transcendental, and intensely dogmatic. As a vent for this varied party, the *Westminster Review* was founded by Mr Bentham, in 1824. Its articles are always well written, and sometimes dangerous, according to our orthodox notions. It is supported by such writers as Mill, Bowring, and Buckle.

Besides these there are numerous quarterlies of more or less limited scope, as in science or art, theology or law; such as *The Eclectic*, *The Christian Observer*, *The Dublin*, and many others.

THE MONTHLIES. Passing from the reviews to the monthlies, we find the range and number of these far greater, and the matter lighter. The first great representative of the modern series, and one that has kept its issue up to the present day, is Cave's *Gentleman's Magazine*, which commenced its career in 1831, and has been continued, after Cave's death, by Henry & Nichols, who wrote under the pseudonym of *Sylvanus Urban*. It is a strong link between past and present. Johnson sent his *queries* to it while preparing his dictionary, and at the present day it is the favorite vehicle of antiquarians and historians. Passing by others, we find Blackwood's *Edinburgh Magazine*, first published in 1817. Originally a strong and bitter conservative, it kept up its popularity by its fine stories and poems. Among the most notable papers in Blackwood are the *Noctes Ambrosianæ*, in which Professor Wilson, under the pseudonym of *Christopher North*, took the greater part.

Most of the magazines had little or no political proclivity, but were chiefly literary. Among them are *Fraser's*, begun in 1830, and the *Dublin University*, in 1832.

A charming light literature was presented by the *New Monthly*: in politics it was a sort of set-off to Blackwood: in it Captain Marryat wrote his famous sea stories; and among other contributors are the ever welcome names of Hood, Lytton, and Campbell. The *Penny Magazine*, of Knight, was issued from 1832 to 1845.

Quite a new era dawned upon the magazine world in the establishment of several new ones, under the auspices of famous authors; among which we mention *The Cornhill,* edited by Thackeray, in 1859, with unprecedented success, until his tender heart compelled him to resign it; *Temple Bar,* by Sala, in 1860, is also very successful.

In 1850 Dickens began the issue of *Household Words,* and in 1859 this was merged into *All the Year Round,* which owed its great popularity to the prestige of the same great writer

Besides these, devoted to literature and criticism, there are also many monthlies issued in behalf of special branches of knowledge, art, and science, which we have not space to refer to.

Descending in the order mentioned, we come to the weeklies, which, besides containing summaries of daily intelligence, also share the magazine field in brief descriptive articles, short stories, and occasional poems.

A number of these are illustrated journals, and are of great value in giving us pictorial representations of the great events and scenes as they pass, with portraits of men who have become suddenly famous by some special act or appointment. Their value cannot be too highly appreciated; they supply to the mind, through the eye, what the best descriptions in letterpress could not give; and in them satire uses comic elements with wonderful effect. Among the illustrated weeklies, the *Illustrated London News* has long held a high place; and within a short period *The Graphic* has exhibited splendid pictures of men and things of timely interest. Nor must we forget to mention *Punch,* which has been the grand jester of the realm since its origin. The best humorous and witty talent of England has found a vent in its pages, and sometimes its pathos has been productive of reform. Thackeray, Cuthbert Bede, Mark Lemon, Hood, have amused us in its pages, and the clever pencil of Leech has made a series of etching which will never grow tiresome. To it Thackeray contributed his *Snob Papers*, and Hood *The Song of the Shirt*.

THE DAILIES. — But the great characteristic of the age is the daily newspaper, so common a blessing that we cease to marvel at it, and yet marvellous as it is common. It is the product of quick intelligence, of great energy, of concurrent and systematized labor, and, in order to fulfil its mission, it seems to subsidize all arts and invade all subjects — steam, mechanics, photography, phonography, and electricity. The news which it prints and scatters comes to it on the telegraph; long orations are phonographically reported; the very latest mechanical skill is used in its printing; and the world is laid at our feet as we sit at the breakfast-table and read its columns.

I shall not go back to the origin of printing, to show the great progress that has been made in the art from that time to the present; nor shall I attempt to explain the present process, which one visit to a press-room would do far better than any description; but I simply refer to the fact that fifty years ago newspapers were still printed with the hand-press, giving 250 impressions per hour — no cylinder, no flying Hoe, (that was patented only in 1847.) Now, the ten-cylinder Hoe, steam driven, works off 20,000 sheets in an hour, and more, as the stereotyper may multiply the forms. What an emblem of art-progress is this! Fifty years ago mail-coaches carried them away. Now, steamers and locomotives fly with them all over the world, and only enlarge and expand the story, the great facts of which have been already sent in outline by telegraph.

Nor is it possible to overrate the value of a good daily paper: as the body is strengthened by daily food, so are we built up mentally and spiritually for the busy age in which we live by the world of intelligence contained in the daily journal. A great book and a good one is offered for the reading of many who have no time to read others, and a great culture in morals, religion, politics, is thus induced. Of course it would be impossible to mention all the English dailies. Among them *The London Times* is pre-eminent, and stands highest in the opinion of the ministerial party, which fears and uses it.

There was a time when the press was greatly trammelled in England, and license of expression was easily charged with constructive treason; but at present it is remarkably free, and the great, the government, and existing abuses, receive no soft treatment at its hands.

The London Times was started by John Walter, a printer, in 1788, there having been for three years before a paper called the *London Daily Universal Register*. In 1803 his son, John, went into partnership, when the circulation was but 1,000. Within ten years it was 5,000. In 1814, cleverly concealing the purpose from his workmen, he printed the first sheet ever printed by steam, on Kœnig's press. The paper passed, at his death, into the hands of his son, the third John, who is a scholar, educated at Eton and Oxford, like his father a member of Parliament, and who has lately been raised to the peerage. The *Times* is so influential that it may well be called a third estate in the realm: its writers are men of merit and distinction; its correspondence secures the best foreign intelligence; and its travelling agents, like Russell and others, are the true historians of a war. English journalism, it is manifest, is eminently historical. The files of English newspapers are the best history of the period, and will, by their facts and comments, hereafter confront specious and false historians. Another thing to be observed is the impersonality of the British press, not only in the fact that names are withheld, but that the articles betray no authorship; that, in short, the paper does not appear as the glorification of one man or set of men, but like an unprejudiced relator, censor, and judge.

Of the principal London papers, the *Morning Post* (Liberal, but not Radical,) was begun in 1772. The *Globe* (at first Liberal, but within a short time Tory), in 1802. The *Standard* (Conservative), in 1827. The *Daily News* (high-class Liberal), in 1846. The *News* announced itself as pledged to *Principles of Progress and Improvement. The Daily Telegraph* was started in 1855, and claims the largest circulation. It is also a *Liberal* paper.

INDEX OF AUTHORS.

THE END.

www.ingramcontent.com/pod-product-compliance
Lightning Source LLC
LaVergne TN
LVHW020918110826
845150LV00004B/705